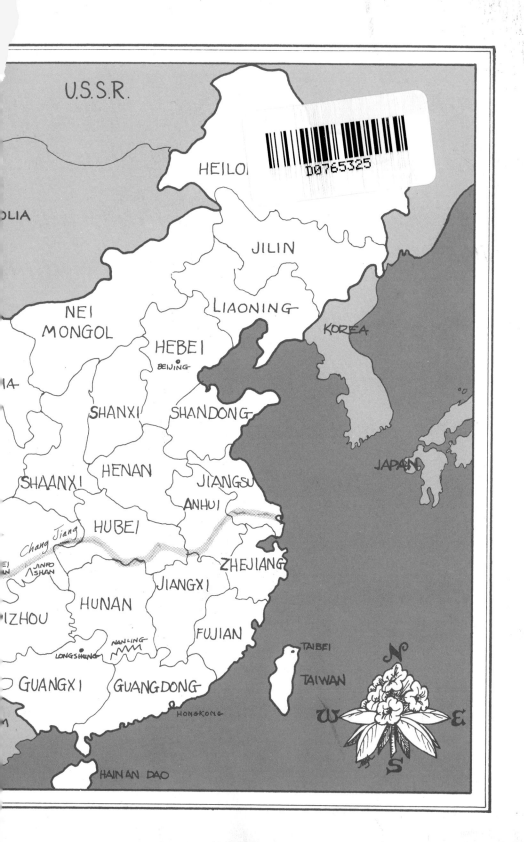

Rhododendrons *of* CHINA

杜鵑花

American Rhododendron Society

Rhododendron Species Foundation

Rhododendrons *of* CHINA

Species Descriptions and Key from Volume III,
ICONOGRAPHIA CORMOPHYTORUM SINICORUM
Beijing Botanical Research Institute
of Academia Sinica, 1974

With the Original Illustrations

Translated from the Chinese
by Judy Young and Dr. Lu-sheng Chong

Binford & Mort
Thomas Binford, Publisher
2536 S.E. Eleventh, Portland, Oregon 97202

American Rhododendron Society
14635 Bull Mountain Road SW
Tigard, Oregon 97223

Rhododendron Species Foundation
P.O. Box 3798
Federal Way, Washington 98003

Printed in the United States of America
Library of Congress Catalog Card Number: 80-68082
ISBN: 0-8323-0373-9
First Printing 1980

PREFACE

The immense and diverse flora of China is considered by many to be unexcelled by any other geographical region in the world. Within the boundaries of this great country the total indigenous plant species number in the many thousands.

The wild and rugged region of southwestern China contains the world's greatest concentration of rhododendron species, exclusive of the Malesian types. China is undoubtedly the primary center of origin of the genus as exemplified by the high levels of polyploid species found there. Among the Chinese species are tetraploids $(2n = 52)$, hexaploids $(2n = 78)$, octoploids $(2n = 104)$ and dodecaploids $(2n = 156)$. In general, polyploidy in natural species is an indication of a relatively recent origin because polyploid plants are basically derived from ancentral diploids $(2n = 26)$ or lower ploidy types. Hence this book is especially useful for geneticists, horticulturists, and hobbyists alike.

Although the introduction of plants from China has been underway for nearly three centuries, few new introductions have reached the Western world in recent decades. The early botanists searching in that country have provided a rich horticultural treasure. In the extensive mountain masses with their tremendous ecologic diversities, there undoubtedly yet remain opportunities for present day plant explorers to extend further our botanical knowledge and to enrich our gardens still further. Perhaps this book will provide stimulus to additional explorations in the near future.

v

While in the People's Republic of China in June 1977 I had the good fortune to visit the Botanical Research Institute of the National Academy of Sciences at Beijing (Peking) University. It was a special privilege to see work in full swing in the taxonomy laboratory on the native flora of China. Species were being illustrated with superb and detailed pen and ink botanical drawings, including enlargements of significant features of each species, all drawn from fresh specimens or from herbarium mounts. This ambitious and valuable project will eventually be published in the Chinese language.

This book, *Rhododendrons of China*, represents an English translation of the rhododendron section of the Ericaceae as published in Volume 3 of the *Iconographia Cormophytorum Sinicorum*. It has descriptions of 283 species, many of which are not in cultivation outside of China. For serious students of the genus, the pen and ink drawings are unmatched in all present day rhododendron literature as a basis for species identification.

If this book proves to be successful, the success reflects the mutually satisfactory cooperation of the Rhododendron Species Foundation and the American Rhododendron Society. May such cooperation continue to prosper. In addition to these two groups, the Botanical Research Institute of Beijing (Peking) University deserves much credit, for without their initial efforts the original source material would not have been available for the American organizations to translate and publish. May such cooperation also continue to prosper.

In a book review of the *Iconographia Cormophytorum Sini-*

corum in the *Bulletin of the American Rhododendron Society* I made the somewhat whimsical suggestion that it would be nice to have a translation of the section on rhododendron species. Upon reading the review Judy Young, who was at the time taking lessons in Chinese, offered to undertake the translation with the assistance of her teacher, Dr. Lu-sheng Chong. Special credit must go to these two fine people for their arduous task in translation. Subsequently Dr. Roy Taylor of the University of British Columbia arranged to have translated the 34-page taxonomic key, and hence deserves recognition and thanks.

Above all, the cooperation of Dr. Li An-ren, Director of the Botanical Research Institute, Academia Sinica, Beijing, is appreciated. We give warm thanks to Dr. Yu-Chen Ting, my former student, for making the formal translation arrangements with Dr. Li. Likewise credit is given to Kendall W. Gambrill and Karen S. Gunderson of the Rhododendron Species Foundation for handling the many essential details of preparing and printing the book. And finally, my congratulations to each member of the ICS Committee.

August E. Kehr
Hendersonville, North Carolina

ACKNOWLEDGMENTS

In the belief that the primary objective of this publication is the furtherance of cooperation between individuals, organizations and institutions concerned with the conservation and study of the Genus Rhododendron and as a result of an unprecedented mutual endeavor, the ICS Project Committee offers this book. The following acknowledgements express our appreciation and give credit to those who made this book possible:

The Rhododendron Species Foundation acknowledges with great appreciation the assistance of the following individuals and organizations for their specific supporting roles which culminated in the successful effort of translating the rhododendron section of the *Iconographia Cormophytorum Sinicorum*. The RSF Publication Committee: Dr. August E. Kehr, Mrs. Thomas P. Binford, Mrs. Robert Berry, Judy Young, Dr. Lu-sheng Chong, Karen S. Gunderson, Kendall W. Gambrill. Translation of the text and key: Judy Young and Dr. Lu-sheng Chong, Seattle, Washington. Assistance with translation of the rhododendron key: Mrs. Annie Y. M. Cheng, Dr. Roy L. Taylor of The University of British Columbia, Botanical Garden, Vancouver, B.C. For financial assistance to the translation project: ARS Research Foundation, Tacoma Rhododendron Study Club, Species Associate Group, Seattle Rhododendron Society, Portland Chapter of ARS, Mr. Gary Van Winkle, Lady Anne Kerr McDonald, Col. and Mrs. Claud Farrow, Frank D. Mossman,

M.D., Mrs. Cyrus Walker, Mr. Ted Van Veen, Mr. and Mrs. Cecil Smith.

In February of 1979 a joint committee was appointed by the Boards of Directors of the American Rhododendron Society and the Rhododendron Species Foundation. This Committee was charged with the task of publishing the translated rhododendron section of the *Iconographia Cormophytorum Sinicorum*. The following individuals, organizations and institutions are recognized as having participated in this important work: Original authors: Beijing Botanical Research Institute of Academia Sinica, Dr. Li An-ren, Director. Presidents of the co-sponsoring organizations at the time of the project's inception: Edwin C. Brockenbrough, M.D., President, The American Rhododendron Society; Lawrence J. Pierce, President, Rhododendron Species Foundation. Financial contributors to the publication: American Rhododendron Society, Rhododendron Species Foundation, and Mr. and Mrs. Lawrence J. Pierce. The Technical Review Panel: Dr. Rupert Barneby, New York Botanical Garden, Bronx, New York; Carlton B. Lees, Senior Vice President, New York Botanical Garden; Dr. James L. Luteyn, Associate Curator, New York Botanical Garden; Dr. Mildred E. Mathias, Emeritus Professor of Botany, University of California Botanical Garden, Los Angeles, California; Dr. Fredrick G. Meyer, Supervisory Botanist, U.S. National Arboretum, Washington, D.C.

For providing technical assistance: Dr. Y. Chen Ting,

Boston College, Department of Biology, Chestnut Hill, Massachusetts; Mr. Joseph Witt, Curator, University of Washington Arboretum, Seattle, Washington; Mr. Brian O. Mulligan, Director Emeritus, University of Washington Arboretum, Seattle, Washington.

Judy Young and Dr. Lu-sheng Chong, Seattle, Washington, for compilation of the glossary, Pinyin guide, geographic index, and map research. Nancy Goerin Hill, graphic illustration of the map and jacket. Dr. Lu-sheng Chong, calligraphy for graphics and text.

The ICS Project Committee: Mrs. Robert Berry, Mrs. Thomas P. Binford, Dr. Lu-sheng Chong, Kendall W. Gambrill, Karen S. Gunderson, Dr. August E. Kehr, Dr. L. Keith Wade, Judy Young.

CONTENTS

INTRODUCTION

"For more than two thousand years Mount Omei has been well known as a sacred mountain to the Chinese people. It is situated in Omei-hsien, which lies in the southwestern corner of Szechuan province . . . " In smooth professorial English, the Editor's Preface continues to describe the mountain, the land which surrounds it, and the botanists who have collected its rich flora. The British and European names are familiar enough, but those that follow are not. Chen, Wang, and Yu head a long list of Chinese botanists and collectors who have worked on Mount Omei during the previous sixteen years. Among them is the editor of this remarkable publication; the year is 1944, the place is National Szechuan University.

Seven years after his return from Europe, Dr. Wen-pei Fang had already published and distributed the first half of Volume I, *Icones Plantarum Omeiensium*, though the world was at war and China was in chaos. The printing difficulties were obvious, on paper curiously soft and fibrous, but the work was thorough and enthusiastic. The first set of fifty folio-sized botanical drawings included twenty rhododendron species, all described in Chinese and English, with new species also in Latin. Copies had somehow been received abroad, for the preface to the second set was accompanied by letters of congratulation from Kew, Edinburgh, and the Arnold Arboretum.

There were no letters from Europe, though, and symbolically so; in Berlin the fires of war had recently destroyed Dr. Hermann Sleumer's specimens and papers outlining a taxonomic revision of the genus *Rhododendron*.

Many rhododendron enthusiasts know that Dr. Sleumer was able to reconstruct his manuscript; it was published in German and Latin in 1949. That first discussion and taxonomic key were published in English just this year, along with his more recent work and that of several other botanists on major reclassification within the genus.* But few have known that a synopsis of Dr. Sleumer's key of 1949 was also published in Chinese as a framework for the classification of rhododendron species in China. Prepared by the taxonomists of that country, this detailed adaptation appeared in 1974. It is part of a five-volume general survey of Chinese plants which describes and illustrates the more common and important species. This is the key which we have translated for *Rhododendrons of China*, along with the species descriptions which precede it in Volume III of *Iconographia Cormophytorum Sinicorum*.

Over three decades have passed since Dr. Fang fought the tide of history to share Emei Shan with the outside world. Now, as then, he is working is Sichuan, but this time in the mainstream of Chinese botany. Involved in the preparation of the *Rhododendron* section of the eighty-volume flora of China, he is one among a great many

*See bibliography addenda.

botanists at work on that national project and countless other studies and publications.* Today the response to this renewed activity is clear, world-wide, and resounding far beyond the walls of the herbarium and botanic garden. We who grow and love some of China's very special plants, and have long imagined the fascination of its mountains, thank and congratulate the botanists of China.

August 1980   J. Y.

大云锦杜鹃
Rhododendron faithae Chun

常绿灌木，高 4—8 米；幼枝无毛。叶集生枝顶，厚革质，边缘有软骨质，椭圆状矩圆形，长 20—25 厘米，宽 7—9 厘米，顶端急尖，有短尖头，基部常圆钝，两面无毛，下面淡绿色，中脉粗而隆起；叶柄长 2.5—4 厘米，上面平，无毛。顶生伞形总状花序有花 8—10 朵，紧密，总轴长 4 厘米，基部粗 1.2 厘米，稍有腺体；花梗向上，长 2.5—3 厘米，稍有腺体；花萼短，几不分裂，外面稍有腺体；花冠白色，无斑点，宽漏斗状钟形，长 9—10 厘米，裂片 7，长 3 厘米；雄蕊 14，花丝无毛；子房 10 室，密生有柄腺体，花柱有腺毛。蒴果长 3.5 厘米，圆柱形，颇直，外面稍有腺体，果柄长达 4 厘米。

分布于广东、广西。生海拔 1000 米的林中。

图 4159 （杜鹃花科）

波叶杜鹃
Rhododendron hemsleyanum
　　Wils.

常绿灌木或小乔木，高 3—6 米；小枝粗壮，稍有疏微毛。叶厚革质，矩圆状卵形，长 15—20 厘米，中部宽 6—8 厘米，顶端钝尖，基部耳状心形，无毛，中脉上面呈沟状，下面隆起，边缘多少呈波状；叶柄粗壮，圆柱形，长 3.5—4.5 厘米，有疏长柄腺毛。顶生总状花序有花 10—12 朵，总轴长 5 厘米，有疏短毛和腺毛；花梗粗壮，长 2—3 厘米，有同样的毛；花萼短，5—10 浅裂，有密腺体；花冠钟状，长 5.5—6.5 厘米，白色，无毛，7 裂；雄蕊 14，花丝无毛；子房密生短腺毛，花柱通体有腺毛。蒴果长椭圆形，长 2—2.5 厘米，有密腺毛。

产四川西部。生林中。产于峨眉山的变种**无腺杜鹃** var. **chengianum** Fang，极近本种，但叶通常较宽，叶柄和花梗光滑，不具腺体。

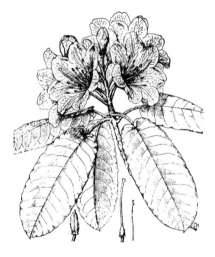

图 4160 （杜鹃花科）

TRANSLATED SPECIES DESCRIPTIONS

WITH LATIN NAMES
AND
PINYIN PRONUNCIATION AND TRANSLATION
OF CHINESE NAMES

ACCOMPANIED BY THE ILLUSTRATIONS
WITH ORIGINAL PLATE NUMBERS
AND NAMES IN CHINESE

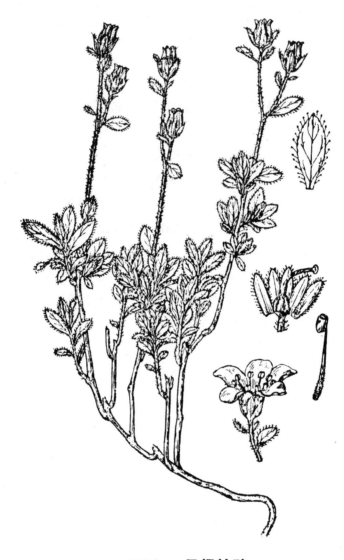

4002　云间杜鹃

THERORHODION REDOWSKIANUM
(Maxim.) Hutch.

yún jiān dùjuān   *"in the clouds rhododendron"*

Dwarf deciduous undershrub about 10 cm high; shoots sparsely glandular-hairy.

Leaves clustered, chartaceous, linguiform-oblanceolate, 5-15 mm long, 3-6 mm broad, apex obtuse and glandular-mucronate, base attenuate and decurrent onto the short petiole, margin glandular-ciliate.

Flowers terminal on the new shoots, in 2-3-flowered racemes, rachis to 3 cm long; pedicels 5-10 mm long, glandular-hairy throughout, with a few hairy leaflike bracts; calyx large, lobes 5, linear-oblong, 5 mm long, glandular-hairy; corolla about 1.5 cm long, purplish red, corolla tube 7-8 mm long, lobes 5, broadly oblong, 6 mm long, more deeply cleft on one side, almost to the base; stamens 10, filaments pubescent on the lower third; ovary densely hairy, style pubescent on the lower half, bent at the corolla sinus and exserted.

Capsule ovoid, about 6 mm long, 5-loculed, loculicidally dehiscent.

Distributed in northeast China; also Korea, USSR. Grows on high mountains.

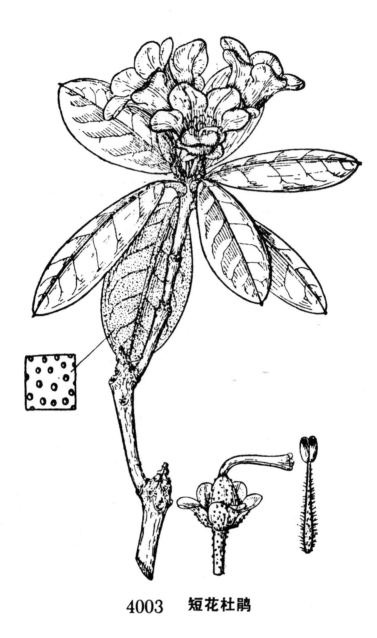

4003　短花杜鹃

RHODODENDRON BRACHYANTHUM
Franch.

duǎn huā dùjuān   *"short-flowered rhododendron"*

Evergreen shrub about 1 meter high; branches of the previous year finely scaly, new shoots more densely scaly, the scales yellow.

Leaves scattered toward the branch tips, firm-coriaceous, elliptic, 2-4 cm long, 1-2 cm broad, upper surface green and clad with inconspicuous glandlike scales, lower surface conspicuously gray-white and sparsely scaly, midrib strongly prominent on the lower surface and not gray-white, lateral veins somewhat obscure; petiole 4-5 mm long, scaly.

Terminal umbelliform inflorescence of 3-4 flowers; pedicels erect, about 2 cm long, scaly; calyx large, leaflike, scaly outside toward the base, deeply 5-lobed, lobes about 8 mm long, slightly scaly on the dorsal surface; corolla light yellow, corolla tube broadly campanulate, 1 cm long, lobes 5, broadly ovate, 6 mm long; stamens 10, filaments densely hairy on the lower part; ovary densely green-scaly, style short and thick, glabrous.

Capsule 6 mm long, enclosed within the calyx.

West Yunnan (Dali). Grows in pine forests at 2800 meters.

4004   绿柱杜鹃

4

RHODODENDRON HYPOLEPIDOTUM
Balf. f. et Forrest

lǜ zhù dùjuān   *"green style rhododendron"*

Evergreen aromatic shrub to 1.5 meters high; shoots more or less scaly.

Leaves coriaceous, oblong, 2.5-4 cm long, 1-2 cm broad, apex obtuse and mucronate, base cuneate, lower surface clad with many scattered mostly pale scales (a few brown), midrib prominent on the lower surface; petiole 5 mm long, scaly.

Terminal umbelliform inflorescence of 3-10 flowers, rachis 5 mm long, sparsely pubescent; pedicels 2.5-4 cm long, scaly; calyx large, 5-cleft almost to the base, lobes round-ovate, about 5 mm long, green, more or less scaly on the dorsal surface; corolla campanulate, about 1.5 cm long, yellow, not scaly, corolla tube 8 mm long, finely hairy within, lobes 5, about 7 mm long, rounded; stamens 10, filaments hairy overall; ovary 5-loculed, densely clad with scalelike glands, style thick, green, reflexed, glabrous.

Northwest Yunnan, southeast Xizang. In thickets at 4000 meters.

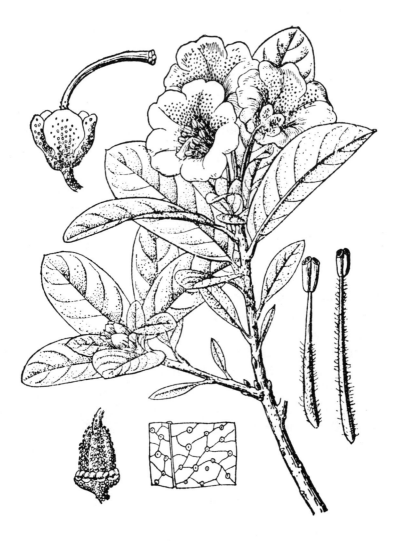

4005　雅容杜鹃

6

RHODODENDRON CHARITOPES
Balf. f. et Farrer

yǎ róng dùjuān   *"pretty face rhododendron"*

Evergreen undershrub about 75 cm high; twigs sparsely scaly, internodes short.

Leaves aromatic, few and scattered (the lower leaves reduced to leaflike bracts), obovate-elliptic or obovate, 4-7 cm long, 1.5-3 cm broad, acute at the apex, slightly tapering toward the base, base obtuse, upper surface scaly, lower surface gray-white and densely clad with glandlike scales of unequal size, the scales less than a diameter apart; petiole 5 mm long, scaly.

Terminal inflorescence of usually 3(-5) flowers; pedicels about 1.5 cm long, densely clad with red and white scales; calyx large, almost 1 cm long, deeply 5-lobed, lobes broad, leaflike, finely scaly outside; corolla apple-blossom pink with dark red spots on the upper 3 lobes, corolla tube campanulate, 1 cm long, sparsely pubescent outside, lobes 5, spreading, emarginate; stamens 10, filaments hairy nearly to the top; ovary densely scaly, style as long as the stamens, curved downward, slightly scaly only at the base.

Distributed in Yunnan, southeast Xizang; also Burma. Grows on rocky cliffs.

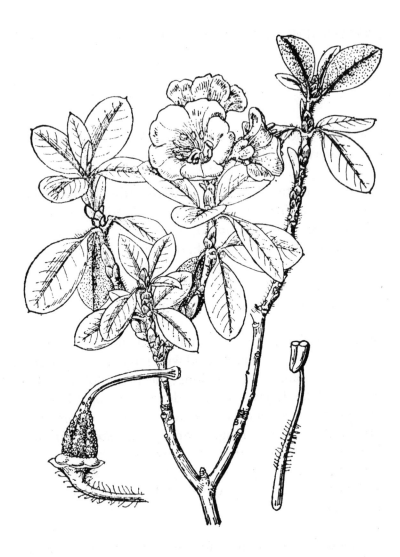

4006　招展杜鹃

RHODODENDRON MEGERATUM
Balf. f. et Forrest

zhāo zhǎn dùjuān   *"waving rhododendron"*

Evergreen undershrub to 50 cm high; shoots setose at first, the hairs light red and spreading.

Leaves quite clustered, coriaceous, oblong-elliptic, to 3 cm long, 1.5 cm broad, apex rounded and mucronulate, base short cuneate, lower surface gray-white, densely papillate, scattered with hollow golden scales, and glabrous except for a few light brown hairs near the base and at the margin; petiole 6 mm long, setose.

Terminal raceme of 1-3 flowers, rachis to 12 mm long, closely wrapped with large and small flower-bud scales; pedicels to 1 cm long, setose; calyx large, 5-lobed, lobes oblong-elliptic, to 12 mm long, glabrous, slightly scaly; corolla broadly campanulate, 3 cm in diameter at the mouth, yellow, sparsely scaly outside, corolla tube 1 cm long, 1 cm broad, upper interior orange-red spotted; stamens 10, hairy at the middle; ovary gray-white, densely stipitate-scaly; style thick, reflexed.

Capsule ovoid, enclosed by the calyx.

Distributed in Yunnan, southeast Xizang; also Burma.

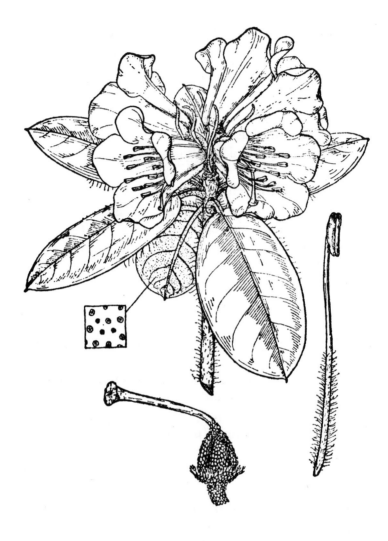

4007 纯黄杜鹃

RHODODENDRON CHRYSODORON
Tagg

chún huáng dùjuān *"pure yellow rhododendron"*

Evergreen undershrub; branches glossy green in the first year, almost without scales but sparsely clad with long soft bristles.

Leaves coriaceous, elliptic, 4.5-8 cm long, 3-4 cm broad, apex obtuse and mucronate, base rounded, lower surface gray-green, sparsely clad with fine scales of unequal size, the scales a diameter apart; petiole 1.5 cm long, sparsely clad with fine appressed scales, with slender bristles distributed along both sides and up to the upper middle leaf margins.

Terminal clusters of about 5 flowers; calyx discoid, with 5 shallow angular lobes, densely scaly, densely white-hairy at the margin; corolla broadly campanulate, bright light yellow, not spotted, corolla tube 2 cm long, exterior glabrous or slightly hairy at the base, lobes 5, with a few medial scales; stamens 10, light yellow-green, hairy on the lower part; ovary 6-loculed, densely white-hairy, style green, conspicuously bent at the base, slightly scaly at the base.

Northwest Yunnan. Grows in forests.

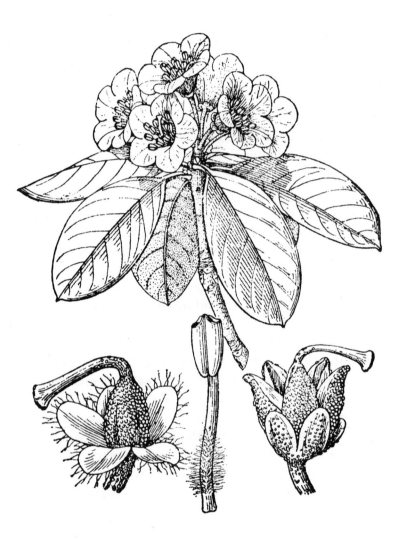

4008　硫黄杜鹃

RHODODENDRON SULFUREUM
Franch.

liú huáng dùjuān *"sulfur rhododendron"*

Evergreen shrub, 0.6-1.2 meters high; branchlets glabrous, branches of the current year green, clad at first with dark red scales, older branches light brown.

Leaves coriaceous, elliptic, 4-7 cm long, 2.5-3.5 cm broad, apex obtuse and stiffly mucronate, base obtuse, upper surface green and scaly, lower surface gray-white and scaly, the scales extremely small, of uniform size, and about a diameter apart; petiole thick, cylindric, 7-12 mm long, densely scaly.

Terminal compact umbelliform inflorescence of 5-8 flowers; pedicels to 1.8 cm long, densely scaly; calyx well developed, deeply 5-lobed, lobes 3.5-5.5 mm long, membranaceous, yellow-green, scaly outside, sparsely long-ciliate; corolla broadly campanulate, bright yellow with orange-yellow spots on the upper lobes, more or less scaly outside, lobes 5, suborbicular, about 1 cm long; stamens 10, filaments pubescent on one part above the base; ovary scaly, style short and thick, bent upward.

Capsule ovoid, 1 cm long.

West Yunnan (Cang Shan). Grows at 3000 meters on rocky cliffs.

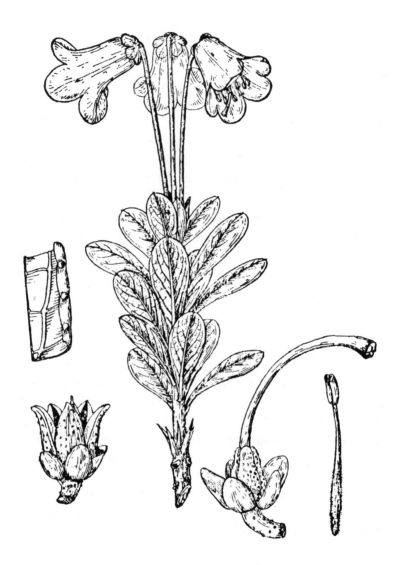

4009　弯柱杜鹃

RHODODENDRON CAMPYLOGYNUM
Franch.

wān zhù dùjuān   *"bent style rhododendron"*

Evergreen cushion-shaped shrub about 1 meter high; year-old branchlets short, sparsely scaly.

Leaves scattered, thick-coriaceous, obovate to obovate-lanceolate, 2-2.5 cm long, 1-1.3 cm broad, apex rounded and bluntly mucronate, base cuneate and decurrent onto the petiole, margin conspicuously recurved, scalloped by tightly-attached sessile glands, upper surface smooth and glossy, lower surface slightly scaly; petiole broad, 2 mm long, not scaly.

Terminal inflorescence of 1-4 flowers, flowers turned downward; pedicels 3-4 cm long, erect, reddish, sparsely scaly; calyx large, deeply 5-lobed, lobes 5-6 mm long, subglabrous, initially glandular at the margin; corolla campanulate, fleshy, purplish red, gray-whitish outside but glabrous, corolla tube 1-1.3 cm long, short-hairy within at the base, lobes 5, 5-6 mm long; stamens usually 8, filaments hairy on the lower half; ovary 5-loculed, scattered with globose scaly glands, style thick, bent downward, glabrous.

Capsule glabrous.

Distributed in Yunnan, southeast Xizang; also Burma. Grows on high mountains.

4010　鳞腺杜鹃

RHODODENDRON LEPIDOTUM
Wall.

lín xiàn dùjuān   *"scaly-glandular rhododendron"*

Evergreen undershrub about 0.5-1 meter high; branchlets slender, scabrous, and verrucose.

Leaves in terminal clusters, thin-coriaceous, varying greatly from narrowly oblanceolate to broadly obovate or obovate elliptic, 1.2-3 cm long, 5-15 mm broad, apex bluntly acute, mucronate, upper and lower surfaces scaly, the scales of the lower surface contiguous, uniform, and light yellow-green; petiole about 2 mm long.

Terminal umbelliform inflorescence of usually 1-3 flowers (rarely 4); pedicels slender, 1.8-2.5 cm long, quite densely scaly; calyx well developed, 5-lobed, scaly outside and at the margin; corolla broadly campanulate, from pink, purple, or dark red to light yellow, light green, or white, scaly outside, 5-lobed; stamens 8, exserted, filaments thick, densely pubescent on the lower half; ovary scaly, style short and thick, curved, scaly, glabrous, and shorter than the stamens.

Capsule 5 mm long, densely scaly.

South Xizang; also Nepal, Sikkim, Bhutan. Grows in thickets above 3000 meters.

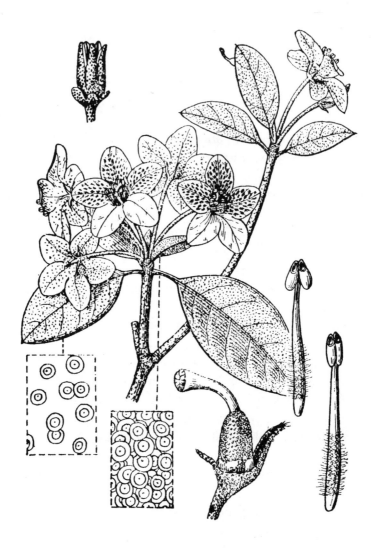

4011　辐花杜鹃

18

RHODODENDRON BAILEYI
Balf. f.

fú huā dùjuān   *"wheel flower rhododendron"*

Evergreen dwarf shrub, densely branched; branches densely scaly at first, later sparsely so.

Leaves coriaceous, oblong or elliptic-oblong, 2-4 cm long, 1-2 cm broad, obtuse and mucronate at the apex, broadly cuneate at the base, the lower leaves comparatively larger (to 6.5 cm long), thinner, and dropping earlier, lower surface yellow-green at first, later changing to cinnamon, upper and lower surfaces scaly, the scales discoid and crenulate, soon separate on the upper surface, remaining contiguous or imbricate on the lower surface.

Terminal inflorescence of 5-9 flowers or more, rachis 5-15 mm long, sparsely white-hairy; pedicels 1.5-2.5 cm long, red; calyx deeply 5-lobed, the lobes unequal in length, red, and densely scaly; corolla reddish purple with dark purplish blue dots on the 3 upper lobes, corolla tube cuplike, 5-6 mm long, the mouth 5-lobed, rotate, scaly outside except at the lobe margins; stamens 10; ovary densely scaly, style thick, reflexed, red.

Capsule 7 mm long.

South Xizang; also Bhutan. Grows on rocky cliffs.

4012　灰白杜鹃

RHODODENDRON GENESTIERIANUM
Forrest

huī bái dùjuān   *"gray-white rhododendron"*

Evergreen sparse shrub, 1-3 meters high or more; branchlets green, glabrous.

Leaves in terminal clusters of 5-10, thin-coriaceous, lanceolate or oblong-lanceolate, 3-15 cm long, 1.2-3.5 cm broad, apex acuminate, base cuneate, upper surface glossy green and sparsely scaly, lower surface gray-white and sparsely clad with fine evenly-distributed shining yellow scales or light brown hollow dots (scale remnants); petiole 0.5-2.5 cm long, very sparsely scaly.

Erect terminal raceme of 10-12 flowers, rachis thick, green or purplish, finely white-powdery, up to 5 cm long; pedicels 2-3 cm long, light red-purple, white-powdery, subglabrous; calyx a shallow cup, reddish, unequally 5-lobed; corolla campanulate, about 1.4 cm long, fleshy, deep red-purple, conspicuously white-powdery, 5-lobed; stamens 10, filaments glabrous, red at the base; ovary densely scaly, style thick, reflexed.

Capsule ovoid, 6 mm long, gray.

Distributed in Yunnan, southeast Xizang. Grows in open thickets.

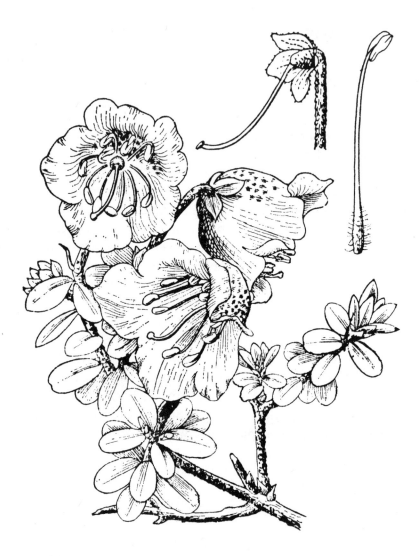

4013　广口杜鹃

22

RHODODENDRON LUDLOWII
Cowan

guǎng kǒu dùjuān   *"broad-mouthed rhododendron"*

Evergreen dwarf shrub about 30 cm high; shoots clad with prominent glands.

Leaves subsessile, coriaceous, obovate or obovate-elliptic, 9-17 mm long, 5-10 mm broad, apex rounded and mucronate, base rounded-cuneate, margin crenulate, upper and lower surfaces scaly, the scales separate, leaf veins evident.

Flowers terminal, solitary or in pairs; pedicels 1.8-2.5 cm long, densely clad with prominent scales; calyx large, about 7 mm long, 5-lobed, lobes broadly ovate, scaly outside, ciliolate; corolla cuplike, 2.5-3 cm long, about 4 cm in diameter, yellow slightly tinged light red, corolla-tube interior dark purple spotted on the upper part, densely hairy at the bottom, exterior hairy and scaly, more densely so at the base, lobes to 1.5 cm long; stamens 10, filaments densely hairy at the base, ovary scaly, style glabrous, reflexed, the tip curved upward.

Capsule 8 mm long.

Southeast Xizang. Grows at 4000 meters in moss- and lichen-covered rocky soil.

4014　矮小杜鹃

RHODODENDRON PUMILUM
Hook.f.

ǎi xiǎo dùjuān   *"dwarf rhododendron"*

Evergreen dwarf shrub about 20 cm high with semirepent scaly branchlets.

Leaves thin-coriaceous, oblong to obovate-elliptic, 8-18 mm long, 4-8 mm broad, apex mucronulate, only the lower surface scaly, the scales sparse, 2 or more diameters apart, usually gray-white; petiole 2 mm long.

Terminal umbelliform inflorescence of 1-3 flowers; pedicels to 2.5 cm long, sparsely scaly; calyx deeply 5-lobed, lobes to 3 mm long, pink or light purplish red, sparsely scaly outside; corolla campanulate, 1.3-1.8 cm long, nearly pure pink, dotted on the back, exterior sparsely pubescent overall and sometimes slightly scaly, lobes 5; stamens 10, filaments pubescent at the base; ovary 5-loculed, densely scaly, style short and thick, glabrous, about half as long as the corolla.

Capsule about 1 cm long, about 4 mm thick, scaly.

Distributed in southwest Yunnan, south Xizang; also Sikkim and Burma. Grows abundantly in mountain thickets at about 4000 meters.

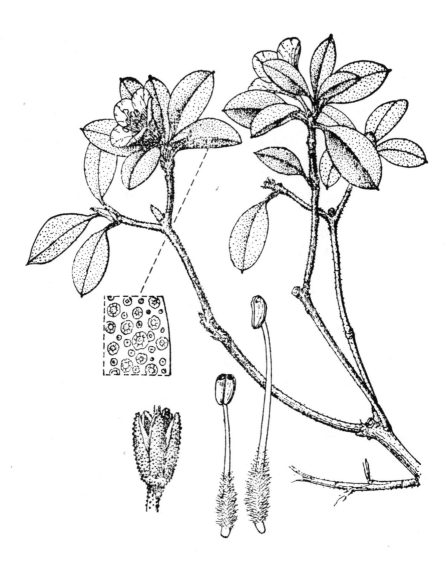

4015　　一朵花杜鹃

RHODODENDRON MONANTHUM
Balf. f. et W. W. Sm.

yīduǒ huā dùjuān   *"one-flowered rhododendron"*

Evergreen undershrub to 1.2 meters high; twigs short and close, densely scaly.

Leaves coriaceous, elliptic to obovate, usually 2.6-5 cm long, 1.2-2.5 cm broad, apex short acute and mucronate, upper surface sparsely scaly, lower surface grayish green and densely scaly, the scales of unequal size and less than a diameter apart; petiole to 1.2 cm long, densely scaly.

Terminal inflorescence of one flower; pedicel 6 mm long, densely scaly; calyx small, less than 1 mm long with 5 undulate shallow lobes, scaly; corolla broadly funnel-form, 1.8 cm long, bright yellow, glabrous, very sparsely scaly outside, shallowly 5-lobed; stamens 10, shorter than the corolla, filaments densely pubescent on the lower part; ovary 5-loculed, densely scaly, style glabrous, slightly longer than the stamens, shorter than the corolla.

Capsule 1.2 cm long, 3.5 mm thick, narrowly elliptic, very densely scaly.

Distributed in Yunnan, southeast Xizang. Grows in thickets below 4000 meters.

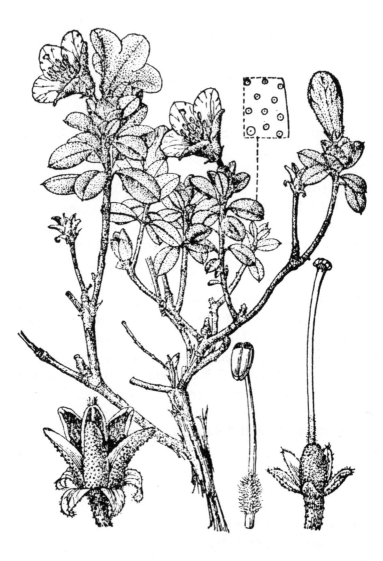

4016　假单花杜鹃

RHODODENDRON PEMAKOENSE
Ward

jiǎ dān huā dùjuān   *"false solitary flower rhododendron"*

Evergreen dwarf shrub, erect or semierect, 20-30 cm high; shoots sparsely scaly.

Leaves coriaceous, obovate-elliptic, about 1 cm long, about 6 mm broad, apex rounded and mucronate, upper surface sparsely scaly, lower surface gray-white and sparsely scaly, the scales 1½ to 2 diameters apart; petiole 3 mm long, slightly scaly.

Terminal inflorescence of 1(-2) flowers; flower-bud scales persistent during flowering; pedicels about 5 mm long, sparsely scaly; calyx well developed, lobes about 4 mm long, densely scaly outside, also scaly at the margin; corolla broadly funnelform, about 2.5 cm long, purple or purplish pink, exterior pubescent, rather densely so on the corolla tube, lobes shallow, sparsely scaly outside; stamens 10, filaments densely pubescent near the base; ovary scaly, style sparsely hairy at the base.

Southeast Xizang. Grows on grassy slopes.

A closely related species also from Xizang is *R. uniflorum* Hutch. et Ward (dān huā dùjuān, "solitary flower rhododendron"), in which the scales of the lower leaf surface are 3 to 6 diameters apart, the flowers are purple, and the style is glabrous.

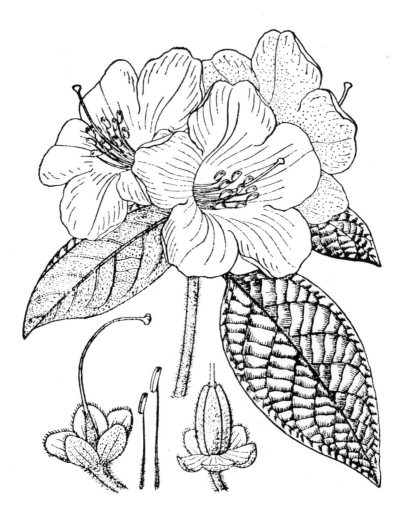

4017　泡泡叶杜鹃

RHODODENDRON BULLATUM
Franch.

pàopào yè dùjuān   *"bubble leaf rhododendron"*

Evergreen shrub to 8 meters high, sparsely branched; branchlets densely clad with a thick layer of yellowish brown woolly hairs.

Leaves coriaceous, ovate-elliptic, 5-10 cm long, 3-4.8 cm broad, apex acute or short acuminate, base rounded, upper surface conspicuously bullate, lower surface densely clad with a thick layer of loose and soft yellowish brown woolly hairs, with scales and irregular hollow dots concealed beneath the indumentum along with the prominent lateral veins and veinlets.

Terminal inflorescence of 1-3 fragrant flowers; pedicels 1.2-1.8 cm long, woolly; calyx large, 1.2-1.6 cm long, deeply 5-lobed, lobes very densely woolly-ciliate, scaly outside; corolla broadly tubular, 5-6.2 cm long, white or pinkish, scaly outside, 5-lobed; stamens 10, filaments hairy on the lower part; ovary 5-6 loculed, densely woolly, style finely scaly and sparsely hairy toward the base.

Capsule 2 cm long, scaly and hairy.

Distributed in west Yunnan, southeast Xizang. Grows in forests at 2800 meters.

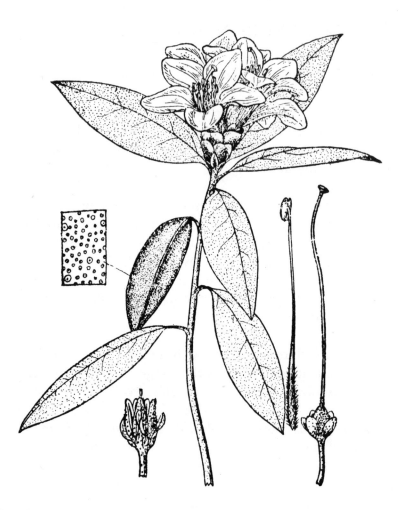

4018　鲜黄杜鹃

RHODODENDRON XANTHOSTEPHANUM

Merr.

xiān huáng dùjuān   *"bright yellow rhododendron"*

Evergreen shrub, 0.6-3 meters high; twigs slender and rigid, glabrous, slightly scaly.

Leaves scattered, coriaceous, lanceolate-oblong to lanceolate, 5-10 cm long, 2-4 cm broad, glabrous, upper surface densely clad with detersile scales, lower surface gray or gray-white and scaly, the scales very fine and borne within hollow dots about a diameter apart, lateral veins obscure on the lower surface; petiole 6-9 mm long, densely scaly.

Terminal racemose-umbelliform inflorescence of 3-5 flowers; pedicels 6-14 mm long, densely scaly; calyx large, deeply 5-lobed, lobes rounded, about 6 mm long, scaly throughout; corolla campanulate, about 2.5 cm long, bright yellow, exterior sparsely but uniformly scaly, lobes 5; stamens 10, filaments pubescent on the lower part; ovary densely scaly, style light green, glabrous, slightly scaly only at the base.

Capsule about 8 mm long, scaly.

Distributed in Yunnan, southeast Xizang; also north Burma. Grows in shade on rock cliffs at about 3000 meters.

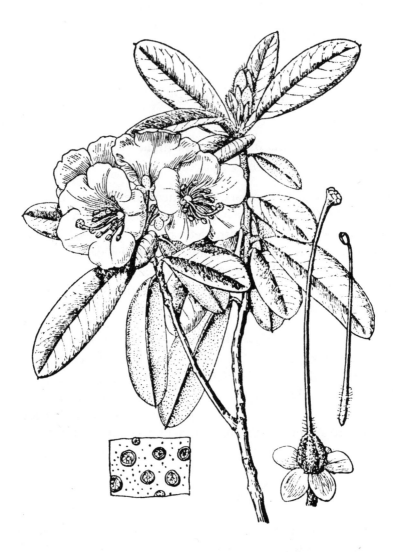

4019　灰被杜鹃

RHODODENDRON TEPHROPEPLUM

Balf. f. et Farrer

huǐ bèi dùjuān   *"gray-clad rhododendron"*

Evergreen undershrub to 1.3 meters high, sparsely branched; shoots quite densely scaly.

Leaves few and scattered, coriaceous, oblong-oblance-olate to obovate-elliptic, 3-5 cm long, 1-2 cm broad, apex obtuse and mucronate, narrowed abruptly at the base to short cuneate, upper surface scaly when young, soon nearly smooth and glossy, lower surface gray-white and densely scaly, the scales less than a diameter apart; petiole 5 mm long, slightly scaly.

Terminal umbelliform inflorescence of 3-4 flowers; pedi-cels 1-1.5 cm long, sparsely scaly; calyx large, spreading, 5-lobed almost to the base, lobes green, finely vein-lined, sparsely scaly outside, ciliolate; corolla broadly tubular, 3.2 cm long, bright carmine-rose, corolla tube 2 cm long, glabrous outside and within, not scaly outside, lobes 5, spreading, reflexed, emarginate; stamens 10, filaments finely hairy on the lower part; ovary densely scaly, style scaly on the lower half.

Capsule 6 mm long, enclosed by the calyx.

Southeast Xizang. Grows on limestone cliffs.

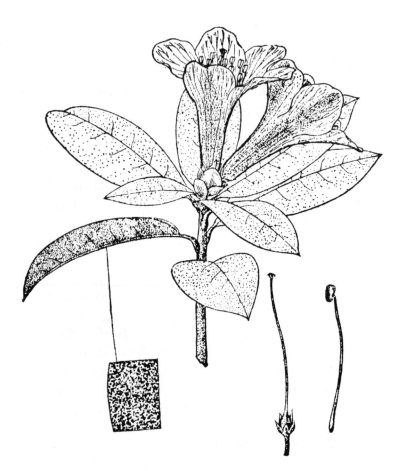

4020　隐脉杜鹃

RHODODENDRON MADDENII
Hook. f.

yǐn mài dùjuān   *"hidden vein rhododendron"*

Evergreen shrub to 6 meters high; shoots clad with ferrugineous scales.

Leaves coriaceous, broadly lanceolate to oblong-lance-olate, 10-13 cm long, 2.5-3.5 cm broad, apex acute, base broadly cuneate, upper surface dark green, scaly at first, lower surface densely clad with imbricate brown scales, lateral veins slightly visible on the upper surface, rather inconspicuous on the lower surface; petiole 1.2-2.5 cm long.

Terminal umbelliform inflorescence of 2-4 flowers; pedicels about 1.2 cm long, densely scaly; calyx 5-lobed, lobes of unequal size, usually 5 mm long but sometimes as long as 1.6 cm, scaly outside, not ciliate; corolla broadly tubular, fleshy, white lightly pink-tinged outside on the lobes, corolla tube 4-5 cm long, densely scaly outside, the scales about a diameter apart, lobes 5, undulate, scaly outside; stamens 20, glabrous, as long as the corolla; ovary 10-loculed, densely scaly, style exserted, scaly except at the tip.

Capsule 2.5 cm long, thick, scaly.

South Xizang; also Sikkim, Bhutan. Grows in forests.

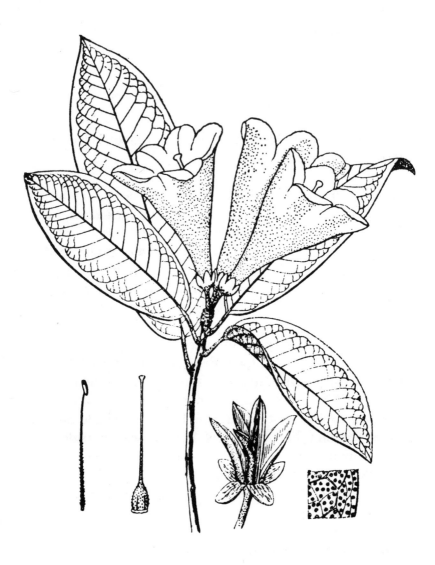

4021　大喇叭杜鹃

RHODODENDRON EXCELLENS
Rehd. et Wils.

dà lăba dùjuān   *"large trumpet rhododendron"*

Evergreen shrub about 3.3 meters high; branches densely scaly in the first year, the scales fine and dark rusty yellow.

Leaves large, coriaceous, oblong-elliptic, 15-19 cm long, 4-5.5 cm broad, apex bluntly acute, base rounded, upper surface smooth and glossy, lower surface somewhat gray-white and rather densely scaly, the scales a diameter or less than a diameter apart, epidermis densely papillate; petiole cylindric, 2.5-4 cm long, clad with small scales.

Terminal umbelliform inflorescence of 3-4 flowers; pedicels 2 cm long, densely clad with dark red scales; calyx well developed, 1-1.6 cm long, slightly scaly outside at the base, lobes oblong, not scaly; corolla funnelform, white, quite densely scaly outside, corolla tube about 8 cm long, lobes 5, about 2.5 cm long; stamens 15, shorter than the corolla tube, filaments densely hairy on the lower 2/3; ovary densely clad with light red scales, style scaly on the lower part.

Capsule 4 cm long.

Southeast Yunnan (Hong He valley). Grows in forests.

4022　大萼杜鹃

RHODODENDRON MEGACALYX
Balf. f. et Ward

dà è dùjuān   *"large calyx rhododendron"*

Evergreen shrub or small tree, 2-4 meters high; shoots stout, densely fine-scaly at first.

Leaves scattered, coriaceous, elliptic to oblong, 9.5-15 cm long, 3-6.5 cm broad, apex obtuse, base narrowly rounded, upper surface densely clad at first with detersile scales, lower surface clad with numerous small scales a diameter apart, midrib impressed on the upper surface; petiole 1-2 cm long, scaly, shallowly grooved on the upper surface.

Inflorescence a very short terminal raceme of 4-6 fragrant flowers, rachis thick, 1 cm long; pedicels 2-3.7 cm long, quite smooth and glossy; calyx large, broadly campanulate, to 2.5 cm long, chartaceous, green, glabrous, lobes 5, broadly ovate; corolla funnelform, quite oblique at the mouth, 5 cm long, 9 cm in diameter, white, sparsely scaly outside, lobes 2.5 cm long, spreading; stamens 10, filaments hairy at the base; ovary white-scaly, style curved upward.

Capsule 1.8 cm long, enclosed by the persistent calyx.

Southeast Xizang; also Burma. Grows in forests.

4023　南岭杜鹃

RHODODENDRON LEVINEI
Merr.

nán lǐng dùjuān   *"Nan Ling rhododendron"*

Evergreen shrub to 4 meters high; twigs long, shoots sparsely clad at first with scales and long coarse appressed hairs which are later lost.

Leaves coriaceous, elliptic-obovate, 4-7 cm long, 1.8-2.5(-3) cm broad, apex broadly rounded, usually retuse and mucronate, base obtuse, upper surface lustrous and scaly, the scales 2-3 diameters apart, the upper surface also sparsely clad overall with long gray bristles, the margin similarly bristly, the hairs later gradually lost, lower surface glabrous and densely scaly, the scales slightly more than a diameter apart; petiole 5-10 mm long, convex on the upper surface, clad with sparse scales and long coarse hairs which are later lost.

Terminal inflorescence of usually 2-3 flowers; pedicels about 2 cm long, scaly, sparsely coarse-hairy at first; calyx large, 10 mm long, deeply 5-lobed; corolla broadly funnelform, 8-9 cm long, white, smooth and glossy; stamens 10, filaments pubescent on the lower part; ovary densely scaly, style densely scaly at the base.

Capsule oblong, to 2 cm long, scaly.

Distributed in Guangxi, Guangdong, Hunan, Fujian. Grows in forests.

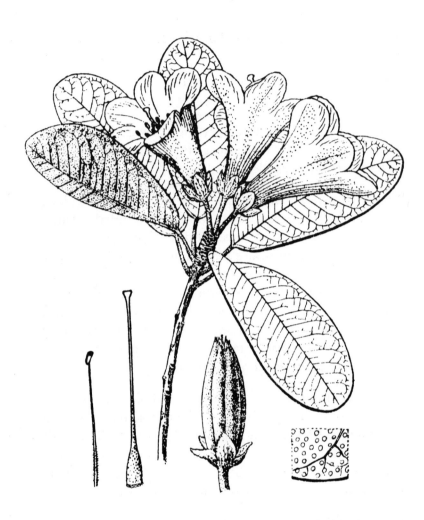

4024　百合花杜鹃

RHODODENDRON LILIIFLORUM
Lévl.

bǎi hé huā dùjuān   *"lily rhododendron"*

Evergreen shrub, 3-8 meters high; shoots and flower-bud scales clad with reddish brown scales, glabrous.

Leaves coriaceous, oblong-lanceolate, 6-11 cm long, 2.5-3.5 cm broad, obtuse at the apex, narrowing slightly downward, rounded at the base, upper surface smooth and glossy, lateral veins inconspicuous, lower surface clad with fine reddish brown scales about a diameter apart; petiole 2-2.5 cm long, convex on the upper surface, densely scaly.

Terminal umbelliform inflorescence of 3-5 fragrant flowers; pedicels about 1.5 cm long, scaly; calyx large, about 8 mm long, 5-lobed nearly to the base, sparsely scaly outside; corolla broadly funnelform, white, corolla tube about 7 cm long, quite densely scaly outside, lobes 5, slightly short-ciliate; stamens 10, rather short, filaments pubescent on the lower third, anthers about 5 mm long; ovary densely scaly, style rather densely scaly on the lower half.

Capsule about 3.5 cm long, 1.2 cm thick, densely scaly.

Distributed in Guizhou, Hunan, Guangxi. Grows in open forests.

45

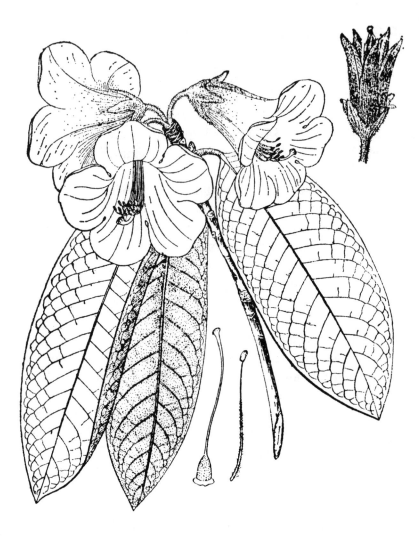

4025　大果杜鹃

RHODODENDRON SINONUTTALLII
Balf. f. et Forrest

dà guǒ dùjuān   *"large-capsuled rhododendron"*

Evergreen shrub to 4 meters high or more; twigs stout, about 8 mm thick, scaly.

Leaves and flowers similar to those of *R. nuttallii* Booth. (mù lán dùjuān, "magnolia rhododendron"), this species mainly differentiated by the inflorescence of 3 flowers, the stouter pedicels which are pubescent as well as scaly, the calyx lobes which are narrower, oblong, and pubescent outside, the corolla exterior which is more or less scaly overall, and the much larger capsule, to 6 cm long and 2.2 cm thick.

Distributed in southeast Xizang, northwest Yunnan. Grows in forests at 1700 meters.

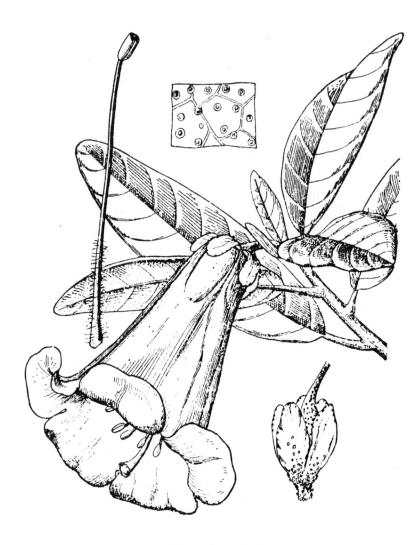

4026　独花杜鹃

48

RHODODENDRON HEADFORTIANUM
Hutch.

dú huā dùjuān   *"lone-flowered rhododendron"*

Evergreen shrub, 1-2 meters high; shoots sparsely scaly.

Leaves scattered, coriaceous, narrowly oblong or oblong-lanceolate, 7-12 cm long, 2-4.5 cm broad, apex obtuse or bluntly acute, base obtuse, margin recurved, upper surface slightly scaly when young, lower surface gray-white and scaly, the scales of unequal size and 2-3 diameters apart; petiole 1.5-2 cm long, not grooved on the upper surface, scaly.

Terminal inflorescence of one flower; pedicel 2 cm long, densely scaly; calyx large, 5-lobed nearly to the base, lobes 1.5 cm long, sparsely scaly at the middle and on the lower part, also scaly at the upper margin; corolla cream, corolla tube very slightly pink-tinged outside at the top, lobes 5; stamens 10, rather long compared to the corolla tube, filaments hairy on the lower third, anthers 5 mm long, dark brown; ovary densely scaly, style scaly on the lower part.

Capsule 5 cm long, scaly.

Southeast Xizang (Yarlung Zangbo Jiang valley).

4027　白喇叭杜鹃

RHODODENDRON TAGGIANUM
Hutch.

bái lǎba dùjuān   *"white trumpet rhododendron"*

Evergreen shrub about 2 meters high; shoots rather densely glandular-scaly.

Leaves scattered, coriaceous, oblong or oblong-lanceolate, 10-16 cm long, 3-5 cm broad, acute at the apex, tapering downward, upper surface quite scaly toward the midrib, lower surface gray and glandular-scaly, the scales small and 2-3 diameters apart, lateral veins prominent on the upper and lower surfaces; petiole 2-3 cm long, upper surface not grooved.

Terminal inflorescence of usually 3 fragrant flowers, rachis 1 cm long; pedicels 2 cm long, densely scaly; calyx large, leaflike, green, scaly at the base, deeply 5-lobed, lobes 1.5 cm long; corolla funnelform-campanulate, 6-7 cm long, white with 2 yellow elliptic spots between the nectary sacs, densely scaly at the base, lobes 5, broadly emarginate; stamens 10, as long as the corolla tube, filaments hairy on the lower half; ovary densely scaly, style densely scaly on the lower part.

Capsule straight, 5 cm long, densely clad with fleshy fine scaly glands.

Southeast Xizang; also Burma. Grows in thickets.

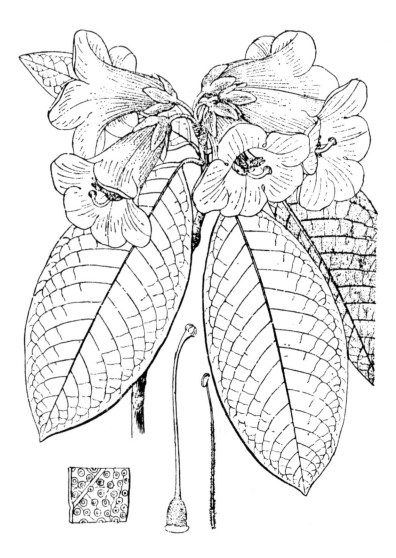

4028　木兰杜鹃

RHODODENDRON NUTTALLII
Booth.

mù lán dùjuān   *"magnolia rhododendron"*

Evergreen shrub to small tree to 10 meters high, sometimes epiphytic; branchlets nearly smooth and glossy.

Leaves stiff-coriaceous, elliptic, 12-20 cm long, 5.6-10 cm broad, apex mucronate, upper surface strongly and coarsely bullate-reticulate, lower surface densely scaly, the scales of unequal size and 1½ to 2 diameters apart, midrib and lateral veins prominent on the upper surface, very prominent on the lower surface; petiole 1.8 cm long, cylindric, convex on the upper surface, scaly.

Terminal umbelliform inflorescence of about 5 flowers (sometimes more); pedicels curved downward, 3 cm long, scaly; calyx large, to 2.5 cm long, 5-lobed nearly to the base, smooth and glossy; corolla funnelform, 10 cm long or longer, white with yellowish corolla tube and slightly pinkish lobes, corolla tube scaly mainly toward the base, lobes 5; stamens 10; filaments pubescent; ovary densely scaly, style densely scaly at the base.

Capsule 3.5 cm long, 1.2 cm thick, densely scaly, fruit-stalk to 5 cm long.

South Xizang; also Bhutan. Grows in forests at 1200 to 1600 meters.

4029　金鳞杜鹃

RHODODENDRON CHUNIENII
Chun et Fang

jīn lín dùjuān   *"golden scale rhododendron"*

Evergreen large shrub; branches of the current year purplish brown, with brown appressed scales persisting into the second year.

Leaves terminal, coriaceous, elliptic-lanceolate, 9-12 cm long, 3-3.5 cm broad, apex obtuse and mucronate, base obtuse, upper surface smooth and glossy, lower surface yellow-green with extremely small golden scales about 2-3 diameters apart, midrib flat and smooth on the upper surface, very prominent on the lower surface; petiole 2-2.5 cm long, not grooved on the upper surface, densely scaly.

Terminal umbelliform inflorescence of 1-3 flowers; pedicels thick, 1-1.5 cm long, densely scaly; calyx large, glabrous, lobes leaflike, of unequal size, the larger to 1.4 cm long and 9 mm broad, the smaller 9-10 mm long; corolla campanulate, large, 9-10 cm long, white, not scaly, corolla tube 3-4 cm in diameter, lobes 5, flatly and obliquely spreading, finely undulate; stamens 5, clad with soft stellate hairs on the lower part; ovary densely scaly, style stout, scaly on the lower third.

North Guangxi (Longsheng). Grows in mountaintop open forests.

55

4030　大花杜鹃

RHODODENDRON LINDLEYI

T. Moore

dà huā dùjuān   *"large-flowered rhododendron"*

Evergreen shrub, often epiphytic, to 1.5 meters high; branches few, shoots light green and scaly.

Leaves scattered, coriaceous, elliptic, 10-16 cm long, 3.3-6.2 cm broad, apex abruptly acute to sharply acute, base obtuse, upper surface dark green and sparsely scaly, lower surface nearly gray-white and sparsely scaly, the scales fine and evenly distributed 2-3 diameters apart; petiole 2-3.5 cm long, convex on the upper surface, more or less scaly.

Terminal subumbelliform inflorescence of 4-6 fragrant flowers; pedicels 1.2-2 cm long, densely scaly; calyx large, 2-2.5 cm long, light blue-green, deeply 5-lobed, lobes oblong-lanceolate, ciliolate; corolla campanulate-funnelform, 9-10 cm long and in diameter, white, yellow-dotted within the corolla tube at the base, slightly pink outside at the lobe tips, corolla tube sparsely scaly only at the base; stamens 10, filaments hairy at the base; ovary 1 cm long, densely scaly.

Capsule 5 cm long.

Southeast Xizang; also Sikkim, Bhutan. Grows in forests.

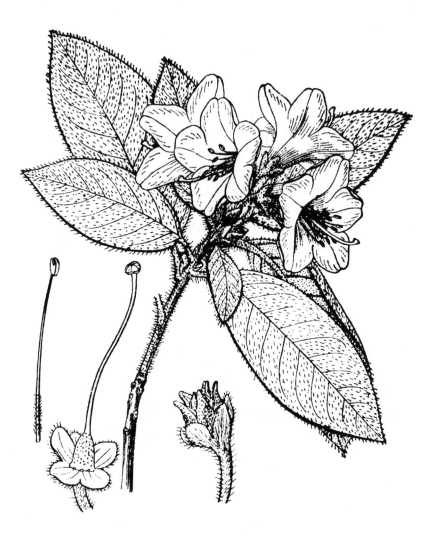

4031　睫毛杜鹃

RHODODENDRON CILIATUM
Hook. f.

jié máo dùjuān   *"eyelash rhododendron"*

Evergreen shrub to 2 meters high, often trailing on rocks; shoots setose.

Leaves coriaceous, elliptic, 3.7-8.2 cm long, 1.6-3.7 cm broad, upper surface setose, lower surface slightly setose at the midrib and sparsely scaly, the scales small and 2-3 diameters apart; petiole 6 mm long, long-setose.

Terminal short raceme of 2-4 flowers; pedicels 8 mm long, densely setose and scaly; calyx large, 8 mm long, deeply 5-lobed, lobes broadly ovate, vein-lined, sparsely scaly outside at the base, densely and stiffly long-ciliate; corolla funnelform, 3.7-5 cm long, white tinged rose, corolla tube broad, smooth and glossy outside, lobes 5, emarginate; stamens 10, filaments densely pubescent at the base; ovary 5-loculed, scaly, style smooth and glossy.

Capsule 1.6 cm long.

South Xizang; also Sikkim. Grows in mountainous areas at 2800-3500 meters.

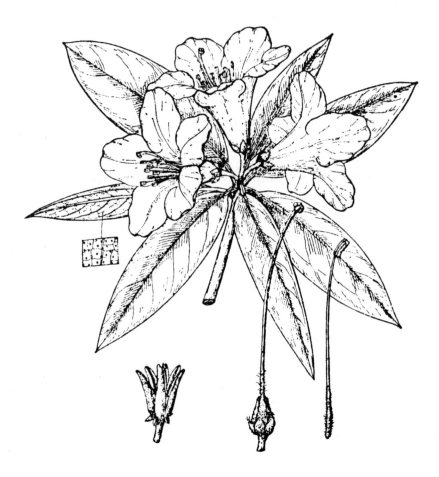

4032　石峰杜鹃

RHODODENDRON SCOPULORUM
Hutch.

shí fēng dùjuān   *"rocky cliff rhododendron"*

Evergreen shrub to more than 4 meters high; shoots sparsely scaly at first.

Leaves thick-coriaceous, elliptic-lanceolate, 7-8 cm long, 2.5-3 cm broad, apex mucronate, base bluntly cuneate, upper surface devoid of scales except when very young, lower surface very sparsely scaly, the scales fine and about 3-4 diameters apart, lateral veins evident; petiole 1 cm long, grooved on the upper surface, sparsely scaly.

Terminal inflorescence of 3 flowers; pedicels 5-15 mm long, sparsely clad with loose scurfy scales; calyx deeply 5-lobed, the lobes broadly ovate, sparsely scaly outside, and sparsely ciliate; corolla 6 cm long, white tinged pink, the color deepest outside toward the middle of each lobe, corolla tube funnelform, clad outside with sparse fine scales and fine soft hairs; stamens 10, filaments hairy on the lower part; ovary densely scaly, style green and scaly with a few soft hairs near the base.

Capsule 2 cm long, clad with wrinkled scales.

Xizang (Yarlung Zangbo Jiang valley). Grows on rocky cliffs.

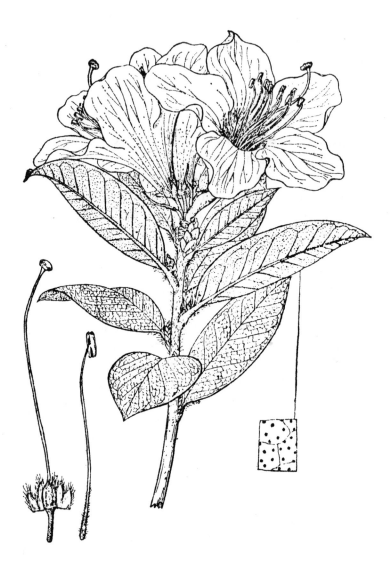

4033　睫毛萼杜鹃

RHODODENDRON CILIICALYX
Franch.

jié máo è dùjuān   *"ciliate calyx rhododendron"*

Evergreen shrub to 3.5 meters high; shoots sparsely fine-scaly, sometimes also stiff-hairy.

Leaves scattered, coriaceous, elliptic or obovate-elliptic, 6.5-11 cm long, 2.4-3.4 cm broad, apex acute, base obtuse, upper surface reticulate, lower surface gray-white and scaly, the scales 2-4 diameters apart; petiole 1.2-1.7 cm long, scaly, often sparsely setose along both sides.

Terminal umbelliform inflorescence of about 3 flowers; pedicels 1.2-1.7 cm long, densely scaly; calyx variable, 5-lobed almost to the base, lobes to 6.5 mm long, sparsely scaly outside, long-setose at the margin; corolla broadly campanulate, white or rose, corolla tube shorter than the lobes, 2.5-3.2 cm long, scaly outside, lobes 5, 3.2 cm long, sometimes golden-scaly on the back; stamens 10; ovary densely scaly, style scaly and pubescent at the base.

Capsule 1.5 cm long, stout, densely scaly.

West and northwest Yunnan. Grows in thickets on rocky hills.

4034　长柱杜鹃

RHODODENDRON LYI
Lévl.

cháng zhù dùjuān *"long-styled rhododendron"*

Evergreen shrub to 2 meters high; shoots sparsely clad with scurfy scales, with spreading soft bristles on the upper part.

Leaves subterminal, firm-coriaceous, lanceolate to elliptic-oblong, 7-10 cm long, 2.5-4 cm broad, apex acute or acuminate, base cuneate, upper surface smooth and glossy, lower surface white-papillate and scaly, the scales rusty brown, scurfy, of unequal size, sunken, and less than a diameter apart, midrib finely grooved on the upper surface, thick and prominent on the lower surface; petiole 6 mm long, pubescent and scaly.

Terminal umbelliform inflorescence of as many as 5 fragrant flowers; pedicels 5-10 mm long, clad with scurfy scales; calyx 2-3 mm long, densely clad with scurfy scales, lobes 5, of equal or unequal size; corolla broadly funnelform, 5 cm long, white with light lemon yellow spots and dots on the upper part of the throat, finely hairy outside below the middle, lobes 5, undulate, very sparsely scaly on the back; stamens 10; ovary and lower 2/3 of style clad with scurfy scales, style very long, far beyond the corolla.

Capsule oblong, 2.5 cm long, the enlarged calyx persistent at the base.

Guizhou. Grows on limestone hills.

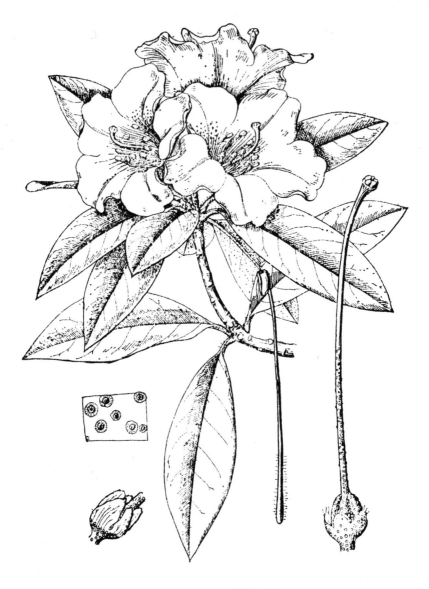

4035　波瓣杜鹃

RHODODENDRON SCOTTIANUM
Hutch.

bō bàn dùjuān   *"wavy petal rhododendron"*

Evergreen shrub to 3 meters high; shoots densely scaly.

Leaves in terminal clusters, coriaceous, broadly lance-olate to elliptic-oblong, 7-14 cm long, 3-5 cm broad, apex acute, base short cuneate, upper surface clad with deter-sile scales, lower surface powdery white and scaly, the scales ferrugineous and mostly 2 diameters apart, with a few white hairs remaining on the immature leaves, mid-rib slightly impressed on the upper surface, slender and prominent on the lower surface, lateral veins rather inconspicuous on both surfaces; petiole 5-8 mm long, clad with scales and caducous bristles.

Terminal raceme of 2-4 fragrant flowers (occasionally more), rachis thick, to 5 mm long; pedicels 1-1.5 cm long, scaly; calyx varying in size from nearly obsolete to 8 mm long, more or less deeply cleft, lobes of unequal size, sparsely scaly and sparsely ciliate; corolla broadly funnel-form, 6-10 cm long, pure white or sometimes rose-tinged outside, scaly and hairy outside at the base, lobes 5, deeply undulate; stamens 10, filaments hairy on the lower fourth; ovary scaly, style scaly on the lower half.

West Yunnan. Grows in thickets.

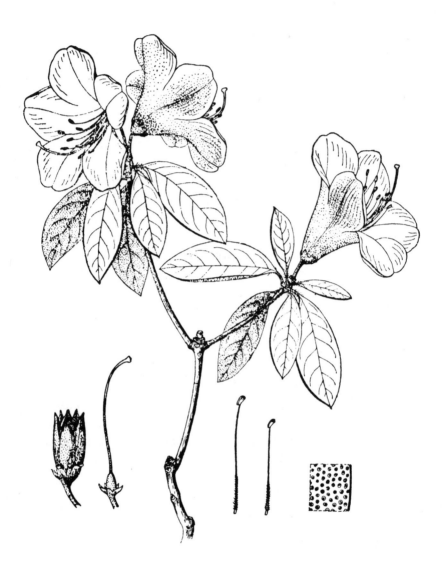

4036　云上杜鹃

RHODODENDRON SUPRANUBIUM
Hutch.

yún shàng dùjuān   *"above-the-clouds rhododendron"*

Evergreen shrub about 1 meter high; branches slender, shoots densely scaly.

Leaves stiff-coriaceous, oblanceolate or obovate-oblanceolate, 3.9-9 cm long, 1.3-3.3 cm broad, upper surface quite densely scaly and ciliate when young, smooth and glossy at maturity, lower surface gray-white and quite densely scaly, the scales golden, somewhat unequal in size, and less than a diameter apart; petiole 5-10 mm long, quite densely scaly, often sparsely setose along both sides, broadly grooved on the upper surface.

Terminal inflorescence of as many as 3 flowers (often 1); pedicels 1 cm long, densely scaly; calyx somewhat orbicular, to 2 mm long, shallowly lobed, scaly; corolla broadly funnelform, white slightly red-tinged, corolla tube 2.5 cm long, rather densely scaly outside and pubescent toward the base, lobes 5, scaly; stamens 10, filaments densely hairy on the lower half; ovary densely scaly, style densely scaly on the lower half.

Capsule oblong, 1.6 cm long, 1 cm thick, scaly.

West Yunnan. Grows on rocky cliffs at 3500 meters.

4037 肉色杜鹃

RHODODENDRON CARNEUM
Hutch.

ròu sè dùjuān   *"flesh-colored rhododendron"*

Evergreen shrub about 1 meter high; shoots densely brown-scaly.

Leaves elliptic-obovate, 6-12 cm long, 3-4 cm broad, apex acute, base obtuse or broadly cuneate, upper surface dark green, finely reticulate, and glabrous, lower surface gray-white and densely scaly, midrib prominent on the lower surface, about 1.5 mm thick at the base, lateral veins evident on both surfaces; petiole 1-1.5 cm long, densely scaly.

Terminal inflorescence of 3-4 flowers; calyx well developed, 5-lobed, lobes rounded-ovate, setose-ciliate at the tips, densely scaly outside; corolla flesh red, corolla tube 3.5-4 cm long, 3 cm in diameter at the mouth, sparsely scaly outside, glabrous within, lobes 3 cm long, oblong, spreading; stamens usually 12, shortly exserted, filaments hairy on the lower part; ovary densely scaly, style exserted, longer than the stamens, quite densely scaly, rose on the upper part.

Northwest Yunnan; also Burma. Grows on grassy slopes.

4038　薄皮杜鵑

72

RHODODENDRON TARONENSE
Hutch.

bó pí dùjuān   *"thin bark rhododendron"*

Evergreen epiphytic shrub, 3-5 meters high; shoots slightly scaly, the thin bark of the older branches smooth, brown, and peeling off easily.

Leaves coriaceous, narrowly elliptic to elliptic-obovate, 10-14 cm long, 4-5.5 cm broad, apex acute and mucronate, base acute, upper surface not scaly, lower surface sparsely scaly, the scales fine and about 3-5 diameters apart, lateral veins about 10 pair, slender and inconspicuous.

Terminal umbelliform inflorescence of 5 fragrant flowers; pedicels 1.2 cm long, densely scaly; calyx poorly developed, undulate, scaly outside; corolla 5 cm long, somewhat fleshy, white with one large yellow spot near the base, corolla tube sparsely scaly outside, lobes 5; stamens 10, almost the same length as the corolla, filaments pubescent on the lower part; ovary 6-loculed, densely scaly, style scaly on the lower fourth.

Capsule crooked at the base, 3.2 cm long, verrocose, not keeled.

Northwest Yunnan. Grows in river-valley rain forests at about 1500 meters.

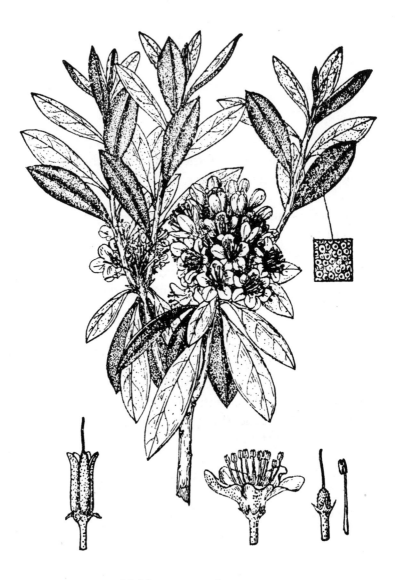

4039　照山白

RHODODENDRON MICRANTHUM
Turcz.

zhào shān bái   *"shining mountain white"*
bái jìngzi   *"white mirror"*

Evergreen shrub, 1-2 meters high; twigs slim and delicate, shoots sparsely scaly.

Leaves scattered, thick-coriaceous, oblanceolate, 3-4 cm long, 8-12 mm broad, bluntly acute at the apex, tapering downward, narrowly cuneate at the base, upper surface slightly scaly, lower surface densely scaly, the scales light brown and more or less imbricate; petiole about 3 mm long.

Terminal dense raceme of many small flowers, rachis 1.8 cm long; pedicels about 8 mm long, scaly; calyx deeply 5-lobed, lobes narrowly triangular, about 3 mm long, ciliate; corolla campanulate, 6-8 mm long, about 1 cm in diameter, milk white, scaly outside; stamens 10, exserted, glabrous; ovary 5-loculed, scaly, style shorter than the stamens, glabrous.

Capsule oblong, to 8 mm long, sparsely scaly.

Broadly distributed in northern and northeastern China, west to Gansu, Sichuan, and Hubei, south to Shandong; also Korea.

Intensely poisonous, especially the young leaves; livestock are easily killed by eating the plant.

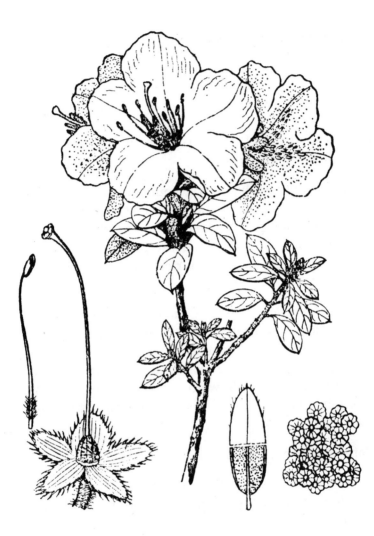

4040　怒江杜鹃

RHODODENDRON SALUENENSE
Franch.

nù jiāng dùjuān   *"Nu Jiang rhododendron"*

Evergreen shrub to 1 meter high; twigs scaly and densely setose; leaf-bud scales subpersistent.

Leaves thick-coriaceous, oblong-elliptic, 1-2 cm long, 8-12 mm broad, apex mucronate, upper surface lustrous and sparsely scaly, lower surface densely covered by imbricate scales, margin long-setose when young; petiole short, densely setose.

Terminal inflorescence of 2-3 flowers; flower-bud scales subpersistent; pedicels 1 cm long, setose and sparsely scaly; calyx large, 8 mm long, lobes 5, purplish red, pubescent on the back and scaly toward the middle, coarsely long-ciliate; corolla broadly campanulate, about 2.5 cm long, deep purplish red with darker spots, exterior densely pubescent and sparsely scaly; stamens 10, exserted, densely villous near the base; ovary scaly, style glabrous, purple.

Capsule ovoid, about 5 mm long, scaly.

Northwest Yunnan. Grows on rocky slopes at 4000 meters.

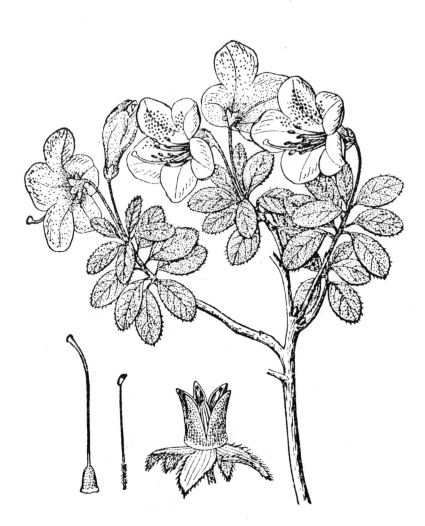

4041　美被杜鹃

RHODODENDRON CALOSTROTUM
Balf. f. et Ward

měi bèi dùjuān   *"beautiful covering rhododendron"*

Evergreen dwarf shrub to 30 cm high; branchlets densely scaly, not setose.

Leaves thin-coriaceous, obovate-elliptic, 1-2.4 cm long, 7-12 mm broad, upper surface densely clad with fleshy scales, lower surface densely scaly, the scales dark chestnut and imbricate; petiole short, densely scaly.

Terminal inflorescence of usually 2 flowers; flower-bud scales caducous; pedicels about 3 cm long, scaly; calyx well developed, 6 mm long, lobes broadly elliptic, ciliate, densely scaly on the back except near the margin; corolla broadly funnelform, about 2.2 cm long, bright light reddish purple, exterior short-pubescent but not scaly; stamens 10, exserted, filaments villous near the base; ovary scaly, style glabrous or villous near the base.

Capsule 6 mm long, scaly, enclosed by the persistent calyx.

Southeast Xizang; also Burma and northern India. Grows on grasslands at about 4000 meters.

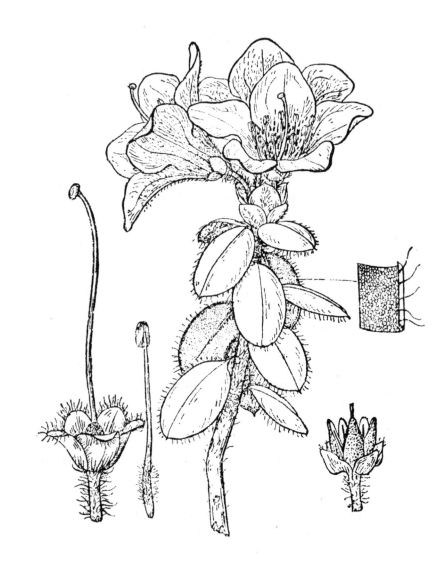

4042　平卧杜鹃

RHODODENDRON PROSTRATUM
W. W. Sm.

píng wò dùjuān   *"trailing rhododendron"*

Evergreen dwarf shrub, 5-10 cm high; twigs numerous and trailing, branchlets green and densely clad with soft white hairs, shoots about 1 cm long, sparsely leaved, clad with gray scales similar to those of the year-old branches.

Leaves thin-coriaceous, oblong-elliptic, 1.5-2 cm long, 6-10 mm broad, margin recurved, clad at first with long soft white hairs, later subglabrous, upper surface glossy green and glabrous, lower surface densely scaly, the scales fine, contiguous, white at first but brown at maturity, midrib impressed on the upper surface, prominent on the lower surface; petiole 2-5 mm long, scaly and setose.

Terminal umbelliform inflorescence of 1-3 flowers; pedicels slightly curved downward, 2 mm long, clad with dense long white hairs and scales; calyx large, 5-lobed to the base, lobes 8 mm long, glabrous on the back, ciliate; corolla broadly funnelform, reddish purple with red dots on the back, pubescent outside; stamens 9-10, filaments hairy at the base, ovary densely fine-scaly, style glabrous.

Capsule 8 mm long.

Northwest Yunnan. Grows on rocky cliffs at about 5000 meters.

4043 树生杜鹃

RHODODENDRON DENDROCHARIS
Franch.

shù shēng dùjuān   *"tree-growing rhododendron"*

Evergreen small epiphytic shrub, usually to 50 cm high; shoots fine, short, and clad with reddish brown bristles, older branches rarely setose.

Leaves thick-coriaceous, elliptic, 10-18 mm long, 5-7 mm broad, apex obtuse and mucronate, margin recurved, ciliate when young, upper surface dark green and glabrous, lower surface white-powdery and scaly, the scales fine, yellow, a diameter apart or nearly contiguous; petiole 3-6 mm long, clad with light red bristles.

Calyx large, deeply 5-lobed, lobes broadly elliptic, scaly on the back, long-ciliate; corolla broadly campanulate, 1.5-2 cm long, rose with dark red dots on the upper interior, minutely hairy within at the base, lobes 5, glabrous; stamens 10, filaments pubescent on the lower part; ovary densely clad with yellow-green scales, style purple and minutely hairy on the lower part.

Capsule elliptic, 1 cm long, 7 mm thick, densely clad with fine fleshy scales.

Distributed in Sichuan, Xizang. Usually epiphytic on tree trunks in forests.

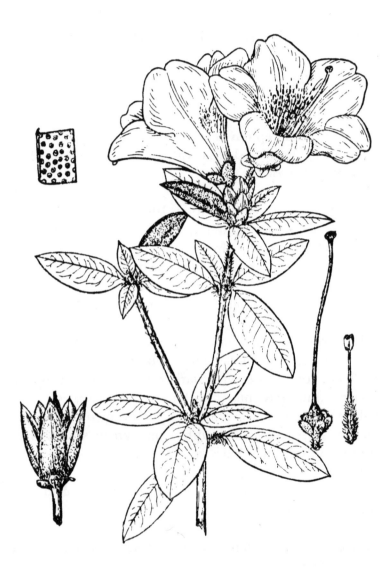

4044　宝兴杜鹃

RHODODENDRON MOUPINENSE
Franch.

bǎo xīng dùjuān   *"Baoxing rhododendron"*

Evergreen small epiphytic shrub about 70 cm high; twigs slender, about 2.5 mm thick, black-setose at first, smooth and glossy at maturity.

Leaves subverticillate, firm-coriaceous, oblong-elliptic or ovate-elliptic, 2-4.5 cm long, 1-2.5 cm broad, apex obtuse and mucronate, base rounded or subcordate, margin strongly revolute and usually ciliate, upper surface sparsely and minutely hairy only on the midrib, lower surface densely clad with yellow scales, lateral veins nearly obscure; petiole 3-5 mm long, usually black-setose.

Terminal inflorescence of 1-3 flowers; pedicels to 7 mm long; calyx well developed, leaflike, 5-lobed, slightly fine-ciliate, and white-glandular outside; corolla broadly funnelform, white with red dots on the lower part of the corolla tube, corolla tube 2.5-3.5 cm long, glabrous outside, pubescent within, lobes 5, about 2.3 cm long, spreading; stamens 10, filaments clad with spreading white hairs on the lower part; ovary densely scaly, style far longer than the stamens, glabrous.

Capsule to 1.3 cm long, scaly.

West Sichuan. Usually epiphytic on tree trunks in forests.

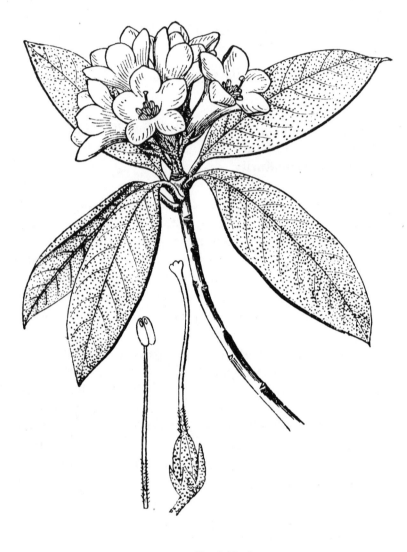

4045　朱砂杜鹃

RHODODENDRON CINNABARINUM
Hook. f.

zhū shā dùjuān *"cinnabar rhododendron"*

Evergreen shrub about 2 meters high; shoots light purple, slightly scaly.

Leaves coriaceous, obovate-elliptic, to 7.5 cm long, 4.5 cm broad, lower surface gray-white and densely scaly, the scales very fine, fleshy, and less than a diameter apart, lateral veins evident on the upper surface; petiole 1.2 cm long, sparsely scaly.

Terminal subumbelliform inflorescence of about 5 flowers; pedicels about 6 mm long, scaly, curved downward; calyx large, lobes unequal, one lobe frequently longer than the others; corolla tubular, gradually enlarged toward the top, 3.7 cm long, cinnabar red, not scaly outside, lobes 5; stamens 10, slightly exserted, slightly pubescent at the base; ovary 5-loculed, scaly.

Capsule 1.2 cm long, densely scaly.

South Xizang; also Sikkim. Grows in forests at 3500 meters.

A closely related species also found in Xizang is *R. igneum* Cowan (ròu hóng dùjuān, "flesh red rhododendron"), which has leaves 3-7 cm long, flesh red corolla 2 cm long, and 10-12 stamens which are longer than the corolla.

4046　管花杜鹃

RHODODENDRON KEYSII

Nutt.

guǎn huā dùjuān   *"tubular flower rhododendron"*

Evergreen shrub about 4 meters high; twigs slender, branchlets densely scaly when young.

Leaves scattered on the shoots, oblong-lanceolate, 7.5-10 cm long, 1.8-4.4 cm broad, apex acute, upper and lower surfaces densely scaly, the scales of the lower surface of unequal size, the larger scales about a diameter apart, broad and fleshy at the center and narrowly rimmed, lateral veins quite evident; petiole 8 mm long.

Racemes produced from clustered lateral buds and terminal buds; pedicels 8 mm long, scaly; calyx small, shallowly 5-lobed, smooth and glossy outside; corolla tubular, slightly ventricose, 1.8 cm long, bright red, sometimes yellowish at the lobe tips (var. *unicolor*) [*sic*], smooth and glossy outside, mouth shallowly 5-lobed, lobes erect; stamens 10, filaments densely pubescent on the lower part; ovary 5-loculed, densely scaly, style pubescent on the lower third.

Capsule 1 cm long, 5-loculed, scaly.

South Xizang; also Bhutan. Grows in mountainous areas at 2800-4500 meters.

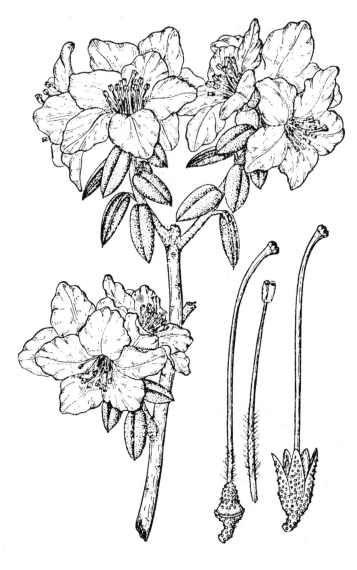

4047　淡黄杜鹃

RHODODENDRON FLAVIDUM
Franch.

dàn huáng dùjuān   *"light yellow rhododendron"*

Evergreen undershrub, 45-80 cm high, densely branched; twigs slender, the plant scaly throughout except on the corolla.

Leaves dense, coriaceous, ovate-oblong, 1.2-2.5 cm long, 6-8 mm broad at the middle, apex obtuse and mucronate, base rounded, embossed, margin recurved, upper and lower surfaces densely scaly, midrib grooved on the upper surface; petiole 2-3 mm long.

Inflorescence a terminal cluster of 3-5 flowers; pedicels abruptly reflexed, 5-7 mm long; calyx sub-bilabiate, the lobes somewhat unequal, 4-6 mm long, ovate, acute, and reflexed at maturity; corolla subregular, nearly rotate, about 3 cm in diameter, light yellow, not scaly, slightly pubescent at the throat, lobes 5, rounded, undulate; stamens 10, shorter than the corolla, filaments villous below the middle; ovary 5-loculed, densely scaly, style pubescent below the middle.

Distributed in Sichuan, east Xizang. Grows beneath forests on the high mountains.

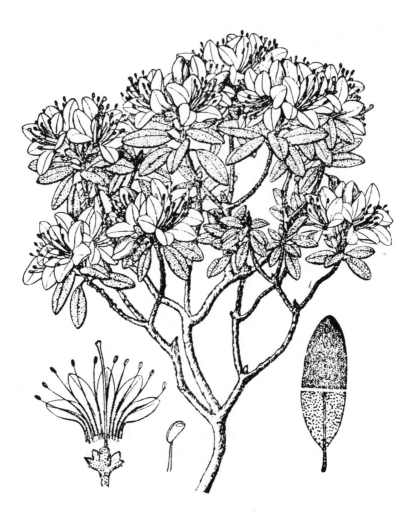

4048 木里杜鹃

RHODODENDRON MULIENSE
Balf. f. et Forrest

mù lǐ dùjuān *"Muli rhododendron"*

Evergreen shrub, 50-85 cm high, densely branched; branchlets densely scaly; leaf-bud scales caducous.

Leaves coriaceous, oblong-elliptic, 1.2 cm long, 8 mm broad, upper and lower surfaces densely scaly, the scales of the lower surface more or less contiguous, of one type but of 2 colors, mostly reddish brown with a few greenish white; petiole 1 mm long, densely scaly.

Terminal inflorescence of about 5-6 flowers; flower-bud scales caducous; pedicels short, densely scaly; calyx well developed, 4 mm long, lobes elliptic, densely scaly outside, short-ciliate; corolla about 1.6 cm long, bright yellow, scaly outside; stamens 10, exserted, filaments villous at the base; ovary scaly, style pubescent at the base, longer than the stamens, stigma deeply cleft.

Capsule small, 3.5 mm long, scaly.

Distributed in southwest Sichuan, north Yunnan. Grows among pine trees on vast rocky grasslands at 3600-3900 meters.

Considered by some to be the same species as *R. chryseum* (jīn huáng dùjuān, "golden rhododendron").

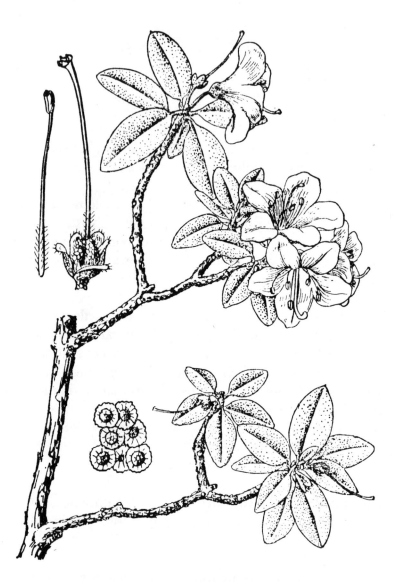

4049　金黄杜鹃

RHODODENDRON CHRYSEUM

Balf. f. et Ward

jīn huáng dùjuān   *"golden rhododendron"*

Evergreen dwarf aromatic shrub, 30-70 cm high; shoots densely clad with dark red scurfy scales.

Leaves in terminal clusters, coriaceous, ovate or obovate-elliptic, 12 mm long, 5-8 mm broad, usually obtuse at the apex and base, mucronulate, slightly recurved at the margin, glabrous, upper and lower surfaces clad with contiguous scales, some scales of the lower surface light green, others rusty brown; petiole 2 mm long, densely scaly.

Terminal compact umbelliform inflorescence of as many as 6 flowers; pedicels 3-5 mm long, densely scaly; calyx well developed, lobes elliptic-oblong, 3-3.5 mm long, often light red, scaly on the back, fringed more or less with soft hairs; corolla 2-2.5 cm in diameter, light yellow to bright yellow, glabrous outside, white-hairy at the throat, corolla tube short funnelform, about 4 mm long, lobes 8-12 mm long, scaly on the back; stamens 5; ovary scaly above the middle, minutely hairy on the lower part; style hairy at the base.

Distributed in northwest Yunnan, south Sichuan. Grows on grassy slopes or in marshes on the high mountains.

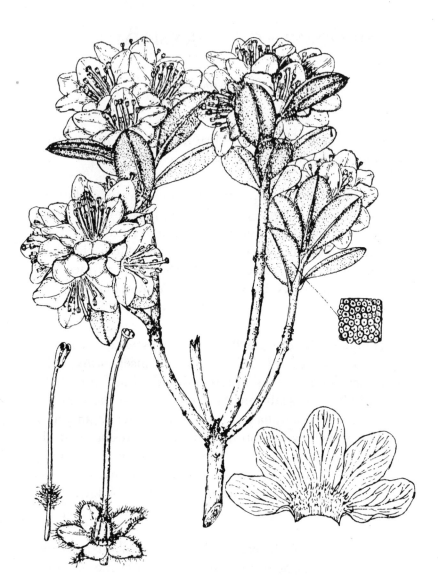

4050　紫蓝杜鹃

RHODODENDRON RUSSATUM

Balf. f. et Forrest

zǐ lán dùjuǎn *"purplish blue rhododendron"*

Evergreen undershrub to 1.2 meters high; shoots densely scaly; leaf-bud scales caducous.

Leaves coriaceous, oblong or ovate-elliptic, about 2.5 cm long, 1.2 cm broad, apex obtuse and mucronate, base obtuse, upper and lower surfaces scaly, the scales of the lower surface rusty red and contiguous or slightly imbricate; petiole to 6 mm long, scaly.

Terminal globose inflorescence of 4-10 flowers; flower-bud scales persistent during flowering; pedicels very short, scaly; calyx well developed, deeply 5-lobed, lobes to 4 mm long, broadly elliptic, nearly smooth and glossy outside, softly long-ciliate; corolla broadly funnelform, about 1.8 cm long, dark purplish blue, pubescent within at the throat, not scaly outside; stamens 10, long-exserted, filaments densely pubescent toward the base; ovary scaly, style red, sparsely pubescent on the lower half, slightly longer than the stamens.

Capsule 4 mm long, scaly.

Northwest Yunnan. Grows on high mountain grasslands at 3500 meters.

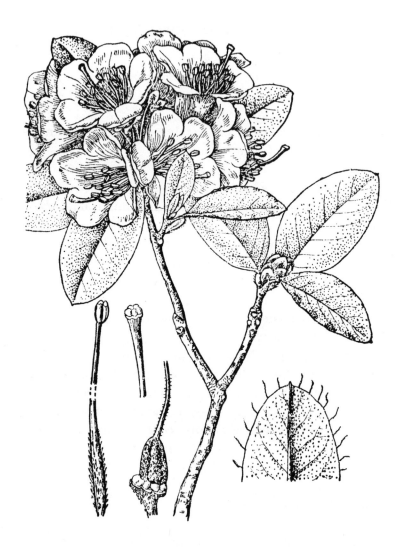

4051　灰色杜鹃

RHODODENDRON RAVUM

Balf. f. et W. W. Sm.

huĭ sè dùjuān *"gray rhododendron"*

Evergreen shrub to 4 meters high; branches sparsely scaly in the first year.

Leaves coriaceous, oblong-elliptic, 4-5 cm long, 2-2.5 cm broad, apex obtuse and mucronate, base broadly cuneate, margin finely long-ciliate when young, glabrous at maturity, upper surface sparsely scaly, lower surface densely clad with imbricate scales; petiole 5-7 mm long, densely scaly.

Terminal umbelliform inflorescence of about 10 flowers; flower-bud scales semipersistent; pedicels about 1 cm long, densely scaly; calyx large, 7 mm long, lobes broadly elliptic, scaly at the middle, long-ciliate; corolla funnelform, 3 cm long, dark rose, not spotted, glabrous within, lobes 5, sparsely scaly outside at the middle; stamens 10, exserted, filaments sparsely pubescent on the lower third; ovary 5-loculed, densely scaly, style longer than the stamens, pubescent at the base.

Northwest Yunnan. Grows in open thickets at about 3200 meters.

4052　毛蕊杜鹃

RHODODENDRON WEBSTERIANUM
Rehd. et Wils.

máo ruĭ dùjuān   *"hairy stamen rhododendron"*

Evergreen undershrub to 1 meter high; branchlets densely scaly; leaf-bud scales caducous.

Leaves narrowly elliptic, about 8 mm long, 3.5-4 mm
broad, upper and lower surfaces densely scaly, the scales
of the lower surface light yellowish gray and imbricate;
petiole 1.5 mm long, scaly.

Terminal inflorescence of usually one flower (sometimes 2), flower-bud scales subpersistent; pedicels 3 mm
long, scaly; calyx well developed, 3.5 mm long, lobes
light purple, scaly from the middle to the base, short-
ciliate; corolla broadly funnelform, 1.8 cm long, purplish
rose, not scaly outside; stamens 10, exserted, densely
pubescent toward the base; ovary scaly, style slightly
longer than the stamens, sparsely pubescent at the base,
sometimes also slightly scaly.

Capsule 4 mm long, 2.2 mm thick, scaly, enclosed at the
base by the persistent calyx.

West Sichuan. Grows on moist grasslands at 3200-4200
meters.

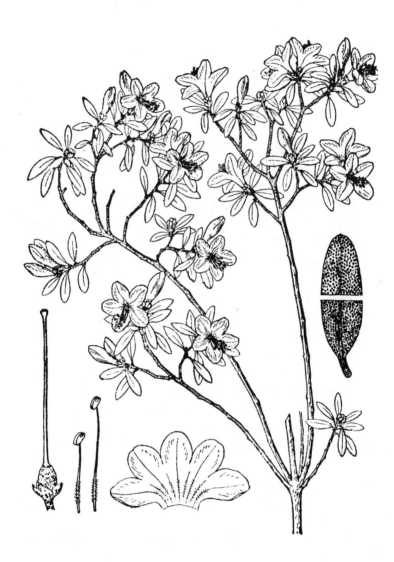

4053　千里香杜鹃

RHODODENDRON THYMIFOLIUM
Maxim.

qiān lǐ xiāng dùjuān *"thousand-li-fragrance rhododendron"**

Evergreen undershrub to 1.2 meters high, densely branched; twigs delicate, grayish brown, and glabrous, shoots densely scaly; leaf-bud scales caducous.

Leaves subcoriaceous, narrowly oblong-lanceolate, about 8 mm long, 2.5-3 mm broad, apex and base obtuse or rounded, upper and lower surfaces densely clad with silvery white scales, the scales of the lower surface of uniform size, imbricate; petiole short and scaly.

Inflorescence terminal, flowers solitary or in pairs; flower-bud scales persistent; petioles short and glabrous; calyx very short, scaly outside; corolla bright purplish blue; stamens 10, exserted, filaments pubescent toward the base; ovary densely scaly, style purple, shorter than the stamens, and glabrous.

Capsule ovoid, 2 mm long, scaly, the style persistent.

Distributed in Gansu, Qinghai. Forms thickets on moist mountain slopes at 2400-3800 meters.

*li = ½ kilometer

4054　隐蕊杜鹃

RHODODENDRON INTRICATUM
Franch.

yǐn ruǐ dùjuān   *"hidden stamen rhododendron"*

Evergreen undershrub to 50 cm high, densely branched; branchlets fine and short, densely scaly; leaf-bud scales caducous.

Leaves small, coriaceous, oblong-elliptic, 8 mm long, 4-5 mm broad, apex and base rounded, upper and lower surfaces densely scaly, the scales of the lower surface light greenish gray and imbricate; petiole very short, scaly.

Terminal subglobose inflorescence of 2-5 flowers; flower-bud scales persistent during flowering; pedicels very short, scaly; calyx very short, lobes triangular, of unequal size, scaly outside, ciliate; corolla narrowly tubular, 8 mm long, purple-violet or lilac-purple, not scaly outside, corolla tube hairy within, lobes 5, oblong, rounded at the tips, spreading; stamens 10, not exserted, filaments hairy at the base; ovary densely scaly, style very short and thick, glabrous, slightly shorter than the stamens.

Capsule ovoid, about 3 mm long, scaly, fruitstalk as long as or slightly longer than the capsule.

Distributed in west Sichuan, northwest Yunnan. Grows on grasslands and moist meadows above 4000 meters.

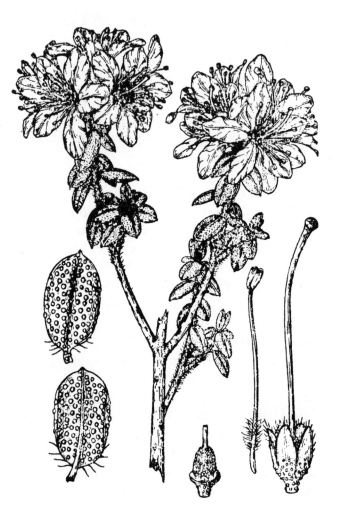

4055　刚毛杜鹃

RHODODENDRON SETOSUM
D. Don

gāng máo dùjuān   *"bristly rhododendron"*

Evergreen undershrub to 1.2 meters high; twigs fine, obliquely spreading, shoots clad with spreading detersile bristles.

Leaves coriaceous, oblong or elliptic-obovate, 7-12 mm long, 4-8 mm broad, apex rounded and mucronate, base rounded, margin revolute and sparsely setose, the bristles more numerous on the lower part, upper surface sparsely scaly, lower surface clad with scales a diameter apart and dense detersile bristles; petiole short and scaly.

Inflorescence a terminal cluster of 3-8 flowers; pedicels to 3 mm long, minutely hairy and sparsely scaly; calyx large, 5-lobed nearly to the base, lobes 3.5-5 mm long, red, ciliate, scaly on the lower part of the dorsal surface; corolla broadly funnelform, purplish rose, corolla tube 7 mm long, short-pubescent within, lobes 5, 11 mm long, spreading; stamens 10, filaments pubescent on one section above the base; ovary densely scaly, style glabrous.

Capsule about 5 mm long, scaly, enclosed by the persistent calyx.

Southeast Xizang; also Sikkim. Grows on high mountain grass slopes at 3800-4500 meters.

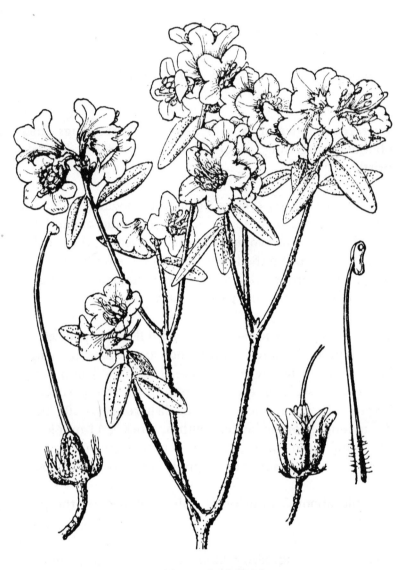

4056　小叶杜鹃

RHODODENDRON PARVIFOLIUM

Adams.

xiǎo yè dùjuān   *"small-leaved rhododendron"*

Evergreen undershrub to 1 meter high, densely branched; twigs slender, straight and upright, clad with dense rusty brown scales and fine hairs, smooth and glossy at maturity.

Leaves scattered at the ends of the twigs, coriaceous, oblong or ovate-elliptic, 1-2.5 cm long, 4-9 mm broad, apex obtuse and mucronate, base rounded, upper surface clad with white-margined subcontiguous scales, lower surface scaly and papillate, the scales contiguous, the papillae white and waxy.

Terminal umbelliform inflorescence of 2-5 flowers; pedicels 2-6 mm long; calyx purple, 5-lobed, lobes 1.5 mm long, subacute, densely scaly outside; corolla rotate-funnelform, 10-13 mm long, rose to purplish rose, not scaly, hairy at the base, 5-lobed; stamens 10, filaments hairy at the base; ovary scaly, style glabrous.

Capsule 5 mm long, oblong, densely scaly, fruitstalk to 8 mm long.

Distributed in northeast China, Nei Mongol; also Korea and USSR. Grows on high mountain grasslands or forest meadows.

4057　灰背杜鹃

RHODODENDRON HIPPOPHAEOIDES
Balf. f. et W. W. Sm.

huĭ bèi dùjuān   *"gray-backed rhododendron"*

Evergreen dwarf shrub to 1.5 meters high; shoots slender, yellow-brown, fastigiate, densely clad with brownish yellow scales.

Leaves scattered, subcoriaceous, oblong to elliptic, 1.5-2.5(-3) cm long, 7-10 mm broad, obtuse or rounded at the apex, broadly cuneate at the base, glabrous, upper surface dark green and scaly, the scales light yellow and mostly contiguous, lower surface light yellowish gray and scaly, the scales compactly contiguous, leaf veins not evident on the lower surface; petiole 3-5 mm long, densely scaly.

Compact terminal umbelliform inflorescence of as many as 8 flowers; pedicels 3-4 mm long and densely scaly; calyx lobes unequal, to 1.5 mm long, densely scaly, the tips sparsely fringed with long hairs; corolla varying in color from purple-lilac to purple to rose-pink, corolla tube short campanulate, 2-4 mm long, not scaly, hairy at the base, lobes 5, rounded; stamens 10, exserted; ovary green and scaly.

Capsule ovoid-oblong, 7 mm long.

Northwest Yunnan. Grows among trees on moist grasslands.

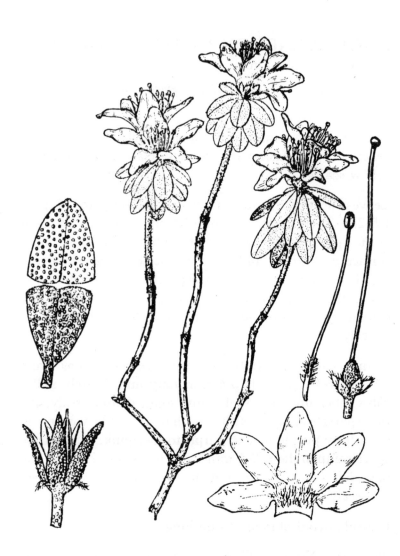

4058　密枝杜鹃

RHODODENDRON FASTIGIATUM
Franch.

mì zhī dùjuān   *"densely branched rhododendron"*

Evergreen dwarf shrub to 70 cm high, densely branched; shoots short and scaly; leaf-bud scales caducous.

Leaves small, in terminal clusters on the branchlets, coriaceous, long-elliptic, 8 mm long, 4 mm broad, apex obtuse and bluntly mucronate, base obtuse, upper and lower surfaces densely scaly, the scales of the lower surface uniform, yellowish brown, contiguous or often slightly separate (less than a diameter apart); petiole very short, scaly.

Terminal inflorescence of 4-5 flowers; flower-bud scales caducous; pedicels very short, scaly; calyx well developed, about 4 mm long, 5-lobed, lobes broadly elliptic, scaly outside, softly long-ciliate; corolla about 1.3 cm long, purplish blue, slightly scaly outside; stamens 10, long-exserted, filaments white-tomentose at the base; ovary scaly, style glabrous, slender, and longer than the stamens.

Capsule oblong, 4 mm long, scaly.

Distributed in west and northwest Yunnan, southwest Sichuan. Grows in thickets on rocky hills at about 3000 meters.

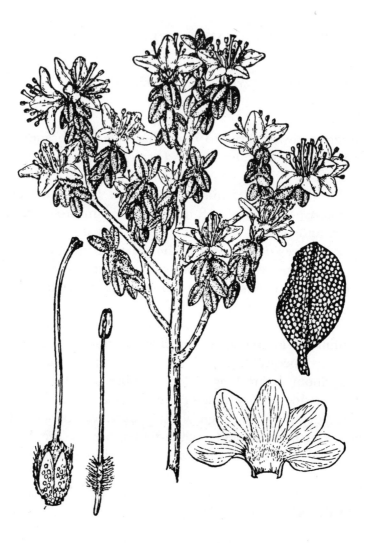

4059　黑鳞杜鹃

RHODODENDRON NIGROPUNCTATUM

Bur. et Franch.

hēi lín dùjuān   *"black scale rhododendron"*

Evergreen undershrub to 35 cm high; twigs fine and dark-scaly, shoots leafy, short, and golden-scaly; leaf-bud scales caducous.

Leaves thick-coriaceous, elliptic or obovate, 5-10 mm long, 3-6 mm broad, apex obtuse, base short cuneate, upper and lower surfaces very densely scaly.

Terminal inflorescence of 1-2 flowers; flower-bud scales subpersistent; pedicels very short; calyx lobes oblong, to 2 mm long, sparsely ciliate on the upper part, scaly on the back; corolla broadly funnelform, 8 mm long, purple, not scaly outside, corolla tube short, pubescent within on the upper part, lobes 5, of unequal size, ovate, rounded at the tips, spreading, glabrous; stamens 10, long-exserted, filaments white-pubescent toward the base; ovary densely scaly, style as long as the stamens, glabrous.

West Sichuan. Grows in grassland thickets at 3200-4600 meters.

4060　头花杜鹃

116

RHODODENDRON CAPITATUM
Maxim.

tóu huā dùjuān *"head-flower rhododendron"*

Evergreen shrub to 1 meter high, much-branched; twigs erect, branchlets densely scaly; bud scales caducous.

Leaves aromatic, subcoriaceous, elliptic, to 1.8 cm long, 6-8 mm broad, apex and base obtuse, upper and lower surfaces densely clad with uniform contiguous scales of 2 colors, light green and dark brown; petiole 2-3 mm long, scaly.

Terminal capitate inflorescence of 5-8 flowers; pedicels very short, scaly; calyx well developed, deeply 5-lobed, lobes 3 mm long, elliptic, not scaly outside, not ciliate; corolla narrowly funnelform, 1.5 cm long, purplish blue, glabrous outside, lobes 5, rounded, quite spreading, overlapping at the base; stamens 10, exserted, filaments pubescent on the lower part; ovary scaly, style as long as the stamens (a little shorter than the longest stamens), glabrous.

Capsule ovoid, about 4 mm long, 3 mm thick, scaly, the calyx persistent.

Distributed in Qinghai, Gansu. Forms thickets on high mountain grasslands at 2500-3600 meters.

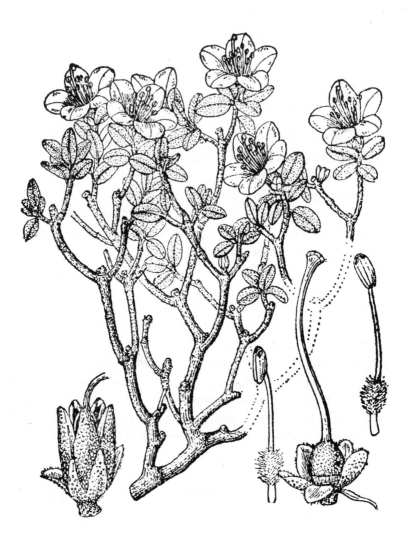

4061　光亮杜鹃

RHODODENDRON NITIDULUM
Rehd. et Wils.

guāng liàng dùjuān   *"shiny rhododendron"*

Evergreen shrub to 1.5 meters high; branchlets dense, short, and scaly; leaf-bud scales caducous.

Leaves broadly elliptic, 7-11 mm long, 4-6 mm broad, upper and lower surfaces densely scaly, the scales of the lower surface of equal size and somewhat imbricate; petiole 2 mm long, scaly.

Terminal inflorescence of 1-2 flowers; flower-bud scales subpersistent; pedicels very short, scaly; calyx well developed, 3 mm long, densely scaly outside, lobes broadly ovate, scaly at the margin, not ciliate; corolla broadly funnelform, 1.2 cm long, purplish blue, not scaly outside; stamens 10(8), exserted, the filaments densely tomentose on one section above the base; ovary scaly, style glabrous and longer than the stamens.

Capsule ovoid, about 3 mm long, scaly.

West Sichuan. Grows on grassy slopes at 3200-3800 meters.

Found on a 4500-meter mountain near Kangding, Sichuan, var. *nubigenum* Rehd. et Wils. (yún shēng dùjuān, "cloud-growing rhododendron") is a dwarf form with smaller leaves and frequently reddish calyx.

4062　紫丁杜鹃

RHODODENDRON VIOLACEUM
Rehd. et Wils.

zǐ dīng dùjuān   *"purple-lilac rhododendron"*

Evergreen undershrub to about 1 meter high, much-branched and dense; branchlets short, straight, upright, and scaly; leaf-bud scales caducous.

Leaves coriaceous, narrowly oblong-elliptic, 8 mm long, to 4 mm broad, apex obtuse, base obtuse or slightly attenuate, upper and lower surfaces densely scaly.

Terminal inflorescence of 1-3 subsessile flowers; flower-bud scales caducous; calyx short, 5-lobed, lobes 1-2 mm long, ovate, scaly outside, ciliate toward the tips; corolla broadly funnelform, about 1.2 cm long, purplish blue, not scaly outside; stamens 10, exserted, filaments densely villous toward the base; ovary scaly, style glabrous and longer than the stamens.

Capsule ovoid, 4 mm long, scaly.

West Sichuan. Grows on moist grasslands at 3800-4200 meters.

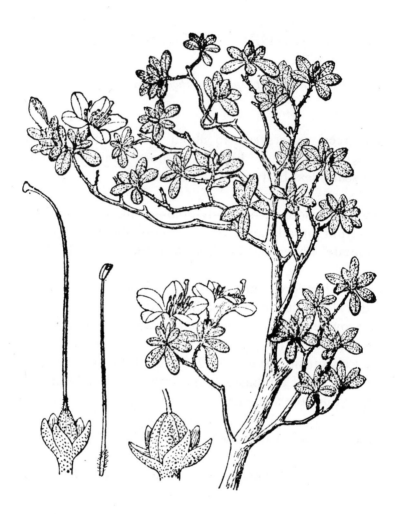

4063　雪层杜鹃

RHODODENDRON NIVALE
Hook. f.

xuě céng dùjuān   *"snow layer rhododendron"*

Evergreen dwarf procumbent shrub to 30 cm high, often cushion-shaped; branches densely scaly; leaf-bud scales caducous.

Leaves coriaceous, elliptic, very small, less than 6 mm long, upper and lower surfaces clad with imbricate scales; petiole very short, scaly.

Flowers terminal and solitary, sometimes opposite; pedicels very short, scaly; calyx well developed, 3 mm long, lobes oblong-elliptic, scaly outside and at the margin; corolla broadly funnelform, about 1.2 cm long, varying in color from bright purple, light red, or bright purplish blue to lilac-purple, corolla tube very short, hairy within, lobes 5, deep, slightly scaly outside; stamens 10, long-exserted, filaments villous near the base; ovary scaly, style curved on the upper part, slightly longer than the stamens, glabrous or sparsely hairy at the base.

Capsule ovoid, 4 mm long, scaly.

South Xizang; also Sikkim. Grows on grasslands at 4800 meters.

4064　多色杜鹃

RHODODENDRON ACHROANTHUM

Balf. f. et W. W. Sm.

duó sè dùjuān   *"multicolor rhododendron"*

Evergreen shrub less than 1 meter high; branchlets short and strong, densely scaly; leaf-bud scales caducous.

Leaves oblong-elliptic, 1.6 cm long, to 8 mm broad, upper and lower surfaces densely scaly, the scales of the lower surface brown and light green, imbricate; petiole 1.5-2 mm long, scaly.

Terminal inflorescence of 3-5 flowers; pedicels very short, scaly; calyx well developed, 3 mm long, 5-lobed, lobes broadly elliptic, densely scaly on the back except at the densely ciliate light purple margin; corolla openly funnel-form, about 1.2 cm long, varying in color from purple, deep carmine, or plum-purple to dark bluish purple, short-pubescent within, quite densely scaly outside from the middle of the lobes downward; stamens 5(-6), exserted, filaments densely pubescent toward the base; ovary densely scaly, style longer than the stamens, hairy at the base.

Capsule ovoid, about 4 mm long, scaly.

Northwest Yunnan. Grows on rocky mountains at 3800 meters.

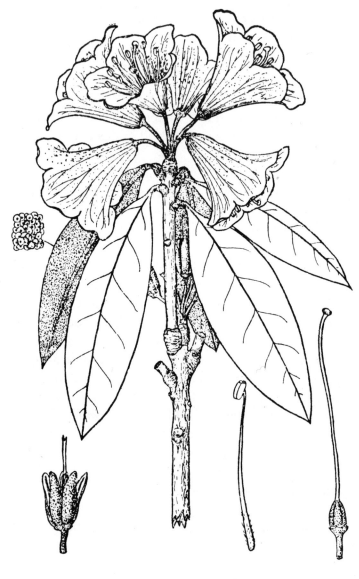

4065　红棕杜鹃

RHODODENDRON RUBIGINOSUM

Franch.

hóng zōng dùjuān   *"reddish brown rhododendron"*

Evergreen shrub or small tree to 10 meters high; twigs rather stout, shoots light purple and scaly.

Leaves in terminal clusters, coriaceous, elliptic-lanceolate, about 6.5 cm long, 2.5 cm broad, apex acute, base rounded-cuneate, lower surface densely clad with rusty brown imbricate scales; petiole 1.2 cm long, scaly.

Terminal umbelliform inflorescence of 4-8 flowers; pedicels 1.2 cm long, densely scaly; calyx very short, undulate, scaly outside; corolla funnelform, 3.2 cm long, rose tinged lilac-purple or pink, brown-dotted, scaly outside, the scales most numerous on the lobes; stamens 10, slightly exserted, filaments pubescent toward the base; ovary 5-loculed, densely scaly, style glabrous.

Capsule oblong, to 1.5 cm long, scaly.

Distributed in west Yunnan, southwest Sichuan (Jiulong). Grows in open forests at 2400-3000 meters.

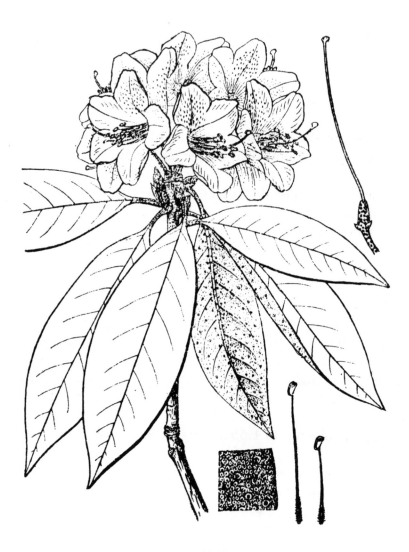

4066　茶花叶杜鹃

RHODODENDRON DESQUAMATUM

Balf. f. et Forrest

chá huā yè dùjuān   *"camellia-leaved rhododendron"*

Evergreen shrub or small tree to 8 meters high; shoots densely scaly; leaf-bud scales caducous.

Leaves broadly oblong-elliptic, about 8 cm long, 2.6-3.5 cm broad, apex acute or acute-acuminate, base cuneate, upper surface not scaly, lower surface densely clad with scales of unequal size, the largest scales darker brown, lateral veins somewhat prominent; petiole 1.2 cm long, densely scaly.

Terminal many-flowered inflorescence, flower-bud scales caducous; pedicels 1.2 cm long, scaly; calyx very short, scaly; corolla broadly funnelform, 3.7 cm long, purplish blue, streaked, sparsely scaly outside; stamens 10, exserted, of unequal length, filaments pubescent toward the base; ovary densely scaly, style glabrous, long-exserted.

West Yunnan; also north Burma. Grows in forests at about 3000 meters.

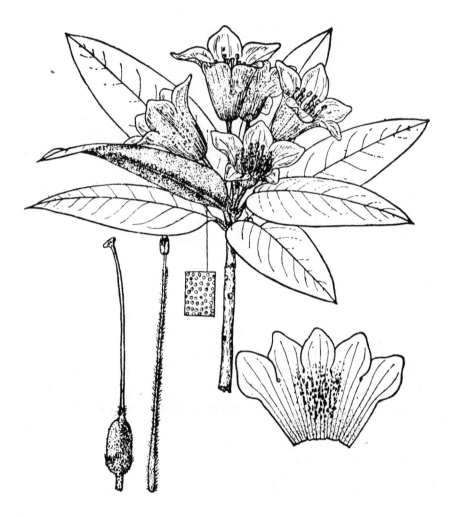

4067　短柱杜鹃

RHODODENDRON BREVISTYLUM

Franch.

duǎn zhù dùjuān   *"short-styled rhododendron"*

Evergreen shrub to 3.6 meters high; shoots densely clad with contiguous scales.

Leaves coriaceous, ovate-lanceolate to ovate-oblong, 5-8 cm long, 2-3 cm broad, apex acute and mucronate, base rounded or sometimes acute, upper surface glabrous, with a few scales or scale remnants, lower surface sparsely scaly, the scales more than a diameter apart; petiole 1-1.5 cm long, densely scaly.

Terminal raceme of about 5 flowers; pedicels spreading, 1.5-3 cm long, more or less scaly; calyx orbicular, to 4 mm long, densely scaly; corolla broadly campanulate, to 3 cm long, rose or purplish, red-dotted on the upper interior, glabrous but very scaly outside, minutely hairy within, lobes 5; stamens 10, filaments pubescent; ovary densely scaly, style red, glabrous or sparsely hairy at the base, not longer than the longest stamens.

Northwest Yunnan. Grows on high mountain grasslands at 4000 meters.

4068　亮鳞杜鹃

RHODODENDRON HELIOLEPIS

Franch.

liàng lín dùjuān   *"bright scale rhododendron"*

Evergreen shrub about 2 meters high; branchlets scaly.

Leaves soft-coriaceous, oblong-elliptic, 7.5-10 cm long, 3-3.8 cm broad, apex acute and long-mucronate, base obtuse, upper surface smooth and glossy, densely rugulose, lower surface clad with golden and darker scales of equal size about ½-1 diameter apart; petiole about 1.2 cm long, scaly.

Terminal umbelliform inflorescence of 4-6 flowers; pedicels 1.2 cm long, densely scaly; calyx short, about 1.5 mm long, shallowly 5-lobed, scaly outside; corolla funnelform, 2.5 cm long, red or rose, exterior densely scaly throughout, lobes 5, sparsely scaly at the middle; stamens 10, filaments densely pubescent on the lower half; ovary densely scaly, style as long as the stamens, pubescent on the lower half.

West and northwest Yunnan. Grows in open forests.

Found in south Gansu, *R. invictum* Balf. f. et Farrer (jué lún dùjuān, "matchless rhododendron") is very similar to this species except that the flowers are purple, the style is pubescent only at the base, and the corolla exterior is scaly only on one side.

4069　苍山杜鹃

RHODODENDRON PHOLIDOTUM
Balf. f. et W. W. Sm.

cāng shān dùjuān   *"Cang Shan rhododendron"*

Evergreen shrub to 3 meters high; branchlets light red and scaly; leaf-bud scales caducous.

Leaves coriaceous, ovate-oblong, 5-6.2 cm long, 2.5-3.2 cm broad, apex acute, base obtuse, upper surface smooth and glossy at maturity, net veins impressed, lower surface densely scaly, the scales contiguous or about ½ diameter apart, lateral veins somewhat evident; petiole about 1 cm long, sparsely scaly.

Terminal short raceme of 4-5 flowers; flower-bud scales caducous; pedicels 1.5 cm long, sparsely scaly; calyx short, shallowly 5-lobed, densely scaly outside; corolla broadly funnelform, to 2.5 cm long, rose or purplish, dotted, densely scaly outside; stamens 10, filaments densely pubescent on the lower part; ovary scaly, style short (not quite as long as the stamens), sparsely pubescent at the base.

Capsule cylindric, 1.2 cm long, scaly.

West Yunnan. Grows in forests at about 3500 meters.

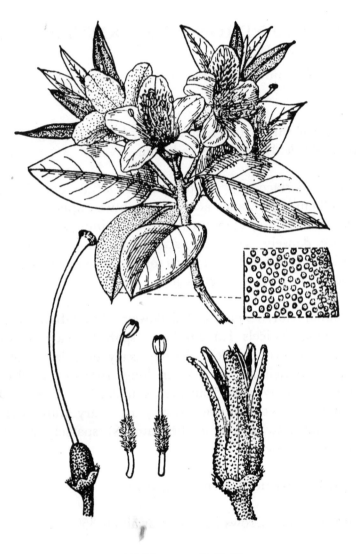

4070　三花杜鹃

RHODODENDRON TRIFLORUM
Hook. f.

sān huā dùjuān   *"three-flowered rhododendron"*

Evergreen shrub to 2.6 meters high; branchlets clad with small black scales.

Leaves coriaceous, lanceolate or oblong-lanceolate, 3.2-5.2 cm long, 1.2-3 cm broad, apex very acute, base obtuse or rounded, upper surface smooth and glossy, lower surface densely scaly, the scales small, uniform, and less than a diameter apart; petiole 6 mm long, scaly.

Terminal umbelliform inflorescence of 3 fragrant flowers; pedicels 8-12 mm long, densely scaly; calyx small, shallowly 5-lobed, densely scaly outside, with a few very short hairs at the margin; corolla about 3.7 cm long, light yellow with green dots on the upper part, corolla tube and lobes quite densely scaly outside, lobes 5; stamens 10, exserted, filaments pubescent on one section above the base; ovary 5-loculed, densely scaly, style glabrous.

Capsule 1.2 cm long, thickly cylindric, densely scaly.

South Xizang; also Sikkim, Bhutan. Grows in pine forests at 2500 meters.

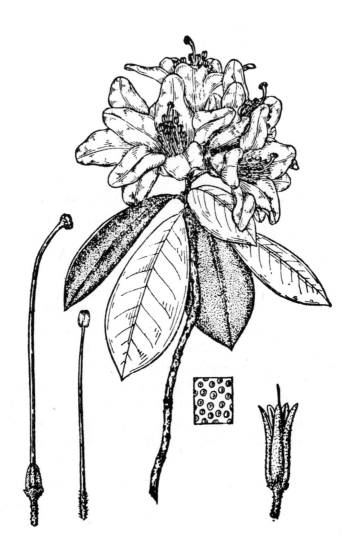

4071 问客杜鹃

138

RHODODENDRON AMBIGUUM
Hemsl.

wèn kè dùjuān   *"greet visitor rhododendron"*

Evergreen shrub to 1.8 meters high; twigs slender, quite densely scaly.

Leaves coriaceous, obovate-lanceolate, 4-8 cm long, 1.8-3 cm broad, apex acute and stiffly mucronate, base obtuse, upper surface soon glabrous, lower surface densely scaly, the scales of unequal size and less than a diameter apart, some nearly black, leaf veins obscure; petiole to 6 mm long, scaly.

Terminal raceme of usually 5-7 flowers; pedicels 1.5-2 cm long, slightly curved, densely scaly; calyx small, undulate, scaly outside; corolla broadly campanulate, about 5 cm in diameter, greenish yellow or light yellow with green dots on the upper part of the corolla tube interior, sparsely scaly outside, corolla tube sparsely pubescent within at the base, lobes 5, spreading; stamens 10, exserted, filaments villous on the lower part; ovary densely scaly, style glabrous.

Capsule about 1.5 cm long, densely scaly.

Distributed in Sichuan, Guizhou. Grows in open forests.

4072　拟黄花杜鹃

RHODODENDRON CHENGSHIENIANUM
Fang

nǐ huáng dùjuān   *"imitation yellow rhododendron"*

Evergreen shrub, 2-3 meters high; branchlets quite slender, glabrous, densely scaly and black-glandular.

Leaves coriaceous, oblong-elliptic, 4-5.5 cm long, 1.8-2.2 cm broad, apex acute or short acuminate, base broadly cuneate, upper surface glabrous at maturity, not scaly, lower surface bluish green, white-powdery, and clad with brown scales a diameter apart; petiole 6-10 mm long, scaly.

Terminal umbelliform inflorescence of 3-4 flowers; pedicels 10-14 mm long, densely scaly; calyx small, about 2 mm long, shallowly 5-lobed, scaly; corolla funnelform, about 3 cm long, yellow or light yellow, corolla tube minutely hairy within, scaly outside, lobes 5, acute; stamens 10, filaments pubescent on the lower part; ovary scaly, style glabrous.

Capsule cylindric, about 7 mm long, scaly.

Southwest Sichuan (Emei Shan). Grows in thickets.

4073　黄花杜鹃

RHODODENDRON LUTESCENS
Franch.

huáng huā dùjuān *"yellow-flowered rhododendron"*

Evergreen shrub, 2-3 meters high; shoots slender, sparsely yellow-scaly.

Leaves scattered, chartaceous, broadly lanceolate to oblong-lanceolate, 6-12 cm long, 2.5-3.5 cm broad, apex caudate-acuminate, base broadly cuneate, upper surface dark green, lower surface pale, both surfaces clad with fine scales 4-6 diameters apart; petiole 8-10 mm long, scaly.

Flowers solitary, terminal or simultaneously terminal and subterminal-axillary, rarely a cluster of 2-3 produced from one terminal bud; pedicels about 1 cm long, slightly scaly and sparsely pubescent; calyx small, pubescent, and scaly; corolla broadly funnelform, 2 cm long, light yellow, white-hairy and slightly scaly outside, lobes 5, spreading; stamens 10, exserted, filaments hairy at the base (fewer hairs on the longer filaments); ovary densely white-scaly, style smooth and glossy.

Capsule cylindric, densely scaly.

Distributed in Sichuan, Yunnan, Guizhou. Grows in open thickets.

143

4074 疏叶杜鹃

RHODODENDRON HANCEANUM
Hemsl.

shū yè dùjuān   *"sparsely leaved rhododendron"*

Evergreen shrub, 1-2 meters high; shoots slender and scaly, older branches nearly smooth and glossy.

Leaves coriaceous, ovate-lanceolate to obovate, 5-12 cm long, 2-4 cm broad at the middle, apex acute to short acuminate, upper surface glossy green and glabrous, lower surface whitish green, clad with fine yellow scales 2 diameters apart, lateral veins impressed on the upper surface, obscure on the lower surface; petiole 4-8 mm long, scaly.

Terminal raceme of 7-9 flowers, rachis 1-1.4 cm long, sparsely glandular and minutely hairy; pedicels 1-1.2 cm long, scaly and minutely hairy; calyx large, deeply 5-lobed, lobes 8 mm long, sparsely scaly outside, ciliate; corolla funnelform, 2.5 cm long, white, sparsely scaly outside, sparsely short-hairy within, 5-lobed; stamens 10, densely white-villous below the middle; ovary densely scaly.

Capsule 1 cm long, densely scaly, enclosed by the persistent calyx.

West Sichuan. Grows in thickets at 2500 meters.

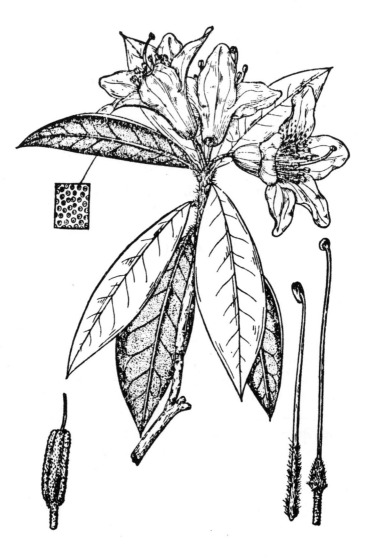

4075　毛肋杜鹃

RHODODENDRON AUGUSTINII
Hemsl.

máo lè dùjuān   *"hairy rib rhododendron"*

Evergreen shrub, 1-1.5 meters high; shoots pubescent and scaly.

Leaves scattered, subcoriaceous, broadly lanceolate to broadly oblanceolate, 4-6.2 cm long, 1.3-2.2 cm broad, apex acute to short acuminate, mucronate, base cuneate, upper surface thinly villous at first, soon glabrous, lower surface glabrous except on the densely villous lower part of the midrib, lower surface scaly, the scales not quite a diameter apart; petiole 3-7 mm long, pubescent.

Terminal umbelliform inflorescence of usually 3 flowers; pedicels 1.1-1.7 cm long, scaly; calyx very short, densely scaly outside, lobes rounded, ciliate; corolla campanulate, purplish blue or lilac-purple with yellow-green dots on the upper part, corolla tube 1.4 cm long, lobes 5, 2.3 cm long, obtuse, spreading; stamens 10, filaments villous on the lower third; ovary densely scaly, pubescent or glabrous, style glabrous.

Capsule 1.2-1.6 cm long, cylindric, densely clad with small scales.

Distributed in Hubei, Sichuan, south Shaanxi. Grows in forests.

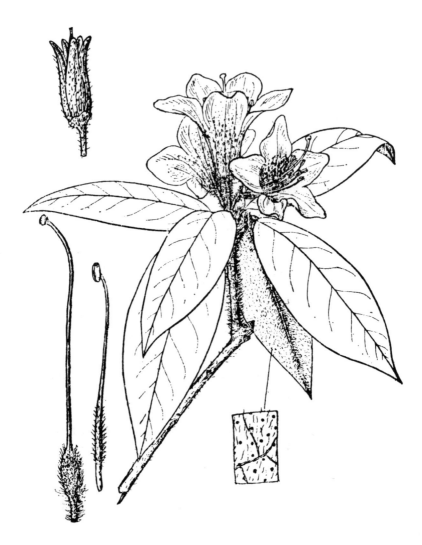

4076　长毛杜鹃

RHODODENDRON VILLOSUM
Hemsl.

cháng máo dùjuān   *"long-haired rhododendron"*

Evergreen bushy shrub, 1-5 meters high; twigs slender, shoots sparsely scaly and densely long-setose, older branches smooth and glossy.

Leaves in terminal clusters, coriaceous, narrowly elliptic to oblong-lanceolate, sometimes subovate, 4.5-10 cm long, 2-4.5 cm broad, apex acute or short acuminate, stiffly mucronate, base rounded or rounded-cuneate, upper surface of the young leaves sparsely or densely scaly, with or without appressed soft bristles or sparse downy hairs, the bristles or hairs persistent on the midrib, upper and lower surfaces of the older leaves sparsely scaly, the scales of the lower surface 3-4 diameters apart; petiole densely setose.

Terminal umbelliform inflorescence of usually 3 flowers, pedicels 1.2 cm long, densely setose; calyx small, shallowly 5-lobed, densely clad with long soft hairs and bristles; corolla pale purple to rose, corolla tube funnelform, 1.2-2 cm long, sparsely scaly outside, setose on the lower part, lobes 5; stamens 10; ovary densely scaly, more or less setose.

Capsule cylindric, 1.8 cm long, scaly and sparsely setose.

West Sichuan. Grows in forests at about 3500 meters.

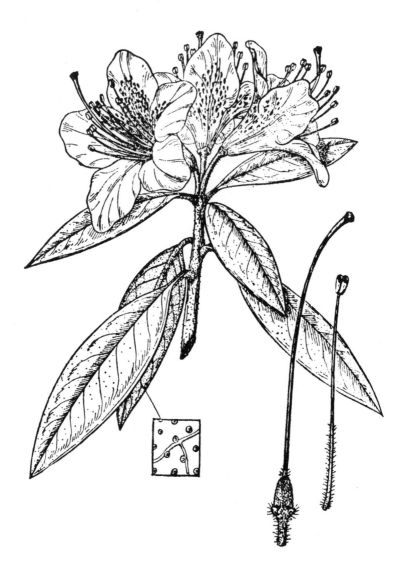

4077　张口杜鹃

RHODODENDRON CHASMANTHUM
Diels

zhāng kǒu dùjuān   *"open-mouthed rhododendron"*

Evergreen shrub, 1-7 meters high; branchlets scaly, glabrous or minutely hairy.

Leaves coriaceous, lanceolate or oblong-lanceolate, 6.5-10 cm long, 1.8-3.6 cm broad, apex acute, base broadly cuneate, upper surface smooth and glossy, lower surface sparsely clad with fine scales 4-5 diameters apart, midrib pubescent on the lower surface, lateral veins numerous and conspicuous; petiole 8 mm long.

Terminal subumbelliform inflorescence of 3-4 flowers; pedicels 2.5 cm long, sparsely scaly; calyx small, about 3 mm long, unequally 5-lobed, scaly outside; corolla 3.7 cm long, pale rose-purple streaked with light olive, sparsely scaly on one side; stamens 10, long-exserted, filaments pubescent on the lower part; ovary densely scaly, style glabrous, longer than the stamens.

Capsule 1.8 cm long, sparsely white-scaly, very crooked at the base, calyx persistent.

Distributed in northwest Yunnan, southeast Xizang. Grows in unforested mountain valleys at 3200 meters.

4078　苞叶杜鹃

RHODODENDRON BRACTEATUM
Rehd. et Wils.

bāo yè dùjuān　*"bract-leaf rhododendron"*

Evergreen shrub, 1-3 meters high; twigs slender, not scaly.

Brown leaf-bud bracts persistent for several years on the lower part of the branches, strap-shaped or lanceolate, 6-15 mm long, revolute at the margin.

Leaves in terminal clusters, chartaceous, oblong to ovate, 2-3.5 cm long, 1.2-1.8 cm broad, apex acute and mucronate, base rounded, upper surface sparsely scaly, lower surface more densely scaly, the scales of unequal size and 1-2 diameters apart; petiole about 4-6 mm long.

Terminal umbelliform inflorescence of 3-6 flowers; pedicels slender, 1.2-2.5 cm long, slightly scaly, bracteate at the base, the bracts caducous, strap-shaped, to 8 mm long, hairy; calyx small, to 2 mm long, 5-lobed, scaly; corolla campanulate, 1.8 cm long, white with red dots, hairy on the upper part of the throat, sparsely scaly outside, 5-lobed; stamens 10, filaments pubescent below the middle; ovary densely scaly, style sparsely hairy at the base.

Capsule about 2.5 cm long, sparsely scaly.

West Sichuan. Grows in conifer forests at 2500-3200 meters.

153

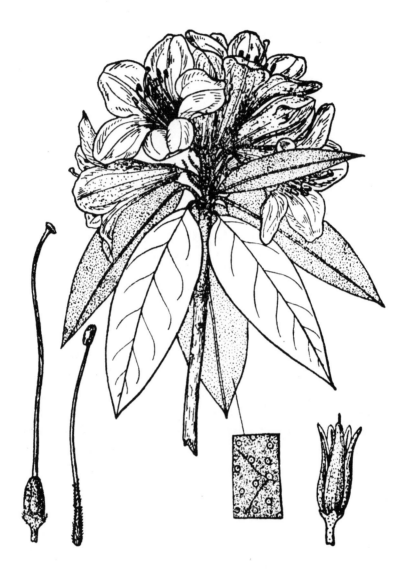

4079　白面杜鹃

RHODODENDRON ZALEUCUM
Balf. f.

bái miàn dùjuān *"white-surfaced rhododendron"*

Evergreen shrub or small tree to 10 meters high; twigs slender, brown, and scaly.

Leaves mostly in terminal clusters, chartaceous, broadly lanceolate to lanceolate-oblong, 3-7.5 cm long, 1.2-2.5 cm broad, apex acute and stiffly mucronate, base rounded-cuneate, margin recurved and sometimes clad with a few long fine detersile bristles, upper surface smooth and glossy, the young leaves very minutely hairy along the midrib at the base, lower surface gray-white (conspicuously so on the older leaves) and scaly, the scales uniform and 1½-2 diameters apart; petiole to 1.2 cm long, scaly.

Terminal umbelliform inflorescence of 3-4 slightly fragrant flowers (rarely more); pedicels 1.5 cm long, scaly; calyx small, shallowly 5-lobed, densely scaly outside, ciliate; corolla broadly funnelform, 3.5 cm long, white or rose, scaly outside, 5-lobed; stamens 10, exserted, short-pubescent on the lower part; ovary scaly, style glabrous.

Capsule 1.2 cm long, scaly, fruitstalk to 2.5 cm long.

West Yunnan; also Burma. Grows in river-valley rain forests.

155

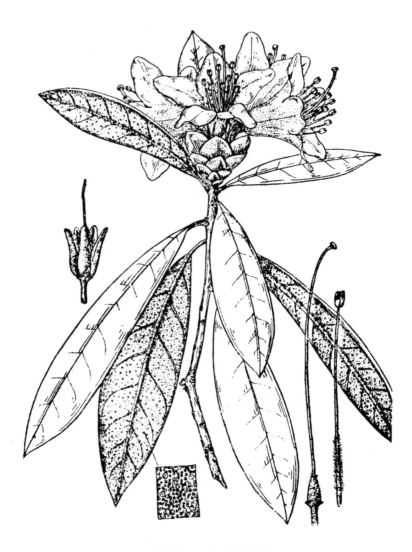

4080　多鳞杜鹃

RHODODENDRON POLYLEPIS

Franch.

duō lín dùjuān   *"very scaly rhododendron"*

Evergreen shrub to 4 meters high; twigs slender, straight and upright, quite densely clad with scurfy scales.

Leaves scattered, coriaceous, lanceolate, 3-7 cm long, 1.5-2.2 cm broad at the middle, apex acute, base cuneate, margin recurved, upper surface glossy green and smooth, the midrib impressed, lower surface densely clad with imbricate brown scales, the veins coarse and prominent; petiole 4-8 mm long, thick.

Terminal umbelliform inflorescence of 3-5 flowers; pedicels 1.5-2 cm long, reddish, white-scaly; calyx very short, the margin smoothly cleft or inconspicuously undulate; corolla campanulate, 2-2.5 cm long, lilac-purple, reddish purple outside on the lower part and light yellow dotted within on the upper lobes, white-scaly, lobes 5, broad, bluntly acute; stamens 10, exserted, filaments pubescent from above the base to below the middle; ovary densely scaly, style glabrous.

Capsule 8 mm long, densely scaly.

Distributed in west Sichuan, north Yunnan. Grows in thickets at 2200-2600 meters, common.

157

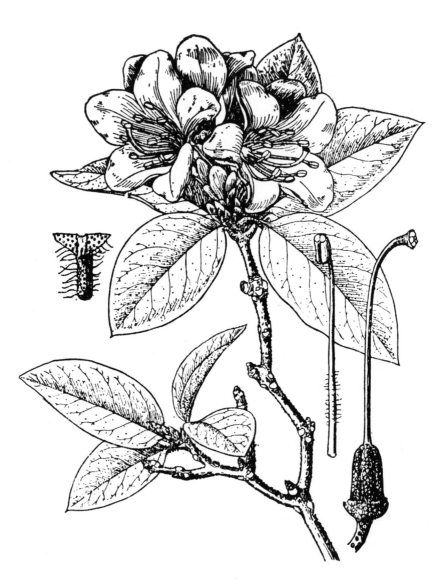

4081　紫花杜鹃

158

RHODODENDRON AMESIAE
Rehd. et Wils.

zǐ huā dùjuān   *"purple-flowered rhododendron"*

Evergreen shrub, 2-4 meters high; twigs flexuose, more or less verrucose.

Leaves subterminal in clusters of about 5, coriaceous, ovate or oblong-elliptic, 4.5-5.5 cm long, 2-3.5 cm broad, apex acute and mucronulate, base rounded, upper surface sparsely scaly, glabrous except for some reddish brown bristles on the midrib at the base, lower surface clad with many light yellow scales a diameter apart, the scales blackish at maturity, lateral veins obscure; petiole 5-10 mm long, scaly, clad with reddish brown bristles along both sides of the upper surface.

Terminal false umbel of as many as 5 flowers; pedicels to 1.5 cm long, scaly; calyx a shallow cup, scaly, lobes rounded and ciliolate; corolla funnelform, 3-4 cm long, deep purplish carmine, very sparsely scaly outside; stamens 10, filaments red, villous from below the middle to above the base; ovary dark green and scaly, style red and glabrous.

Capsule about 1.5 cm long.

West Sichuan. Grows in forests at 2200 to 3000 meters.

4082　秀雅杜鹃

RHODODENDRON CONCINNUM
Hemsl.

xiù yǎ dùjuān *"elegant rhododendron"*
chòu pípa *"fetid loquat"*

Evergreen shrub to 3.5 meters high; twigs glabrous, branches of the current year clad with subglobose glandular scales.

Leaves coriaceous, broadly lanceolate to elliptic-lanceolate, 3-8 cm long, 1.5-3 cm broad, apex acute and conspicuously long-mucronate, base rounded, upper surface rather sparsely clad with blackish wartlike scales, lower surface densely yellow-scaly with fewer blackish scales, midrib minutely hairy on the upper surface; petiole 5-10 mm long, scaly.

Terminal umbelliform inflorescence of usually 5 flowers; pedicels 1.5-2 cm long, partly sessile-glandular; calyx very short, undulate, scaly; corolla broadly funnelform, carmine, corolla tube 1.5 cm long, sparsely scaly outside, minutely hairy within, lobes 5, 2 cm long, glabrous; stamens 10; ovary densely scaly, short-hairy at the base and on the top, style purple and glabrous.

Capsule cylindric, 1.5 cm long, scaly.

Distributed in Yunnan, Sichuan, Shaanxi, Henan. Grows in forests.

4083　紫蕊杜鹃

RHODODENDRON PSEUDOYANTHINUM

Hutch.

zǐ ruǐ dùjuān   *"purple pistil rhododendron"*

Evergreen shrub; shoots glabrous, sparsely clad with subglobose scaly glands.

Leaves coriaceous, broadly lanceolate or elliptic-lanceolate, 3-7.5 cm long, 1.6-3 cm broad, apex bluntly acute and sharply long-mucronate, base obtuse or rounded, upper surface conspicuously verrucose and sparsely clad with blackish scales, lower surface scaly, the scales dense but not contiguous, dark yellowish brown with a few black, midrib minutely hairy on the upper surface, prominent on the lower surface and glabrous but scaly, lateral veins rather inconspicuous on the lower surface; petiole 3-6 mm long, scaly.

Terminal subumbelliform inflorescence of usually 5 flowers; pedicels 1.6-1.8 cm long, partly scaly; corolla broadly funnelform, 3.2 cm long, dark red, corolla tube sparsely scaly outside, minutely hairy within, lobes 5; stamens 10, exserted, filaments pubescent on one small section above the base; ovary densely scaly, short-pubescent at the base and on the top, style purple and glabrous.

West Sichuan. Grows in open forests.

163

4084　二郎山杜鹃

RHODODENDRON HUTCHINSONIANUM

Fang

èr láng shān dùjuān   *"Erlang Shan rhododendron"*

Evergreen shrub, 40-70 cm high; twigs quite slender, shoots purple, yellow-scaly.

Leaves coriaceous, elliptic or long-ovate, 5-6 cm long, 3-4 cm broad, apex acute, base nearly rounded, upper surface smooth and glossy, lower surface densely clad with yellow scales less than a diameter apart, midrib impressed on the upper surface, prominent on the lower surface, lateral veins obscure; petiole 5 mm long, grooved on the upper surface, scaly.

Terminal inflorescence of 2-3 flowers; pedicels 5-8 mm long, densely scaly; calyx 4 mm long, 5-lobed, lobes ovate, acute, scaly outside, ciliate; corolla campanulate-funnelform, 1.5-1.8 cm long, purple, yellow-scaly outside, 5-lobed; stamens 10, of unequal length, filaments sparsely villous at the base; ovary 5-loculed, purple and scaly, style purple, glabrous, to 3 cm long.

West Sichuan (Erlang Shan). Grows in forests.

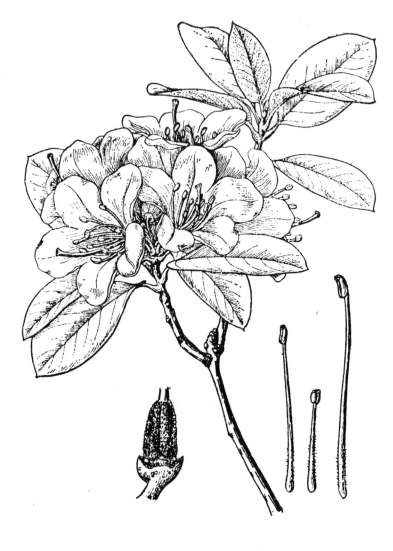

4085　优美杜鹃

RHODODENDRON EXQUISITUM
Hutch.

yōu měi dùjuān   *"exquisite rhododendron"*

Evergreen shrub about 1.3 meters high; shoots purple, slightly scaly, produced at the time of flowering.

Leaves coriaceous, broadly elliptic, 5-6 cm long, 3-3.5 cm broad, apex obtuse and mucronulate, base rounded, upper surface smooth and glossy, lower surface gray-green and scaly, the scales of one type and 2-3 diameters apart; petiole 8-10 mm long, upper surface purple, grooved, and scaly at the groove margins.

Terminal lax umbelliform inflorescence of 8-10 flowers, rachis very short, glabrous; pedicels about 3 cm long, light purple, slightly scaly only toward the top; calyx short, undulate, slightly scaly on the back but densely scaly at the margin; corolla broadly funnelform, pale pink, not spotted, not scaly outside, corolla tube about 2 cm long, lobes 5, 3 cm long; stamens 10, filaments hairy on the lower part; ovary densely scaly, style glabrous.

Distributed in southwest Sichuan, Yunnan. Grows in forests.

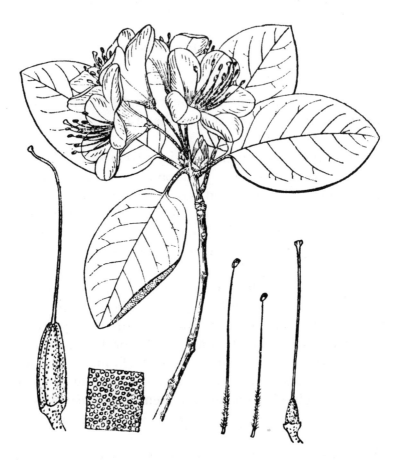

4086 微心杜鹃

RHODODENDRON ARTOSQUAMEUM

Balf. f. et Forrest

wéi xīn dùjuān   *"tiny heart rhododendron"*

Evergreen shrub, 1-3 meters high, annual twigs short; branchlets sparsely scaly.

Leaves strongly aromatic, thin-coriaceous, broadly ovate or suborbicular, 3-4.2 cm long, 1.8-3.2 cm broad, apex bluntly acute, base more or less cordate, upper surface smooth and glossy, lower surface quite densely scaly, the scales fleshy, of one type, and ½ to ¾ diameter apart, lateral veins nearly obscure; petiole 8-12 mm long, sparsely scaly.

Terminal umbelliform inflorescence of 3-4 flowers; pedicels 1.2 cm long, slightly scaly; calyx short, undulate, scaly outside; corolla funnelform, to 3.1 cm long, rose, not spotted, quite smooth and glossy outside; stamens 10, as long as the corolla, filaments sparsely short-pubescent on the lower part; ovary 5-loculed, densely scaly, style glabrous, stigma deeply cleft.

Capsule cylindric, about 1 cm long, 3 mm thick, scaly.

Distributed in northwest Yunnan, southeast Xizang. Grows in thickets at 3800 meters.

4087 基毛杜鹃

RHODODENDRON RIGIDUM

Franch.

jī máo dùjuān   *"basal hair rhododendron"*

Semi-evergreen or evergreen shrub, 1-2 meters high; branchlets slender and strong, sparsely scaly, smooth and glossy at maturity, gray-white.

Leaves firm-coriaceous, elliptic-oblanceolate, 3-5 cm long, 1-1.8 cm broad, apex bluntly acute and mucronate, base cuneate, margin clad with a few long fine bristles toward the base, upper and lower surfaces scaly, the scales of the lower surface 1½-2 diameters apart; petiole about 4 mm long, clad with long fine bristles along both sides when young.

Terminal inflorescence of as many as 4 flowers; pedicels 1 cm long, slightly scaly; calyx poorly developed, undulate, sparsely scaly outside; corolla 1.8 cm long, pale rose with dark red dots, corolla tube not scaly, lobes 5, deep, with an occasional scale; stamens 10, exserted, filaments densely pubescent at the base; ovary scaly, style glabrous.

Northwest Yunnan (Lijiang). Grows on rocky cliffs in pine forests at 2800 meters.

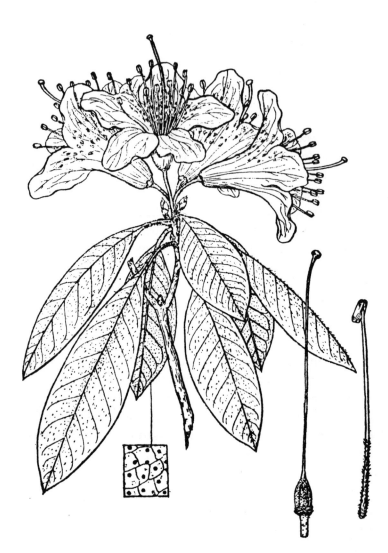

4088 云南杜鹃

RHODODENDRON YUNNANENSE
Franch.

yún nán dùjuān   *"Yunnan rhododendron"*

Semi-evergreen or evergreen shrub, 1-2 meters high; twigs slender, shoots sparsely clad with blackish glands.

Leaves scattered, inclining or reflexed, coriaceous, oblanceolate or obovate-oblanceolate, 5-6.5 cm long, 1.2-2.5 cm broad, acute and mucronate at the apex, tapering toward the base to cuneate, setose on the upper surface and at the margin, especially when young, upper and lower surfaces scaly, the scales of the lower surface 2-4 diameters apart; petiole to 8 mm long.

Inflorescences terminal or terminal and lateral, each flower bud producing 3-5 flowers in a very short raceme; pedicels sparsely scaly; calyx short, undulate, scaly outside; corolla about 3.7 cm long, slightly asymmetric, light pink or nearly white with red dots, corolla tube not scaly outside, lobes 5; stamens 10, long-exserted, filaments short-pubescent on the lower part; ovary 5-loculed, densely scaly, with a conspicuous hairy disc at the base, style glabrous.

Capsule 1.8 cm long, sparsely scaly.

West and north Yunnan, southwest Sichuan. Grows in thickets.

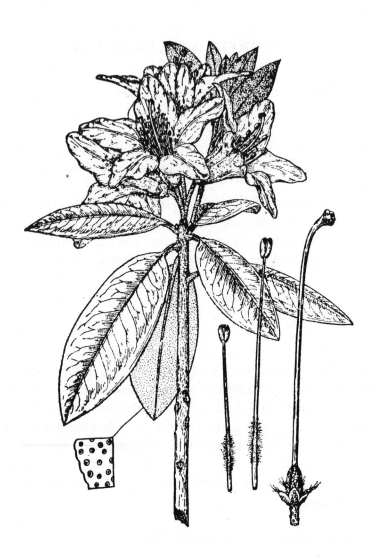

4089 绿点杜鹃

RHODODENDRON SEARSIAE

Rehd. et Wils.

lǜ diǎn dùjuān   *"green-spotted rhododendron"*

Evergreen shrub to 2.5 meters high; twigs slender, shoots densely clad with light yellow scales, older branches verrucose.

Leaves in terminal clusters, coriaceous, oblong-lanceolate, 4-8 cm long, 1.2-2.5 cm broad, apex acute, margin crenulate toward the tip, upper surface sparsely scaly, lower surface bluish gray and scattered with yellow to reddish brown scales of unequal size; petiole 6 mm long, quite densely scaly.

Terminal umbelliform raceme of 4-8 flowers; pedicels 8 mm long, quite densely scaly; calyx large, unequally 5-lobed, the front lobe and back lobe sometimes much larger, about 4 mm long, densely scaly, and long-ciliate; corolla crooked-funnelform, 3.2 cm long, white or purplish pink, sparsely hairy outside, lobes 5, spreading, the lower lobes longer; stamens 10, filaments densely pubescent on one section above the base; ovary densely scaly, style glabrous.

Capsule to 1.2 cm long, densely scaly.

West Sichuan (Wa Shan). Grows in thickets above 2400 meters.

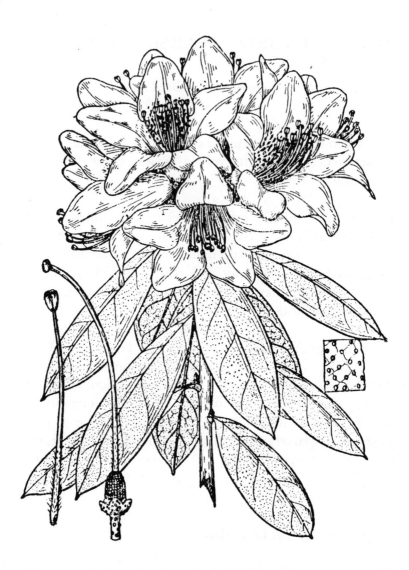

4090　淑花杜鹃

RHODODENDRON CHARIANTHUM
Hutch.

shú huā dùjuān *"fair-flowered rhododendron"*

Evergreen shrub, sparsely branched; branchlets slender, sparsely scaly toward the tips.

Leaves scattered, thin-coriaceous, oblanceolate to oblanceolate-elliptic, 2.5-5 cm long, 1-2 cm broad, apex bluntly acute and long-mucronate, base cuneate, margin inconspicuously crenulate, upper and lower surfaces clad with golden scales 3-5 diameters apart, glabrous, lateral veins prominent on both surfaces, conspicuously so on the lower surface; petiole 3-6 mm long, sparsely scaly.

Terminal flat-globose corymb of 9-10 flowers; pedicels slender, 1-1.5 cm long, sparsely glandular; calyx short and undulate; corolla pink and densely red-spotted on the upper interior, corolla tube broadly spreading, about 1 cm long, glabrous, lobes 5, 1.5-2 cm long; stamens 10, filaments hairy on the lower part; ovary densely scaly, style very minutely hairy on the lower part.

Capsule 1 cm long, finely scaly.

Distributed in Hubei, Sichuan. Grows in forests.

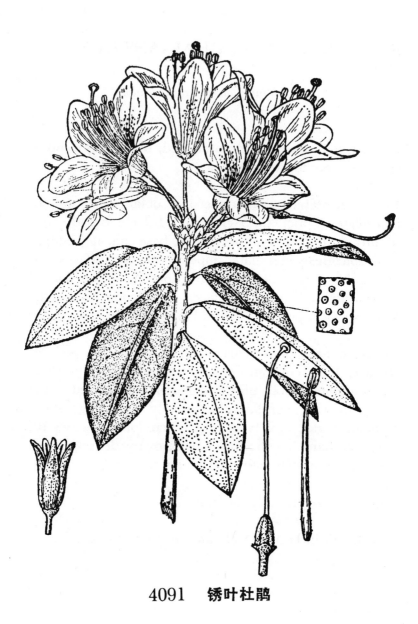

4091 锈叶杜鹃

RHODODENDRON SIDEROPHYLLUM

Franch.

xiù yè dùjuān   *"rusty-leaved rhododendron"*

Evergreen shrub, 1.2-3 meters high, sparsely branched; branchlets densely scaly.

Leaves stiff-chartaceous, lanceolate or oblong-lanceolate, 3-6 cm long, 1-2 cm broad, apex acute, base broadly cuneate, upper surface sparsely black-scaly, lower surface densely clad with rusty yellow scales ¾ to 1½ diameters apart, lateral veins nearly obscure; petiole about 8 mm long, scaly.

Inflorescences terminal and upper-lateral, 3-4(-5) flowers produced from each bud to form umbelliform racemes; pedicels 1.5-2 cm long, scaly; calyx degenerate, undulate, densely scaly; corolla campanulate, white to rose, corolla tube about 1 cm long, finely dark-dotted on the upper part, not scaly outside, lobes 5, spreading, slightly scaly outside; stamens 10, long-exserted, only 2 filaments slightly short-pubescent on the lower part; ovary densely scaly, style glabrous.

Capsule 1.3 cm in length, long oblong, scaly.

Central, west, and north Yunnan. Grows in open forests at 1700 to 2400 meters.

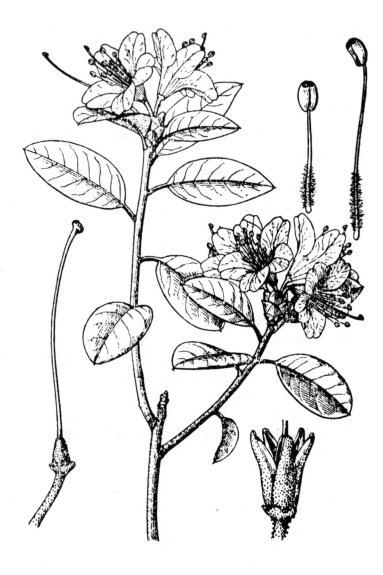

4092   硬叶杜鹃

RHODODENDRON STEREOPHYLLUM

Balf. f. et W. W. Sm.

yìng yè dùjuān   *"stiff-leaved rhododendron"*

Evergreen shrub to 2 meters high; branchlets densely clad with small resinous scales.

Leaves scattered, stiff-coriaceous, elliptic-ovate or obovate, 3.7-5 cm long, 1.2-3.7 cm broad, upper and lower surfaces of the young leaves densely scaly, the scales of the lower surface small and uniform, 1-1½ diameters apart; petiole 6 mm long, scaly.

Terminal (often also axillary) inflorescence of 3-4 flowers, flower-bud scales persistent during flowering; pedicels 4 mm long, densely scaly; calyx short, rimlike, scaly; corolla funnelform, 2-2.4 cm long, light rose, not spotted, lobes 5, slightly scaly outside; stamens 10, exserted, filaments minutely hairy on the lower third; ovary scaly, style glabrous.

Capsule cylindric, 1-1.3 cm long, about 3 mm thick, scaly.

Northwest Yunnan. Grows in open thickets in mountain valleys at 1800 to 2400 meters.

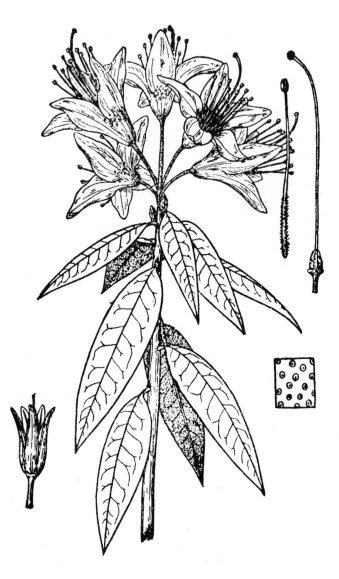

4093　凹叶杜鹃

RHODODENDRON DAVIDSONIANUM
Rehd. et Wils.

āo yè dùjuān   *"concave leaf rhododendron"*

Evergreen shrub, 1-3 meters high; twigs slender and spreading, gray-brown.

Leaves stiff chartaceous, usually with both sides bent upward from the midrib in a V, lanceolate or oblong-oblanceolate, 2.5-5.5 cm long, 1-2 cm broad, apex acute and conspicuously mucronate, base obtuse or rounded, upper surface sparsely black-scaly at first, lower surface densely clad with fine scales 1-2 diameters apart, midrib flat, smooth, and inconspicuous on the upper surface, prominent on the lower surface, lateral veins obscure on the upper surface (in dried leaves the upper surface is conspicuously vein-lined), lateral veins and veinlets nearly obscure on the lower surface; petiole 3-5 mm long, sometimes sparsely pubescent.

Terminal umbelliform inflorescence of about 6 flowers; pedicels 1-1.5 cm long, clad with globose glands; calyx very short, undulate; corolla light rose with yellow spots on the upper lobes, corolla tube about 1 cm long, glabrous, lobes 5, 4-4.5 cm long; stamens 10, long-exserted; ovary densely scaly.

Capsule short, about 1 cm long, 4 mm thick.

West Sichuan, in thickets on dry sunny slopes.

4094　黑水杜鹃

RHODODENDRON HEISHUIENSE
Fang

hēi shuǐ dùjuān   *"Heishui rhododendron"*

Evergreen shrub about 3 meters high; shoots very sparsely scaly.

Leaves coriaceous, oblong-lanceolate, 5.5-7 cm long, 2.5-3 cm broad, apex acute and very sharply mucronate, base nearly rounded, upper surface not scaly or rarely somewhat scaly, lower surface densely clad with yellow scales 2 diameters apart; petiole purple, 5 mm long, upper surface grooved, lower surface rounded.

Terminal umbelliform inflorescence of 2-3 flowers; pedicels 1 cm long, rose, scaly; calyx 2 mm long, scaly outside, lobes 5, obtuse; corolla campanulate-funnelform, rose, corolla tube 1 cm long, lobes 5, 1.2 cm long, 8-10 mm broad; stamens 10, long-exserted, of unequal length, filaments minutely hairy on one small section below the middle; ovary yellow-scaly, style 2.5-3 cm long, rose, glabrous.

North Sichuan (Heishui He valley). Grows in forests.

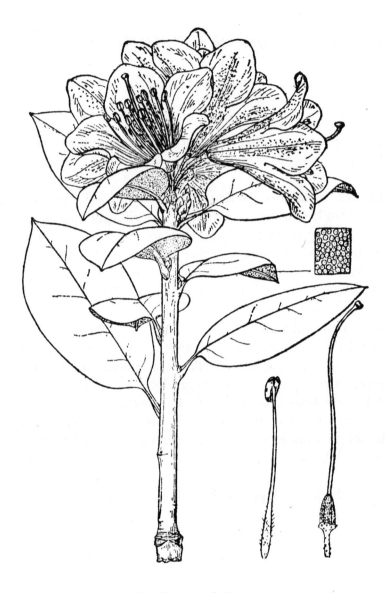

4095　山育杜鹃

RHODODENDRON OREOTREPHES
W. W. Sm.

shān yù dùjuān   *"mountain-born rhododendron"*

Evergreen shrub to 2.5 meters high; shoots sparsely scaly.

Leaves stiff-coriaceous, broadly elliptic, 3-4.5 cm long, 2.5-3 cm broad, apex rounded and bluntly mucronate, base rounded, upper surface brownish green and glabrous, lower surface gray-white and densely scaly, the scales of nearly equal size, from contiguous to less than a diameter apart, leaf veins inconspicuous; petiole 8-12 mm long, grooved on the upper surface, transversely wrinkled on the lower surface, sparsely scaly or nearly smooth and glossy.

Short terminal raceme of 5-8 flowers; pedicels 1-2 cm long, sparsely scaly; calyx degenerate, about 1 mm high, undulate; corolla broadly funnelform, about 3.2 cm long, usually rose, lobes 5, broadly ovate, slightly spreading, not scaly outside; stamens 10, filaments sparsely pubescent toward the base; ovary 5-loculed, densely scaly, style long-exserted, glabrous, light red.

Capsule about 1.2 cm long, sparsely scaly.

Distributed in Yunnan, southeast Xizang. Grows in forests at about 3000 meters.

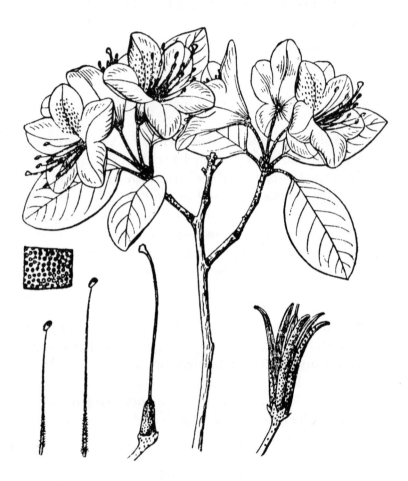

4096　可敬杜鹃

RHODODENDRON TIMETEUM

Balf. f. et Forrest

kě jìng dùjuān   *"respected rhododendron"*

Evergreen shrub about 1 meter high; branchlets short, slender, smooth and glossy, usually with a cluster of 3 leaves at the tip.

Leaves coriaceous, oblong-elliptic, 3-4 cm long, 1.8-2.4 cm broad, apex obtuse and mucronate, base obtuse, upper surface smooth and glossy, lower surface densely scaly, the scales about 2(-3) diameters apart; petiole 6-8 mm long, sometimes slightly scaly.

Terminal inflorescence of usually 3 flowers; pedicels about 1.5 cm long, smooth and glossy; calyx short, very slightly undulate, scaly outside; corolla funnelform, about 2.5 cm long, rose tinged with light purple and dark purple-dotted on the upper part, not scaly outside, lobes 5; stamens 10, slightly exserted, filaments pubescent on the lower part; ovary scaly, style glabrous.

Capsule 1.2-1.5 cm long, cylindric, scaly.

Distributed in southwest Sichuan (Muli), northwest Yunnan, southeast Xizang. Grows in sparse pine forests at 3400 meters.

4097   纸叶杜鹃

RHODODENDRON CHARTOPHYLLUM
Franch.

zhǐ yè dùjuān *"papery-leaved rhododendron"*

Semi-evergreen shrub, 1-2 meters high, the leaves of the previous year dropping just before or after flowering; twigs slender, slightly scaly.

Leaves thick-chartaceous, elliptic-lanceolate, about 4 cm long, about 1.4 cm broad, apex acute, base short cuneate, upper surface very slightly scaly only in the young leaves, lower surface scattered with scales 4-5 diameters apart; petiole to about 8 mm long, not scaly.

Terminal umbelliform inflorescence of 3-5 flowers; flower-bud scales caducous; pedicels 1.5-2.5 cm long, not scaly; calyx small, undulate, slightly scaly; corolla slightly asymmetric, 2.5 cm long, rose with dark red dots on the upper part, not scaly outside, deeply 5-lobed; stamens 10, exserted, filaments minutely hairy on the lower part, glabrous at the base; ovary densely scaly, style as long as the stamens, glabrous.

Distributed in west and north Yunnan, south Sichuan. Grows in open thickets at 1800 to 2600 meters.

4098 矛头杜鹃

RHODODENDRON AECHMOPHYLLUM

Balf. f. et Forrest

máo tóu dùjuān   *"spearhead rhododendron"*

Evergreen shrub about 1 meter high; shoots slightly scaly.

Leaves stiff-coriaceous, elliptic-lanceolate, 3-4.8 cm long, 1-1.5 cm broad, apex acute, base cuneate, upper surface smooth and glossy, midrib slightly impressed only on the lower part, lateral veins obscure, lower surface sparsely scaly, the scales about 3 or more diameters apart; petiole 4-8 mm long, slightly scaly.

Terminal umbelliform inflorescence of 3-6 flowers; pedicels 1-1.4 cm long, slightly scaly; calyx short, undulate, glabrous, with an occasional scale; corolla 3 cm long, rose, not scaly, deeply 5-lobed, lobes ovate and spreading; stamens 10, long-exserted, filaments glabrous; pistil much longer than the stamens, ovary scaly, style smooth and glossy.

Distributed in southwest Sichuan, north Yunnan. Grows on riverside rock debris.

Also from Sichuan and very similar to this species is *Rhododendron longistylum* Rehd. et Wils. (cháng zhóu dùjuān, "long-axis rhododendron"), but it is easily distinguished by the calyx which is well developed, deeply 5-lobed, and densely scaly outside, and by the stamen filaments which are hairy on the lower part.

193

4099　　　鬈花杜鹃

RHODODENDRON ANTHOPOGON
D. Don

rán huā dùjuān   *"bearded-flower rhododendron"*

Evergreen shrub to 1 meter high; branchlets short and strong, sparsely short-setose and scaly; leaf-bud scales caducous.

Leaves coriaceous, obovate-elliptic, 2.5-3.2 cm long, 1.3-2 cm broad, apex rounded and mucronate, upper surface sparsely scaly, lower surface very densely clad with dark yellowish brown scales of two types, the larger scales raised and resembling dry brown snowflakes; petiole about 5 mm long, scaly on the upper surface.

Terminal subumbelliform inflorescence of several flowers; pedicels about 4 mm long, slightly scaly; calyx well developed, deeply 5-lobed, lobes elliptic, about 5 mm long, ciliolate; corolla narrowly tubular, 1.8 cm long, pink, densely pubescent at the throat, not scaly outside; stamens 6-8, included, filaments glabrous; ovary scaly, 4-5-loculed, style smooth and glossy, short and stout.

Capsule 3 mm long, enclosed by the persistent calyx.

South Xizang; also Sikkim and Nepal. Grows in thickets on mountain slopes at 4000 meters.

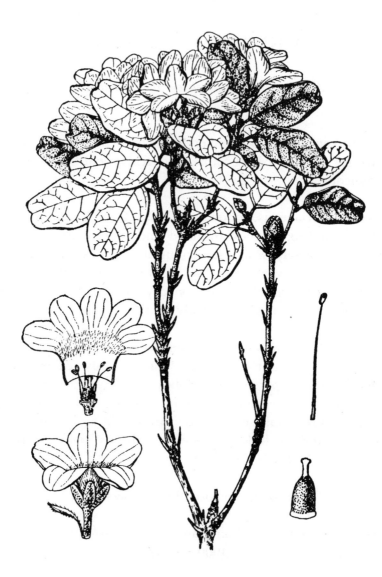

4100　毛花杜鹃

RHODODENDRON HYPENANTHUM
Balf. f.

máo huā dùjuān   *"hairy-flowered rhododendron"*

Evergreen undershrub about 50 cm high; branchlets short, sparsely coarse-hairy and scaly; leaf-bud scales persistent for several years.

Leaves coriaceous, obovate-elliptic, 2.5-3.5 cm long, to 1.6 cm broad, apex rounded and mucronate (but often recurved, appearing emarginate), upper surface smooth and glossy, lower surface densely clad with dark yellowish brown snowflakelike scales of one type and color; petiole about 4 mm long, scaly.

Terminal subumbelliform inflorescence of 5-7 flowers; pedicels about 3 mm long, scaly; calyx well developed, deeply 5-lobed, lobes broadly elliptic, about 5 mm long, densely ciliate; corolla narrowly tubular, about 1.8 cm long, yellow, not scaly outside; stamens 5, filaments glabrous; ovary scaly, style short and stout, smooth and glossy.

Capsule 3 mm long, enclosed by the persistent calyx.

South and southeast Xizang; also Sikkim and Nepal. Grows in thickets on mountain slopes at 3800 meters.

4101　　毛喉杜鹃

198

RHODODENDRON CEPHALANTHUM
Franch.

máo hóu dùjuān   *"hairy-throated rhododendron"*

Evergreen dwarf shrub about 30 cm high; twigs short and stout, pubescent and setose when young; leaf-bud scales persistent for many years.

Leaves stiffly thick-coriaceous, oblong-elliptic, to 2.3 cm long, about 8 mm broad, apex obtuse and mucronulate, base bluntly cuneate, margin revolute, upper surface smooth and glossy, the net veins impressed, lower surface densely clad with yellowish brown flaky scales; petiole about 3 mm long.

Terminal dense capitate inflorescence of 4-9 flowers; flower-bud scales persistent during flowering; pedicels very short; calyx large, about 4 mm long, deeply 5-lobed, lobes scaly outside and long-ciliate; corolla narrowly tubular, 1.6 cm long, white, not scaly outside, densely villous within at the throat, 5-lobed; stamens 5, included within the corolla tube, filaments slightly hairy at the base; ovary scaly, style very short, turbinate, glabrous.

Capsule 4 mm long, scaly, the short style persistent.

Distributed in west Yunnan, southeast Xizang, southwest Sichuan. Grows on rocky mountains at 3000-3500 meters.

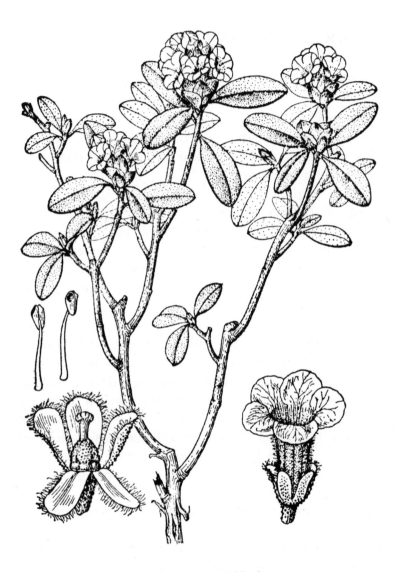

4102　毛冠杜鹃

RHODODENDRON LAUDANDUM
Cowan

máo guān dùjuān   *"hairy corolla rhododendron"*

Evergreen erect shrub about 1 meter high; shoots slender, straight and upright, light yellow, scaly.

Leaves coriaceous, oblong to oblong-elliptic, 1.2-1.8 cm long, 6-8 mm broad, margin recurved, upper surface densely clad with subcontiguous scales, lower surface scaly, the scales dark chestnut, dry and flaky, imbricate; petiole 2-3 mm long, scaly.

Terminal capitate inflorescence of 3-6 flowers; pedicels 1.5 mm long, scaly; calyx well developed, 4 mm long, lobes oblong, densely scaly and hairy outside, densely long-ciliate; corolla 1.2 cm long, pale pink or nearly white, corolla tube tubular, about 6 mm long, densely hairy within, densely gray-white-pubescent outside, lobes 5, rounded, subglabrous outside, sparsely scaly; ovary scaly, style short and thick, sparsely pubescent, shorter than the stamens.

Southeast Xizang. Grows in thickets above 4000 meters.

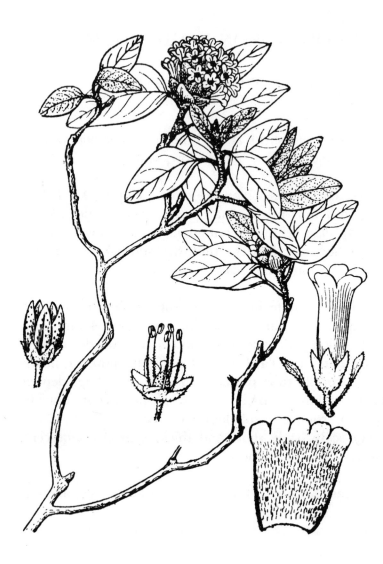

4103　烈香杜鹃

RHODODENDRON ANTHOPOGONOIDES

Maxim.

liè xiāng dùjuān   *"intensely fragrant rhododendron"*

Evergreen shrub about 1.2 meters high; twigs strong and erect, shoots densely scaly and slightly pubescent.

Leaves soft-coriaceous, broadly elliptic, about 2.5 cm long, 1.2-1.7 cm broad, upper surface glabrous, not scaly at maturity, lower surface sparsely brown-scaly, midrib prominent; petiole 3-4 mm long, sparsely scaly, upper surface grooved and ciliate.

Terminal capitate inflorescence of 10 or more intensely fragrant flowers; flower-bud scales persistent during flowering; pedicels glabrous; calyx large, to 4 mm long, lobes broadly oblong, light green, not scaly outside, long-ciliate; corolla narrowly tubular, 1.2 cm long, light yellow-green, exterior clad with a few minute hairs, not scaly, interior densely villous; stamens 5, included, filaments pubescent; ovary scaly, style very short, turbinate, glabrous.

Distributed in Gansu, Qinghai, north Sichuan. Forms thickets in the high mountains.

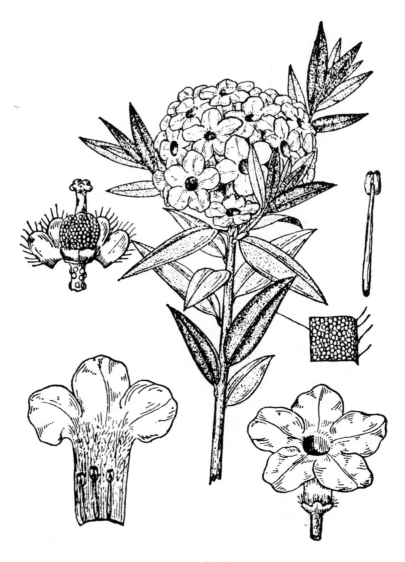

4104　筒花杜鹃

RHODODENDRON LEDOIDES
Balf. f.

tŏng huā dùjuān   *"tubular flower rhododendron"*

Evergreen dwarf undershrub to 30 cm high; twigs clad with peltate scales and with bristles which are residual stalks of the scales; bud scales caducous.

Leaves scattered, coriaceous, elliptic-lanceolate, 2-3.5 cm long, 7-12 mm broad, apex acute and stiffly mucronate, margin somewhat revolute, upper surface densely scaly at first, soon smooth and glossy, lower surface dark rusty brown, covered with 2 scurfy layers of peltate and dentate scales, lateral veins obscured; petiole 3-5 mm long.

Terminal capitate inflorescence of as many as 10 flowers, 4.5 cm in diameter; pedicels 3-5 mm long, scaly; calyx cuplike, green, 5-lobed, lobes sparsely scaly outside, tomentose at the margin; corolla tubular-campanulate, 2.5 cm in diameter, white, corolla tube narrowly cylindric, 1.4 cm long, lobes 5, about 1 cm long; stamens 5, filaments glabrous; ovary green and scaly, style short, stout, and smooth.

Capsule 4 mm long, scaly.

Distributed in Yunnan, west Sichuan. Grows in thickets on the high mountains.

Regarded by some as a variety of *Rhododendron trichostomum* Franch. (máo zuĭ dùjuān, "hairy-mouthed rhododendron").

205

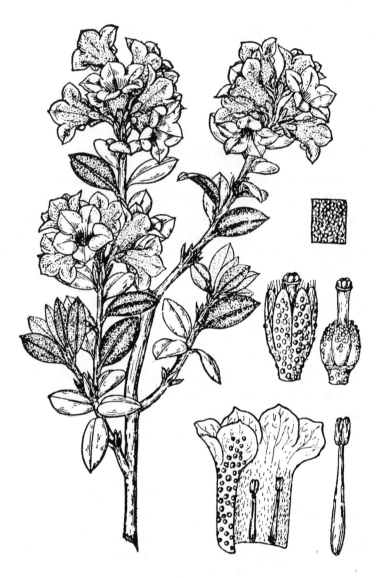

4105　水仙杜鹃

RHODODENDRON SARGENTIANUM
Rehd. et Wils.

shuĭ xiān dùjuān   *"narcissus rhododendron"*

Evergreen undershrub to 60 cm high, erect and densely branched; shoots very short, finely setose and scaly; bud scales persistent on the older branches.

Leaves aromatic, scattered, coriaceous, broadly elliptic, 8-15 mm long, 5-8 mm broad, apex obtuse and stoutly mucronate, base broadly cuneate, upper surface scaly at first, soon smooth and glossy, lower surface clad with scurfy scales, midrib impressed on the upper surface, prominent and nearly smooth and glossy on the lower surface.

Terminal lax umbelliform raceme of 6-8 flowers; bud scales subpersistent, as long as the pedicels; pedicels 5-8 mm long, yellow-scaly; calyx quite well developed, 4 mm long, green, 5-lobed, lobes oblong, sparsely scaly on the back, long-ciliate; corolla salverform, light yellow, scaly outside except at the margin, corolla tube broadly cylindric, about 1 cm long, pubescent within, lobes 5, rounded, slightly spreading; stamens 5, glabrous; ovary yellow-scaly, style glabrous.

West Sichuan. Grows on rock cliffs above 3000 meters.

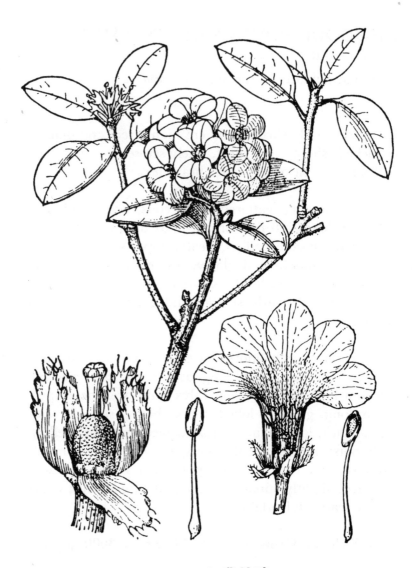

4106　红背杜鹃

RHODODENDRON RUFESCENS
Franch.

hóng bèi dùjuān   *"red-backed rhododendron"*

Evergreen shrub, less than 1 meter high; branchlets slender, clad with scales and a few minute bristles; leaf-bud scales caducous.

Leaves strongly aromatic, coriaceous, ovate-oblong, to 2.5 cm long, 1.2 cm broad, upper surface dark green and lustrous, not scaly, lower surface densely clad with spongy brownish-cinnamon scales; petiole about 4 mm long, scaly.

Terminal inflorescence of 6-8 flowers; flower-bud scales persistent during flowering; pedicels 2 mm long, slightly scaly; calyx light purple, well developed, deeply 5-lobed, lobes 3 mm long, oblong-elliptic, smooth and glossy on the back, long-ciliate and scaly at the margin; corolla narrowly tubular, 1.7 cm long, rose, not scaly outside, corolla tube about 8 mm long, lobes 5, suborbicular, spreading; stamens 5, included, filaments glabrous; ovary scaly, style very short and thick, glabrous.

North and northwest Sichuan. Grows in forest undergrowth at about 4000 meters.

4107　　樱草杜鹃

RHODODENDRON PRIMULAEFLORUM

Bur. et Franch.

yĭng căo dùjuān   *"primrose rhododendron"*

Evergreen shrub about 1 meter high; shoots short, densely clad with scales and short coarse hairs; leaf-bud scales caducous.

Leaves coriaceous, oblong-elliptic, 1.8-2.4 cm long, 8-12 mm broad, upper surface smooth and lustrous, lower surface densely scaly, the scales flaky and gray-brown to light yellowish brown; petiole 2 mm long, scaly.

Terminal capitate inflorescence of 5-8 flowers; flower-bud scales caducous; pedicels 2 mm long, nearly smooth and glossy; calyx well developed, 4 mm long, 5-lobed, lobes oblong, more or less scaly outside, ciliate; corolla narrowly tubular, 1.2-1.6 cm long, yellow, white, or rose, not scaly outside, pubescent within; stamens 5, included, filaments glabrous; ovary scaly, style short and thick, turbinate, glabrous.

Capsule 4 mm long, scaly.

Distributed in Yunnan, Sichuan, Xizang. Grows in high mountain meadows.

From the same area, *Rhododendron primulaeflorum* var. *cephalanthoides* (Balf. f. et W. W. Sm.) Cowan (wéi máo dùjuān, "minutely hairy rhododendron") is a variety in which the corolla exterior is densely clad with minute hairs.

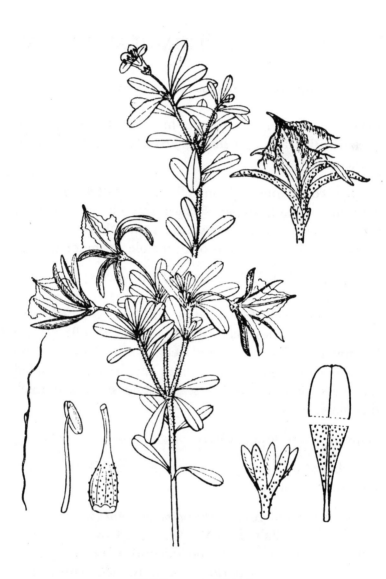

4108　越橘杜鹃

RHODODENDRON VACCINIOIDES
Hook. f.

yuè jú dùjuān   *"vaccinium rhododendron"*

Delicate dwarf evergreen epiphytic or saxatile shrub, 0.3-1 meter high; twigs slender, often pendulous, branchlets very scabrous, densely verrucose-glandular, branches densely clad with stipitate glands in the first year, with semipersistent bud scales at the base.

Leaves scattered, occasionally in pseudoverticillate clusters, thick-coriaceous, spatulate-oblanceolate, 1.3-2 cm long, 5-8 mm broad on the upper part, rounded, emarginate, and mucronate at the apex, tapering toward the base, decurrent along the thick winged petiole, upper surface glabrous, lower surface sparsely clad with punctate scales, lateral veins obscure; petiole about 2 mm long.

Terminal inflorescence of 1-2 flowers; pedicels 1-1.5 cm long, glandular-scaly; calyx large, lobes 3 mm long, with a few scales on the back; corolla campanulate, 8 mm long, purplish pink or pinkish white, corolla tube 5 mm long, sparsely glandular-scaly outside, 5-lobed; stamens 10, ovary scaly, style short and thick.

Capsule 2 cm long, splitting from the reflexed tip; seeds long-tailed at both ends, the tails threadlike and about 7 mm long.

Distributed in Xizang, Yunnan; also Sikkim, Burma.

4109　缺顶杜鹃

214

RHODODENDRON EMARGINATUM
Hemsl.

quē dǐng dùjuān   *"notched tip rhododendron"*

Evergreen shrub to 1 meter high; twigs spreading and strong, branchlets very scabrous and densely clad with small wartlike scales; winter-bud scales caducous.

Leaves in whorls of 3-4, firm-coriaceous, long obovate, 2-3.5 cm long, 1-1.5 cm broad at the widest upper part, broadly rounded and emarginate at the apex, tapering downward, cuneate at the base, upper surface smooth and glossy, lower surface light yellow and clad with small punctate scales about 3 diameters apart, midrib and lateral veins impressed on the upper surface, conspicuously prominent on the lower surface.

Flowers terminal and solitary, with a few bracts at the base; pedicels about 2 cm long, sparsely scaly; calyx very small, undulate, sparsely scaly outside; corolla campanulate, 1.3 cm long, yellow, sparsely scaly outside, 5-lobed; stamens 10, exserted, filaments pubescent; ovary scaly, style smooth and glossy.

Capsule 1.3 cm long, cylindric, clad outside with small raised scales.

Southeast Yunnan. Grows in forests at 1700 meters.

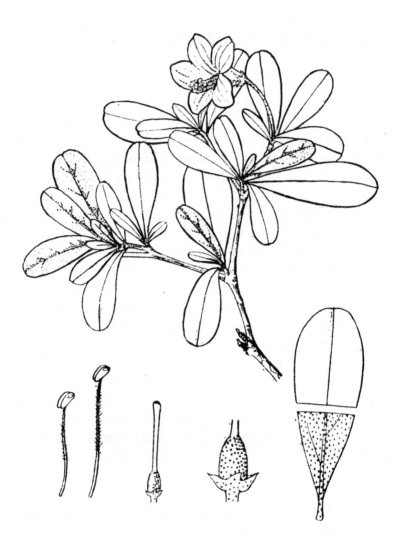

4110　卫矛叶杜鹃

RHODODENDRON EUONYMIFOLIUM

Lévl.

wèi máo yè dùjuān   *"euonymus-leaved rhododendron"*

Evergreen shrub about 1 meter high; twigs more or less bent, internodes short, shoots sparsely clad with fine glandular hairs and scales.

Leaves in terminal clusters, thick-coriaceous, narrowly cuneate-oblanceolate or spatulate, 2-4 cm long, 8-12 mm broad at the widest place above the middle, apex broadly rounded and very shortly mucronate, emargination slight or nearly absent, upper and lower surfaces glabrous and slightly scaly, the scales fine, within small hollow dots, and broadly separated, midrib and lateral veins obscure on both surfaces; petiole very short, slightly scaly.

Flowers terminal and solitary; pedicels about 2 cm long, sparsely fine-scaly; calyx lobes small, sparsely scaly outside; corolla campanulate, about 2 cm long, fleshy, yellow, sparsely scaly outside, glabrous within, 5-lobed; stamens 10, filaments pubescent on the upper 2/3; ovary 5-loculed, finely scaly, style shorter than the stamens, the upper part gradually thickened and abruptly reflexed.

Capsule 1.2 cm long.

Distributed in Guizhou, north Guangxi. Grows in dense forests. Blooms in November.

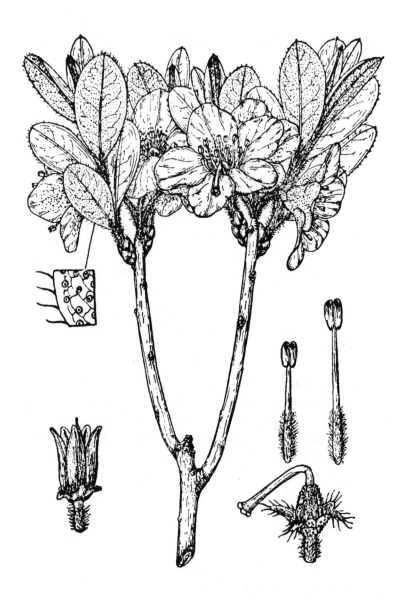

4111　糙毛杜鹃

RHODODENDRON TRICHOCLADUM
Franch.

cāo máo dùjuān   *"coarse-haired rhododendron"*

Deciduous or late-deciduous shrub about 1 meter high; twigs quite fine but straight and upright, shoots clad with long stiff pale yellow hairs which persist into the second year.

Leaves scattered, opening with the flowers, firm-chartaceous, broadly oblong, 2.4-4 cm long, 1.5-2 cm broad, rounded and mucronulate at the apex, tapering toward the base to short cuneate, more or less clad at the margin with long stiff hairs, upper surface sparsely hairy and scaly when young, lower surface glabrous and more densely scaly, the scales fine and 3-4 diameters apart; petiole about 4 mm long, stiff-hairy.

Flowers in terminal clusters of 3-5; pedicels clad with somewhat curly pale yellow hairs; calyx well developed, deeply 5-lobed, 5 mm long, lobes scaly outside, long-ciliate; corolla broadly funnelform, about 2.5 cm long, yellow with a trace of green, green-dotted at the throat, scaly outside; stamens 10, filaments hairy on the lower part; ovary scaly, style thick and reflexed.

Capsule oblong, about 7 mm long, erect, scaly.

West Yunnan; also Burma. Grows on rocky slopes.

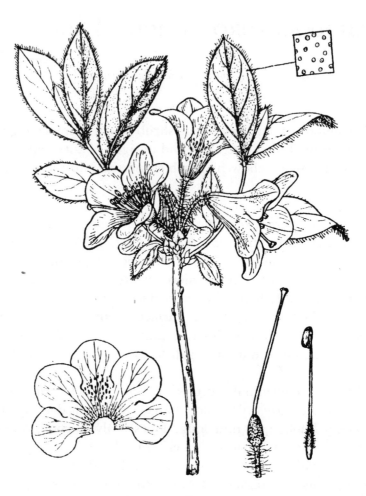

4112　蜜花杜鹃

220

RHODODENDRON MELINANTHUM

Balf. f. et Ward

mì huā dùjuān   *"honey flower rhododendron"*

Deciduous shrub to 2.5 meters high; twigs slender, straight, and upright, shoots clad with spreading stiff yellow hairs which are mostly shed during the first year.

Leaves chartaceous, opening with the flowers, oblong to oblong-obovate, about 3 cm long, 1.2 cm broad, apex bluntly acute, base short cuneate, margin long-ciliate (at least in youth), upper surface smooth and glossy even when young, lower surface somewhat gray-white and sparsely scaly, the midrib and lateral veins stiff-hairy; petiole 4-6 mm long, stiff-hairy.

Flowers in terminal clusters of 3-5; pedicels to 2 cm long, more or less sparsely scaly and sparsely stiff-hairy or glabrous; calyx poorly developed, shallowly and un-equally 5-lobed, usually glabrous; corolla short, broadly campanulate, to 3 cm in diameter, lemon yellow, sparsely scaly outside, lobes 5, rounded; stamens 10, filaments hairy; ovary scaly, style glabrous throughout.

Distributed in Yunnan, southeast Xizang; also northern Burma. Grows around glacial areas at about 4000 meters.

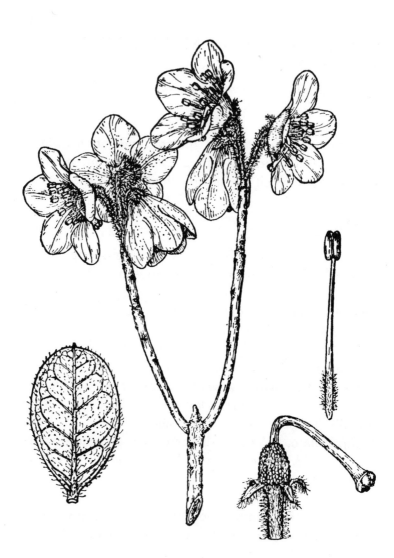

4113　卷毛杜鹃

RHODODENDRON OULOTRICHUM

Balf. f. et Forrest

quán máo dùjuān *"curly-haired rhododendron"*

Deciduous undershrub about 1 meter high; branchlets nearly smooth and glossy; leaf-bud scales caducous.

Leaves obovate-elliptic, about 2.5 cm long, 1.8 cm broad, apex rounded and mucronate, margin brown-ciliate, upper surface smooth and glossy, lower surface sparsely clad with fine scales several diameters apart, midrib quite densely brown-villous on the lower surface when young.

Terminal inflorescence of about 3 flowers which open before the leaves; flower-bud scales caducous; pedicels 1.2 cm long, villous but not scaly; calyx well developed, 4 mm long, 5-lobed, lobes oblong, densely long-ciliate; corolla broadly funnelform, 1.8 cm long, yellow, sparsely scaly outside; stamens 10, exserted, densely pubescent toward the base; ovary densely scaly, style thick, curved downward, smooth and glossy.

Capsule 8 mm long, sparsely scaly.

West Yunnan. Grows on dry rocky grasslands at 3000 meters.

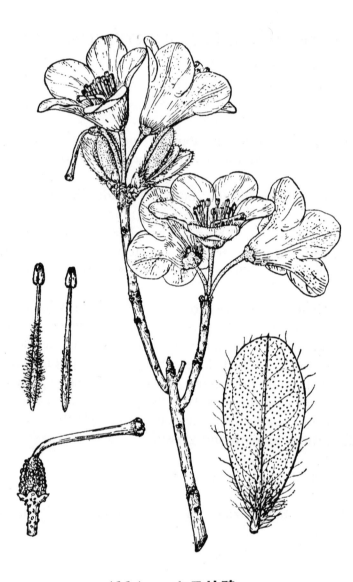

4114　弯月杜鹃

RHODODENDRON SEMILUNATUM

Balf. f. et Forrest

wān yuè dùjuān   *"curved moon rhododendron"*

Deciduous undershrub about 1 meter high; branchlets grayish green, nearly smooth and glossy or clad with coarse gray hairs; leaf-bud scales subpersistent.

Leaves in terminal clusters, thin-chartaceous, oblong-oblanceolate, 1.8 cm long, 8 mm broad, apex rounded and mucronulate, margin sparsely ciliolate when young, upper surface smooth and glossy, lower surface quite densely glandular-scaly, the scales fine and about 1-2 diameters apart, midrib sometimes villous on the lower surface; petiole very short, villous.

Terminal inflorescence of 3 flowers; flower-bud scales caducous; pedicels 8 mm long, scaly but not villous; calyx very short, undulate, not ciliate, scaly outside; corolla broadly tubular, 1.8 cm long, dark yellow, lobes sparsely scaly outside; stamens 10, exserted, about half of the filaments pubescent on the lower part, the others very sparsely short-pubescent; ovary scaly, style bent to the side, glabrous.

Distributed in northwest Yunnan, southeast Xizang. Grows in thickets on rocky areas at about 3800 meters.

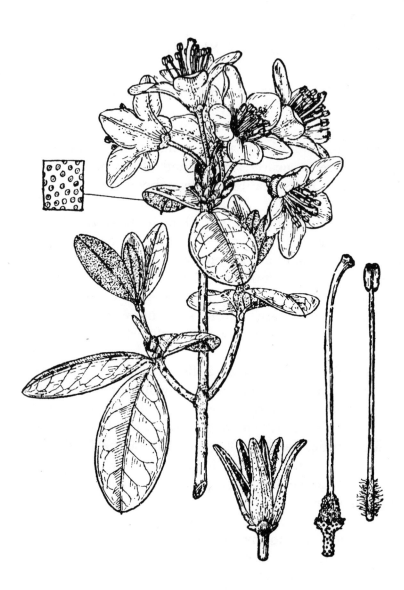

4115 红线杜鹃

RHODODENDRON RUBROLINEATUM

Balf. f. et Forrest

hóng xiàn dùjuān   *"red-lined rhododendron"*

Semi-evergreen shrub to about 1.5 meters high; shoots slender and scaly; leaf-bud scales caducous.

Leaves chartaceous, obovate-elliptic, about 3 cm long, about 1.6 cm broad, apex rounded and mucronulate, upper surface smooth and glossy, lower surface densely clad with fine scales about a diameter apart; petiole about 3 mm long, slightly coarse-hairy.

Inflorescences terminal and lateral, about 3 flowers each; flower-bud scales caducous; pedicels about 2 cm long, sparsely scaly; calyx short and undulate, scaly outside; corolla yellow, exterior streaked with rose; stamens 10, exserted, filaments pubescent near the base; ovary densely scaly, style straight, smooth and glossy.

Capsule 8 mm long, oblong, sparsely scaly.

Northwest Yunnan. Grows on grassy areas in forests at 3200-3500 meters.

Since this species is closely related to Subsection Triflorum, it may be just as appropriate to include it in that subsection.

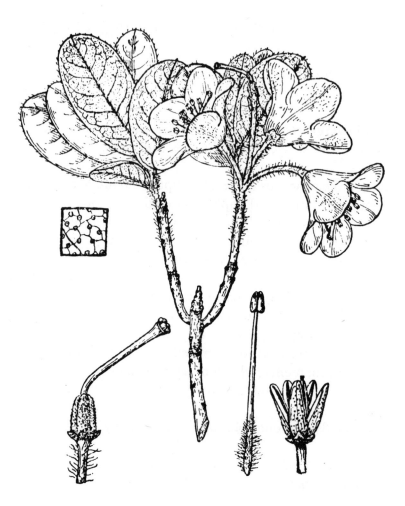

4116 黄绿杜鹃

RHODODENDRON CHLORANTHUM

Balf. f. et Forrest

huáng lǜ dùjuān   *"yellow-green rhododendron"*

Deciduous undershrub about 1 meter high; branchlets clad with spreading long coarse hairs; leaf-bud scales caducous.

Leaves obovate or oblong-obovate, 2.5-3 cm long, about 2 cm broad, apex rounded and mucronate, upper surface smooth and glossy, lower surface scaly, the scales fine and about 2-3 diameters apart, the young leaves clad with long coarse hairs on the lower surface of the midrib and at the margin; petiole 3 mm long, densely clad with long coarse hairs.

Terminal inflorescence of 4 flowers which open before the leaves (or at the same time); pedicels about 2 cm long, clad with spreading long coarse hairs; calyx small, lobes triangular, sparsely scaly at the margin, smooth and glossy outside; corolla funnelform, 1.8 cm long, yellow, greenish toward the base, smooth and glossy, sparsely scaly outside only on the lobes; stamens 10, filaments pubescent on the lower part; ovary sparsely scaly, style thick, slightly curved, smooth and glossy.

Capsule about 1 cm long, cylindric, sparsely scaly, fruit-stalk glabrous.

Distributed in northwest Yunnan, southeast Xizang. Grows on expanses of open land.

4117　耳叶杜鹃

230

RHODODENDRON AURICULATUM

Hemsl.

ěr yè dùjuān   *"eared-leaf rhododendron"*

Evergreen shrub or small tree to 9.5 meters high; new branches densely clad with very long glandular hairs, hair remnants remaining on the year-old branches, older branches glabrous.

Leaves chartaceous, oblong or elliptic-lanceolate, 15-25 cm long, 4.5-7 cm broad, apex obtuse and short-mucronate, base rounded and usually cordate, upper surface and especially the lower surface densely pubescent at first, later subglabrous with hairs only on the midrib, net veins evident on the lower surface; petiole 2.5-4 cm long, densely glandular-hairy.

Terminal short raceme of 5-10 fragrant flowers, to 22 cm in diameter; pedicels thick, 2-3 cm long, densely clad with very long glandular hairs; calyx variable, shallowly or deeply divided, lobes to 7 mm long, glandular-hairy on the back; corolla funnelform, 6-10 cm long, silvery white, sparsely glandular-hairy outside, lobes 7, spreading; stamens 14; ovary 7-8-loculed, densely pubescent.

Capsule to 4 cm long, 1.4 cm thick, glandular-hairy.

Distributed in Hubei, Sichuan, Guizhou. Grows in forests at 2000 meters.

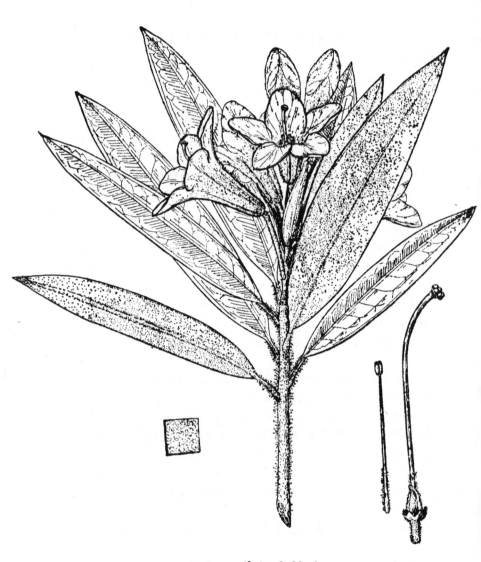

4118　朱红大杜鹃

RHODODENDRON GRIERSONIANUM
Balf. f. et Forrest

zhū hóng dà dùjuān   *"vermilion large rhododendron"*

Evergreen shrub to 2.5 meters high; branchlets densely clad with branching long soft yellowish hairs and long-stalked glandular hairs.

Leaves quite scattered, coriaceous, lanceolate, 11-14 cm long, 2.5-3 cm broad, apex short acuminate, base acute, upper surface glabrous at maturity, lower surface clad with more or less persistent yellowish brown felted hairs; petiole 1.5-2.5 cm long, grooved on the upper surface, clad with hair similar to that of the young branches.

Terminal lax raceme of 5-6 flowers (rarely 10), rachis 2 cm long, with strap-shaped bracts to 5.5 cm long; pedicels to 3.5 cm long; calyx small, lobes 5, triangular, densely glandular-hairy; corolla dark red to vermilion, corolla tube quite narrowly cylindric, 2-2.5 cm long, gradually expanding upward, the rim of the corolla funnelform and spreading, corolla exterior densely clad with branching soft hairs and long-stalked glands, interior minutely hairy; stamens 10; ovary clad with dense appressed hairs and sparse glands.

West Yunnan; also Burma. Grows in thickets.

4119 硬刺杜鹃

RHODODENDRON BARBATUM
Wall.

yìng cì dùjuān   *"stiff-thorned rhododendron"*

Evergreen tree to 20 meters high, branching from the base; shoots long-setose, the bristles stiff and thornlike, sometimes persisting for several years.

Leaves coriaceous, elliptic-lanceolate, 10-20 cm long, 4-7 cm broad, apex acute and long-mucronate, lower surface clad at first with woolly indumentum, glabrous and light yellow-green at maturity, the midrib very prominent and clad near the base with long thornlike bristles; petiole 1-1.5 cm long, similarly setose.

Terminal compact globose-umbelliform inflorescence of 10-15 flowers, rachis glabrous; pedicels 1-1.5 cm long, smooth and glossy; calyx large, 1-1.5 cm long, glabrous, lobes shallow and irregular, dark red; corolla tubular-campanulate, 3.5 cm long, blood red, fleshy, 5-lobed; stamens 10, filaments white, glabrous; ovary light greenish white, densely clad with stipitate glands, style white and glabrous.

Capsule 2-2.5 cm long, 6 mm thick, setose.

South Xizang; also Sikkim, Nepal.

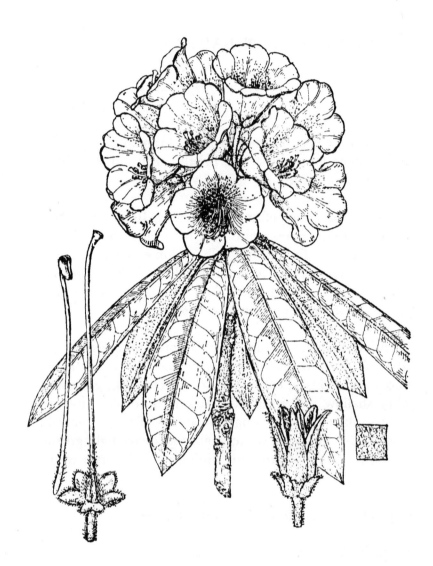

4120   长粗毛杜鹃

RHODODENDRON CRINIGERUM
Franch.

cháng cū máo dùjuān   *"long coarse hair rhododendron"*

Evergreen shrub to 4 meters high; shoots densely clad with long gland-tipped bristles.

Leaves coriaceous, oblong or oblanceolate, 10-15 cm long, 3-4.5 cm broad, apex acute, base rounded or slightly cordate, upper surface somewhat bullate-reticulate, lower surface clad with dense woolly indumentum; petiole 1-2 cm long, clad with gland-tipped bristles.

Terminal lax inflorescence of 12-15 flowers, bud scales persistent during flowering; pedicels 3 cm long, densely clad with long gland-tipped bristles; calyx large, lobes unequal, to 8 mm long, clad with gland-tipped soft hairs, ciliate; corolla broadly campanulate, pink, corolla tube 2.5 cm long, dark red dotted within on the upper part, the dots joining in a blotch toward the base, lobes spreading, glabrous; stamens 10, inclining, filaments hairy on the lower part; ovary and lower part of the style densely clad with gland-tipped bristles.

Capsule 1.5 cm long, densely clad with stipitate glands.

Distributed in west Yunnan, southeast Xizang. Grows in open forests.

4121 粘毛杜鹃

RHODODENDRON GLISCHRUM

Balf. f. et W. W. Sm.

nián máo dùjuān   *"sticky-haired rhododendron"*

Evergreen shrub or small tree to 8 meters high; new shoots, petioles, and midrib bases densely clad with gland-tipped bristles of unequal length, the glands blackish and viscid, with eglandular bristles and detersile branching felted hairs as well.

Leaves subcoriaceous, narrowly oblong-lanceolate, to 20 cm long, 4-6 cm broad, apex abruptly acuminate, base rounded, margin ciliolate, upper surface glabrous at maturity, lower surface clad along the midrib and lateral veins with partially gland-tipped fine stiff hairs; petiole 2-2.5 cm long, clad with gland-tipped bristles.

Terminal umbelliform raceme of 10-15 flowers; pedicels to 4 cm long, densely clad with long yellow hairs and glands; calyx large, 1.5 cm long, deeply 5-lobed, pubescent and glandular; corolla light purple-lilac, 3-4 cm long; stamens 10, filaments glandular on the lower half; ovary and style densely clad with gland-tipped fine bristles.

Capsule oblong, 1.5 cm long, viscid, enclosed within the persistent calyx lobes.

Distributed in Yunnan, Sichuan, southeast Xizang. Grows in thickets.

239

4122 芒刺杜鹃

RHODODENDRON STRIGILLOSUM
Franch.

máng cì dùjuān   *"prickly rhododendron"*

Evergreen shrub, 2-3 meters high; shoots straight and upright, densely clad with gland-tipped bristles.

Leaves in terminal clusters, coriaceous, oblong-lanceolate, 8-14 cm long, 2-3 cm broad, apex abruptly short acuminate and mucronate, base nearly rounded, margin densely ciliate when young, upper surface glabrous, lower surface scattered with a few crooked hairs, often clad only at the midrib with dark purple soft hairs and gland-tipped light purple bristles; petiole about 1 cm long, clad with hairs similar to those of the midrib.

Terminal racemose-umbelliform inflorescence of 8-12 flowers, rachis about 8 mm long, sparsely glandular; pedicels 10-15 mm long, clad with hairs similar to those of the petioles; calyx small, 3 mm long, clad with gland-tipped bristles, shallowly 5-lobed; corolla campanulate, 4.5-5.5 cm long, dark red, 5-lobed, lobes spreading and emarginate; stamens 10, filaments glabrous; ovary densely clad with light brown gland-tipped bristles, style light purple and glabrous.

Capsule oblong-cylindric, about 2.5 cm long, clad with long red bristles.

Distributed in Sichuan, Yunnan. Grows in forests at 2000-3000 meters.

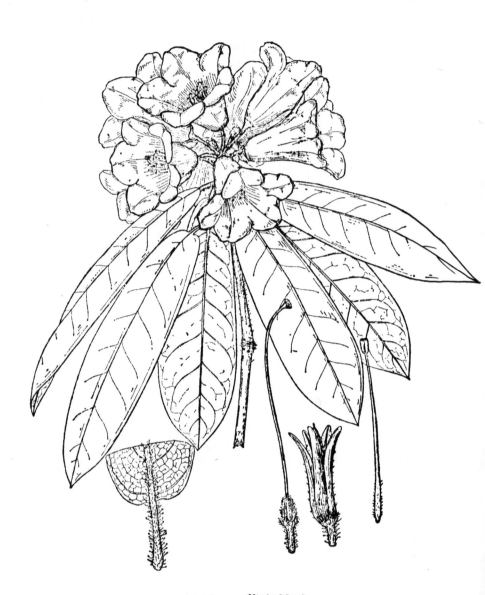

4123　紫斑杜鹃

242

RHODODENDRON MONOSEMATUM
Hutch.

zǐ bān dùjuān   *"purple-spotted rhododendron"*

Evergreen shrub to small tree, 2-7 meters high; new shoots subglabrous toward the base, leafy on the upper part and densely hairy, the hairs long, stiff, spreading, blackish, and gland-tipped.

Leaves firm-coriaceous, oblong, 8-11 cm long, 2-3.5 cm broad, apex acute, base subcordate, upper surface glabrous, with dense fine net veins, lower surface glabrous, only the midrib slightly setose, lateral veins slightly prominent; petiole 1.5 cm long, with gland-tipped bristles similar to those of the shoots.

Terminal racemose-umbelliform inflorescence of about 12 flowers; pedicels 1.5-2 cm long, densely clad with stiff hairs tipped with black glands; calyx short, inconspicuously 5-lobed, glandular-hairy outside; corolla broadly funnelform, white tinged pink with one large purple blotch within above the base, red outside at the base, corolla tube 3 cm long, glabrous, lobes 5, spreading; stamens 10, included, filaments pubescent at the base; ovary densely clad with reddish brown hairs tipped with black glands.

Capsule about 2 cm long, slightly curved, glandular-hairy.

West Sichuan. Grows in forests.

4124　龙胜杜鹃

RHODODENDRON CHIHSINIANUM

Chun et Fang

lóng shèng dùjuān   *"Longsheng rhododendron"*

Evergreen small tree about 4 meters high; branchlets stout, sparsely brown-setose at first, the bristles 3-4 mm long, spreading, and gland-tipped.

Leaves stiff-coriaceous, long elliptic, 19-23 cm long, 5-7 cm broad, bluntly acute and short-mucronate at the apex, tapering asymmetrically toward the base, the base obtuse, rarely subcordate, lower surface clad with detersile powdery pubescence; petiole 1.5-2 cm long, stout, clad with gland-tipped bristles.

Terminal racemose-umbelliform inflorescence of about 8 flowers, rachis 2 cm long, densely clad with long crooked rusty yellow soft hairs; pedicels and calyces similarly hairy; calyx poorly developed, orbicular, undulate, long-ciliate; corolla funnelform-campanulate, 4 cm long, glabrous, 7-lobed;* stamens 15, filaments glabrous; ovary densely clad with long yellow glandular hairs, style sparsely stipitate-glandular.

North Guangxi. Grows in forests.

*No corolla color given; see key.

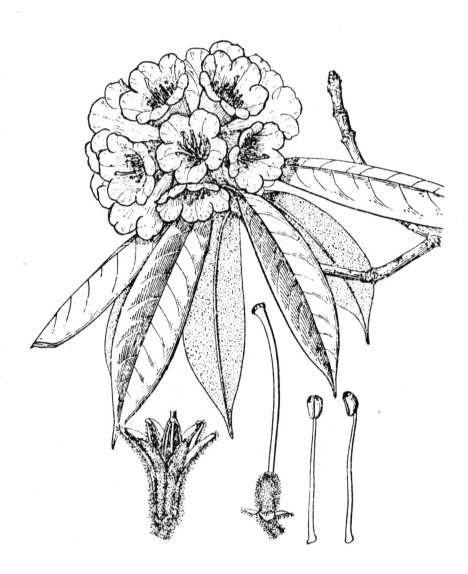

4125　峨马杜鹃

RHODODENDRON OCHRACEUM
Rehd. et Wils.

é mǎ dùjuān   *"E-Ma rhododendron"**

Evergreen shrub to 3.5 meters high; twigs slender, shoots densely setose, the bristles brown, of unequal length, and gland-tipped, older branches smooth and glossy.

Leaves thin-coriaceous, narrowly oblanceolate, 5-8 cm long, 1.5-2.5 cm broad, apex abruptly acuminate, base rounded, upper surface setose when young, smooth and glossy at maturity, lower surface clad with a thick layer of loose woolly yellow indumentum, the midrib prominent, the lateral veins concealed by the indumentum; petiole 1-1.5 cm long, pubescent and setose when young, the bristles light yellow and gland-tipped.

Terminal umbelliform inflorescence of 8-12 flowers, rachis about 5 mm long, pubescent; pedicels 6-12 mm long, densely clad with short gland-tipped bristles; calyx cuplike, 5-lobed, lobes triangular, 2.5 mm long, pubescent; corolla broadly campanulate, about 3 cm long, dark red, not spotted, 5-lobed; stamens 10-12, filaments glabrous; ovary densely glandular-hairy.

Capsule cylindric, 2.5 cm long.

Southwest Sichuan. Grows in thickets.

*Possibly a geographic reference to two neighboring areas.

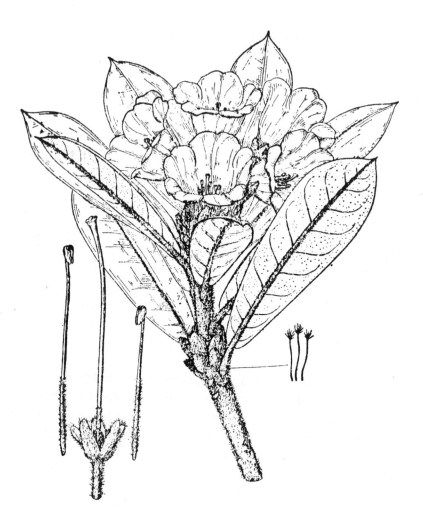

4126　长鳞杜鹃

RHODODENDRON LONGESQUAMATUM
Schneid.

cháng lín dùjuān *"long-scaled rhododendron"*

Evergreen shrub to 3 meters high or more; shoots and one- to two-year-old branches densely hairy, the hairs rusty yellow, very long, and branching; leaf-bud scales persistent for one to two years.

Leaves coriaceous, oblong-oblanceolate to narrowly obovate, 7-12 cm long, 2.4-4 cm broad, apex acute, base narrowly rounded, margin fringed with curly hairs when young, upper surface glabrous except on the midrib, lower surface bullate and finely glandular, the midrib and petiole densely clad with long branching hairs.

Terminal lax inflorescence; flower-bud scales persistent during flowering; pedicels 2-3 cm long, densely white-pubescent; calyx variable, usually large, lobes to 1 cm long, pubescent and glandular; corolla broadly campanulate, 5 cm long, about 4 cm in diameter, bright pink with dark red dots, corolla tube hairy within, lobes 5; stamens 10, filament hairy on the lower half; ovary densely clad with bristlelike hairs.

Capsule curved, 1.5 cm long, finely setose, the calyx persistent.

West Sichuan (Baoxing, Kangding). Grows in thickets above 3500 meters.

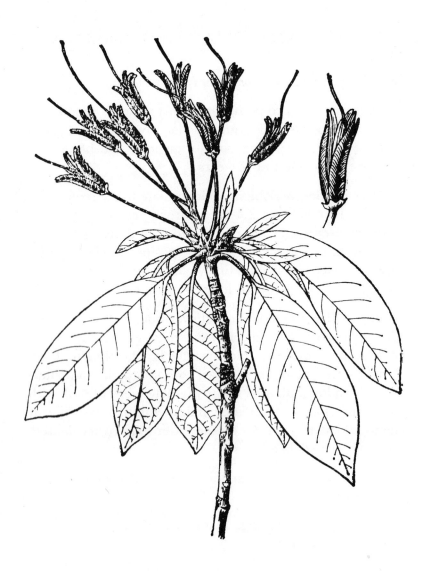

4127　黄山杜鹃

RHODODENDRON ANWHEIENSE
Wils.

huáng shān dùjuān   *"Huangshan rhododendron"*

Evergreen shrub to 2 meters high; twigs sparsely floccose when young.

Leaves in terminal clusters, coriaceous, ovate-lanceolate, 3-6 cm long, 1.5-3 cm broad, apex acute and mucronate, upper surface glabrous, bright green, and conspicuously reticulate, lower surface glabrous; petiole 5-10 mm long, grooved on the upper surface, sparsely floccose.

Terminal umbelliform inflorescence of 6-10 flowers; pedicels erect, 1.7-2.5 cm long, slightly floccose; calyx small, orbicular, with 5 small triangular teeth, glandular-ciliate; corolla campanulate, 2-2.5 cm long, white to light purple, 5-lobed, one upper lobe red-dotted within on the lower part; stamens 10, filaments hairy at the base; pistil longer than the stamens, ovary sparsely floccose and glandular, style slightly hairy at the base, stigma large, purple.

Capsule cylindric, 1.2-1.7 cm long, about 4 mm thick, glandular-hairy when young.

Distributed in Jiangxi, south Anhui. Grows in forests at 1000 meters.

251

4128　绒毛杜鹃

RHODODENDRON PACHYTRICHUM

Franch.

róng máo dùjuān   *"tomentose rhododendron"*

Evergreen shrub, 2-8 meters high; shoots straight and upright, densely clad with light brown branching hairs which are distributed up onto the petioles; older branches slightly hairy or glabrous.

Leaves in terminal false whorls, coriaceous, narrowly oblong to oblanceolate, 6-12 cm long, 2.5-3.5 cm broad, apex abruptly acuminate and mucronate, base rounded, upper and lower surfaces glabrous at maturity, only the lower surface of the midrib densely clad with brown branching hairs; petiole 1.5-2 cm long, similarly hairy.

Terminal racemose-umbelliform inflorescence of 7-10 flowers, rachis 1.5-2 cm long, sparsely pubescent; pedicels 1-2 cm long, brown-hairy; calyx small, 2 mm long, sparsely hairy, shallowly 5-lobed; corolla campanulate, broad at the base, 3.5 cm long, white or rose, dark purple spotted within at the base; stamens 10, included, filaments pubescent near the base; ovary densely brown-tomentose, style glabrous.

Capsule cylindric, 2.5 cm long, densely clad with short brown bristles.

West Sichuan. Grows in forests at 2400-3500 meters.

4129 麻花杜鹃

RHODODENDRON MACULIFERUM

Franch.

má huā dùjuān   *"pocked flower rhododendron"*

Evergreen shrub or small tree to 10 meters high; shoots slightly whitish-tomentose.

Leaves coriaceous, oblong-long-ovate to elliptic, 6-11 cm long, 2.5-4.5 cm broad, apex acute, base rounded or slightly cordate, margin more or less ciliate (glabrous at maturity), upper surface glabrous, only the prominent midrib of the lower surface thickly clad with interwoven floccose light brown hairs, the hairs most dense toward the base and distributed upward slightly more than 2/3 the length of the midrib, net veins evident; petiole 1.5-2.5 cm long, cylindric, thinly floccose.

Terminal lax umbelliform raceme of 7-10 flowers, rachis 1.5-2.5 cm long, pubescent; pedicels 1.5-2 cm long, clad with brown subsetose fluffy floccose hairs; calyx small, 2-3 mm long, 5-lobed, similarly hairy; corolla broadly campanulate, about 3.5 cm long, white or tinged light red, deep purple spotted at the base, 5-lobed; stamens 10, filaments sparsely pubescent only at the base; ovary brown-tomentose.

Capsule 2 cm long, cylindric.

Distributed in Hubei, Sichuan, Guizhou, Shaanxi. Grows in forests.

255

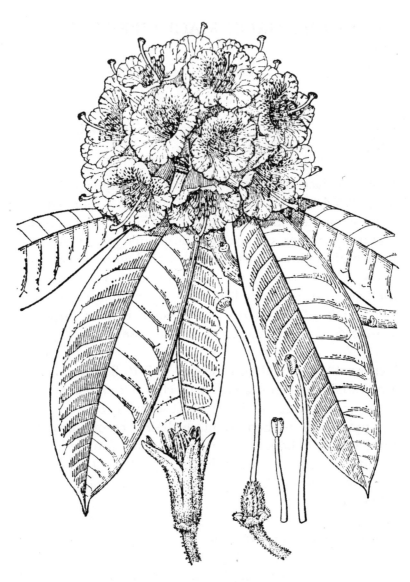

4130　树形杜鹃

RHODODENDRON ARBOREUM
Sm.

shù xíng dùjuān   *"treelike rhododendron"*

Evergreen tree, 7-14 meters high, much-branched from above the base.

Leaves coriaceous, oblong-lanceolate, 10-20 cm long, 3-6 cm broad, apex acute, base cuneate, upper surface bright green, glabrous at maturity, lower surface tomentose, the hairs white to yellowish brown, in a thin layer or more thickly woolly and felted, leaf veins slightly impressed on the upper surface, prominent and subglabrous on the lower surface; petiole 1-2 cm long, cylindric, very shallowly grooved on the upper surface, floccose at first, glandular on the lower surface.

Terminal compact inflorescence of about 20 flowers, rachis about 2 cm long, tomentose; pedicels about 8 mm long, tomentose and glandular; calyx small, tomentose and glandular, 5-lobed; corolla tubular-campanulate, 4-5 cm long, dark blood red (varieites may be white, rose, etc.) with 5 black nectaries at the base, corolla tube interior abundantly dark-dotted within, lobes 5, emarginate; stamens 10, filaments white; ovary white-tomentose.

Capsule cylindric, 3 cm long.

Xizang; also Bhutan, India, Sri Lanka.

4131　马缨杜鹃

RHODODENDRON DELAVAYI
Franch.

mǎ yīng dùjuān   *"Lantana rhododendron"*

Evergreen shrub to small tree, sometimes as high as 12 meters; twigs thick, strong, and erect, at first floccose.

Leaves in terminal clusters, coriaceous, oblong-lanceolate, 8-15 cm long, 2.5-3 cm broad, acute at the apex and base, upper surface glossy green and glabrous at maturity, lower surface clad with grayish white to light brown spongy thinly-felted hairs, midrib and lateral veins impressed on the upper surface, prominent on the lower surface; petiole 1-2 cm long, glabrous at maturity.

Terminal compact umbelliform inflorescence of 10-20 flowers, rachis hairy; bracts thick, elliptic, and mucronate; pedicels about 1 cm long, densely clad with reddish brown hairs; calyx small, about 2 mm long, 5-lobed, tomentose and glandular; corolla campanulate, 4-5 cm long, fleshy, dark red, with 5 basal nectaries; stamens 10, filaments glabrous; ovary densely clad with reddish brown flat hairs, style glabrous.

Capsule cylindric, 1.8 cm long, glabrous.

Distributed in Yunnan, Guizhou; also Burma. Grows in thickets.

4132　悦人杜鹃

RHODODENDRON PERAMOENUM

Balf. f. et Forrest

yuè rén dùjuān   *"delightful rhododendron"*

Evergreen shrub, 2-4 meters high; twigs strong and upright, white-floccose and sparsely glandular at first, smooth and glossy at maturity.

Leaves stiff-coriaceous, very narrowly lanceolate, 7-15 cm long, 1-2 cm broad, upper surface glabrous, lower surface thinly clad with a persistent and slightly agglutinate layer of pale yellow indumentum composed of interwoven branching hairs and small glands, midrib impressed on the upper surface, prominent on the lower surface, lateral veins slightly impressed on the upper surface, somewhat evident on the lower surface; petiole 1-1.5 cm long, grooved on the upper surface.

Terminal racemose-umbelliform inflorescence of 15-20 flowers, rachis densely brown-tomentose; pedicels about 6 mm long, densely tomentose and sparsely glandular; calyx small, about 2 mm long, with 5 broadly triangular teeth, tomentose; corolla campanulate, 5 cm long, fleshy, bright dark red, with 5 basal nectaries, lobes 5, emarginate; stamens 10, filaments glabrous; ovary densely yellow-tomentose, style glabrous.

Capsule 2 cm long.

West Yunnan. Grows in forests at 3000 meters.

4133　串珠杜鹃

RHODODENDRON HOOKERI
Nutt.

chuàn zhū dùjuān   *"string of pearls rhododendron"*

Evergreen large shrub to 4.5 meters high; shoots at first grayish white, clad with a waxy white powder, later green, old branches light brown.

Leaves coriaceous, oblong, 8-14 cm long, 3-5 cm broad, apex obtuse and mucronate, upper surface dark green and smooth, the midrib impressed and resembling a light green thread, lower surface light grayish green, the midrib prominent, smooth, and glossy, the lateral veins slightly prominent and dotted with separate clusters of hairs like a string of pearls, the hairs white at first, brown at maturity; petiole 2-3 cm long, slightly flattened on the upper surface, not grooved, clad with a thin layer of waxy white powder.

Terminal umbelliform inflorescence of 10-15 flowers; pedicels 1 cm long, smooth and glossy; calyx large, 1-2 cm long, smooth and glossy, unequally 5-lobed, the 2 lower lobes largest; corolla tubular-campanulate, about 4 cm long, dark red, 5-lobed; stamens 10, filaments glabrous; pistil glabrous.

Capsule cylindric-ovoid, 2-2.5 cm long, enclosed at the base by the persistent calyx.

South Xizang; also Bhutan. Forms forests in mountain areas.

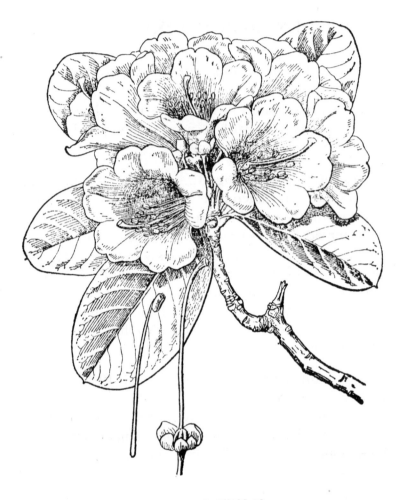

4134　红尊杜鹃

RHODODENDRON MEDDIANUM
Hutch.

hóng è dùjuān   *"red calyx rhododendron"*

Evergreen shrub about 2 meters high; bark of branches in the second year is gray, smooth and glossy, shoots very short with several terminal leaves.

Leaves coriaceous, broadly obovate-elliptic, 6-12 cm long, 4-6 cm broad, rounded and bluntly mucronate at the apex, abruptly tapered toward the base, glabrous, upper and lower surfaces densely net-veined; petiole 1.5 cm long, flat and smooth on the upper surface.

Terminal racemose umbelliform inflorescence of 8-10 flowers, rachis 1 cm long; pedicels 1.6-2 cm long, glabrous throughout; calyx large, to 8 mm long, dark red, shallowly 5-lobed, lobes rounded, glabrous; corolla funnelform, 3.5 cm long, dark red with darker streaks, dark-spotted within, lobes 5, quite deeply emarginate; stamens 10, filaments glabrous at the base, anthers blackish; ovary 5-loculed, glabrous, style far longer than the stamens, glabrous.

Capsule cylindric, about 2 cm long, slightly curved, glabrous.

West Yunnan. Grows in rhododendron thickets at 3200-3600 meters.

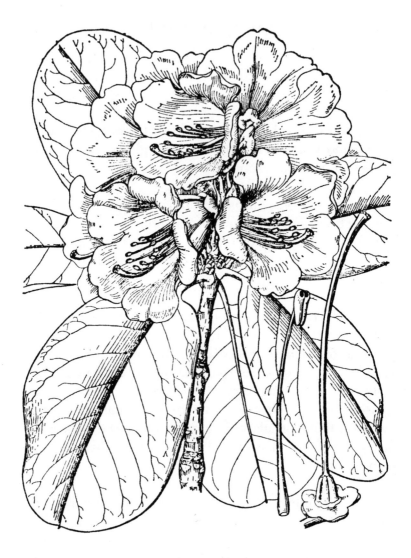

4135　蓝果杜鹃

RHODODENDRON CYANOCARPUM

(Franch.) W. W. Sm.

lán guǒ dùjuān   *"blue-fruited rhododendron"*

Evergreen shrub or small tree, 1.5-5 meters high; branchlets glabrous, pale gray-white.

Leaves coriaceous, broadly elliptic or suborbicular, apex rounded and mucronate, base rounded or slightly cordate, upper surface glabrous, lower surface grayish green, glabrous or sparsely clad with minute hairs, midrib not prominent on the upper surface, slightly prominent on the lower surface, lateral veins on both surfaces evident but not prominent; petiole 1.5-3 cm long, glabrous.

Terminal umbelliform or shortly racemose inflorescence of 6-10 fragrant flowers; pedicels 1-2 cm long, glabrous; calyx cuplike, 0.2-1 cm long, greenish red, glabrous, 5-lobed, lobes of unequal size; corolla campanulate or funnelform-campanulate, 4-6 cm long, white tinged rose, lobes 5, emarginate; stamens 10, of unequal length, filaments glabrous; pistil glabrous.

Capsule thick and oblong, to 2.5 cm long, to 1 cm thick, glabrous, the calyx persistent.

West Yunnan. Grows on mountain summits at 3500 meters.

4136　杂色杜鹃

RHODODENDRON ECLECTEUM

Balf. f. et Forrest

zá sè dùjuān   *"variegated rhododendron"*

Evergreen shrub, 2-3 meters high; twigs thick, stiff, and straight, shoots slightly glandular.

Leaves coriaceous, narrowly long-obovate or oblong, 6.5-14 cm long, 4-5.5 cm broad at the widest place below the apex, apex broadly rounded, mucronate, and often broadly subemarginate, base obtuse, slightly cordate, and somewhat decurrent along both sides onto the broad flat petiole, lower surface glabrous but more or less white-pubescent along both sides of the prominent midrib, the lateral veins slightly impressed and resembling pale threads; petiole about 1 cm long, broad and flat, glabrous or clad with a few stipitate glands.

Terminal racemose umbelliform inflorescence of about 12 flowers; rachis 1.5 cm long, glabrous; pedicels 1-2 cm long, glabrous; calyx well developed, 1-2 cm long, lobes 5, of unequal size, glabrous; corolla tubular-campanulate, 4.5 cm long, fleshy, white to deep rose or sometimes carmine, rarely light yellow, more or less dotted or not, 5-lobed; stamens 10, filaments glabrous or minutely hairy; ovary densely glandular, style glabrous.

Capsule 1.5 cm long, densely glandular.

Distributed in Yunnan, southeast Xizang. Grows in thickets.

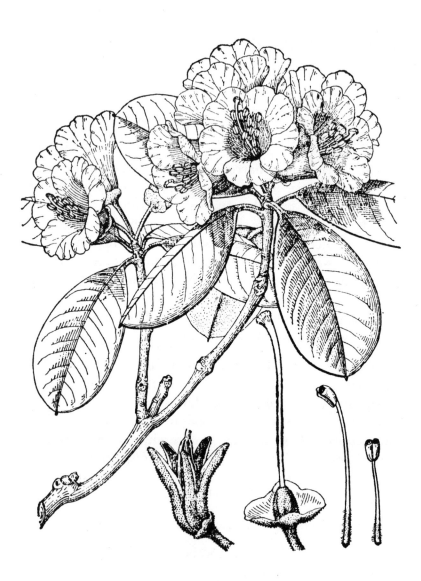

4137 多趣杜鹃

RHODODENDRON STEWARTIANUM
Diels

duō qù dùjuān   *"fascinating rhododendron"*

Evergreen shrub, 1-3 meters high; twigs glabrous.

Leaves coriaceous, long-obovate to elliptic, 5-12 cm long, 3-6.5 cm broad, apex obtuse and mucronate, upper surface glabrous, lower surface finely papillate, covered by a thin smooth layer of cream-colored powdery indumentum (nearly absent at maturity), lateral veins obscure, just faintly impressed traces; petiole 1 cm long, slightly white-powdery, glabrous.

Terminal umbelliform inflorescence of 3-7 flowers; pedicels 1-2.5 cm long, more or less glandular; calyx orbicular, about 1 cm long, smooth and glossy, shallowly 5-lobed, lobes of unequal size, glabrous, rarely glandular at the margin; corolla tubular-campanulate, 4.5 cm long, varying in color from pure white, light yellow, or white tinged rose to deep red and darker at the margin, spotted or not, lobes 5, emarginate; stamens 10, filaments densely clad with minute hairs at the base; ovary usually glandular.

Capsule oblong, 1.5-2.5 cm long, 6-10 mm thick.

Distributed in Yunnan, southeast Xizang; also Burma.

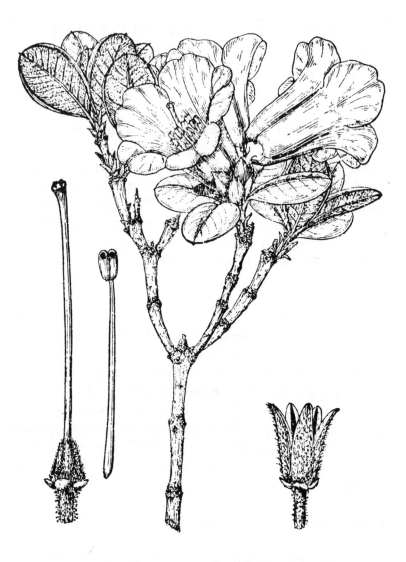

4138　紫背杜鹃

RHODODENDRON FORRESTII
Balf. f. ex Diels

zǐ bèi dùjuān   *"purple-backed rhododendron"*

Evergreen undershrub creeping on rock cliffs, about 50 cm high, stems twining and crooked, growing only about a centimeter per year; branchlets fine, reddish brown, glandular.

As many as 5 leaves in terminal clusters, the leaves coriaceous, oblong-elliptic, sometimes obovate, 2.5 cm long, 1.7 cm broad, sometimes larger, apex rounded and mucronate, base obtuse or cuneate, upper surface clad with caespitose-floccose hairs when young, lower surface gray-green and often purplish or dark purplish, clad at the midrib and lateral veins with short-stalked capitate red glands and often with caducous indumentum; petiole to 12 mm long, light red, floccose, glandular.

Terminal inflorescence of 1-3 flowers; pedicels to 2.5 cm long, dark red, glandular, enclosed at the base by large leaflike bracts; calyx orbicular, 5-lobed, glandular at the margin; corolla tubular-campanulate, to 3.8 cm long, dark red, 5-lobed; stamens 10, filaments glabrous; ovary clad with white glands and a few long hairs.

Capsule 2.5 cm long, setose.

Distributed in Yunnan, southeast Xizang. Grows on mossy lichenous rock cliffs.

4139　火红杜鹃

RHODODENDRON NERIIFLORUM

Franch.

huǒ hóng dùjuān   *"flame red rhododendron"*

Evergreen shrub, 1-3 meters high; shoots white-tomentose at first, later subglabrous, light purple.

Leaves firm-coriaceous, oblong, 5-10 cm long, 2-3.5 cm broad, rounded or obtuse and mucronate at the apex, obtuse at the base, glabrous, upper surface light green, lower surface grayish green, midrib slightly impressed on the upper surface, prominent on the lower surface, lateral veins slender, net veins quite evident; petiole 1.5-2 cm long, purple, subglabrous.

Terminal subcapitate raceme of about 8 flowers; pedicels 1.3 cm long, sparsely light yellow-tomentose; calyx well developed, fleshy, purple, to 1 cm long, glabrous outside, 5-lobed, the lobes of unequal size, short-ciliate; corolla tubular-campanulate, 3.5-4.5 cm long, fleshy, flame red tinged purple, with 5 saccate nectaries at the base, lobes 5, deeply emarginate; stamens 10, slightly shorter than the corolla, filaments flat, white, glabrous; ovary light yellow, style hairy at the base.

Capsule 2 cm long, cylindric, curved, sparsely hairy.

West Yunnan. Grows in forests and on open grasslands.

4140   绵毛杜鹃

RHODODENDRON FLOCCIGERUM
Franch.

mián máo dùjuān   *"woolly rhododendron"*

Evergreen shrub to 1.5 meters high, glandular hairs absent throughout; shoots floccose, soon smooth and glossy.

Leaves in terminal clusters, coriaceous, lanceolate-oblong, 5-8 cm long, 1.5-2 cm broad, apex obtuse or acute, mucronate, upper surface glabrous, lower surface densely clad with rusty yellow radiate-furcate hairs which may drop to reveal the gray-white surface beneath; midrib very prominent on the lower surface.

Terminal false umbel of 4-7 flowers; pedicels to 1 cm long, soon glabrous; calyx orbicular, light green, glabrous, 5-lobed, lobes rounded, caducous, the 5-toothed base remaining; corolla campanulate, to 3 cm long, fleshy, dark red or rose overall or yellow with a wide red or rose margin, with 5 dark red saccate nectaries at the base; stamens 10, filaments white to light yellow, glabrous; ovary densely white-hairy, style more or less floccose at the base.

Capsule 3 cm long, 4 mm thick, slightly curved, covered with red hairs.

Northwest Yunnan. Grows in thickets on the high mountains.

4141　似血杜鹃

RHODODENDRON HAEMATODES

Franch.

sì xiě dùjuān   *"bloodlike rhododendron"*

Evergreen shrub to 3 meters high; shoots tomentose, eglandular.

Leaves coriaceous, elliptic-oblong, 4-6 cm long, 2-3 cm broad, apex obtuse and mucronate, base obtuse or rounded, upper surface glabrous, lower surface clad more or less with ferrugineous branching felted hairs; petiole to 1.5 cm long, somewhat hairy at first, subglabrous at maturity.

Terminal umbelliform inflorescence of as many as 10 flowers; pedicels 2-3 cm long, light red, tomentose; calyx large, light to dark red, deeply 5-lobed, lobes of unequal size, 5-10 mm long but often enlarged to as long as 2 cm, membranaceous, bright red, floccose only near the base; corolla tubular-campanulate, fleshy, mostly dark red, glabrous, corolla tube 2-2.5 cm long, 4-4.5 cm in diameter, lobes 5, spreading; stamens 10, filaments light red, rarely clad with sparse minute hairs on the lower part; ovary densely white-hairy.

West Yunnan. Grows in thickets on the high mountains.

4142　羊毛杜鹃

RHODODENDRON MALLOTUM

Balf. f. et Ward

yáng máo dùjuān   *"woolly rhododendron"*

Evergreen shrub or small tree to 5 meters high; branchlets densely rusty-yellow-tomentose, older branches glabrous.

Leaves in terminal clusters, very thick and coriaceous, elliptic or obovate-elliptic, 7-13 cm long, 3-6 cm broad, apex rounded or subtruncate, mucronate, base more or less cuneate, upper surface bullate, glabrous except at the midrib, lower surface clad with thick yellow indumentum, lateral veins obscure on the lower surface; petiole 2-3 cm long, convex on the upper surface, gray-tomentose.

Terminal compact flat-globose inflorescence of about 20 flowers, about 12 cm in diameter; pedicels slightly less than 1 cm long, tomentose; calyx degenerate, rimlike; corolla tubular-campanulate, waxy, dark red, with black saccate nectaries within at the base, corolla tube 3.5 cm long, lobes 5; stamens 10, filaments glabrous, dark red toward the base; ovary densely woolly-tomentose, style glabrous.

Capsule ovoid, about 1 cm long, densely brown-woolly.

Distributed in Yunnan, southeast Xizang; also north Burma. Grows in thickets.

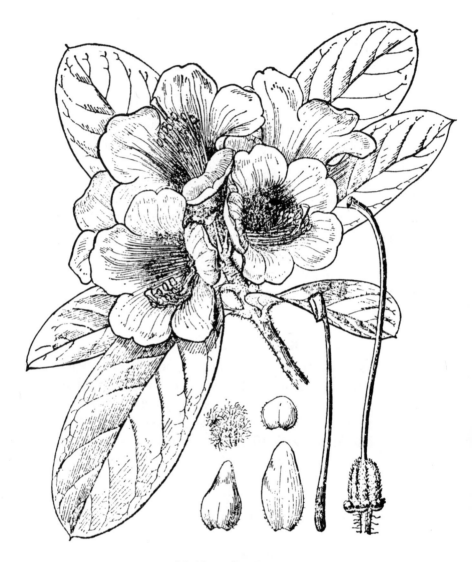

4143　绢毛杜鹃

RHODODENDRON CHAETOMALLUM
Hutch.

juàn máo dùjuān   *"silky rhododendron"*

Evergreen shrub about 1.5 meters high; shoots very short, setose and clad with scalelike glands which are persistent and verrucose on the older branches.

Leaves few, clustered below the inflorescences, obovate or obovate-elliptic, about 7 cm long, 4 cm broad, apex rounded and mucronate, base broadly cuneate or more or less rounded, upper surface soon glabrous, lower surface densely yellowish-brown-tomentose, the lateral veins mostly concealed beneath the indumentum; petiole 1-1.5 cm long, more or less setose.

Terminal umbelliform inflorescence of 4-6 flowers; pedicels 1.5-2 cm long, clad with furcate bristles; calyx to 1 cm long, fleshy, red, glabrous, lobes of unequal length; corolla tubular-campanulate, 4.5 cm long, dark red with darker lines; stamens 10, shorter than the corolla, filaments glabrous, dark red toward the base, anthers blackish; ovary densely hairy, style glabrous.

Capsule to 1.5 cm long, densely clad with long ferrugineous hairs.

Distributed in Yunnan, southeast Xizang. Grows in thickets on rocky slopes.

4144　剌枝杜鹃

RHODODENDRON BEANIANUM

Cowan

cì zhī dùjuān   *"thorny branch rhododendron"*

Evergreen erect undershrub to 2 meters high, much-branched; shoots densely clad with branching bristlelike glandular hairs and floccose hairs.

Leaves coriaceous, short oblong or elliptic-oblong, to 9 cm long, 4 cm broad, apex broadly rounded and emarginate, base obtuse or rounded, upper surface dark green, rugose, and subglabrous, lower surface clad with persistent reddish brown much-branched thickly felted hairs, the midrib prominent and glabrous, the lateral veins obscured by the indumentum; petiole about 2 cm long, light red-tomentose.

Terminal umbelliform inflorescence of 6-10 flowers; pedicels about 2 cm long, densely floccose, long-setose, and glandular; calyx light red, a shallow cup with 5 irregular teeth; corolla tubular-campanulate, 3 cm long, dark red, glabrous, 5-lobed; stamens 10, filaments dark red at the base and pale above, anthers black; ovary densely light yellowish-brown-tomentose, style stellate-hairy only at the base.

Southeast Xizang; also Burma, northern India. Grows in forests or thickets at 3200-3700 meters.

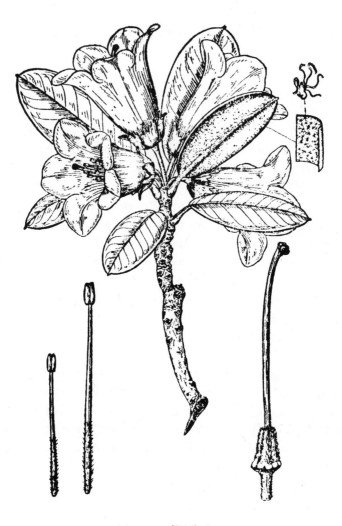

4145　可喜杜鹃

RHODODENDRON APODECTUM

Balf. f. et W. W. Sm.

kě xǐ dùjuān   *"gratifying rhododendron"*

Evergreen shrub to 2.5 meters high; twigs bent, clad with snow-white floccose hairs, year-old branches glabrous.

Leaves thick-coriaceous, elliptic, 3-7 cm long, 1.7-3.5 cm broad, apex obtuse and stiffly mucronate, base rounded or subcordate, margin revolute, upper surface lustrous and glabrous, lower surface light grayish brown, clad with a thin compact indumentum composed of radiate hairs, the single-celled hairs coarse and in groups of 5-10 on very short stalks, leaf veins obscure; petiole 5-15 mm long, floccose at first.

Terminal umbelliform inflorescence of 1-3 flowers, rachis very short; pedicels to 2.5 cm long; calyx cuplike, 5-lobed, lobes of unequal size, crimson, glabrous; corolla tubular-campanulate, somewhat fleshy, orange-red, glabrous, corolla tube 2-3 cm long, lobes 5; stamens 10, filaments minutely hairy on the lower part; ovary green, densely clad with short caespitose hairs, style green.

Northwest Yunnan. Grows at the edge of rhododendron forests and in thickets at 3200 meters.

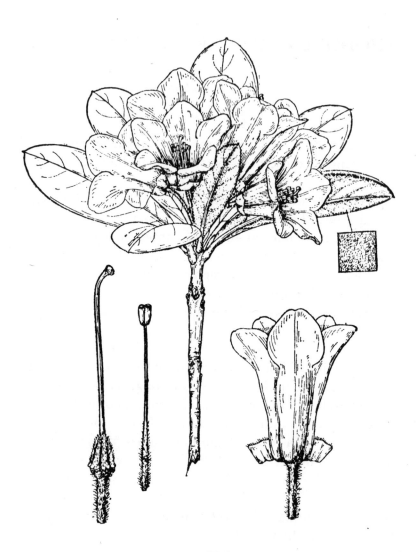

4146 两色杜鹃

RHODODENDRON DICHROANTHUM

Diels

liǎng sè dùjuān   *"bicolored rhododendron"*

Evergreen shrub, 1-2 meters high; year-old branches subglabrous, new shoots thinly clad with white arachnoid hair.

Leaves firm-chartaceous, oblong-oblanceolate, 6-8 cm long, 2-3 cm broad at the upper third, tapering downward, apex rounded and mucronate, upper surface glabrous, the net veins impressed, lower surface clad with white powdery indumentum, the midrib prominent and glabrous; petiole about 1 cm long, subglabrous, grooved on the upper surface.

Terminal short loose umbelliform raceme of 5-7 flowers, rachis about 5 mm long, glabrous; pedicels 1.5 cm long, clad with curly hairs, ultimately curving downward; calyx large, variable, cuplike, to 1.2 cm long, red, shallowly 4-5 lobed, lobes rounded, glabrous, sometimes sparsely and very shortly ciliolate; corolla broadly tubular-campanulate, orangish purple, corolla tube 3-3.5 cm long, glabrous, lobes 5, slightly spreading, emarginate; stamens 10, filaments sparsely clad with minute hairs toward the base; ovary 6-loculed, hairy, style glabrous.

Northwest Yunnan. Grows on grasslands at 3000 meters.

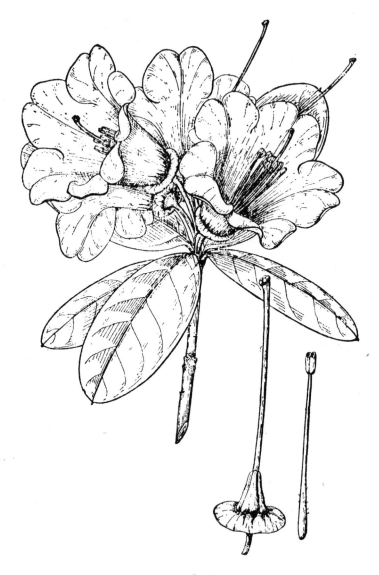

4147　盘萼杜鹃

RHODODENDRON PARMULATUM

Cowan

pán è dùjuān   *"discoid calyx rhododendron"*

Evergreen shrub to 1 meter high; year-old branches glabrous.

Leaves few, borne on the upper part of the twigs, chartaceous, oblong to oblong-elliptic, upper surface glabrous, lower surface glabrous and sparsely papillate, lateral veins about 6 pair; petiole 5-10 long.

Terminal racemose-umbelliform inflorescence of 5-6 flowers; pedicels 1.5-2 cm long, glabrous; calyx discoid, green with a dark red ring at the base, about 1.5 cm in diameter, glabrous; corolla white, shaded and veined light red, with dark red nectary sacs at the base, dark red spotted within on the upper side, corolla tube 3.5 cm long, lobes 5, deeply emarginate; stamens 10, shorter than the corolla, filaments glabrous or very shortly hairy on the lower third, dark red at the base; disc deeply cleft; ovary 5-loculed, glabrous, style as long as the corolla, glabrous.

Southeast Xizang. Grows in forests.

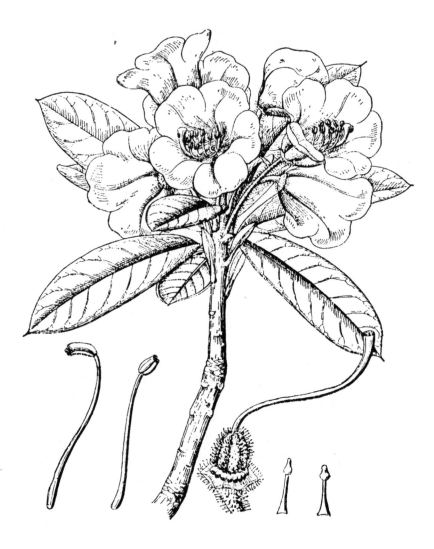

4148　黑红杜鹃

RHODODENDRON DIDYMUM

Balf. f. et Forrest

hēi hóng dùjuān   *"black-red rhododendron"*

Evergreen undershrub, 50-70 cm high; shoots densely clad with spreading caespitose branching hairs and gland-tipped simple hairs.

Leaves coriaceous, spreading almost horizontally, oblanceolate or obovate-oblong, 2.5-7.5 cm long, 1.5-2.7 cm broad, apex bluntly acute and long-mucronate, base cuneate, margin more or less recurved, upper surface clad with spreading long hairs and a few downy hairs when young, lower surface clad with pale arachnoid indumentum; petiole about 5 mm long, subglabrous or slightly glandular.

Terminal umbelliform inflorescence of 4-8 flowers; pedicels to 3.5 cm long, densely glandular-hairy; calyx small, orbicular, irregularly divided, densely glandular-hairy outside; corolla campanulate, blackish dark red, corolla tube 1.6-2 cm long, with 5 nectary sacs at the base, lobes 5, of unequal size, suborbicular, slightly emarginate; filaments red, glabrous; ovary whitish, densely glandular, the glands especially dense at the ridges, style red, glabrous.

Distributed in southeast Xizang, northwest Yunnan. Grows on grasslands.

4149　血红杜鹃

RHODODENDRON SANGUINEUM
Franch.

xiě hóng dùjuān   *"blood red rhododendron"*

Evergreen dwarf shrub to 1 meter high; year-old branches sparsely white-hairy, eglandular.

Leaves in terminal clusters, coriaceous, obovate, broadly ovate, or narrowly elliptic, 4-5 cm long, 2-2.5 cm broad, rounded or obtuse and mucronulate at the apex, tapered toward the base and decurrent onto the petiole, upper surface glabrous, lower surface gray-white, clad with a thin layer of gray indumentum, midrib and lateral veins slightly impressed on the upper surface.

Terminal umbelliform inflorescence of 6-9 flowers; pedicels 2-3 cm long, slender, clad more or less with clusters of fine red hairs; calyx a shallow cup, 2-3.5 mm long, lobes 5, dark red; corolla campanulate, 2.5-3 cm long, fleshy, dark blood red throughout, glabrous, with 5 saccate nectaries at the base; stamens 10, filaments red at the base and white toward the top, glabrous; ovary densely clad with eglandular branching hairs, style glabrous.

Capsule oblong-cylindric, 1.5 cm long, 6.8 mm thick, red-hairy.

Distributed in west Yunnan, southeast Xizang. Grows in pine forests above 3500 meters.

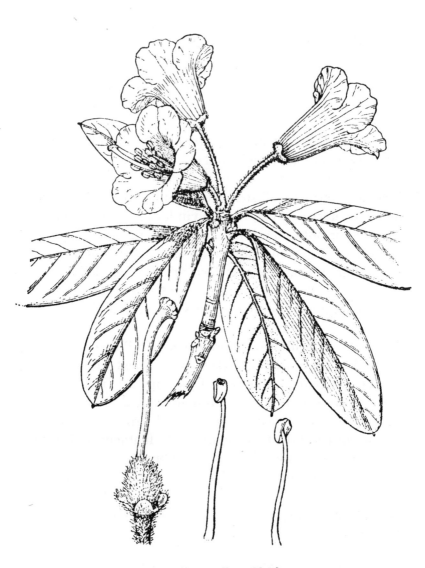

4150　　紫血杜鹃

RHODODENDRON HAEMALEUM

Balf. f. et Forrest

zĭ xiě dùjuān   *"purple blood rhododendron"*

Evergreen undershrub about 1 meter high; twigs slender, stiff, and glabrous.

Leaves coriaceous, oblanceolate or obovate-oblanceolate, 4-8 cm long, 1.5-2.5 cm broad, apex obtuse and short-mucronate, base attentuate and somewhat decurrent onto the petiole, upper surface glabrous, lower surface smoothly clad with compact plastered white or light yellow indumentum, the midrib prominent and subglabrous, the lateral veins conspicuously prominent and more or less hairy; petiole 5-10 mm long, subglabrous.

Terminal umbelliform inflorescence of 3-5 flowers; pedicels 1.2-2.5 cm long, more or less floccose but eglandular; calyx about 3.5 mm long, floccose, lobes about 2 mm long, dark red; corolla tubular-campanulate, 3-4 cm long, fleshy, blackish dark red, 5-lobed; stamens 10, filaments white, with a few minute hairs at the base; ovary densely tomentose, eglandular, style glabrous.

Southeast Xizang. Grows in forest margins at 3800 meters.

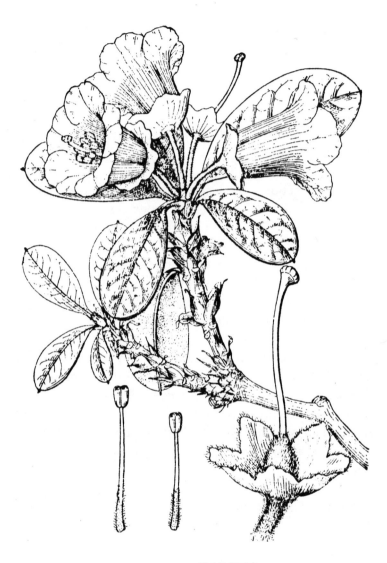

4151　美艳杜鹃

RHODODENDRON HORAEUM
Balf. f. et Forrest

měi yàn dùjuān   *"gorgeous rhododendron"*

Evergreen procumbent dwarf shrub, 15-30 cm high; shoots short and thick, clad with a thin layer of pale appressed soft hairs; leaf-bud scales persistent on the branches for several years.

Leaves in terminal clusters, coriaceous, narrowly obovate, 3-5 cm long, 1-2 cm broad above the middle, apex obtuse and conspicuously mucronate, base cuneate, upper surface glabrous and sub-bullate, lower surface clad with a soft woolly layer of pale yellow to brown indumentum, the lateral veins concealed; petiole 1 cm long, clad with hair similar to that of the shoots.

Terminal umbelliform inflorescence of 4 flowers; pedicels 2 cm long, clad with gland-tipped fine bristles and floccose hairs; calyx cuplike, about 1 cm long, purple, 5-lobed, lobes of unequal size, floccose at the margin, often caducous; corolla tubular-campanulate, 3.5 cm long, fleshy, dark red, 5-lobed, lobes emarginate; stamens 10, filaments minutely hairy on the lower part; ovary tomentose.

Distributed in southeast Xizang, northwest Yunnan. Grows on rocky slopes at 4000 meters.

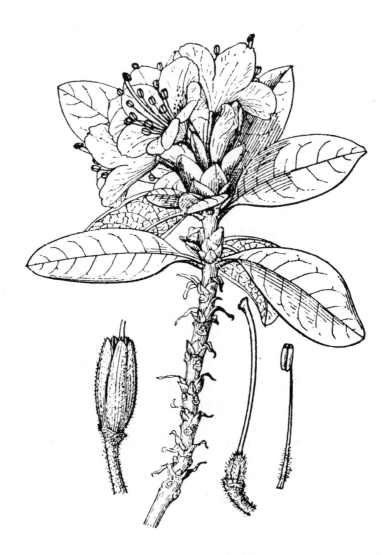

4152　牛皮茶

RHODODENDRON CHRYSANTHUM
Pallas

niú pí chá   *"oxhide tea"*

Evergreen undershrub, stems thick and horizontal, lateral branches obliquely ascending, 10-25 cm high; leaf-bud scales persistent.

Leaves broadly oblanceolate or obovate, 2.5-8 cm long, 1-3.5 cm broad, apex obtuse or rounded, base cuneate, margin recurved, upper surface rugose, lower surface glabrous or clad with juvenile-hair remnants at the midrib and lateral veins, net veins conspicuous; petiole about 5 mm long, glabrous.

Terminal corymb of 5-8 flowers, rachis 1 cm long; pedicels erect, 3 cm long, red-hairy, enclosed by the persistent bud scales and bracts; calyx small, undulate, floccose; corolla broadly campanulate, about 3 cm long, yellow, lobes 5, of unequal size, one upper lobe largest and more or less spotted; stamens 10, filaments hairy on the lower part; ovary ferrugineous-tomentose, style glabrous.

Capsule oblong, 5-lobed, slightly tomentose.

Distributed throughout northeastern China; also Korea, Japan, Mongolia, USSR. Grows on rocky moss-and-lichen strata in the high mountains.

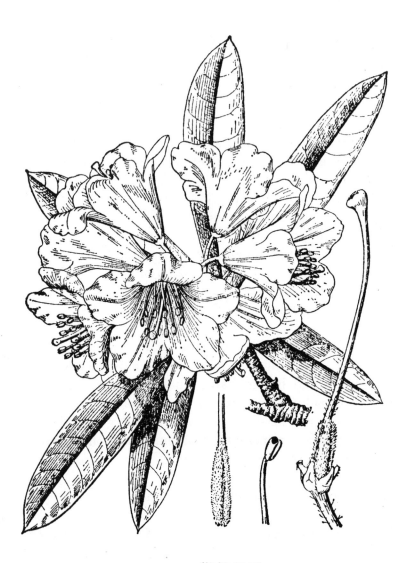

4153　微笑杜鹃

RHODODENDRON HYPERYTHRUM

Hayata

wēi xiào dùjuān   *"smile rhododendron"*

Evergreen shrub to 3 meters high; twigs strong, straight, and glabrous.

Leaves coriaceous, oblong-lanceolate to elliptic lanceolate, 8-10 cm long, 1.8-3 cm broad, apex acute, base obtuse or tapering, upper surface glabrous, lower surface finely brown-dotted, midrib impressed on the upper surface, very prominent on the lower surface; petiole 1.5-2.5 cm long, glabrous.

Terminal racemose-umbelliform inflorescence of 10 flowers; pedicels 2.5-4 cm long, sparsely glandular and floccose; calyx small, 5-lobed, lobes triangular, obtuse, glandular-ciliate; corolla funnelform-campanulate, 3-3.5 cm long, white, lobes 5, rounded; stamens 10(12), shorter than the corolla, filaments densely tomentose on the lower part; ovary 4-6 mm long, densely floccose, style slightly hairy on the lower part.

Endemic to Taiwan. Grows in forests.

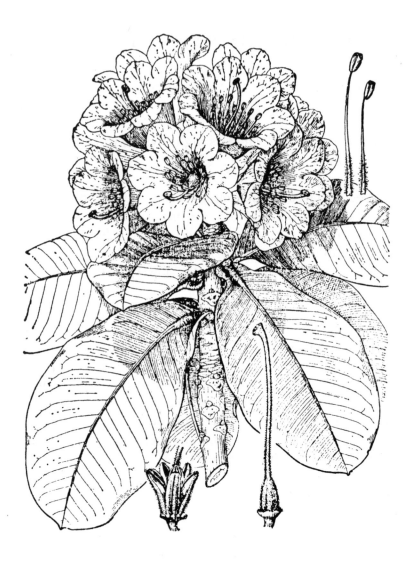

4154　　阔柄杜鹃

RHODODENDRON PLATYPODUM
Diels

kuò bǐng dùjuān   *"broad-stalked rhododendron"*

Evergreen large shrub to 7 meters high; branches very stout, glabrous.

Leaves coriaceous, broadly elliptic to suborbicular, 8-11 cm long, 5-7 cm broad, rounded and bluntly mucronate at the apex, obtuse or rounded at the base, broadly winged and decurrent onto the short petiole, glabrous at maturity, the lower surface clad only with juvenile-hair remnants, lateral veins 16-18 pair, quite close and sharply angled upward, midrib thick on the lower surface, broadening gradually toward the flat and thick petiole, net veins conspicuous.

Terminal lax raceme of about 15 flowers, rachis 4-5 cm long, slightly glandular; pedicels about 2.6 cm long, glabrous; calyx 2 mm long, rimlike with 7 undulate teeth, fleshy; corolla funnelform-campanulate, about 4 cm long, pink without dots, lobes 7, 1.3 cm long; stamens 14, filaments pubescent on the lower part; ovary densely clad with short-stalked glands, style thick, glandular throughout.

Capsule 1.6 cm long, oblong, densely glandular.

Southeast Sichuan (Jinfo Shan). Grows in forests.

4155　大白杜鹃

RHODODENDRON DECORUM

Franch.

dà bái dùjuān   *"great white rhododendron"*

Evergreen shrub to 5 meters high; branchlets stout and glabrous, shoots green, white-powdery at first.

Leaves in terminal clusters, thick-coriaceous, oblong or oblong-elliptic, 7-12 cm long or larger, 3-5 cm broad, rounded and mucronate at the apex, obtuse at the base, glabrous, upper surface densely reticulate, lateral veins slender and slightly prominent on both surfaces; petiole 1-1.5 cm long, thick, nearly smooth and even on the upper surface.

Terminal large racemose-umbelliform inflorescence of about 10 flowers, about 20 cm in diameter, rachis about 3 cm long, glandular; pedicels 3-3.5 cm long, sparsely glandular; calyx quite well developed, cuplike, undulate, sparsely glandular outside and at the margin; corolla white or rose-tinged, sometimes dotted with light green or pink, corolla tube 3-5 cm long, hairy within at the base, lobes 6-8, suborbicular, emarginate; stamens 12-16; ovary 10-loculed, densely glandular, style green, clad overall with white or light yellow glands.

Capsule oblong, 4 cm long.

Distributed in Yunnan, Sichuan. Grows in thickets.

The flowers have been eaten as a vegetable.

4156　高尚杜鹃

RHODODENDRON DIAPREPES

Balf. f. et W. W. Sm.

gāo shàng dùjuān *"noble rhododendron"*

Evergreen shrub or small tree to 8 meters high; branches of the current year glabrous, green.

Leaves coriaceous, oblong to oblong-elliptic, usually 10-15 cm long, 3.5-5.5 cm broad, rounded and mucronate at the apex, nearly rounded at the base and decurrent onto the petiole, glabrous, lateral veins very slender but conspicuous on the lower surface; petiole 2-2.5 cm long, flat, narrowly winged.

Terminal loose raceme of 7-10 subtly fragrant flowers, rachis to 7 cm long, purple; pedicels 3.5-5 cm long, purple, glabrous or clad with a few minute glands; calyx very short, undulate, glabrous; corolla broadly funnelform, about 9 cm long and in diameter, white tinged light red outside the corolla tube and at the dorsal ridge, lobes 7, undulate; stamens 15-20, filaments sparsely short-hairy on the lower part; ovary about 10-loculed, papillate-glandular, style slightly longer than the corolla tube, green, glandular throughout.

Capsule large, oblong-cylindric, to 6.5 cm long, 1.5-2 cm thick.

Southwest Yunnan. Grows in open forests at about 3500 meters.

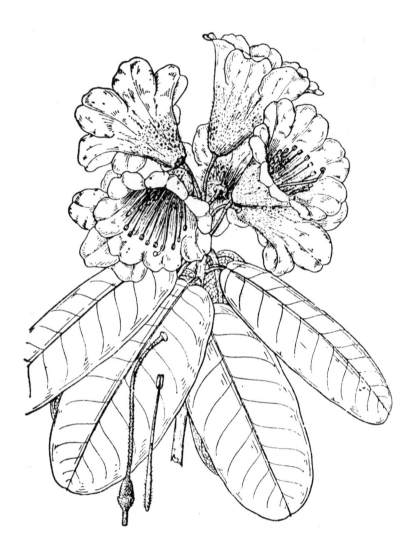

4157　晚花杜鹃

RHODODENDRON SEROTINUM
Hutch.

wǎn huā dùjuān *"late-flowering rhododendron"*

Evergreen shrub to 3 meters high; year-old branches green and lustrous.

Leaves coriaceous, oblong-elliptic, 10-15 cm long, 6-7 cm broad, rounded, emarginate, and mucronate at the apex, asymmetric and shallowly cordate at the base, glabrous, lower surface gray-green and rather inconspicuously papillate, lateral veins conspicuous on the lower surface, spreading nearly at right angles from the midrib, net veins evident; petiole cylindric, 2-3.5 cm long, about 3.5 mm thick, glabrous.

Terminal short raceme of 7-8 fragrant flowers, rachis 3 cm long, finely glandular-papillate; pedicels 3-4.5 cm long, similarly papillate; calyx small, undulately lobed, clad with light red glands outside and at the margin; corolla white tinged pale rose outside, red-spotted within the corolla tube on the upper part, corolla tube broadly funnelform, 4-4.5 cm long, clad outside with stipitate white glands, lobes 7, spreading; stamens 15-16, filaments hairy on the lower part; ovary and style clad throughout with short-stalked glands.

West Yunnan. Grows in open forests. Blooms as late as August.

4158 云锦杜鹃

RHODODENDRON FORTUNEI
Lindley

yún jǐn dùjuān   *"cloud brocade rhododendron"*

Evergreen shrub, 3-4 meters high; twigs stout and light green, shoots glandular at first.

Leaves in terminal clusters, thick-coriaceous, oblong to oblong-elliptic, 7-17 cm long, 3.5-7 cm broad, bluntly acute at the apex, rounded or cordate at the base, glabrous, upper surface dark green and rugose, the midrib impressed, lateral veins inconspicuously impressed on both surfaces; petiole 2-3 cm long, glabrous at maturity.

Terminal lax racemose-umbelliform inflorescence of 6-12 slightly nodding flowers, rachis 3-5 cm long, more or less glandular; pedicels 2-3 cm long, densely glandular; calyx small, shallowly lobed, glandular; corolla funnelform-campanulate, 4-5 cm long, pink, glandular toward the base, 7-lobed; stamens 14, glabrous; ovary 10-loculed, densely glandular, style glandular overall.

Capsule oblong, 2-3 cm long, 1-1.5 cm thick, scabrous.

Distributed in Zhejiang, Jiangxi, Anhui, Hunan. Grows in high-mountain forests.

4159 大云锦杜鹃

RHODODENDRON FAITHAE

Chun

dà yún jǐn dùjuān   *"large cloud brocade rhododendron"*

Evergreen shrub, 4-8 meters high; shoots glabrous.

Leaves in terminal clusters, thick-coriaceous, cartilaginous at the margin, elliptic-oblong, 20-25 cm long, 7-9 cm broad, apex acute and mucronate, base usually obtuse, upper surface glabrous, lower surface light green and glabrous, the midrib thick and prominent; petiole 2.5-4 cm long, smooth on the upper surface, glabrous.

Terminal compact umbelliform raceme of 8-10 flowers, rachis 4 cm long, 1.2 cm thick at the base, somewhat glandular; pedicels upright, 2.5-3 cm long, somewhat glandular; calyx short, subentire, somewhat glandular outside; corolla broadly funnelform-campanulate, 9-10 cm long, white without spots, lobes 7, 3 cm long; stamens 14, filaments glabrous; ovary 10-loculed, densely stipitate-glandular, style glandular-hairy.

Capsule cylindric, quite straight, 3.5 cm long, somewhat glandular outside; fruitstalk to 4 cm long.

Distributed in Guangdong, Guangxi. Grows in forests at 1000 meters.

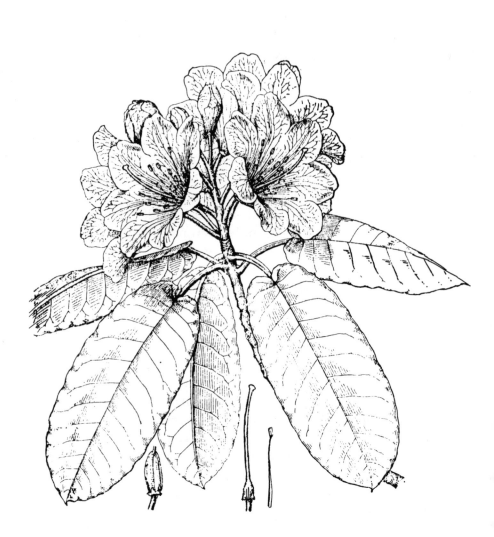

4160　波叶杜鹃

RHODODENDRON HEMSLEYANUM
Wils.

bō yè dùjuān   *"wavy-leaved rhododendron"*

Evergreen shrub or small tree, 3-6 meters high; branchlets stout, sparsely clad with minute hairs.

Leaves thick-coriaceous, oblong-ovate, 15-20 cm long, 6-8 cm broad at the middle, bluntly acute at the apex, auriculate-cordate at the base, more or less undulate at the margin, glabrous, midrib grooved on the upper surface, prominent on the lower surface; petiole stout, cylindric, 3.5-4.5 cm long, sparsely clad with long-stalked glandular hairs.

Terminal raceme of 10-12 flowers, rachis 5 cm long, sparsely short-hairy and glandular-hairy; pedicels stout, 2-3 cm long, similarly hairy; calyx short, with 5-10 shallow lobes, densely glandular; corolla campanulate, 5.5-6.5 cm long, white, glabrous, 7-lobed; stamens 14, filaments glabrous; ovary densely clad with short glandular hairs, style glandular-hairy throughout.

Capsule long elliptic, 2-2.5 cm long, densely glandular-hairy.

West Sichuan. Grows in forests.

A variety found on Emei Shan, var. *chengianum* Fang (wú xiàn dùjuān, "eglandular rhododendron"), closely resembles the type, but the leaves are generally broader and the petioles and pedicels are smooth, glossy, and eglandular.

317

4161 喇叭杜鹃

RHODODENDRON DISCOLOR
Franch.

lǎba dùjuān *"trumpet rhododendron"*

Evergreen shrub or small tree to 6 meters high; branchlets glabrous.

Leaves coriaceous, oblong-elliptic to oblong-oblance-olate, 13-16 cm long, 4-5 cm broad on the upper part, acute at the apex, tapering downward, cuneate at the base, glabrous, upper surface green, lower surface pale green, midrib strongly prominent, lateral veins somewhat prominent; petiole 2-3 cm long.

Terminal racemose-umbelliform inflorescence of 7 fragrant flowers, rachis 1.5 cm long, hairy and glandular; pedicels 2-3.5 cm long, hairy and glandular; calyx ciliate; corolla long funnelform, 6-8 cm long, pink at first, gradually turning white, clad outside with a few long-stalked glands, lobes 7, emarginate; stamens 12-14, filaments glabrous; ovary and style clad throughout with short-stalked glands.

Capsule oblong, 4-5 cm long, 9-12-loculed, covered with withered glands.

Distributed in Hubei, Sichuan. Grows in forests at 1500-2000 meters.

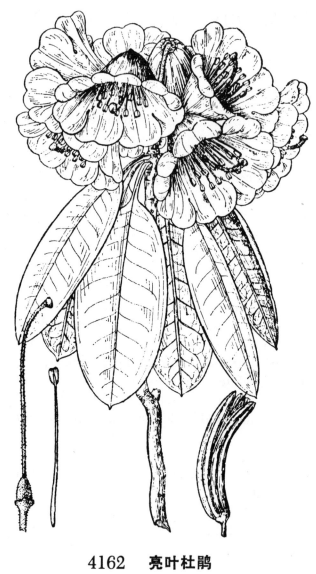

4162　亮叶杜鹃

RHODODENDRON VERNICOSUM
Franch.

liàng yè dùjuān   *"glossy-leaved rhododendron"*

Evergreen shrub to 4.5 meters high; branchlets dark brown, glabrous, somewhat lustrous when dried.

Leaves scattered, thin-coriaceous, elliptic, 6-11 cm long, 2.5-6 cm broad, apex rounded and bluntly mucronate, base asymmetrically rounded or subtruncate, upper surface glossy green, lower surface light green, net veins fine and dense, lateral veins slender and spreading at an obtuse angle from the midrib; petiole 2-2.5 cm long, narrowly grooved on the upper surface, glabrous.

Terminal short raceme of about 10 flowers; pedicels curved downward, 2-2.5 cm long, sparsely clad with light red short-stalked glands; calyx very short, shallowly 7-lobed, densely glandular; corolla broadly funnelform-campanulate, 4 cm long, white to bright rose, dotted or not, 7-lobed, lobes 1.7 cm long, broadly emarginate; stamens 14, glabrous; ovary 6-7-loculed, densely clad with sessile glands, style clad throughout with dark red glands.

Capsule thickly cylindric, slightly curved, 3-4 cm long, 7 mm thick, smooth and glossy.

Distributed in Sichuan and west Yunnan. Grows in open forests or in thickets.

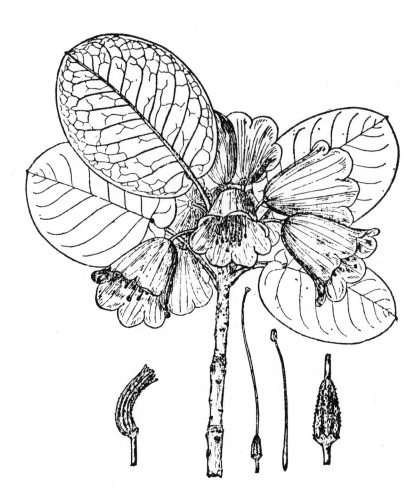

4163　团叶杜鹃

RHODODENDRON ORBICULARE

Decaisne

tuán yè dùjuān　　"*circular-leaved rhododendron*"

Evergreen shrub, 1-3 meters high; twigs stout, glabrous.

Leaves thick-coriaceous, broadly ovate to orbicular, 5-10 cm long, 5-8 cm broad, mucronate, deeply cordate at the base with the auricles slightly overlapping, glabrous, upper surface green, lower surface gray-white, the net veins fine and dense, midrib even and smooth or slightly impressed on the upper surface, strongly prominent on the lower surface, 2.5 mm thick at the base; petiole cylindric, to 6 mm long, lustrous, glabrous.

Terminal lax umbelliform inflorescence of 7-10 pendulous flowers; pedicels 2.5-3.5 cm long, glabrous; calyx small, undulately lobed, glandular at the margin; corolla broadly campanulate, 3.5-4 cm long, rose tinged carmine, 7-lobed, lobes 1 cm long, suberect or slightly spreading; stamens 14, of unequal length, filaments glabrous, white; ovary 7-loculed, clad with sessile glands, style glabrous.

Capsule cylindric, curved, to 2 cm long.

West Sichuan. Grows in forests at 2500-3000 meters.

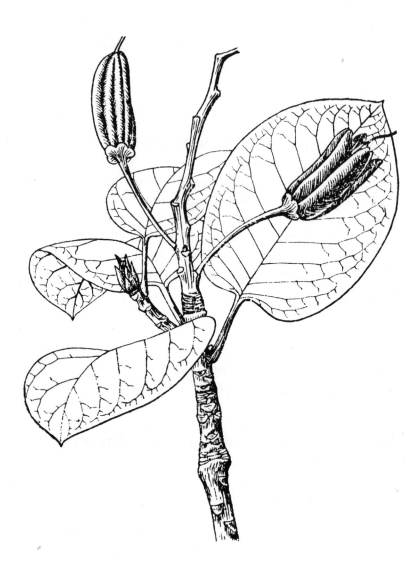

4164　心基杜鹃

RHODODENDRON CARDIOBASIS
Sleumer

xīn jī dùjuān   *"heart-based rhododendron"*

Evergreen small tree over 3 meters high, trunk 10-12 cm in diameter; twigs stout, glabrous.

Leaves sparse on the twigs, subcoriaceous, elliptic or suborbicular-ovate, 8-12 cm long, 5.5-9 cm broad, nearly rounded at the apex and mucronate, conspicuously cordate at the base or sometimes subcordate, glabrous, lower surface light brown and sparsely dotted with fine glands, midrib even and smooth on the upper surface, prominent on the lower surface, lateral veins somewhat evident on both surfaces; petiole 3-4.5 cm long, glabrous.

Terminal corymb of 6-7 flowers, rachis thick, to 6 cm long, glabrous; pedicels thick, 3-4 cm long during flowering; calyx somewhat fleshy, shallowly 5-lobed, lobes obtuse; corolla broadly funnelform, 5.5 cm long, smooth and glossy, lobes 7, rounded, 2 cm long;* stamens 14, filaments glabrous; ovary densely glandular, style 4 cm long, not exserted, glandular, the glands especially numerous toward the tip.

Northeast Guangxi. Grows in forests.

*No corolla color given.

4165　山光杜鹃

RHODODENDRON OREODOXA

Franch.

shān guāng dùjuān   *"mountain glory rhododendron"*

Evergreen shrub or small tree to 7 meters high; shoots thick, at first thinly gray-white-tomentose, soon subglabrous.

Leaves in terminal clusters, subcoriaceous, narrowly elliptic or oblanceolate-elliptic, 5-10 cm long, 2-3.5 cm broad, obtuse at the apex, rounded at the base, glabrous at maturity, lower surface gray-green, with papilliform juvenile-hair remnants which are visible under magnification, midrib impressed on the upper surface, prominent on the lower surface, lateral veins somewhat prominent; petiole 1-2 cm long, shallowly grooved on the upper surface, subglabrous.

Terminal racemose-umbelliform inflorescence of 10-12 flowers, rachis about 5 mm long, glandular and tomentose; pedicels 5-7 mm long, densely or sparsely glandular or nearly smooth and glossy; calyx short, 2-3 mm long, lobes triangular, more or less glandular; corolla broadly campanulate, 4 cm long, pale rose, purple-dotted or not, lobes 7-8; stamens 14, filaments subglabrous; pistil glabrous.

Capsule oblong-cylindric, 2 cm long, 7 mm thick.

Distributed in Hubei, Sichuan, Gansu. Grows in forests.

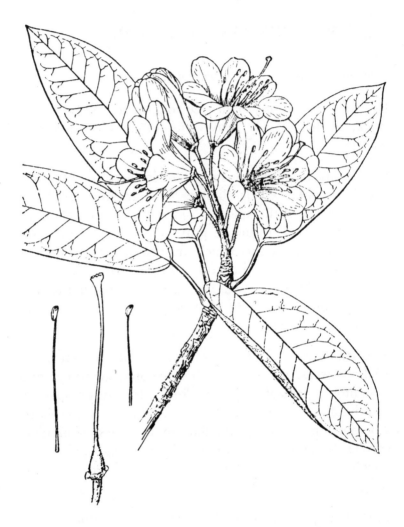

4166　广福杜鹃

RHODODENDRON KWANGFUENSE

Chun et Fang

guǎng fú dùjuān   *"Guangfu rhododendron"*

Evergreen shrub, 3-4 meters high; twigs stout, charcoal brown, glabrous.

Leaves coriaceous, long elliptic to oblanceolate-long-elliptic, 9-14 cm long, 3-4 cm broad, bluntly or sharply acute at the apex and stiffly mucronate, rounded at the base, glabrous even when young, midrib slender on the upper surface and somewhat impressed toward the base, stout on the lower surface and conspicuously prominent, net veins obscure; petiole 1.5-2 cm long, grooved on the upper surface, glabrous.

Racemose-umbelliform inflorescence of 7-9 flowers, terminal on the defoliate shoots of the previous year, rachis 3 cm long, glabrous, slightly glandular when young; calyx small, orbicular, undulate, very sparsely glandular; corolla broadly campanulate, 4.5-5 cm long, rose, not spotted, lobes 7, emarginate; stamens 14, filaments glabrous; ovary densely glandular, style glabrous.

North Guangxi. Grows in forests.

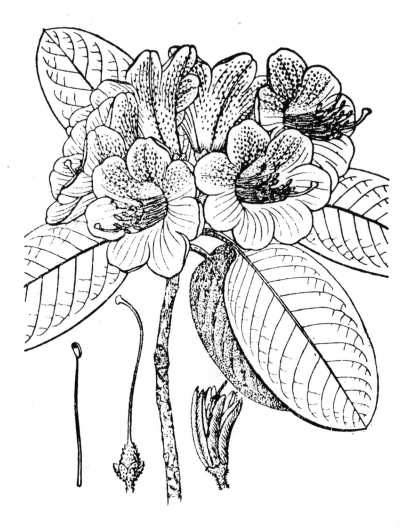

4167　粉红杜鹃

RHODODENDRON FARGESII
Franch.

fěn hóng dùjuān   *"pink rhododendron"*

Evergreen shrub to small tree, 3-8 meters high; twigs lustrous, glabrous, shoots short, purple.

Leaves few, thin-coriaceous, oblong to oblong-elliptic, 5-12 cm long, 2.5-4 cm broad, rounded at the apex and mucronulate, rounded or subcordate at the base, glabrous, lower surface light green, lateral veins slender and numerous, net veins evident; petiole to 2 cm long, light purple.

Terminal umbelliform inflorescence of 6-10 flowers; pedicels about 1 cm long, densely glandular; calyx very short, undulate, glandular outside; corolla broadly campanulate, 4 cm long, carmine in bud, turning rose to white, red-dotted, glabrous outside, lobes 5-7, suborbicular, obliquely spreading; stamens about 14, filaments glabrous; ovary about 8-loculed, densely glandular, style carmine, glabrous.

Capsule elliptic, 2 cm long, glandular; fruitstalk glandular.

Distributed in Sichuan, Hubei, south Shaanxi. Grows in dense forests above 2000 meters.

331

4168 红晕杜鹃

RHODODENDRON ERUBESCENS
Hutch.

hóng yùn dùjuān   *"red halo rhododendron"*

Evergreen shrub about 1 meter high; branchlets straight and upright, purple, glabrous.

Leaves firm-coriaceous, oblong-elliptic, 8-10 cm long, 3-4 cm broad, apex obtuse and conspicuously mucronate, base rounded, upper surface dark green with impressed net veins, lower surface yellow-green and finely papillate; petiole 2 cm long, grooved on the upper surface, purplish red, glabrous.

Terminal inflorescence of about 10 flowers; pedicels 1-1.4 cm long, densely clad with short papillate glands; calyx small, 5-lobed, lobes of unequal size, to 2 mm long, papillate-glandular; corolla campanulate, 3.5-4 cm long, exterior rose tinged dark red, interior white and minutely hairy, lobes 7, somewhat spreading, reflexed, deeply emarginate; stamens 12-14, included, filaments densely pubescent on the lower part; ovary clad with white stipitate glands, usually 6-loculed, style exserted, 3 cm long, glabrous.

Distributed in Sichuan, Hubei. Grows in forests at 1800 meters.

333

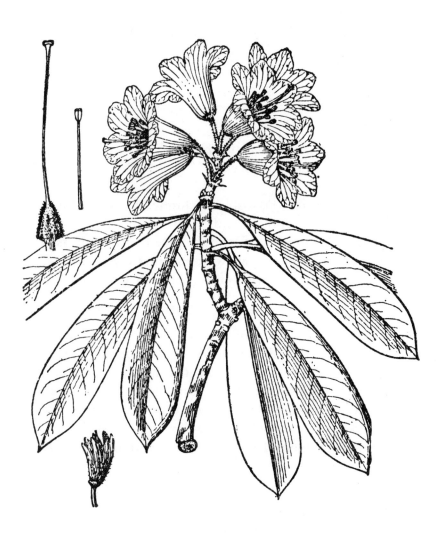

4169　腺果杜鹃

RHODODENDRON DAVIDII

Franch.

xiàn guǒ dùjuān   *"glandular fruit rhododendron"*

Evergreen shrub or small tree, 5-8 meters high; shoots strict, glabrous.

Leaves coriaceous, narrowly oblong-oblanceolate or suboblanceolate, 10-17 cm long, 2.5-4 cm broad, apex acute and mucronate, base cuneate, upper surface green and smooth, lower surface pale green and often yellowish, glabrous, lateral veins evident but not prominent; petiole 1.5-2 cm long, subglabrous.

Terminal long raceme of 6-12 flowers, rachis 5-10 cm long, thick, clad with short-stalked glands; pedicels 1-2 cm long, clad with short-stalked glands; calyx small, discoid, glandular and yellow-hairy, lobes 6, obtuse; corolla campanulate, 3.5-4.5 cm long, 3 cm in diameter, rose to purple, deep purple dotted on one upper lobe, glabrous, lobes 7-8; stamens 13-16, filaments glabrous; ovary clad with short-stalked glands, style slender and glabrous.

Capsule glandular-hairy.

West Sichuan. Grows in forests at 3000 meters.

4170　四川杜鹃

RHODODENDRON SUTCHUENENSE
Franch.

sì chuān dùjuān   *"Sichuan rhododendron"*

Evergreen shrub or small tree to 6 meters high; shoots thinly tomentose at first, later subglabrous, stout, erect.

Leaves numerous, in terminal clusters, thick-coriaceous, oblanceolate-oblong, 8-25 cm long (usually about 18 cm), 3-6 cm broad, acute at the apex, slightly tapering toward the base, base usually broadly cuneate, at maturity the lower surface usually sparsely tomentose only at the midrib, midrib very thick, prominent on the lower surface; petiole thick, 2-4 cm long, flat and smooth on the upper surface, subglabrous at maturity.

Terminal raceme of 8-10 flowers, rachis 1.5-2.5 cm long, glabrous; pedicels 1.5-2 cm long; calyx small, discoid, undulately 5-lobed, subglabrous; corolla broadly campanulate, 5-7.5 cm long, pink tinged rose, dark dotted within, minutely hairy at the base, lobes 5 or rarely 6, deeply emarginate; stamens 13-15, filaments white, pubescent below the middle; ovary glabrous, style red.

Capsule woody, oblong, about 3.5 cm long, 1 cm thick.

Distributed in Sichuan, Hubei, Shaanxi. Grows in forests at about 2000 meters.

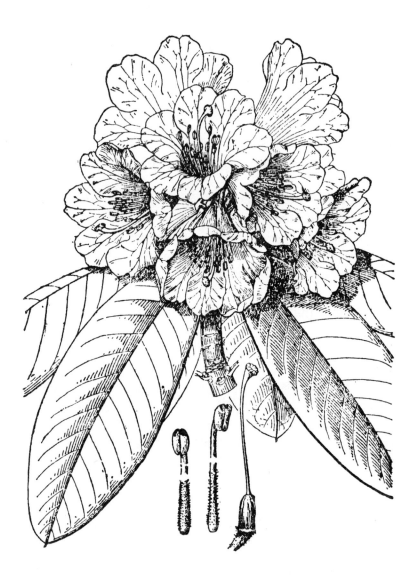

4171　阔口杜鹃

RHODODENDRON PLANETUM
Balf. f.

kuò kǒu dùjuān   *"wide-mouthed rhododendron"*

Evergreen shrub about 3 meters high; twigs stout, shoots clad with caducous woolly white hairs.

Leaves coriaceous, long oblong, to 20 cm long, 6 cm broad, obtuse at the apex and stiffly mucronate, tapering toward the cuneate base, midrib, lateral veins, and veinlets very sparsely clad with stellate-floccose hairs, soon glabrous, midrib thick and prominent on the lower surface; petiole about 2 cm long, nearly flat and smooth on the upper surface, both sides narrowly winged.

Terminal umbelliform inflorescence of as many as 10 flowers, rachis glabrous; pedicels 1.5 cm long, glandular; calyx annular, about 1 mm high, with 5 small teeth; corolla broadly funnelform, to 5.5 cm long, rose, dark red at the base and nearly white at the lobes, usually not spotted, lobes 6-7, of equal size; stamens 12-14, filaments enlarged toward the lower part and minutely glandular-hairy, anthers blackish purple; ovary glabrous, style purple on the lower part, glabrous.

Capsule 3 cm long, 1 cm thick, oblong-cylindric.

Distributed in Sichuan, south Shaanxi. Grows in forests.

4172 早春杜鹃

RHODODENDRON PRAEVERNUM
Hutch.

zǎo chūn dùjuān   *"early spring rhododendron"*

Evergreen shrub to small tree to 7 meters high; twigs quite stout, glabrous at maturity.

Leaves coriaceous, elliptic-oblanceolate, 10-18 cm long, 2.5-6 cm broad, acuminate at the apex, cuneate at the base, glabrous, net veins evident on the lower surface; petiole 1.5-2.5 cm long, somewhat flat on the upper surface, glabrous at maturity.

Terminal umbelliform inflorescence of about 10 flowers, rachis about 1 cm long, slightly floccose; pedicels stout, 2 cm long, glabrous; calyx small, about 2 mm long, with 5 broad triangular teeth, glabrous; corolla campanulate, 5-6 cm long, white or rose-tinged with one large red basal spot and smaller dots above, minutely pubescent within at the base, lobes 5, deeply emarginate; stamens 20, filaments minutely hairy on the lower third; ovary and style glabrous, stigma large, capitate, and shallowly cleft.

Capsule woody, oblong, about 3 cm long, locules 10-20.

Distributed in Hubei, Shaanxi, Sichuan, Yunnan. Grows in forests. Blooms in March, April.

4173 美容杜鹃

RHODODENDRON CALOPHYTUM
Franch.

měi róng dùjuān   *"beautiful face rhododendron"*

Evergreen small tree as high as 10 meters, sometimes shrubby; shoots stout, clad at first with long white hairs.

Leaves thick-coriaceous, oblong-oblanceolate, 20-30 cm long, 5-7 cm broad, acute at the apex, tapering downward, cuneate at the base, glabrous, the lower surface pale green and sparsely clad with short white stellate hairs only when young; petiole 2-2.5 cm long.

Terminal racemose-umbelliform inflorescence of 15-20 flowers or more, rachis 1.5-2 cm long, clad with caespitose yellow hairs; pedicels 3-7 cm long, sparsely long-hairy only when young; calyx small, 5-lobed; corolla broadly campanulate, swollen at the base, 5-6 cm long, white or rose-tinged, dark red dotted within on the lower part, lobes 5-7, of unequal size, one larger lower lobe to 2.5 cm long; stamens 15-20, filaments clad with a few minute hairs only at the base; ovary green, glabrous, 14-loculed, style thick, glabrous, stigma discoid, 8 mm in diameter.

Capsule oblong, 1.5-2.5 cm long.

Distributed in Sichuan, south Shaanxi. Grows in forests at 2000-3000 meters.

4174　尖叶杜鹃

RHODODENDRON OPENSHAWIANUM

Rehd. et Wils.

jiān yè dùjuān   *"sharp-leaved rhododendron"*

Evergreen small tree to 12 meters high; branchlets stout, green, glabrous.

Leaves in terminal clusters, coriaceous, oblong-oblanceolate, 9-15 cm long, 3-5 cm broad above the middle, apex abruptly acuminate, base cuneate, upper surface bright green and glabrous, lower surface glabrous, midrib impressed on the upper surface and resembling a light green thread; petiole 1.5-2 cm long, slightly floccose only when young.

Terminal racemose-umbelliform inflorescence of 9-12 flowers, rachis 1-1.5 cm long, subglabrous, pedicels 1.5-4 cm long, green, glabrous; calyx small, discoid, shallowly divided into 5 ovate teeth, corolla campanulate, 4.5-5 cm long, 3 cm in diameter, white tinged light purple, lobes 5-6, orbicular, deeply emarginate; stamens 20-25, of unequal length, filaments subglabrous or very minutely hairy at the base; ovary glabrous, 14-loculed, style glabrous, stigma large and discoid.

Capsule long ovate, to 3 cm long.

West Sichuan. Grows in forests at 2300-2500 meters.

4175　多变杜鹃

RHODODENDRON SELENSE
Franch.

duō biàn dùjuān   *"variable rhododendron"*

Evergreen undershrub to 2 meters high; branchlets densely clad with short-stalked glands and floccose hairs.

Leaves thin-coriaceous, oblong, 3-7 cm long, 1.5-3.5 cm broad, apex rounded and mucronate, base rounded or obtuse but not cordate, upper and lower surfaces glabrous; petiole 2 cm long, clad at first with short-stalked glands and a few floccose hairs, later nearly smooth and glossy.

Terminal umbelliform inflorescence of 4-6 flowers; pedicels about 1.5 cm long, clad with short-stalked glands and a few floccose hairs; calyx small, to 3 mm long, with 5 broad triangular teeth, densely glandular at the margin; corolla funnelform-campanulate, about 3 cm long, white tinged rose or rose-colored, not spotted in the type although spotted varieties occur, lobes 5; stamens 10, filaments sparsely pubescent on the lower part; ovary clad with short-stalked glands and a few floccose hairs, style glabrous.

Capsule narrowly cylindric, curved, about 1.5 cm long, 4 mm thick, clad with remnants of the glands.

Distributed in Yunnan, southwest Sichuan (Muli). Grows in the high mountains.

4176　黄杯杜鹃

RHODODENDRON WARDII
W. W. Sm.

huáng bēi dùjuān   *"yellow cup rhododendron"*

Evergreen shrub, 4-7 meters high; shoots glandular, later smooth and glossy.

Leaves coriaceous, oblong-elliptic to ovate-elliptic, 5-10 cm long, 2-5 cm broad, apex obtuse and mucronulate, base cordate, truncate, or rounded, upper surface glabrous, lower surface light grayish white and glabrous; petiole 1.5-3 cm long, smooth and glossy at maturity.

Terminal racemose-umbelliform inflorescence of 7-14 flowers, rachis 1-1.5 cm long, tomentose and glandular; pedicels 2.5-4 cm long, more or less glandular; calyx large, 6-12 mm long, more or less glandular, lobes of unequal size, glandular at the margin; corolla cuplike, 3.5-4 cm long, bright yellow very slightly tinged green, lobes 5, emarginate; stamens 10, filaments glabrous; ovary glandular, style glandular overall.

Capsule slightly curved, to 2.5 cm long, to 7 mm thick, clad with gland-tipped hairs, the lower part enclosed by the persistent calyx.

Distributed in Yunnan, southeast Xizang. Grows in thickets at 4000 meters.

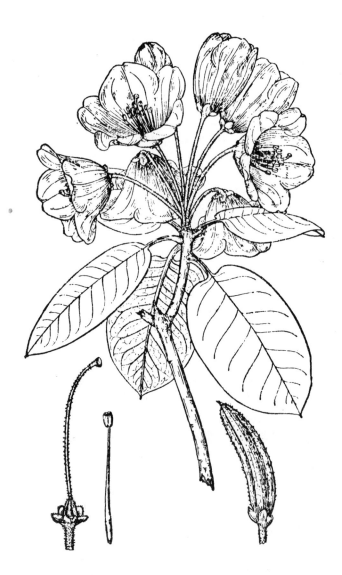

4177　白碗杜鹃

RHODODENDRON SOULIEI
Franch.

bái wǎn dùjuān   *"white bowl rhododendron"*

Evergreen shrub, 2-4 meters high; twigs glabrous, shoots light grayish green to purplish red, clad more or less with stipitate red glands.

Leaves coriaceous, oblong or oblong-elliptic, 4-7 cm long, 2-4 cm broad, rounded and mucronate at the apex, truncate, rounded, or slightly cordate at the base, glabrous, lower surface light grayish green and finely net-veined; petiole 2-2.5 cm long, purple on the lower surface, clad more or less with stipitate glands.

Terminal loose racemose-umbelliform inflorescence of 5-8 flowers, rachis 5 mm long; pedicels 4-5 cm long, densely glandular; calyx about 7 mm long, deeply 5-lobed, lobes broadly ovate, 4-5 mm long, 4-5 mm broad, red-glandular outside, glandular-ciliate; corolla campanulate-bowl-shaped or cuplike, 2.5-3.5 cm long, 5 cm in diameter, white tinged pink, lobes 5-6; stamens 10, filaments white, glabrous; ovary and style densely clad with dark red glands.

Capsule slightly curved, 2 cm long, 5 mm thick, glandular-hairy.

West Sichuan. Grows in thickets above 3000 meters.

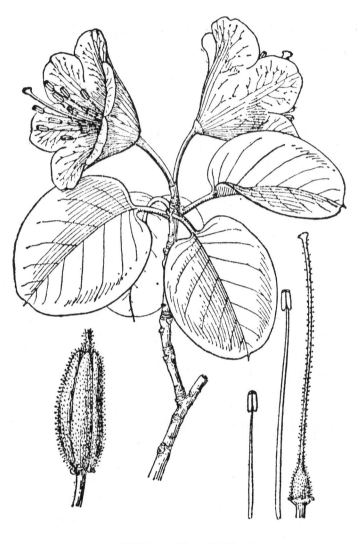

4178　圆叶杜鹃

RHODODENDRON WILLIAMSIANUM
Rehd. et Wils.

yuán yè dùjuān   *"round-leaved rhododendron"*

Evergreen shrub, 1-2 meters high; twigs horizontal, shoots slightly glandular, later smooth and glossy.

Leaves coriaceous, broadly elliptic or suborbicular, 2.5-5 cm long, 2.5-4 cm broad, apex rounded and mucronate, base cordate or subcordate, upper surface glabrous, lower surface gray-white, finely papillate-glandular and hairy, lateral veins obscure on the upper surface, somewhat evident on the lower surface; petiole cylindric, 8-12 mm long, glandular when young.

Terminal racemose-umbelliform inflorescence of 2-5 flowers, rachis 3-5 mm long, rachis, pedicels, and calyx glandular when young; pedicels 1.5-2 cm long; calyx very small, about 2 mm long, 6-lobed; corolla campanulate, 3.5-4 cm long, light rose, 6-lobed; stamens 11-14, glabrous; ovary 6-loculed, green, clad with stipitate green glands, the glands most numerous on the ovary and lower half of the style.

Capsule 1.5 cm long, 6 mm thick, nearly eglandular when mature.

West Sichuan. Grows in thickets at about 3000 meters.

4179 樱花杜鹃

RHODODENDRON CERASINUM

Tagg

yīng huā dùjuān   *"cherry rhododendron"*

Evergreen shrub to 3.5-4 meters high; shoots very sparsely hairy, soon glabrous.

Leaves oblong or oblong-elliptic, 5-6.5 cm long, 2-3 cm broad, upper surface sparsely clad with minute hairs when young, soon hairy only at the midrib, lower surface whitish gray-green, glabrous, finely net-veined; petiole 2 cm long, sparsely pubescent at first, especially on the upper surface, soon glabrous.

Terminal umbelliform inflorescence of 5-6 nodding flowers; pedicels 2-3 cm long, clad with short-stalked glands; calyx small, just an undulate rim, sessile-glandular outside and at the margin; corolla campanulate, 4.5 cm long, 5 cm in diameter, dark red overall or the corolla tube pink with dark red lobes, corolla tube dark-spotted at the base, lobes 1.5 cm long, emarginate; stamens 10, as long as the corolla tube, filaments glabrous; ovary densely clad with clavate glands, style glandular throughout.

Capsule 2.5 cm long.

Southeast Xizang. Grows in rhododendron thickets at 3600 meters.

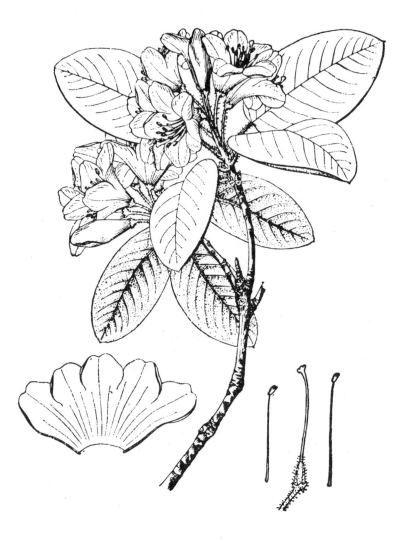

4180　弯果杜鹃

RHODODENDRON CAMPYLOCARPUM
Hook. f.

wān guǒ dùjuān *"curved fruit rhododendron"*

Evergreen subshrub, 1.2-2.5 meters high; branchlets slightly stipitate-glandular.

Leaves coriaceous, ovate to short elliptic, 5-8 cm long, 3-5 cm broad, apex rounded to broadly obtuse, base cordate to truncate or rarely rounded, lower surface grayish green and minutely papillate; petiole 1.5-2 cm long, sparsely stipitate-glandular and minutely hairy, the glands scattered upward onto the leaf margin and the base of the midrib.

Terminal racemose-umbelliform inflorescence of 6-8 flowers; pedicels 2-3 cm long, more or less stipitate-glandular; calyx small, 3 mm long, 5-lobed, glandular outside and at the margin; corolla campanulate, 4 cm long, bright yellow, with or without minute dark red spots at the base, lobes 5, emarginate; stamens 10, filaments glabrous or minutely hairy at the base; ovary densely clad with short-stalked glands, style more or less glandular at the base or eglandular.

Capsule cylindric, curved in a semicircle, 2-2.5 cm long.

South Xizang; also Sikkim and Nepal.

357

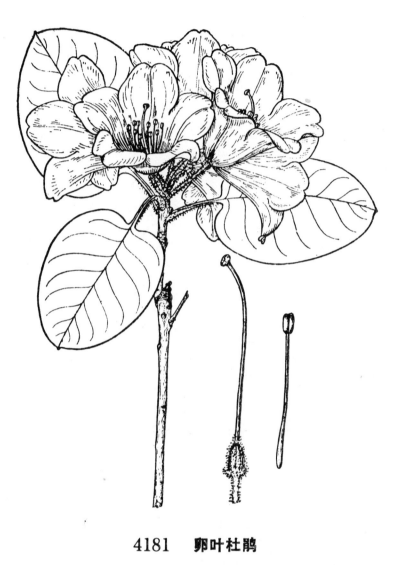

4181　卵叶杜鹃

RHODODENDRON CALLIMORPHUM

Balf. f. et W. W. Sm.

luǎn yè dùjuān   *"ovate-leaved rhododendron"*

Evergreen shrub to 3 meters high; branchlets suberect, shoots sparsely stipitate-glandular in the first year.

Leaves few, thin-coriaceous, ovate to ovate-orbicular, 3-6.5 cm long, 2-4.5 cm broad, apex rounded and bluntly mucronate, base cordate, upper surface glossy green, lower surface gray-white, glabrous except at the sparsely stipitate-glandular midrib, the midrib usually light red; petiole 1-2 cm long, sparsely clad with light red and brownish black stipitate glands which are scattered upward onto the basal leaf margin.

Terminal inflorescence of about 8 flowers; pedicels 2-2.5 cm long, densely clad with stipitate red glands; calyx very short, about 1.2 mm long, 5-lobed, red-glandular outside; corolla campanulate, 4.5 cm long, reddish rose, eglandular, lobes 5, 1.3 cm long, deeply emarginate; stamens 10; ovary 5-loculed, densely clad with stipitate red glands, style as long as the corolla, similarly glandular at the base.

West Yunnan. Grows in thickets on rocky slopes in the mountains.

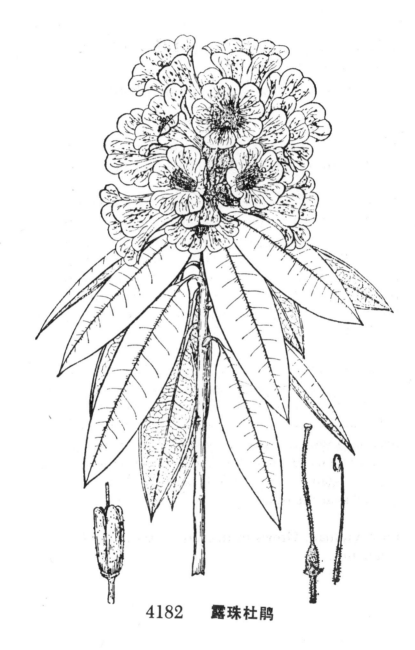

4182　　露珠杜鹃

RHODODENDRON IRRORATUM
Franch.

lù zhū dùjuān   *"dewdrop rhododendron"*

Evergreen shrub or small tree to 8 meters high; shoots thinly tomentose and clad with short-stalked glands which soon wither.

Leaves scattered, thick-coriaceous, lanceolate or narrowly elliptic, 5-12 cm long, 1.5-3 cm broad, tapering at the apex to acute, tapering at the base to cuneate, margin more or less undulate and slightly scabrous, upper surface glabrous at maturity, lower surface glabrous and epapillate (without magnification) at maturity.

Terminal lax racemose-umbelliform inflorescence of about 15 flowers, rachis 1.5-3 cm long, red-glandular; pedicels 1.5-2.5 cm long, densely clad with clavate glands; calyx small, about 2 mm long, 5-lobed, densely glandular; corolla tubular-campanulate, 3-5 cm long, white or cream, usually tinged varying shades of rose and dotted with red or light green, lobes 5; stamens 10, filaments finely pubescent at the base; ovary 5-10-loculed, densely glandular.

Capsule to 3 cm long.

West Yunnan. Grows in pine forests above 2600 meters.

361

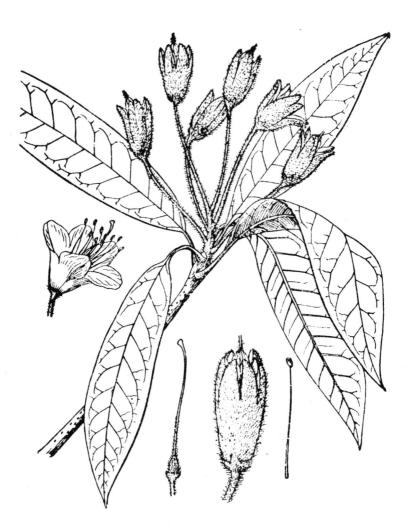

4183　短脉杜鹃

RHODODENDRON BREVINERVE

Chun et Fang

duǎn mài dùjuān   *"short-veined rhododendron"*

Evergreen small tree to 5 meters high; branchlets glabrous.

Leaves thin-coriaceous, lanceolate to elliptic-lanceolate, 8-10 cm long, 2.5-4 cm broad, tapering at the apex to acute, broadly cuneate at the base, glabrous at maturity, midrib conspicuously prominent on the lower surface, lateral veins very slender, somewhat evident only on the lower half; petiole 1.5-2.5 cm long, glabrous.

Terminal raceme of 3-5 flowers, rachis less than 1 cm long, glabrous; pedicels 2 cm long, glandular-hairy; calyx small, with small irregular teeth, stipitate-glandular on the back and at the margin; corolla broadly campanulate, 3-3.5 cm long, purple, not spotted, deeply 5-lobed, each lobe darkly vein-lined down the middle; stamens 10, exserted, filaments glabrous; ovary densely clad with stiff gland-tipped hairs, style similarly hairy on the lower third to half.

Capsule narrowly elliptic, 1.8 cm long, 8 mm thick, densely clad with gland-tipped bristles, the calyx enlarged.

Distributed in Guangdong, Guangxi, Guizhou. Grows in open forests.

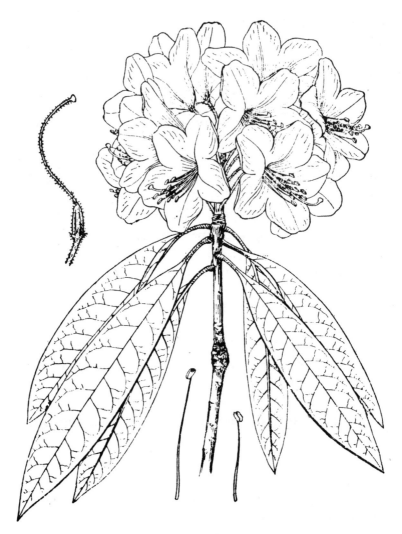

4184　桃叶杜鹃

RHODODENDRON ANNAE
Franch.

táo yè dùjuān   *"peach-leaved rhododendron"*

Evergreen shrub, 1.5-2 meters high; shoots slightly floccose and more or less glandular.

Leaves firm-coriaceous, narrowly long-lanceolate, 7-11 cm long, 1.5-3 cm broad, apex acute or short acuminate, base cuneate, upper and lower surfaces glabrous at maturity, lower surface light green, sparsely and minutely dotted, lateral veins slightly prominent; petiole 1-1.4 cm long.

Terminal raceme of about 10 flowers, rachis about 2.5 cm long, densely glandular and sparsely floccose; calyx small, densely glandular, undulately lobed, and glandular-ciliate; corolla broadly campanulate, about 2.5 cm long, milk white tinged rose and purple-dotted, lobes 1-1.5 cm long, emarginate; stamens 10, filaments glabrous; ovary densely glandular, style densely glandular throughout.

Distributed in Guizhou, Yunnan. Grows in forests at 1400 meters.

4185　川西杜鹃

RHODODENDRON SIKANGENSE

Fang

chuān xī dùjuan   *"west Sichuan rhododendron"*

Evergreen shrub to small tree, 3-5 meters high; shoots clad at first with grayish brown hairs, glabrous when old.

Leaves coriaceous, oblong-lanceolate, 8-10 cm long, 2.5-3 cm broad, apex acute, base obtuse, upper surface glabrous, midrib prominent on the lower surface and slightly brown-floccose on the lower part, lateral veins obscure on both surfaces; petiole 1-1.5 cm long, narrowly grooved on the upper surface, red-brown-tomentose when young.

Terminal racemose-umbelliform inflorescence of about 10 flowers, rachis 2 cm long, densely red-brown-tomentose; pedicels 1.5-2 cm long, similarly hairy; calyx about 2 mm long, undulately 5-lobed, hairy outside; corolla broadly campanulate, 4 cm long, light red, the interior red-blotched above the base and finely purple-dotted on the upper part, lobes 5; stamens 10, filaments minutely hairy at the base; ovary densely tomentose, the hairs red-brown and branched like a tree, style glabrous.

Capsule to 2 cm long, cylindric, red-brown-hairy.

West Sichuan (Erlang Shan). Grows in forests.

4186　团花杜鹃

RHODODENDRON ANTHOSPHAERUM
Diels

tuán huā dùjuān   *"globe-flowered rhododendron"*

Evergreen shrub or small tree to 9 meters high.

Leaves in terminal clusters, thin-coriaceous, oblong-lanceolate to lanceolate, 8-11 cm long, 2-3.5 cm broad, mucronate, narrowly cartilaginous at the margin and somewhat scabrous, quite glabrous at maturity, lower surface dark yellowish brown in the dried leaf and scattered with a few glands, the epidermis papillate and coarsely granular.

Inflorescence a dense globose cluster of as many as 12 flowers, rachis 1 cm long, red-hairy; pedicels 1.5 cm long, sparsely glandular, floccose, or glabrous; calyx degenerate, a fleshy shallow cup, undulate, glandular-pubescent; corolla campanulate, 4-5 cm long, 4-5 cm in diameter, bright deep rose, the color paler toward the lobes, with one purplish black spot on the back at the base, lobes 5-7; stamens 10-14, filaments dark red on the lower part, glabrous or densely pubescent below the middle; ovary green and glabrous, style light green and glabrous.

Northwest Yunnan. Grows in pine forests.

4187 迷人杜鹃

RHODODENDRON AGASTUM
Balf. f. et W. W. Sm.

mí rén dùjuān   *"charming rhododendron"*

Evergreen shrub or small tree to 6.5 meters high; shoots clad with small sessile mucilaginous glands.

Leaves oblong or oblong-elliptic, 10-15 cm long, 4-5 cm broad, apex obtuse and mucronate, base obtuse or rounded, upper surface glabrous, lower surface yellowish green and clad with a scobiform indumentum, lateral veins conspicuously prominent; petiole 2-3 cm long, shallowly grooved on the upper surface, clad with gland remnants and floccose hairs.

Inflorescence a terminal flat-topped umbelliform cluster of many flowers; pedicels 2 cm long, clad with short glandular hairs; calyx small, just an undulate rim, pale red, glandular; corolla funnelform, about 5 cm long, pink with dark red dots or spots on the back of the corolla tube, glabrous, lobes 5-7; stamens 10-14, filaments minutely hairy on the lower part; ovary 10-loculed, reddish green, clad with dense stipitate glands and a few stiff hairs, style sparsely clad with stipitate glands on the lower half or sometimes overall.

West Yunnan. Grows in pine and oak forests.

371

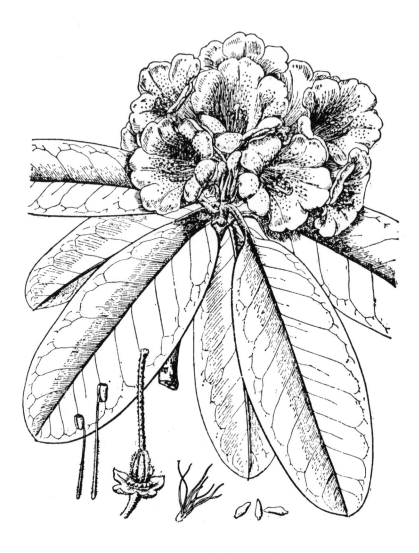

4188　绵毛房杜鹃

RHODODENDRON ERIOGYNUM

Balf. f. et W. W. Sm.

mián máo fáng dùjuān   *"woolly ovary rhododendron"*

Evergreen shrub to 3 meters high; branchlets stout, sparsely clad with long stellate hairs when young.

Leaves coriaceous, narrowly oblong-elliptic, 12-18 cm long, 4-6.5 cm broad, apex rounded and mucronate, base obtuse, lower surface densely clad with much-branched loosely felted brown hairs when young, soon glabrous (midrib hairy at the base); petiole 2-3 cm long, tomentose when young.

Terminal lax raceme of about 12 flowers; rachis 1.5-2 cm long, clad with soft minute simple hairs; pedicels 1-2 cm long, eglandular, stellate-hairy, the hairs dense at first, ultimately sparse; calyx well developed, light reddish, 6-7 mm long, unequally divided to the middle, lobes minutely hairy and ciliate; corolla broadly funnelform, red, finely brown-dotted within, corolla tube 3 cm long, lobes 5, 2 cm long, broadly emarginate; stamens 10, filaments sparsely hairy on the lower part; ovary tomentose, style stellate-hairy.

West Yunnan (Jizu Shan). Grows in open thickets.

4189　粉白杜鹃

RHODODENDRON HYPOGLAUCUM

Hemsl.

fěn bái dùjuān   *"powdery white rhododendron"*

Evergreen large shrub to 6 meters high; shoots dark green, minutely pubescent at first, later glabrous.

Leaves firm-coriaceous, oblong-oblanceolate or oblong-elliptic, 7-11 cm long, 2-4 cm broad, acute at the apex, tapering downward, cuneate at the base, lower surface clad with powdery white indumentum, midrib somewhat impressed on the upper surface, prominent on the lower surface, lateral veins mostly rather inconspicuous.

Terminal raceme of 4-7 flowers; pedicels 2.5-4 cm long, pale red, shortly pubescent; calyx small, 5-lobed, glandular-hairy outside; corolla 4-4.5 cm long, white tinged rose-red, upper interior red-dotted, corolla tube campanulate, 2 cm long, glabrous outside, lobes broadly ovate, about 1.5 cm long; stamens 10, slightly exserted, filaments short-hairy below the middle; ovary subglabrous, style glabrous.

Capsule slightly curved, 1.5-2.5 cm long, 5 mm thick, densely wart-dotted.

Distributed in Sichuan, Hubei, south Shaanxi. Grows in forests.

4190　银叶杜鹃

RHODODENDRON ARGYROPHYLLUM

Franch.

yin yè dùjuān   *"silver-leaved rhododendron"*

Evergreen shrub, 3-7 meters high; twigs slender, green, shortly gray-tomentose when young.

Leaves coriaceous, oblong-lanceolate, 6-13 cm long, 1.5-3 cm broad above the middle, apex acute, base cuneate, upper surface floccose when young, lower surface silvery-white-tomentose or floccose when young, lateral veins rather inconspicuous; petiole 10-15 mm long, subglabrous.

Terminal raceme of 7-9 flowers, rachis about 1 cm long, grayish yellow-floccose; calyx small, 5-lobed, slightly pubescent; corolla broadly campanulate, 3-3.5 cm long, white occasionally rose-tinged, purple-spotted within the corolla tube on the upper part, subglabrous, 5-lobed; stamens 12-14(-16), of unequal length, filaments white-hairy on the lower part; ovary short-hairy.

Capsule cylindric, to 1.5 cm long, glabrous at maturity.

Distributed in Sichuan, Guizhou, northeast Yunnan. Grows in thickets in mountainous areas at about 2000 meters. Highly variable.

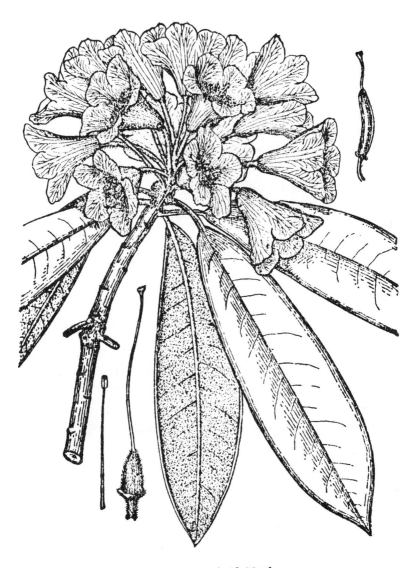

4191　海绵杜鹃

RHODODENDRON PINGIANUM

Fang

hǎi mián dùjuān   *"spongy rhododendron"*

Evergreen shrub or small tree, 4-9 meters high; twigs stout, glabrous at maturity.

Leaves coriaceous, oblanceolate or sublanceolate, 9-12 cm long, 2.5-3.8 cm broad above the middle, acute at the apex, narrowing downward, cuneate at the base, upper surface glabrous, lower surface clad with white to grayish white spongy indumentum, thickest along the sides of the midrib; petiole 1-2 cm long, grooved on the upper surface, smooth and glossy at maturity.

Terminal racemose-umbelliform inflorescence of 12-22 flowers, rachis 1-2 cm long, more or less hairy; pedicels 2-4 cm long, white-pubescent; calyx small, about 2 mm long, with 5 small triangular teeth; corolla campanulate-funnelform, 3-3.5 cm long, 2-2.5 cm in diameter, purple or light purplish red, glabrous, 5-lobed, lobes about 1 cm long, emarginate; stamens 10, filaments glabrous; ovary densely clad with branching hairs, style glabrous.

Capsule cylindric, slightly curved, to 3.5 cm long, ultimately smooth and glossy.

West Sichuan. Grows in forests.

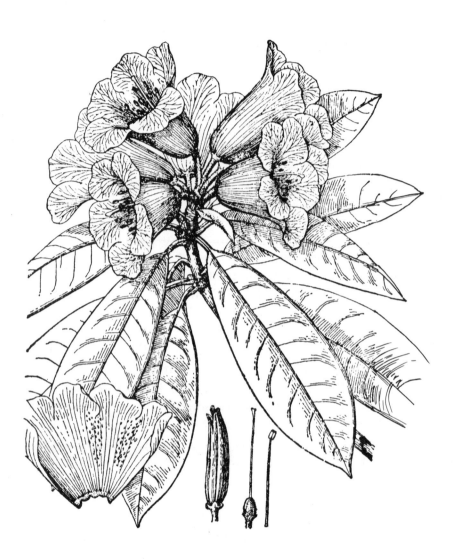

4192　大钟杜鹃

RHODODENDRON RIRIEI
Hemsl. et Wils.

dà zhōng dùjuān   *"great bell rhododendron"*

Evergreen shrub or small tree, 4-7 meters high; shoots stout, curving somewhat, glabrous.

Leaves in terminal whorls of 3-5, coriaceous, oblong-elliptic, 6-12 cm long, 2.8-6.5 cm broad at the middle, apex acute, base broadly cuneate, upper surface dark green and glabrous, lower surface silvery white, clad with a very thin white indumentum, midrib impressed on the upper surface, prominent on the lower surface; petiole thick, glabrous, 1-2 cm long.

Terminal short raceme of 5-10 flowers, rachis 5-8 mm long, woolly, the hairs white or light yellow; calyx about 5 mm long, light red, slightly hairy, unequally lobed; corolla campanulate, broad at the base, 4-5 cm long, light purple, 5-lobed, lobes rounded, emarginate; stamens 10, nearly included, filaments purple, glabrous; ovary densely clad with short gray hairs, style glabrous.

Capsule cylindric, 3-3.5 cm long, hairy or glabrous.

Sichuan (Emei Shan). Grows in forests.

4193　不凡杜鹃

RHODODENDRON INSIGNE
Hemsl.

bù fán dùjuān *"extraordinary rhododendron"*

Evergreen bushy shrub, 1.6-6 meters high; shoots glabrous even at first.

Leaves scattered, thick-coriaceous, oblong-lanceolate, 7.6-11 cm long, 2.5-3.8 cm broad or broader, apex short-acuminate, base cuneate, lower surface densely clad with a woolly indumentum composed of interwoven stellate hairs, white at first, turning a lustrous bronzy light gray, midrib prominent on the lower surface; petiole 1.2-2.5 cm long, flat and smooth on the upper surface.

Terminal compact raceme of 8 flowers or more (to 19), rachis to 1.2 cm long; pedicels spreading, 2.5-3.8 cm long, light red, sparsely and minutely hairy, the hairs denser toward the calyx; calyx poorly developed, annular, shallowly 5-lobed, minutely red-hairy; corolla broadly campanulate, to 3.3 cm long, white or pale pink, often rose-streaked outside and red-dotted on the back, 5-lobed; stamens 13-14; ovary 11-loculed, densely clad with long white hairs.

Capsule subcylindric, 2.5 cm long, slightly tomentose.

West Sichuan. Grows in forests above 2500 meters.

383

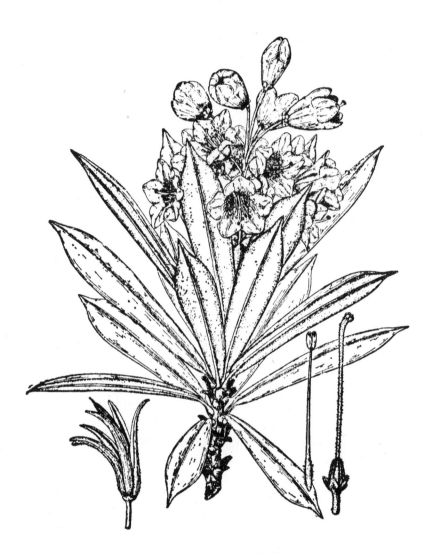

4194　反边杜鹃

RHODODENDRON THAYERIANUM
Rehd. et Wils.

fǎn biān dùjuān   *"reversed margin rhododendron"*

Evergreen shrub, 3-4 meters high; shoots more or less arachnoid-hairy, at maturity glabrous and blackish brown, bud scales persistent at the base for several years.

Leaves in terminal clusters of 10-20, thick-coriaceous, narrowly long-oblanceolate, to 15 cm long, to 2.5(-3) cm broad, short acuminate at the apex, tapering toward the base, broadly recurved at the margin, upper and lower surfaces arachnoid-hairy when young, the upper surface soon glabrous, the lower surface closely clad with a thin layer of light purplish coppery indumentum composed of interwoven caespitose hairs and stipitate multicellular glands; petiole 1.2 cm long, glandular and sparsely floccose when young.

Terminal racemose-umbelliform inflorescence of 10-20 flowers, rachis 3-5 cm long; pedicels 3-5 cm long, densely glandular; calyx small, 2-4 mm long, unequally 5-lobed, densely glandular; corolla broadly funnelform, 2.5-3 cm long, white tinged pink, red-dotted within on the upper part, 5-lobed; stamens 10; pistil glandular throughout.

Capsule oblong-cylindric, 2-3 cm long, glandular.

West Sichuan. Grows in forests at 2800 meters.

385

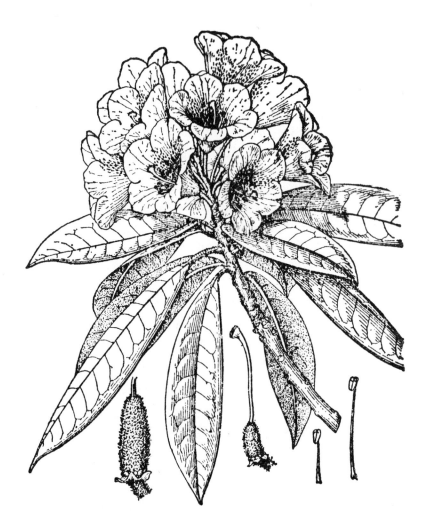

4195　金山杜鹃

RHODODENDRON CHIENIANUM

Fang

jǐn shān dùjuān   *"Jin Shan rhododendron"*

Evergreen small tree to 10 meters high; shoots floccose at first, later glabrous.

Leaves coriaceous, lanceolate or oblanceolate, 5-9 cm long, 1.5-2 cm broad, apex short acuminate, base cuneate or obtuse, upper surface slightly floccose at first, lower surface clad with yellowish brown woolly indumentum, midrib impressed on the upper surface, the lateral veins somewhat impressed or obscure; petiole 8-12 mm long, floccose at first.

Terminal racemose corymb of 8-12 flowers, rachis 1-1.5 cm long, floccose; pedicels 2.5-3 cm long, floccose; calyx small, 5-lobed, floccose; corolla campanulate-funnelform, about 3 cm long, purple, lobes 5, about 1 cm long; stamens 12, 5-15 mm long, filaments glabrous; ovary densely glandular, style glabrous.

Capsule cylindric, 2-2.5 cm long, glandular.

Southeast Sichuan (Jinfo Shan). Common in forests above 2000 meters.

4196 光枝杜鹃

RHODODENDRON HAOFUI
Chun et Fang

guāng zhǐ dùjuān   *"glossy-branched rhododendron"*

Evergreen shrub, 4-6 meters high; shoots green and glabrous.

Leaves coriaceous, lanceolate, 7-10 cm long, 3-4 cm broad, apex bluntly acute and mucronate, base obtuse, upper surface glabrous at maturity, lower surface densely clad with a thickly felted indumentum of light-yellow curled woolly hairs, midrib grooved on the upper surface, strongly prominent on the lower surface, the other veins obscure on the upper surface, lateral veins on the lower surface usually more or less concealed by the indumentum; petiole 1.5-2.2 cm long, nearly flat and smooth on the upper surface, glabrous.

Terminal umbelliform inflorescence of 5-7 flowers, rachis and pedicels more or less white-pubescent; pedicels 2.5-3.5 cm long; calyx small, lobes toothlike, sparsely and minutely hairy; corolla broadly campanulate, 4-4.5 cm long, white slightly tinged rose, 5-lobed; stamens 18-20, filaments minutely hairy on the lower half; ovary densely white-floccose, style glabrous.

Capsule cylindric, about 1 cm long, light yellow-floccose.

North Guangxi. Grows in forests.

4197 福建杜鹃

RHODODENDRON FOKIENENSE

Franch.

fú jiàn dùjuān   *"Fujian rhododendron"*

Evergreen small tree to 7 meters high; twigs slender and glabrous, shoots sparsely pubescent.

Leaves thick-coriaceous, lanceolate or oblong-lanceolate, 5-9 cm long, 1.5-2.5 cm broad, apex acute, base cuneate, upper surface glabrous at maturity or clad at the midrib with downy white hair remnants, lower surface clad with a thin layer of crustaceous white to gray indumentum, subglabrous at the midrib, midrib grooved on the upper surface, prominent on the lower surface, lateral veins rather inconspicuous on the upper surface; petiole 1-2 cm long, glabrous.

Terminal umbelliform inflorescence of 5-10 flowers; pedicels 2 cm long, sparsely clad with floccose hairs and small glands; calyx small, with inconspicuous triangular teeth, more or less glandular; corolla funnelform-campanulate, 3.5-4 cm long, white to pink and red-dotted, minutely hairy within, lobes 5, rounded, undulate; stamens 22, filaments densely hairy below the middle; ovary clad with dense branching hairs as well as small glands.

Capsule oblong, 1.5 cm long, hairy, fruitstalk elongate.

Distributed in Fujian, Zhejiang, Jiangxi, Guangxi. Grows in forests.

4198   弯尖杜鹃

RHODODENDRON YOUNGAE

Fang

wān jiān dùjuān   *"curved point rhododendron"*

Evergreen shrub to 4 meters high; shoots slightly pubescent at first, later glabrous.

Leaves coriaceous, oblong-elliptic or oblong-oblanceolate, 5-12 cm long, 2-4 cm broad, apex acute, usually with a reflexed mucro, base cuneate or obtuse, upper surface glabrous, lower surface thinly clad with a light brownish gray plastered indumentum, the midrib prominent, the lateral veins nearly obscure; petiole 1.3-2 cm long, shallowly grooved on the upper surface, ultimately glabrous.

Terminal umbelliform inflorescence of 6-8 flowers, rachis 1-1.5 cm long, hairy and stipitate-glandular; pedicels about 2 cm long, sparsely pubescent and densely clad with light brown gland-tipped hairs; calyx small, 2 mm long, 5-lobed, slightly glandular outside; corolla funnelform-campanulate; 3.5-4 cm long, pink, upper interior rose-dotted, lobes 5, 2 cm long, rounded; stamens 10, slightly shorter than the corolla, filaments minutely hairy at the base; ovary densely tomentose and glandular-hairy, style glabrous.

Southeast Sichuan (Jinfo Shan). Grows in mixed forests.

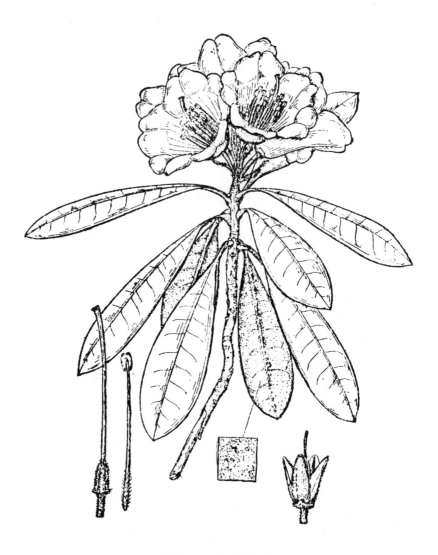

4199　猴头杜鹃

394

RHODODENDRON SIMIARUM

Hance

hóu tóu dùjuān   *"monkey head rhododendron"*

Evergreen shrub, 2-3 meters high; twigs gray-floccose when young, later glabrous.

Leaves in terminal clusters, thick-coriaceous, oblanceolate to oblong-lanceolate, 4-9 cm long, 2-3 cm broad at the upper third, apex obtuse or rounded and mucronate, base cuneate and slightly decurrent onto the petiole, upper surface gray-floccose at first, lower surface clad with a light gray to yellowish brown crustaceous indumentum, the midrib prominent, thinly clad with indumentum and sparsely glandular; petiole 1-1.5 cm long, at first floccose and glandular.

Terminal racemose-umbelliform inflorescence of 4-6 flowers, rachis 1-2 cm long, more or less floccose; calyx discoid, with 5 small triangular teeth, glandular-ciliate; corolla funnelform-campanulate, about 4 cm long, pink, pink-dotted within, lobes 5, spreading; stamens 10-12, filaments sparsely pubescent on the lower part; ovary clad with stellate branching hairs and glands, style glandular at the base.

Capsule long ovoid, 1 cm long, often red-hairy.

Distributed in Guangdong, Guangxi, Hunan, Fujian, Zhejiang. Grows in forests on the high mountains.

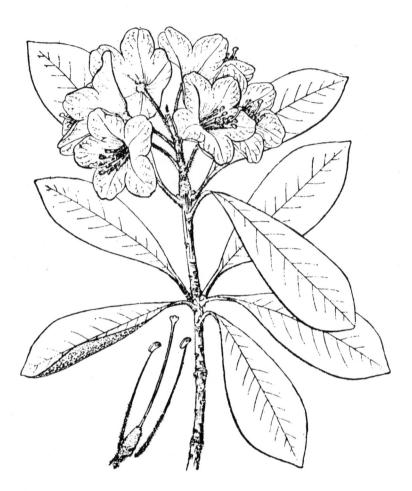

4200 变色杜鹃

RHODODENDRON VERSICOLOR
Chun et Fang

biàn sè dùjuān   *"changing color rhododendron"*

Evergreen small tree to 6 meters high; branchlets glabrous.

Leaves in terminal clusters, coriaceous, oblanceolate or obovate-lanceolate, 8-13 cm long, 3-4 cm broad, rounded, bluntly acute, or occasionally shortly acute at the apex, tapering downward from above the middle, cuneate at the base, upper surface glabrous, lower surface thinly clad with light yellow or pale gray detersile indumentum, midrib gradually obscured toward the apex on the lower surface, lateral veins slender, obscure on both surfaces; petiole 1-1.5 cm long, glabrous, grooved on the upper surface.

Terminal racemose-umbelliform inflorescence of 5-7 flowers, rachis 2 cm long, sparsely short-pubescent; pedicels 1.5-2.2 cm long, minutely white-hairy; calyx small, shallowly 5-lobed, densely clad with minute hairs; corolla funnelform-campanulate, 3 cm long, rose when first opening, white when fully open, lobes 5, beautifully vein-lined at the margin; stamens 10, filaments minutely hairy on the lower third; ovary densely clad with soft mucilaginous hairs.

North Guangxi (Longsheng). Grows in densely forested mountain valleys.

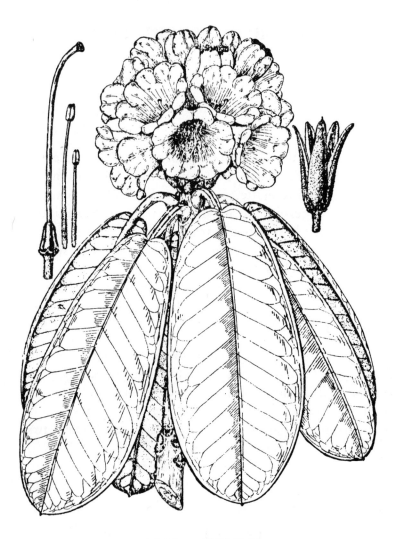

4201　乳黄杜鹃

RHODODENDRON LACTEUM

Franch.

rǔ huáng dùjuān   *"milky-yellow rhododendron"*

Evergreen small tree to 10 meters high; twigs stout, glabrous, light purplish brown.

Leaves in terminal clusters, thick-coriaceous, elliptic-oblong, 8-15 cm long, 4-7 cm broad, apex rounded and mucronate, base rounded and slightly cordate, upper surface glabrous, lower surface densely light yellow-brown-tomentose, the hairs cylindric-oblong, obtuse, thin-walled, and clustered on short stalks, midrib impressed on the upper surface, prominent on the lower surface; petiole thick, 1.5 cm long, upper surface shallowly grooved.

Inflorescence terminal, a tightly crowded cluster of many flowers, rachis short; pedicels 1.2-1.5 cm long, more or less tomentose; calyx small, undulate; corolla broadly campanulate, 3 cm long, 3-4 cm in diameter at the mouth, sulfur-yellow, minutely red-dotted within, glabrous, 5-lobed; stamens 10, of unequal length, shorter than corolla; ovary white-tomentose, style green, glabrous.

Capsule 3 cm long, 6 mm thick, 10-loculed, clad with hair remnants.

Yunnan (west, northwest, northeast). Grows in forests.

4202　宏钟杜鹃

RHODODENDRON WIGHTII
Hook. f.

hóng zhōng dùjuān   *"grand bell rhododendron"*

Evergreen small tree; branches about 1 cm thick and gray-floccose during the first year, older branches glabrous.

Leaves in terminal clusters, coriaceous, oblong to oblong-obovate or oblanceolate, 12-18 cm long, 5-7 cm broad, apex rounded, sometimes mucronate, base nearly rounded, upper surface glabrous, lower surface light green or cinnamon or sometimes light gray (nearly white when young), with a thin layer of uniformly appressed indumentum; petiole 1.2-2 cm long, thick, fleshy, floccose.

Terminal lax capitate-umbelliform inflorescence of 12-20 flowers, with stiff viscid basal bud scales more or less persistent during flowering, rachis short; pedicels 3-4 cm long, yellow-hairy or more or less glandular; calyx extremely small, with 5 short teeth; corolla campanulate and broad at the base, 4-4.5 cm long, light yellow with dense dark red basal dots, 5-lobed; stamens 10, filaments pubescent at the base; ovary densely villous.

Capsule cylindric, slightly curved, with a few hair remnants.

Southeast Xizang; also Bhutan, Sikkim, Nepal.

4203　宽钟杜鹃

RHODODENDRON BEESIANUM
Diels

kuān zhōng dùjuān   *"broad bell rhododendron"*

Evergreen shrub or small tree to 7.5 meters high; branchlets stout, sometimes floccose at first.

Leaves oblong-lanceolate or oblanceolate, 9-30 cm long, 2.6-8.3 cm broad, apex short acuminate, base obtuse or narrowing, upper surface glabrous, lateral veins 16-25 pair and impressed, lower surface clad with a thin layer of cinnamon indumentum composed of stellate hairs; petiole 1.3-3 cm long, glabrous, with bilateral narrow wings.

Terminal racemose-umbelliform inflorescence of 10-25 flowers, rachis 0.5-3 cm long, minutely hairy; pedicels 1.4-2.9 cm long, more or less hairy; calyx extremely short, 5-lobed, glabrous; corolla broadly campanulate, 3.5-5 cm long, white or rose with a few dark red dots; stamens 10, filaments minutely hairy at the base; ovary densely brown-hairy, style glabrous.

Capsule 2-4 cm long, 8 mm thick, slightly hairy.

Distributed in Yunnan, Sichuan, southeast Xizang. Grows in pine forests.

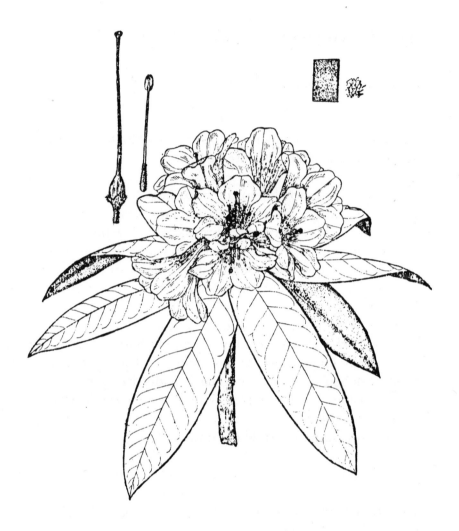

4204　川滇杜鹃

RHODODENDRON TRAILLIANUM

Forrest et W. W. Sm.

chuān diān dùjuān *"Sichuan-Yunnan rhododendron"*

Evergreen shrub or small tree to 10 meters high; twigs stout, young branches gray to light yellow-floccose, soon subglabrous.

Leaves in terminal clusters of 6-10, coriaceous, oblong-lanceolate, 6.5-10 cm long, 3.5-4.5 cm broad, apex acute, base obtuse, upper surface finely rugose, lower surface clad with dense gray to yellow suedelike indumentum composed of stellate hairs, lateral veins obscure on the lower surface; petiole more than 1 cm long, clad with hairs similar to those of the young branches, ultimately subglabrous.

Terminal compact umbelliform inflorescence of 10-15 flowers; pedicels 1-1.6 cm long, sparsely and finely floccose; calyx a shallow cup, 5-lobed, the lobes more or less finely ciliate toward the tips; corolla funnelform-campanulate, about 3.5 cm long, white or rose-tinged with red dots, 5-lobed; stamens 10, filaments hairy at the base; ovary glabrous or clad with short simple hairs or sparsely floccose.

Capsule cylindric, 2 cm long.

Distributed in northwest Yunnan, southwest Sichuan. Grows in rhododendron forests at 3500 meters.

4205　栎叶杜鹃

RHODODENDRON DRYOPHYLLUM

Balf. f. et Forrest

lì yè dùjuān   *"oak leaf rhododendron"*

Evergreen shrub to 3 meters high; young branches clad with a thin layer of light yellow to cinnamon indumentum.

Leaves coriaceous, oblong-elliptic or oblong-lanceolate, 9-14 cm long, 2.5-3.5 cm broad, apex acuminate, base obtuse, upper surface glabrous, lateral veins nearly obscure, lower surface clad with light yellow smooth suede-like indumentum, midrib prominent, lateral veins obscure; petiole 1-2 cm long, clad with hair similar to that of the young branches.

Terminal racemose-umbelliform inflorescence of about 8-15 flowers, rachis about 1 cm long, floccose; pedicels 2-2.5 cm long, pubescent; calyx small, about 2 mm long, shallowly 5-lobed, with a few minute marginal hairs; corolla funnelform-campanulate, about 4 cm long, white with a few dark red dots, minutely hairy within, lobes 5, emarginate; stamens 10, filaments slightly pubescent on the lower part; ovary glabrous or sparsely floccose.

Capsule elliptic, to 2 cm long.

Northwest Yunnan. Grows in pine forests at 3500 meters.

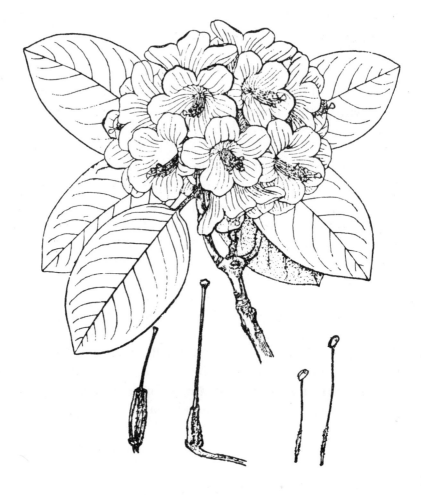

4206　青海杜鹃

RHODODENDRON PRZEWALSKII

Maxim.

qīnghǎi dùjuān   *"Qinghai rhododendron"*
pí pa dùjuān   *"loquat rhododendron"*
lǒng shǔ dùjuān   *"Gansu-Sichuan rhododendron"*

Evergreen shrub to 3 meters high; shoots thick, glabrous.

Leaves in terminal clusters, firm-coriaceous, elliptic to oblong, 7-10 cm long, 3-5 cm broad, apex obtuse and mucronate, base rounded and slightly cordate, upper surface glabrous and finely veined, lower surface clad at first with yellow-brown suedelike thin indumentum composed of long awned stellate hairs, later gradually lost; petiole 1-2 cm long, glabrous.

Corymbose-globose inflorescence of 12-15 flowers; pedicels 1-1.5 cm long, glabrous; calyx short, glabrous, with semicircular teeth; corolla campanulate, 3.5 cm long, white to pink, lobes 5, rounded, emarginate; stamens 10, with a few short thick hairs on lower half of filaments; ovary usually glabrous, style glabrous, slightly longer than stamens, stigma capitate, green.

Capsule to 1.5 cm long, cylindric, smooth and glossy.

Distributed in Qinghai, Gansu, Shaanxi, north Sichuan. Grows on high mountains at about 4000 meters, often forming forests.

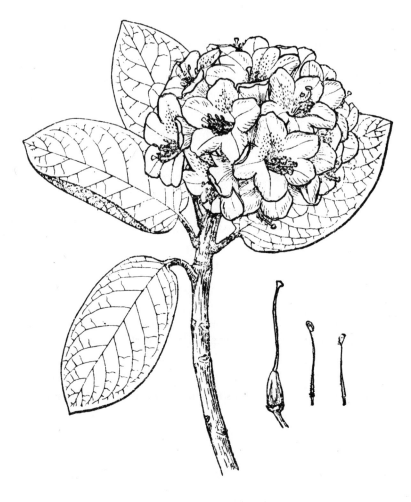

4207 凝毛杜鹃

RHODODENDRON AGGLUTINATUM
Balf. f. et Forrest

níng máo dùjuān   *"congealed hair rhododendron"*

Evergreen shrub, 1.2-5 meters high; twigs short and thick.

Leaves coriaceous, oblong or long ovate, 4-7 cm long, 2-3.5 cm broad, apex bluntly acute, base obtuse or truncate, upper surface glabrous at maturity, lower surface yellow-brown with a thin layer of glutinous indumentum, midrib prominent, clad more or less with similar indumentum or glabrous and light yellow, lateral veins obscure; petiole about 1.5 cm long, usually light yellow, subglabrous.

Terminal compact umbelliform inflorescence of about 10-15 flowers, rachis 5 mm long, minutely hairy; pedicels 1.5 cm long, sparsely floccose; calyx small, lobes 5, obtuse, short-ciliate; corolla funnelform-campanulate, about 3.5 cm long, white or milk white with dark red spots, lobes 5, about 1.5 cm long, emarginate; stamens 10, filaments hairy on the lower part; ovary and style glabrous.

Distributed in Xizang, Yunnan, Sichuan, Gansu. Grows in rhododendron thickets.

411

4208 夺目杜鹃

RHODODENDRON ARIZELUM

Balf. f. et Forrest

duó mù dùjuān   *"eye-catching rhododendron"*

Evergreen shrub to small tree, 3-7 meters high; twigs thick and nodose.

Leaves large, thick-coriaceous, broadly elliptic or obovate or broadly oblanceolate, about 15 cm long, to 8-10 cm broad, apex broadly rounded, retuse, base rounded or slightly cordate, upper surface rugose, lower surface clad with thick cinnamon or reddish brown indumentum composed of cupular compound hairs; petiole 2.5-3 cm long, cylindric, upper surface not grooved, with a few light yellow-brown hairs.

Terminal raceme of 15-25 flowers, rachis 2.5-3.5 cm long, brown-tomentose; pedicels about 2.5 cm long, clad with red-brown hairs, thickened at the top to form the short crooked calyx; calyx tomentose, with 8 small triangular teeth; corolla obliquely campanulate, 4.5 cm long, white or cream or yellow tinged rose with dark red basal spots, 8-lobed; stamens 16, filaments minutely hairy at the base; ovary 12-15-loculed, tomentose, the hairs dense and fasciate.

Capsule thickly cylindric, about 3 cm long, clad with ferrugineous hairs.

Distributed in Yunnan, Xizang; also Burma. Grows in forests.

413

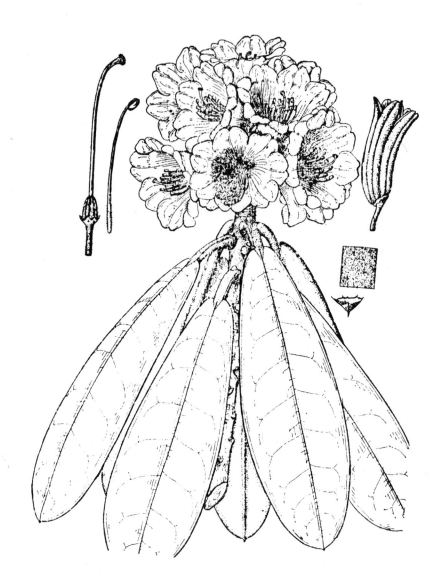

4209　假乳黄杜鹃

RHODODENDRON FICTOLACTEUM

Balf. f.

jiǎ rǔ huáng dùjuān   *"false milky-yellow rhododendron"*

Evergreen tree to 15 meters high; twigs stout, shoots hairy, the hairs light brown and appressed.

Leaves thick-coriaceous, oblong-obovate to oblong-oblanceolate, 15-30 cm long, 6-12 cm broad above the middle, apex obtuse to rounded, mucronate, base rounded or subcordate, upper surface ultimately glabrous, smooth, lower surface clad with rusty-yellow or yellow-brown two-layered indumentum, the upper layer composed of cupular or funnelform hairs, lateral veins obscure; petiole 2.5-4 cm long, cylindric, hairy, upper surface not grooved.

Inflorescence terminal, a corymb of 12-15 flowers, rachis 1.5-2 cm long; pedicels to 3 cm long, with red-brown short hairs; calyx small, a thickened rim with 7-8 undulate teeth, hairy; corolla crooked-campanulate, 3-4 cm long, 6.5 cm in diameter, white or rose-tinged with dark purple basal spots, lobes 7-8, emarginate; stamens 14-16, filaments minutely hairy at the base; ovary densely hairy, the hairs fasciate.

Capsule 3 cm long.

Distributed in Yunnan, Sichuan. Grows in pine forests at 3000 meters.

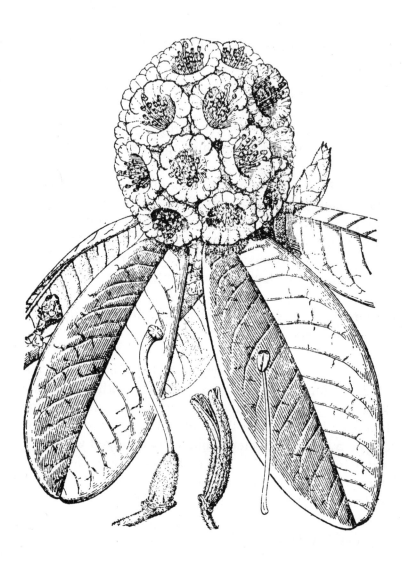

4210 多裂杜鹃

RHODODENDRON HODGSONII
Hook. f.

duō liè dùjuān   *"many-lobed rhododendron"*

Evergreen shrub to small tree, 4-7 meters high; twigs stout, shoots gray-tomentose.

Leaves thick-coriaceous, oblong-elliptic, 18-30 cm long, 7-12 cm broad, apex rounded, sometimes emarginate, base obtuse, upper surface glabrous, somewhat rugose, lower surface clad with appressed gray or light yellow indumentum, midrib prominent, lateral veins slightly visible; petiole 4 cm long, upper surface convex, tomentose at first.

Terminal compact globose-umbelliform inflorescence of 15-20 flowers, rachis to 5 cm long; pedicels 3-4 cm long, densely tomentose; calyx small, fleshy, cuplike, with 7 small triangular teeth; corolla tubular-campulate, 3-4 cm long, fleshy, deep carmine when first open, later somewhat faded and lilac-purplish, lobes 7-8 (occasionally 6 or as many as 10); stamens 15-18 (usually 16), filaments glabrous; ovary densely hairy, the hairs fasciate, locules 9-12.

Capsule 4 cm long, 7 mm thick, yellow-hairy.

South Xizang; also Sikkim, Bhutan, Nepal.

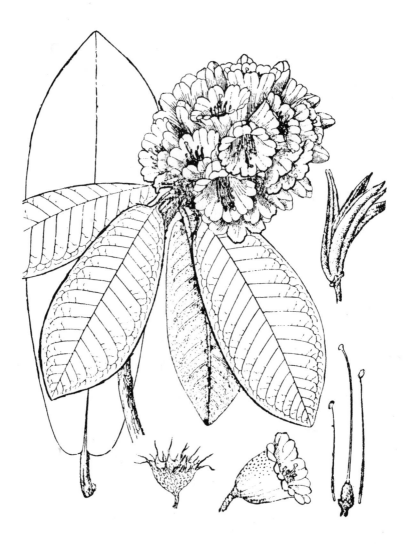

4211　大王杜鹃

RHODODENDRON REX

Lévl.

dà wáng dùjuān   *"king rhododendron"*

Evergreen small tree to 7 meters high; twigs stout, gray-white when young, tomentose.

Leaves coriaceous, to 25 cm long, 8 cm broad, broadly obtuse at the apex, tapering downward, obtuse at the base, upper surface dark green, lower surface gray to light yellow, clad with more or less persistent indumentum, the upper layer composed of bowl-shaped or campanulate-cupular hairs, the surface consequently appearing pitted, lateral veins prominent; petiole 4-4.5 cm long, cylindric, not grooved on the upper surface, clad with hair similar to that of the young branches.

Terminal globose-umbelliform raceme of 20-30 flowers, rachis 2 cm long, tomentose; pedicels 1.5-2 cm long, tomentose; calyx small, tomentose, divided into 8-9 broad triangular teeth; corolla tubular-campanulate, 5 cm long, rose, dark-spotted at the base and dark-dotted upward, lobes 8, emarginate; stamens 16, filaments minutely hairy at the base; ovary 9-10-loculed, clad with caespitose gray hairs, style glabrous.

Capsule to 4 cm long, 1 cm thick, slightly curved, densely hairy, the hairs coarse, brown, and detersile.

Distributed in northeast Yunnan, southwest Sichuan. Grows in forests.

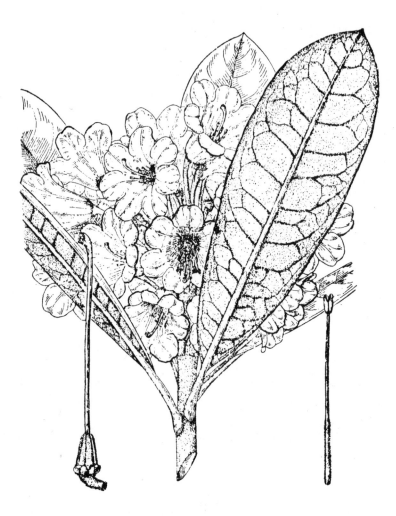

4212　革叶杜鹃

RHODODENDRON CORIACEUM

Franch.

gé yè dùjuān   *"leather-leaf rhododendron"*

Evergreen shrub or small tree to 8 meters high; shoots stout, silvery gray-tomentose, old branches subglabrous.

Leaves scattered, coriaceous, oblanceolate, 10-18 cm long, 3-6 cm broad, apex rounded and mucronate, base cuneate, upper surface smooth and glossy, lower surface clad with dense spongy 2-layered indumentum, silver-gray gradually becoming gray-brown, the upper layer more or less detersile and composed of shallowly bowl-shaped hairs; petiole 3-4.5 cm long, hairy at first.

Terminal large inflorescence of 15-20 flowers, a lax globose raceme to 17 cm in diameter, rachis 1-1.5 cm long, with ferrugineous hairs; pedicels to 4 cm long, similarly hairy; calyx small, with 7 small teeth, pubescent; corolla funnelform-campanulate, 3.5 cm long, white tinged rose with dark red basal spots, lobes 5-7, 1.5 cm long, emarginate; stamens 10-14, filaments minutely hairy on the lower part; ovary densely floccose, the hairs light yellow.

Capsule cylindric, 2 cm long, with coarse ferrugineous hairs.

Distributed in Yunnan, southeast Xizang. Grows in thickets.

4213 乳黄叶杜鹃

RHODODENDRON GALACTINUM
Balf. f.

rŭ huáng yè dùjuān   *"milky-yellow leaf rhododendron"*

Evergreen large shrub or small tree to 8 meters high; shoots long and straight, gray-tomentose at first.

Leaves large, thick-coriaceous, to 22 cm long, 7 cm broad, oblong-ovate to elliptic-lanceolate, apex obtuse and mucronate, base rounded, often asymmetric, upper surface light-gray-tomentose when young, glabrous at maturity, lower surface clad with dense 2-layered persistent pale yellow indumentum, the hairs of the upper layer funnelform and fine-stalked, the hairs of the lower layer lotus-flowerlike and nearly sessile; petiole 3.5 cm long, upper surface slightly grooved, ultimately glabrous.

Terminal racemose-umbelliform inflorescence of 15 flowers; pedicels to 2.5 cm long, hairy; calyx a shallow cup with 7 triangular teeth; corolla campanulate, to 3 cm long, green or light rose with dark red irregular basal spots, 7-lobed; stamens 14, filaments hairy at the base; ovary and style glabrous.

Capsule cylindric, slightly curved, 2.5-3.5 cm long, glabrous.

West Sichuan. Grows in forests.

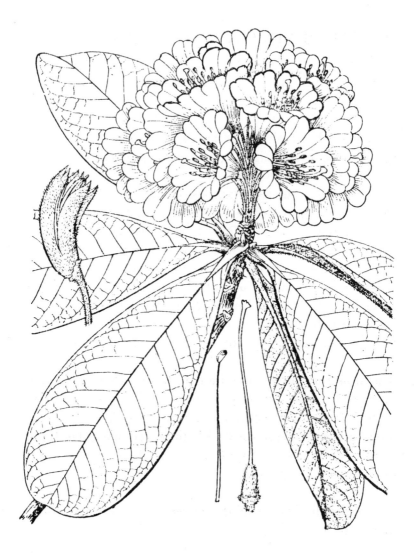

4214 大叶杜鹃

RHODODENDRON BASILICUM
Balf. f. et W. W. Sm.

dà yè dùjuān *"great-leaved rhododendron"*

Evergreen small tree to 10 meters high, shoots red-brown-tomentose.

Leaves thick-coriaceous, broadly obovate to broadly oblanceolate, 13-30 cm long, 8-17 cm broad above the middle, apex broadly rounded, slightly retuse, base cuneate, upper surface glabrous, lower surface clad with thick cinnamon to gray-brown indumentum, slightly spongy and two-layered, the hairs of the upper layer cupular, the lower layer a grayish skin-color; petiole 2-3 cm long, flat and broad, upper surface flat and smooth, both sides narrowly winged or ridged.

Terminal large corymbose raceme of about 20 flowers, rachis 3.5 cm long; pedicels about 3 cm long, tomentose; calyx small, with small triangular teeth; corolla broadly campanulate, 3.5 cm long, fleshy, light yellow or tinged dark red with dark red basal spots, lobes 8, deeply emarginate; stamens 16; ovary clad with dense caespitose hairs.

Capsule 4 cm long, 1 cm thick, straight or slightly curved, clad with dense red-brown hairs.

Northwest Yunnan. Grows in rhododendron forests at 3200 meters.

4215　大树杜鹃

RHODODENDRON GIGANTEUM

Forrest et Tagg

dà shù dùjuān   *"big tree rhododendron"*

Evergreen large tree to 25 meters high; trunk thick and straight, shoots clad with a thin layer of gray-white felted hairs.

Leaves large, 12-37 cm long, 4-12 cm broad, elliptic or oblanceolate, obtuse at the apex, tapering toward the base, base slightly auriculate, upper surface light yellow on the midrib and lateral veins, lower surface pale-yellow-floccose, midrib very prominent; petiole 2-5.4 cm long, upper surface slightly grooved.

Terminal racemose-umbelliform inflorescence of 20-25 flowers, to 16 cm high and 20 cm in diameter; pedicels 1.5-3 cm long, hairy; calyx degenerate, a shallowly lobed irregular disc with 8 small triangular teeth, densely woolly; corolla campanulate, to 7 cm long, bright rose tinged purple, the color deepest on the lobes and corolla-tube interior, lobes 8; stamens 16, extremely variable in length, glabrous; ovary densely tomentose, style glabrous.

Capsule oblong, 4 cm long, 1.5 cm thick, slightly curved, clad with ferrugineous hairs.

West Yunnan. Grows in open forests at 2800 meters.

Found in the same area is *R. protistum* Balf. f. et Forrest (qiáo shǒu dùjuān, "raise-one's-head rhododendron"), in which the lower surface of the leaves is glabrous or very thinly clad with gray-white hairs.

427

4216 巨魁杜鹃

RHODODENDRON GRANDE
Wight

jù kuí dùjuān   *"giant rhododendron"*

Evergreen tree about 10 meters high; shoots as thick as a finger.

Leaves coriaceous, oblong-lanceolate to oblanceolate, 14-30 cm long, 8-13 cm broad, apex bluntly acute or sharply acute, base broadly cuneate, upper surface glossy green, lower surface clad with a thin layer of silvery-white indumentum composed of agglutinate hairs, midrib and lateral veins conspicuously prominent; petiole 4-5 cm long, cylindric, sparsely white-hairy, upper surface slightly grooved.

Terminal large globose corymb of 20-25 flowers, rachis 4-5 cm long; pedicels 2-3 cm long, glandular; calyx small, 1-2 mm long, with 8 undulate teeth; corolla ventricose-campanulate, 5-7 cm long, white or milk white (light rose when in bud), lobes 8, deeply emarginate; stamens 16, filaments white, hairy at the base; ovary densely glandular or glandular-tomentose, 16-loculed.

Capsule large, 4.5 cm long, 1.4 cm thick, scabrous.

South Xizang; also Sikkim, Bhutan. Forms forests.

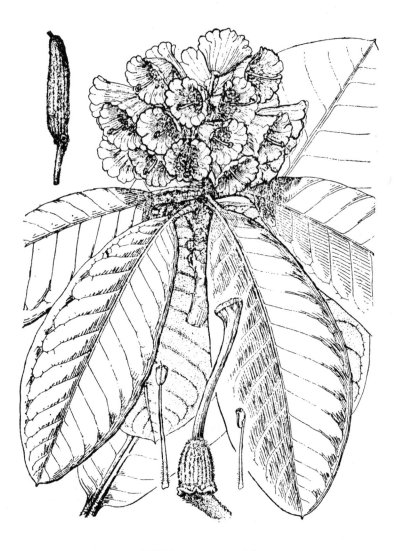

4217　凸尖杜鹃

RHODODENDRON SINOGRANDE
Balf. f. et W. W. Sm.

tú jiān dùjuān   *"mucronate rhododendron"*

Evergreen tree, 6-10 meters high; shoots 1.5-2 cm thick, thinly gray-tomentose.

Leaves very large, stiff-coriaceous, oblong-oblanceolate or oblong-elliptic, 20-70 cm long, 8-25 cm broad, apex rounded and stiffly mucronate, base rounded, upper surface smooth and glossy, rugose, lower surface silver-gray or light yellow, lustrous, clad with compact skinlike indumentum composed of two different layers of stellate hairs, midrib strongly prominent on the lower surface, about 1.3 cm thick at the base, glabrous; petiole 3-5 cm long, 1.5 cm thick, upper surface quite flat and smooth.

Terminal umbelliform raceme of about 20 flowers, to 20 cm in diameter, rachis thick, 3-6 cm long; pedicels thick, 3-4 cm long, densely light-yellow-tomentose; calyx crooked, short, woolly, only a rim with 6-10 undulate fine teeth; corolla pendulous, broadly campanulate, fleshy, milk white with dark red basal spots, lobes 8-10, broadly emarginate; stamens 18-20, filaments hairy on the lower part; ovary woolly.

Capsule 3 cm long, hairy.

Distributed in Yunnan, southeast Xizang. Grows in rhododendron forests at 3200-4000 meters.

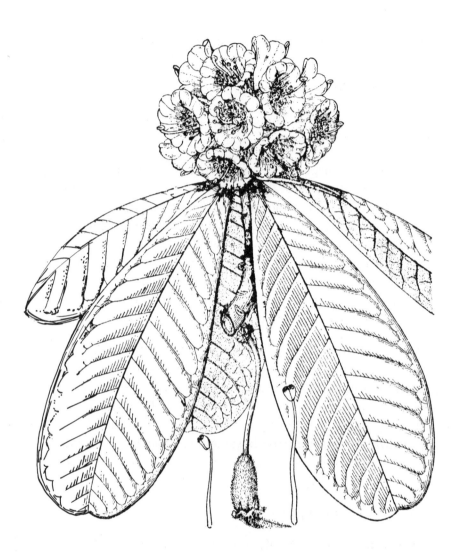

4218 优秀杜鹃

RHODODENDRON PRAESTANS
Balf. f. et W. W. Sm.

yōu xiù dùjuān   *"outstanding rhododendron"*

Evergreen shrub to small tree, 7-10 meters high.

Leaves subsessile, thick-coriaceous, oblong-oblanceolate to oblong-obovate, 18-38 cm long, 7-14 cm broad, broadest near the apex and tapering downward, the apex rounded and sometimes emarginate, base cuneate with broad wings decurrent onto the petiole, upper surface smooth and glabrous, lower surface gray-white to gray-brown, with one thin layer of skinlike or somewhat scurfy indumentum composed of stellate hairs, midrib strongly prominent, glabrous; petiole short, both sides broadly winged, upper surface nearly flat and smooth.

Terminal racemose-umbelliform inflorescence of about 15 flowers, rachis 3-4 cm long, slightly tomentose; pedicels 3 cm long, tomentose; calyx small, with 8 short teeth; corolla oblique-campanulate, 3.5-4.5 cm long, carmine, 8-lobed; stamens as many as 16, glabrous; ovary yellow-tomentose, locules 8-12.

Capsule 3 cm long, slightly curved, tomentose.

Northwest Yunnan. Grows in forests.

From the same area, *Rhododendron coryphaeum* Balf. f. et Forrest (kuí dǒu dùjuān, ''Big Dipper rhododendron'') is differentiated mainly by its milk white flowers.

433

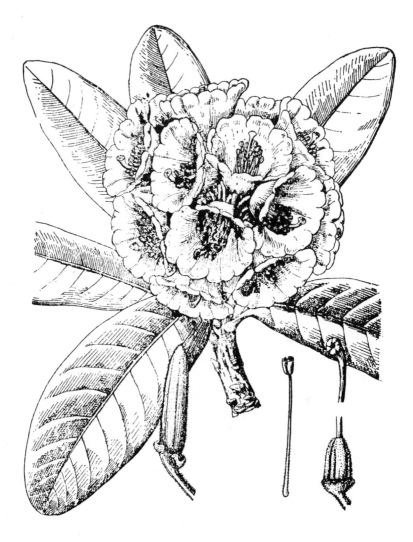

4219　圆头杜鹃

RHODODENDRON SEMNOIDES
Hutch.

yuán tóu dùjuān *"round-headed rhododendron"*

Evergreen small tree, 5-6 meters high; twigs stout, pubescent, the hairs short and gray.

Leaves sessile, coriaceous, in terminal pseudoverticillate clusters, narrowly long obovate, 10-25 cm long, 4-11 cm broad, rounded at the apex, tapering toward the base, with narrow wings decurrent onto the upper part of the thick petiole, upper surface soon glabrous, lower surface clad with a thin layer of brown felted detersile indumentum, net veins obscure.

Terminal short raceme of 15-20 flowers, densely globose, 12 cm in diameter, rachis pubescent; pedicels 3 cm long, similarly pubescent; calyx crooked, only an undulate rim; corolla broadly campanulate, 3 cm long, milk white, dark red at the base with one darker spot, lobes 8, broadly emarginate; stamens 16, shorter than the corolla, filaments slightly pubescent; ovary densely hairy, style thick, glabrous.

Capsule to 3.5 cm long, 8 mm thick, with dense ferruginous hairs.

Distributed in southeast Xizang, northwest Yunnan. Grows in forests.

435

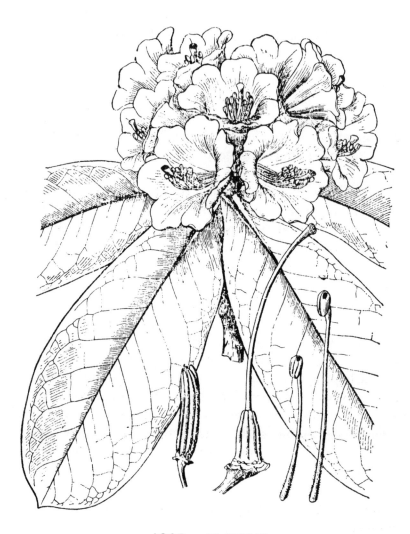

4220　无柄杜鹃

RHODODENDRON WATSONII
Hemsl. et Wils.

wú bǐng dùjuān   *"sessile rhododendron"*

Evergreen shrub to 3.5 meters high; branches bent, shoots stout, slightly gray-brown-tomentose.

Leaves subsessile, coriaceous, obovate or oblong-elliptic or broadly oblanceolate, 15-25 cm long, 5-10 cm broad, acute at the apex, tapering downward, base more or less rounded with broad wings decurrent onto the short petiole, upper surface glabrous, midrib impressed and resembling a pale green thread, lower surface clad with a thin layer of silvery-white or light-brownish skinlike indumentum, midrib prominent, midrib and lateral veins hairy.

Terminal lax umbelliform inflorescence of about 15 flowers, rachis to 3 cm long, gray-white-sericeous; pedicels to 3 cm long, thinly tomentose; calyx crooked, short, with 7 teeth; corolla campanulate, to 3.5 cm long, white, slightly red-tinged and dark red spotted at the base, 7-lobed; stamens 14, filaments minutely hairy on the lower part; ovary glabrous, 7-loculed, style glabrous.

Capsule to 2.5 cm long, 4 mm thick, cylindric, slightly curved, smooth and glossy.

West Sichuan. Grows at about 3000 meters, forming forests.

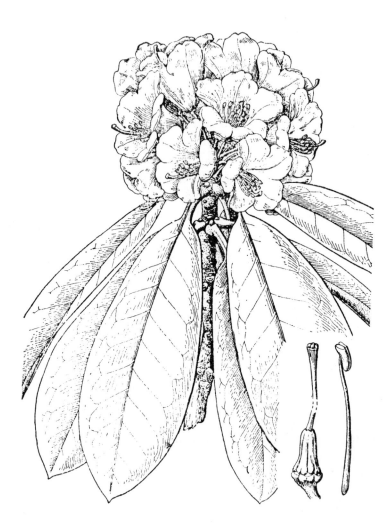

4221　镰果杜鹃

RHODODENDRON FULVUM
Balf. f. et W. W. Sm.

lián guǒ dùjuān *"sickle-capsule rhododendron"*

Evergreen small tree to 8 meters high, branching from the base; shoots tomentose, the hairs rusty-yellow or gray.

Leaves coriaceous, obovate to narrowly oblong-oblance-olate, 10-16 cm long, 4-6 cm broad, bluntly acute at the apex, narrowing toward the rounded base, upper surface glabrous, lower surface clad with light brown to dark cinnamon suedelike indumentum, finely granular on the surface, composed of long-stalked stellate hairs; petiole 1.5-2.5 cm long, granular-tomentose.

Terminal lax globose-umbelliform inflorescence of about 20 flowers, rachis about 1 cm long, slightly floccose; pedicels 1.5-2 cm long, sparsely pubescent; calyx small, with 5 short teeth, glabrous; corolla funnelform-campanulate, to 5 cm long, pink, exterior tinged dark red, interior dark red spotted at the base, lobes 5, emarginate; stamens 10, glabrous; ovary 8-loculed, glabrous.

Capsule 4 cm long, cylindric, falcate at maturity.

Distributed in Yunnan, Xizang; also Burma. Grows at forest margins.

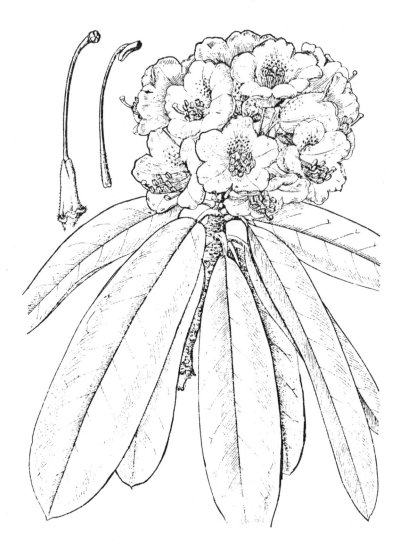

4222　紫玉盘杜鹃

RHODODENDRON UVARIFOLIUM
Diels

zǐ yù pán dùjuān   *"Uvaria rhododendron"*

Evergreen small tree to 8 meters high; shoots stout, soon glabrous.

Leaves coriaceous, oblong or oblong-elliptic, 10-20 cm long, 3.6-6 cm broad, apex obtuse and mucronate, base obtuse, upper surface glabrous, lower surface clad with a thin detersile layer of white arachnoid felted hairs, lateral veins gradually obscured beneath the indumentum toward the outside; petiole 1-1.5 cm long, subglabrous when old.

Terminal subglobose inflorescence of 15-18 flowers, rachis about 1 cm long, more or less floccose; pedicels 2 cm long, more or less floccose; calyx small, about 1 mm long, with 5 shallow undulate lobes, subglabrous; corolla campanulate, 3.5 cm long, white tinged pink with dark red spots at the base and streaks on the lower part; lobes 5, emarginate; stamens 10, filaments hairy at the base; ovary sparsely pubescent, style glabrous.

Capsule curved, 4-5 cm long, 4 mm thick, slender, glabrous, locules 5-6.

Distributed in northwest Yunnan, southeast Xizang. Grows in pine forests.

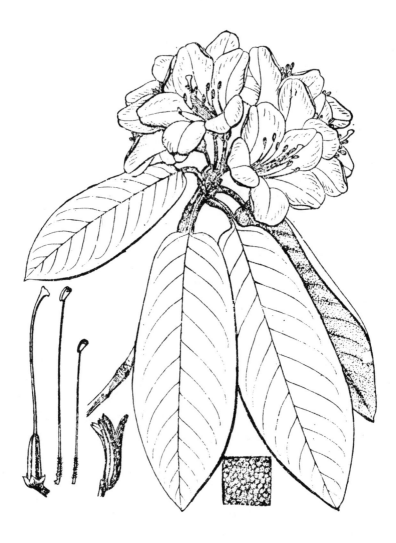

4223　簇毛杜鹃

RHODODENDRON WALLICHII
Hook. f.

cù máo dùjuān   *"clustered-hair rhododendron"*

Evergreen shrub, 2-4 meters high; shoots glabrous.

Leaves coriaceous, elliptic, 7-10 cm long, 2.5-5 cm broad, apex bluntly acute, mucronate, base cordate, margin revolute, upper surface ultimately glabrous, lower surface clad with scattered tufts of powdery ferrugineous hairs, not forming a continuous unbroken indumentum, more or less detersile; petiole 1-1.5 cm long, glabrous, often reddish.

Terminal raceme of 6-12 flowers, rachis 2 cm long, glabrous; pedicels 1.5-2.5 cm long, glabrous or slightly floccose; calyx small, with 5 small triangular lobes, glabrous or floccose; corolla broadly campanulate, 4-5 cm long, lilac-purple, more or less dark rose dotted, lobes 5, emarginate; stamens 10, filaments white, minutely hairy at the base; ovary glabrous, style white, glabrous.

Capsule 1.5 cm long, cylindric, slightly curved, smooth and glossy.

South Xizang; also Sikkim. Grows in thickets at 3300 meters.

4224 钟花杜鹃

RHODODENDRON CAMPANULATUM

D. Don

zhōng huā dùjuān   *"bell-flowered rhododendron"*

Evergreen shrub, 3-6 meters high; shoots green, glabrous.

Leaves coriaceous, broadly elliptic or broadly ovate, 7-15 cm long, 3-6 cm broad, apex obtuse and mucronate, base rounded or slightly cordate, upper surface glabrous, lower surface clad with thin light-yellow or rusty-brown or yellow-brown felted indumentum; petiole 1.5-2 cm long, tomentose at first.

Terminal racemose-umbelliform inflorescence of about 8 flowers, rachis 2-2.5 cm long, glabrous or with a few minute hairs; pedicels 2-2.5 cm long, glabrous; calyx small, with 5 small triangular lobes, glabrous; corolla broadly campanulate, about 4 cm long, white or rose-tinged, upper interior more or less purple dotted, lobes 5, emarginate; stamens 10, filaments minutely hairy at the base; ovary and style glabrous.

Capsule 3 cm long, cylindric, slightly curved, smooth and glossy.

South Xizang; also Bhutan, Sikkim, Nepal. Grows in open forests on mountain slopes at 3400 meters.

445

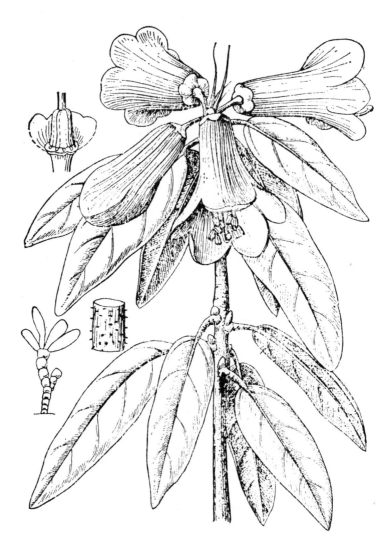

4225　红钟杜鹃

RHODODENDRON SHERRIFFII
Cowan

hóng zhōng dùjuān   *"red bell rhododendron"*

Evergreen shrub or small tree, 2-7 meters high; twigs spreading and strong, shoots sparsely setose, the hairs short, black, and detersile.

Leaves coriaceous, oblong, 5-6.5 cm long, 2.3-3.2 cm broad, apex subacute to bluntly acute, base rounded or subcordate, upper surface glabrous, lower surface (except the midrib) clad with thick brown floccose indumentum composed of stellate hairs at the tips of long multicellular stalks, the stellate hairs short, thick, and obtuse; petiole 1-1.6 cm long, lower surface sparsely black-setose.

Terminal umbelliform inflorescence of 3-4 flowers; pedicels about 1.5 cm long; calyx dark red, unequally 5-lobed, cuplike, about 4 mm long; corolla tubular-campanulate, 4.5 cm long, about 4 cm in diameter, somewhat fleshy, dark red, lobes 5, slightly reflexed, rounded, slightly retuse; stamens 10, filaments glabrous, pink; ovary smooth and glossy, style glabrous overall.

Capsule straight, 1.3 cm long, 7 mm thick, enclosed within the persistent calyx.

Southeast Xizang. Grows on steep slopes at 3800 meters.

4226　大理杜鹃

RHODODENDRON TALIENSE
Franch.

dà lǐ dùjuān   *"Dali rhododendron"*

Evergreen shrub, 1.5-2.5 meters high, sparsely branched; twigs stout, woolly-tomentose when young, later subglabrous.

Leaves oblong-ovate, 4-10 cm long, 2-3.5 cm broad, apex short acute, base rounded to slightly cordate, margin often more or less revolute, upper surface rugose, glabrous, lower surface clad with yellow or light yellow felted indumentum, the surface loose and soft, not agglutinate and without a pellicle, lateral veins concealed beneath the indumentum; petiole 1-1.5 cm long, with felted indumentum.

Terminal compact umbelliform inflorescence of 10-15 flowers, rachis about 1 cm long, pubescent; pedicels 1.5-2 cm long, densely tomentose; calyx small, 2-3 mm long, with 5 triangular lobes; corolla funnelform-campanulate, 3.5 cm long, cream to milk white tinged rose, dark red spotted, lobes 5, undulate; stamens 10, filaments hairy on the lower third; ovary hairy, style glabrous, slightly longer than corolla tube, not exserted.

Capsule 1.5 cm long, narrowly oblong.

West and northwest Yunnan. Grows in fir forests.

449

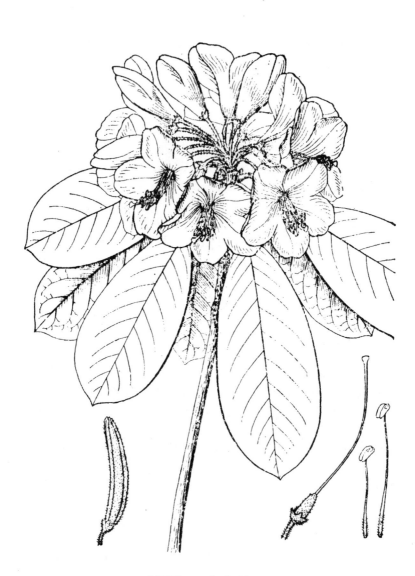

4227　太白杜鹃

RHODODENDRON PURDOMII
Rehd. et Wils.

tài bái dùjuān   *"Taibai rhododendron"*

Evergreen shrub to 3 meters high; twigs stout, shoots somewhat minutely hairy.

Leaves coriaceous, oblong-lanceolate to oblong-elliptic, 6-8 cm long, 2.5-3.5 cm broad, apex acute or obtuse, base cuneate, margin recurved, upper surface smooth and glossy, finely rugose, glabrous, midrib impressed, lateral veins slightly impressed, lower surface light green, glabrous, net veins evident, lateral veins slightly visible; petiole thick, 1-1.5 cm long, minutely hairy at first, later glabrous.

Terminal racemose-umbelliform inflorescence with as many as 16 flowers, rachis about 1 cm long, red-tomentose; pedicels 1-1.6 cm long, densely gray-white-tomentose; calyx small, cuplike, shallowly 5-lobed, sparsely pubescent; corolla campanulate, 2.5-3 cm long, white, lobes 5, rounded; stamens 10, filaments short-hairy at the base; ovary sparsely white-tomentose, style glabrous.

Capsule 1.5 cm long, cylindric, smooth and glossy.

Distributed in Gansu, Shaanxi (Taibai Shan), Henan. Grows in forests.

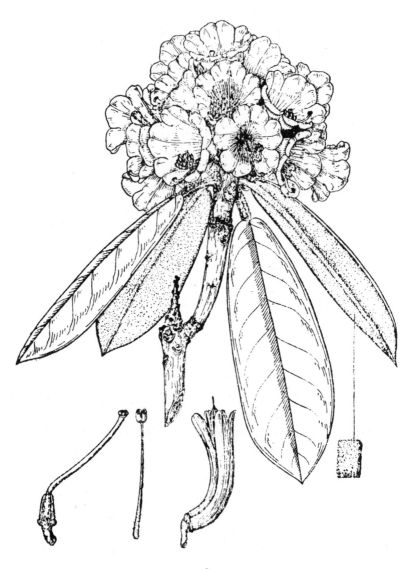

4228　白毛杜鹃

RHODODENDRON VELLEREUM
Hutch. et Tagg

bái máo dùjuān   *"white-haired rhododendron"*

Evergreen shrub, 2-5 meters high; twigs stout, thinly clad at first with floccose hairs which quickly disappear.

Leaves thick-coriaceous, oblong-elliptic to oblong-lanceolate, 6-11 cm long, 2-4.5 cm broad, apex acute or obtuse, base rounded, often slightly cordate, upper surface smooth and glossy, finely rugose, lower surface clad with smooth silvery-white to gray-yellow thick spongy indumentum, the surface a single-layered pellicle tending to crack with age, midrib more or less similarly hairy, lateral veins concealed beneath the indumentum; petiole 1.5-2 cm long, upper surface grooved and white-floccose, lower surface subglabrous.

Terminal short umbelliform raceme of 15-20 flowers, rachis about 1 cm long; pedicels red, 1.5-2 cm long, glabrous; calyx small, about 1 mm long, shallowly 5-lobed to form an undulate rim, slightly short-floccose; corolla funnelform-campanulate, 3.5 cm long, white tinged rose with purple or dark red dots, 5-lobed; stamens 10, filaments sparsely hairy on the lower part; pistil glabrous.

Capsule cylindric, to 3 cm long, curved.

Southeast Xizang. Grows in forests at 3000 meters.

4229 麻点杜鹃

RHODODENDRON CLEMENTINAE
Forrest

má diǎn dùjuān   *"pockmarked rhododendron"*

Evergreen shrub to 3 meters high; shoots glabrous, somewhat white-powdery.

Leaves coriaceous, broadly elliptic or oblong-elliptic, 10-15 cm long, 4-8 cm broad, apex obtuse and mucronate, base most often auriculate-cordate, lower surface clad with dense cinnamon skinlike felted indumentum, midrib prominent near the base on the lower surface and subglabrous, lateral veins visible; petiole 1.5-3 cm long, glabrous, conspicuously and narrowly winged, upper surface narrowly grooved.

Short flat-globose raceme of about 15 flowers, rachis glabrous; pedicels 2.5-3 cm long, glabrous; calyx short, 7-lobed, glabrous; corolla broadly campanulate, about 5 cm long, deep pink with many small dark red dots, glabrous, lobes (6)-7; stamens 14-15, filaments short-hairy on the lower part; ovary 6-8-loculed, glabrous, style glabrous, brick red.

Capsule narrowly elliptic, 2 cm long, black.

Distributed in Yunnan, Sichuan. Grows in open thickets.

455

4230　皱皮杜鹃

RHODODENDRON WILTONII
Hemsl. et Wils.

zhòu pí dùjuān *"wrinkled skin rhododendron"*

Evergreen shrub, 2-3 meters high; shoots stout, yellow-gray-hairy, old branches glabrous.

Leaves thick-coriaceous, obovate-oblong or oblanceolate, 5-9 cm long, 2-3.5 cm broad, apex acute, base cuneate, margin recurved, upper surface coarsely bullate-rugose with deeply impressed veins, light yellow-hairy and glandular when young, glabrous in the second year, lower surface clad with thick light brown indumentum composed of stellate hairs, veins prominent; petiole 1.5-2 cm long, similarly hairy when young.

Terminal racemose-umbelliform inflorescence of 8-10 flowers, rachis 8 mm long, with light yellow hairs; pedicels 1.5-2 cm long, similarly hairy; calyx small, 2 mm long, similarly hairy, 5-lobed; corolla funnelform-campanulate, 2.5-3 cm long, white or pale flesh red, red spotted within; stamens 10, filaments sparsely hairy at the base; ovary clad with dense light brown hairs.

Capsule cylindric, 1.5-2 cm long, slightly curved, clad with dense gland-tipped hairs.

West Sichuan. Grows in thickets at about 3000 meters.

4231　麻叶杜鹃

RHODODENDRON COELONEURUM
Diels

má yè dùjuān   *"pocked leaf rhododendron"*

Evergreen shrub or small tree about 4 meters high; twigs slender, shoots densely red-brown-tomentose.

Leaves coriaceous, oblanceolate to oblong-elliptic, 9-12 cm long, 2.5-3.5 cm broad above the middle, apex bluntly acute or sharply acute, base broadly cuneate, upper surface glabrous at maturity, midrib and lateral veins and net veins conspicuously and deeply impressed, lower surface clad with thick red-brown detersile indumentum, 2-layered, the upper layer thickly felted and composed of red-brown stellate hairs, the lower layer gray-white and composed of short-stalked semi-agglutinate floccose hairs; petiole 1.5-2 cm long, cylindric, densely tomentose.

Terminal umbelliform inflorescence of 4-8 flowers, rachis very short, tomentose; pedicels about 1 cm long, densely brown-tomentose; calyx short, similarly hairy, shallowly 5-lobed; corolla funnelform, 3.5-4 cm long, pink, 5-lobed; stamens 10; ovary densely tomentose.

Capsule to 2.5 cm long, cylindric, hairy.

Southeast Sichuan (Jinfo Shan). Grows in mixed forests.

4232　异色杜鹃

RHODODENDRON WASONII

Hemsl. et Wils.

yì sè dùjuān   *"unusually colored rhododendron"*

Evergreen shrub, 1-2 meters high; branches soon sub-glabrous.

Leaves coriaceous, ovate-lanceolate to ovate or ovate-elliptic, 5-7.5 cm long, 2.3-4 cm broad, apex acute, base rounded, upper surface smooth and glossy, lower surface clad more or less with dense rust-brown woolly indumentum composed of stellate hairs; petiole thick, 5-11 mm long, upper surface grooved, more or less short-tomentose when young.

Terminal short corymbose raceme of 6-8 flowers, rachis 5-7 mm long, more or less villous or glabrous; pedicels suberect, 1.5-2.5 cm long, long-tomentose; calyx extremely small, with 5 small triangular lobes, short-hairy; corolla broadly campanulate, 3-3.5 cm long, white or cream or lemon yellow, rose-tinged and dark red dotted on the upper part, lobes 5, somewhat spreading, imbricate; stamens 10, filaments clad with extremely short hairs on the lower half; ovary densely villous, style glabrous.

Capsule to 1.9 cm long, cylindric, hairy.

West Sichuan. Grows in forests at about 3000 meters.

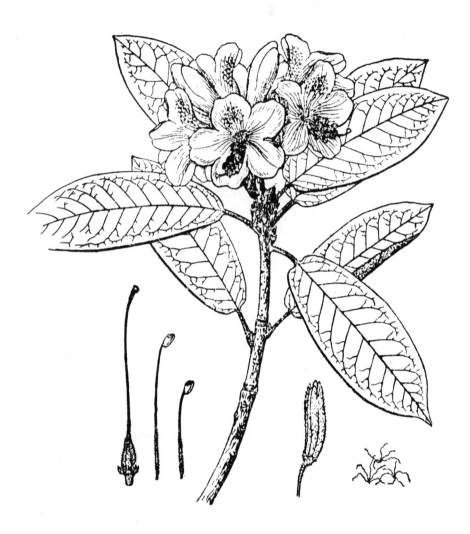

4233　黄毛杜鹃

RHODODENDRON RUFUM
Batal.

huáng máo dùjuān   *"yellow-haired rhododendron"*

Evergreen shrub or small tree to 7 meters high; shoots stout, white-floccose when young, soon glabrous.

Leaves coriaceous, elliptic or oblong-ovate, 7-11 cm long, 3-4.5 cm broad, apex obtuse or subacute, base obtuse or nearly rounded, upper surface glabrous at maturity, lower surface clad with thick loose rusty-yellow or yellow-brown indumentum, the prominent midrib similarly clad, lateral veins concealed by the indumentum; petiole thick, 1.5-2 cm long, thinly red-gray-floccose or sub-glabrous.

Terminal racemose-umbelliform inflorescence of 6-10 flowers, rachis about 6 mm long, pedicels 1.5 cm long, densely floccose, the hairs red or gray; calyx small, about 1 mm long, with 5 broad teeth, exterior similarly hairy; corolla funnelform-campanulate, 2.5-3 cm long, white or pinkish purple with dark red dots, lobes 5, of unequal size; stamens 10, filaments sparsely hairy at the base; ovary densely gray-brown-woolly, style more or less hairy at the base.

Capsule 2.5 cm long.

Distributed in Qinghai, Gansu, north Sichuan. Grows in forests.

463

4234 腺房杜鹃

RHODODENDRON ADENOGYNUM
Diels

xiàn fáng dùjuān   *"glandular calyx rhododendron"*

Evergreen shrub to 2.5 meters high; shoots stout, glabrous.

Leaves thick-coriaceous, lanceolate to oblong-lanceolate, 6-9 cm long, 2-4 cm broad, apex acuminate or acute, base rounded, slightly cordate, upper surface glabrous at maturity, finely rugose, lower surface densely clad with thick cinnamon or yellow-brown woolly indumentum, also clad with a layer of minute glands, midrib impressed on the upper surface, prominent on the lower surface; petiole to 2 cm long, tomentose and glandular.

Terminal compact racemose-umbelliform inflorescence of 5-10 fragrant flowers, rachis about 1 cm long; pedicels about 2 cm long, tomentose and glandular throughout; calyx large, about 1.5 cm long, deeply 5-lobed almost to the base, lobes glandular throughout the dorsal surface and at the margin; corolla broadly funnelform, 4 cm long, light rose to white with dark red dots; stamens 10, filaments densely glandular on the lower half; ovary green, similarly glandular.

Capsule 2 cm long, 7 mm thick, straight, clad with remnants of the glands.

Distributed in Yunnan, southwest Sichuan. Grows on forest-margin grasslands.

465

4235　落毛杜鹃

RHODODENDRON DETONSUM

Balf. f. et Forrest

luò máo dùjuān   *"dropped-hair rhododendron"*

Evergreen shrub about 4 meters high; twigs quite stout, glabrous.

Leaves scattered, thick-coriaceous, oblong-elliptic, 10-14 cm long, 3-4.5 cm broad, apex acute, base rounded, upper surface glabrous, lower surface clad with a thin layer of loose light brown indumentum, somewhat detersile, net veins evident beneath the indumentum; petiole 1.5-4 cm long, glabrous.

Terminal racemose-umbelliform inflorescence, flowers as many as 11, rachis 2.6 cm long, subglabrous; pedicels to 3 cm long, stout, glandular-hairy; calyx unequally 5-lobed, lobes 2.5-4 mm long, glandular-hairy outside and at the margin; corolla funnelform-campanulate, about 4.5 cm long, pink, sparsely dark-dotted on the dorsal surface of the corolla tube, exterior glabrous, interior subglabrous, lobes 5-7, rounded, broadly emarginate; stamens 10-14, filaments clad with sparse minute hairs on the lower third; ovary papillate-glandular, style glandular on the lower third.

Northwest Yunnan. Grows in forests at 3000 meters.

4236　康定杜鹃

RHODODENDRON PRATTII
Franch.

kāng dìng dùjuān   *"Kangding rhododendron"*

Evergreen shrub about 5 meters high; twigs stout, minutely hairy, old branches glabrous.

Leaves clustered, stiff-chartaceous, elliptic to elliptic-obovate, 7-15 cm long, 4-7 cm broad, apex acute, base rounded or slightly cordate, upper surface glabrous at maturity, lower surface clad with a two-layered indumentum, the thin upper layer gray-brown, woolly, and detersile, the lower layer gray; petiole 3-4 cm long, sparsely tomentose and glandular.

Terminal racemose-umbelliform inflorescence of 12-20 flowers, rachis about 1 cm long, light yellow-hairy; pedicels 1.5-2.5 cm long, densely brown-hairy and glandular; calyx large, about 1 cm long, deeply 5-lobed, lobes oblong, with sessile glands at the margin; corolla broadly campanulate, 5-6 cm long, white with deep pink spots, corolla tube pubescent within, lobes 5; stamens 10, filaments pubescent on the lower part, ovary glandular.

Capsule cylindric, 3-4 cm long, 1.2 cm thick, densely glandular, calyx persistent.

Northwest Sichuan. Grows in thickets at 3000 meters.

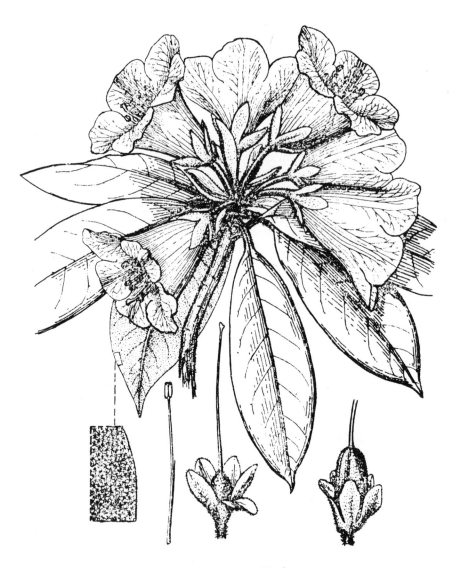

4237　金顶杜鹃

RHODODENDRON FABERI

Hemsl.

jīn dǐng dùjuān *"Jinding rhododendron"*

Evergreen shrub, 1-2 meters high; shoots densely tomentose, the hairs short and brown.

Leaves coriaceous, oblong-ovate, 7-12 cm long, 2.5-4 cm broad, apex acute with a small slightly curved sharp point, upper surface clad at first with short yellow hairs, later glabrous, lower surface clad with a 2-layered indumentum, the upper layer thick, red-brown, and mostly shed at maturity, the inner layer very thin, gray, and persistent; petiole 1-1.5 cm long, clad with short gray hairs.

Terminal racemose-umbelliform inflorescence of 6-10 flowers, rachis 5 mm long, clad with soft gray hairs and a few glandular hairs; pedicels 1.5-2 cm long, similarly hairy; calyx large, green, leaflike, 12 mm long, deeply 5-lobed, lobes glandular-hairy outside, fringed at the margin with gland-tipped hairs; corolla campanulate, 4 cm long, white; stamens 10, filaments somewhat hairy at the base, the hairs minute; ovary densely hairy, the hairs stiff and gland-tipped.

Capsule oblong, 1.5 cm long, densely glandular-hairy.

Southwest Sichuan. Grows in thickets.

From the same area, *Rhododendron faberioides* Balf. f. (nǐ jīn dǐng dùjuān, "imitation Jinding rhododendron") is very closely allied with this species, differing only in that the pedicels, calyx, and ovary are hairy and glandular-hairy.

4238　紫腺杜鹃

RHODODENDRON LEEI

Fang

zǐ xiàn dùjuān   *"purple gland rhododendron"*

Evergreen shrub, 1-2 meters high; shoots clad with minute gray hairs and sparse glands.

Leaves thick-coriaceous, oblong-elliptic, 8-14 cm long, 5.5-6.5 cm broad, apex bluntly acute, base slightly cordate, upper surface glabrous, lower surface densely yellow-brown-tomentose, midrib impressed on the upper surface, prominent on the lower surface; petiole 2 cm long, upper surface grooved, somewhat minutely hairy.

Terminal umbelliform inflorescence of 12 flowers; rachis 5 mm long, minutely hairy; pedicels 2.5-3 cm long, glandular and minutely hairy; calyx large, lobes long obovate, 1.3-1.5 cm long, glandular only at the margin; corolla funnelform-campanulate, 3.5-4 cm long, white or slightly pinkish, glabrous, lobes 5, obovate, 1.5-2 cm long; stamens 10, included, filaments minutely hairy on the lower part; ovary densely purple-glandular, style glabrous, yellow, stigma large.

Northwest Sichuan (Heishui He basin). Grows in forests.

473

4239 卷叶杜鹃

RHODODENDRON ROXIEANUM
Forrest

jŭan yĕ dùjuān   *"rolled leaf rhododendron"*

Evergreen shrub about 2 meters high; twigs short, thick, and flexuose, leaf-bud scales persistent, branches densely tomentose in the first year.

Leaves thick and stiff-coriaceous, lanceolate, 10-12 cm long, about 1.5-2 cm broad, tapering toward the tip to a stiff sharp point, base narrowly cuneate, margin markedly revolute, upper surface finely rugose and clad with fine stiff hairs, lower surface densely clad with thick rusty-yellow indumentum except on the prominent and finely glandular midrib, lateral veins obscure; petiole 1-1.5 cm long, with the leaf base decurrent along both sides of the upper part, densely rusty-yellow-tomentose.

Inflorescence compact and globose, flowers about 20, rachis short; pedicels 2-2.5 cm long, clad toward the top with sparse branching soft hairs and glands; calyx small, a degenerate undulate rim, pubescent; corolla campanulate, 4-4.5 cm long, white tinged deep pink on the lobes, with many U-shaped dark red spots on the upper corolla-tube interior, lobes 5; stamens 10; ovary sparsely hairy, the hairs clavate and glandular.

Capsule cylindric, about 4 cm long.

Distributed in Xizang, Yunnan, Sichuan. Grows on rocky cliffs.

475

4240　繁花杜鹃

RHODODENDRON FLORIBUNDUM

Franch.

fán huā dùjuān *"abundantly flowering rhododendron"*

Evergreen shrub to 5 meters high; branches pubescent in the first year.

Leaves scattered, coriaceous, oblong-oblanceolate to broadly lanceolate, 8-15 cm long, 3-5 cm broad, apex acute, with a long thornlike sharp point, base rounded or subacute, upper surface bullate, glabrous, lower surface clad with white tomentose indumentum composed of long-stalked stellate hairs; petiole 1.5-2 cm long, tomentose, the hairs concealing the narrow groove of the upper surface.

Terminal racemose-umbelliform inflorescence of 8-12 flowers; rachis 7 mm long, clad with stellate-floccose hairs; pedicels 2 cm long, white-tomentose; calyx small, lobes small, triangular, and ciliate; corolla broadly campanulate, 4 cm long, pink with dark red streaks and dense spots, glabrous, 5-lobed; stamens 10, filaments glabrous or somewhat minutely hairy on the lower part; ovary densely white-hairy, the hairs simple, silky, and appressed, style glabrous or minutely hairy at the base.

Capsule thickly cylindric, 2-3 cm long, 1 cm thick, hairy.

Distributed in Sichuan, east Yunnan. Grows in forests at about 2000 meters.

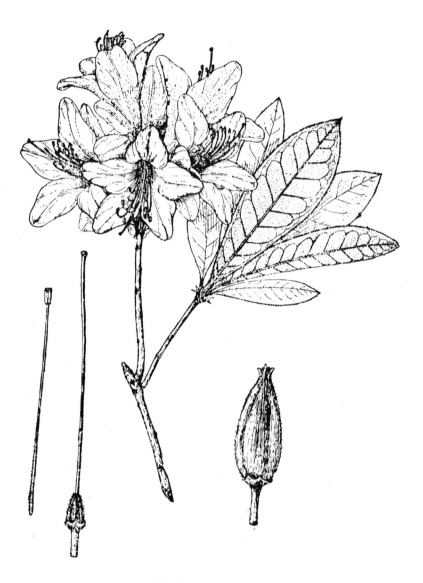

4241　羊踯躅

RHODODENDRON MOLLE
G. Don

yáng zhí zhú   *"sheep azalea"*
nào yáng huā   *"trouble-sheep flower"*
liù zhóuzi   *"six axis"*

Deciduous shrub, 0.3-1.4 meters high, sparsely branched; twigs erect, pubescent when young and often setose.

Leaves chartaceous, oblong to oblong-lanceolate, 6-12 cm long, 2.4-5 cm broad, apex obtuse and mucronate, base cuneate, margin ciliate, upper surface pubescent (at least when young), lower surface densely gray-pubescent, sometimes hairy only on the leaf veins; petiole 2-6 mm long, pubescent.

Terminal umbelliform inflorescence of many flowers (to 9), the flowers opening before the leaves or at nearly the same time; pedicels 1.2-2.5 cm long, short-pubescent, without (or with a few) bristles; calyx small, pubescent and long-ciliate, also slightly setose; corolla broadly campanulate, 5-6.2 cm in diameter, golden yellow, light green spotted on the upper part, exterior tomentose; stamens 5, the same length as the corolla, filaments villous below the middle; ovary pubescent, style glabrous.

Capsule cylindric-oblong, to 2.5 cm long, finely pubescent and sparsely setose.

Broadly distributed throughout the Chang Jiang valley provinces, south to Guangdong, Fujian. Grows in hilly areas.

Possesses an intense toxin used as a narcotic drug and pesticide.

479

4242　丁香杜鹃

RHODODENDRON FARRERAE

Tate

dīng xiāng dùjuān   *"lilac rhododendron"*

Deciduous bushy shrub, 1-2 meters high; twigs short and stiff, shoots clad at first with straight long soft appressed hairs, gradually becoming glabrous.

Leaves usually in terminal clusters of 3, subcoriaceous, ovate, 2.5-3 cm long, 1.3-2 cm broad, apex bluntly acute, base rounded, upper surface glabrous or subglabrous, lower surface conspicuously net-veined; petiole 2-3 mm long, densely pubescent.

Terminal inflorescence of 1-2 flowers which open before the leaves; pedicels 6 mm long, not longer than the bud scales, densely clad with soft red or gray hairs; calyx small, 5-lobed, pubescent; corolla rotate-funnelform, with a short narrow corolla tube and spreading undulate lobes, pale lilac-purple with purplish red dots, glabrous; stamens 8-10, shorter than the corolla, filaments glabrous; ovary densely pubescent, the hairs red-brown and appressed, style curved, glabrous.

Capsule oblong-ovoid, 1.2 cm long, densely hairy, fruit-stalk densely clad with long red-brown hairs.

Distributed in Fujian, Jiangxi, Guangdong, Guangxi.

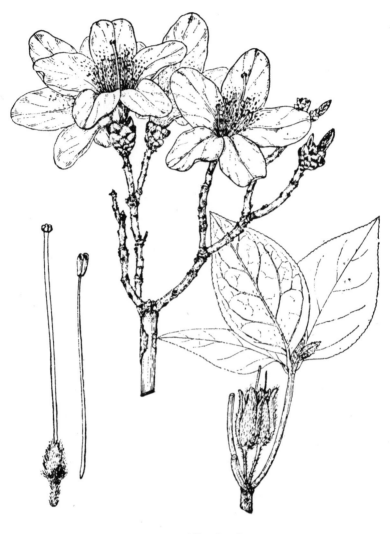

4243 满 山 红

RHODODENDRON MARIESII
Hemsl. et Wils.

mǎn shān hóng   *"whole mountain red"*

Deciduous shrub, 1-2 meters high; twigs verticillate, shoots yellow-sericeous at first, later glabrous.

Leaves 2-3 in terminal whorls, subcoriaceous or chartaceous, ovate-lanceolate, (3-)5-7 cm long, 2-3.5 cm broad, apex acute, base obtuse, margin crenulate on the upper half, upper surface sericeous when young, the hairs long and light yellow, lower surface sparsely pubescent, mature leaf subglabrous; petiole 3-8 mm long, subglabrous; bud scales broadly ovate, acute, pubescent.

Flowers terminal, usually in pairs (rarely 3), opening before the leaves; pedicels erect, 5-10 mm long, stiffhairy; calyx small, 5-lobed, clad with brown appressed hairs; corolla rotate-funnelform, purplish rose with reddish purple dots on the upper lobes, deeply 5-lobed, glabrous outside and within; stamens 10, filaments glabrous; ovary densely brown-villous, style glabrous.

Capsule about 1.2 cm long, densely villous.

Distributed throughout the lower Chang Jiang provinces, south to Fujian, Taiwan. Grows in open thickets in hilly areas.

4244　大字杜鹃

RHODODENDRON SCHLIPPENBACHII
Maxim.

dà zì dùjuān *(The flowers are similar in shape to the character* 大 *"dà".)*

Deciduous shrub, 1-3.5 meters high; twigs verticillate, shoots glandular-hairy and light brown, branches glabrous and gray in the second year.

Leaves in terminal whorls of 5, chartaceous, obovate or broadly obovate, 5-9 cm long, 3-6.5 cm broad, apex rounded, emarginate and mucronate, base cuneate, margin slightly undulate, both surfaces sparsely pubescent at first, later glabrous (major veins hairy on the lower surface), upper surface dark green, in autumn turning yellow, orange, or red; petiole 2-4 mm long, flat, setose or glandular-hairy.

Inflorescence of 3-6 flowers which open before the leaves or at the same time; pedicels 0.6-1.2 cm long, glandular-hairy; corolla broadly rotate-funnelform, 5.6-8 cm in diameter, light pink with red-brown dots on the 3 upper lobes, lobes spreading, broadly ovate; stamens 10, filaments pubescent below the middle; ovary glandular-hairy, style glandular-hairy below the middle.

Capsule oblong-ovoid, about 1.8 cm long, glandular-hairy.

Distributed in northeast China, Nei Mongol; also Korea, Japan.

4245　台北杜鵑

486

RHODODENDRON KANEHIRAI
Wils.

tái běi dùjuān   *"Taibei rhododendron"*

Subevergreen shrub to 2.5 meters high, densely branched; twigs slender, clad with flat chestnut brown appressed hairs.

Leaves dimorphic: Spring leaves linear-lanceolate, 1.8-5 cm long, 5-15 mm broad, acute and mucronate at the apex, tapering toward the base, margin inconspicuously crenulate, with lustrous brown coarse appressed hairs on the upper and lower surfaces; summer leaves linear-oblanceolate to narrowly ovate, 1.5-3.2 cm long, 2-6 mm broad, apex acute or rounded, otherwise similar to the spring leaves; petiole 1-5 mm long, with dense appressed bristles.

Flowers 1-2, terminal; pedicels erect, 3-6 mm long, densely clad with chestnut appressed hairs; calyx usually well-developed, 5-lobed, lobes erect, green, 1-5 mm long, similarly hairy; corolla narrowly funnelform, 3.2-4 cm long, carmine to dark red, lobes ovate-rounded; stamens 10, shorter than the corolla, filaments pubescent below the middle; ovary densely clad with brown coarse appressed hairs.

Capsule 6 mm long, setose.

Taiwan. Grows in hilly areas.

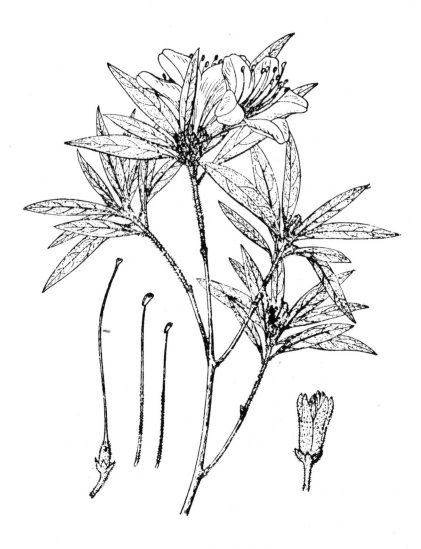

4246　海南杜鹃

RHODODENDRON HAINANENSE
Merr.

hǎi nán dùjuān   *"Hainan rhododendron"*

Semi-evergreen shrub, 2-3 meters high, many-branched; twigs erect, shoots clad with flat brown appressed hairs.

Leaves subcoriaceous, linear-lanceolate, 1.8-3.8 cm long, 3-9 mm broad, apex acute and mucronate, base cuneate, upper surface subglabrous, midrib and lateral veins impressed, lower surface pale gray-white, leaf veins prominent, with a few scattered coarse appressed hairs; petiole 3-5 mm long, compressed, clad with gray-brown appressed hairs.

Terminal inflorescence of 1-3 flowers; pedicels 5-8 mm long, densely clad with coarse appressed hairs; corolla funnelform, 3.2-3.7 cm long, red, deeply 5-lobed, lobes spreading; stamens 10, filaments minutely hairy below the middle; ovary densely clad with stiff hairs, style longer than the stamens, glabrous.

Capsule ovoid, 6 mm long, subglabrous.

Guangdong (Hainan Dao); also Vietnam. Grows in forests.

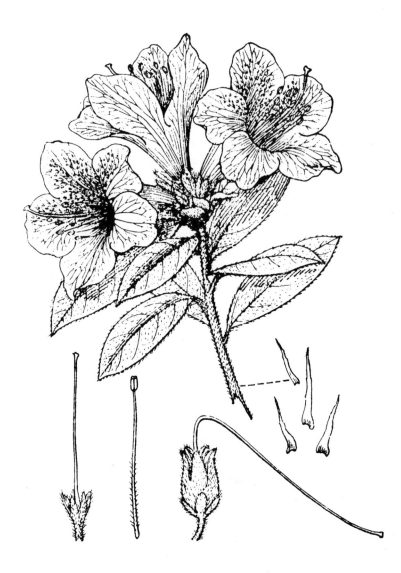

4247　杜鹃

RHODODENDRON SIMSII

Planch.

dùjuān   *"cuckoo"*, *"azalea"*, *"rhododendron"*

yìng shān hóng   *"reflect mountain red"*, *"azalea"*

Deciduous shrub about 2 meters high, many-branched; twigs fine and straight, clad with flat shining brown coarse appressed hairs.

Leaves chartaceous, ovate, elliptic-ovate, or obovate, the spring leaves relatively short, the summer leaves longer, 3-5 cm long, 2-3 cm broad, apex acute, base cuneate, upper surface sparsely clad with coarse appressed hairs, lower surface more densely hairy; petiole 3-5 mm long, densely clad with coarse appressed hairs.

Flowers 2-6 in terminal clusters; calyx 4 mm long, deeply 5-lobed, densely clad with coarse appressed hairs, ciliate; corolla broadly funnelform, 4-5 cm long, rose, bright red, or dark red, lobes 5, upper 1-3 lobes dark red spotted within; stamens 10, filaments minutely hairy below the middle; ovary densely clad with coarse appressed hairs, 10-loculed, style glabrous.

Capsule ovoid, to 8 mm long, densely clad with coarse hairs.

Broadly distributed throughout the Chang Jiang valley provinces, east to Taiwan, west to Sichuan, Yunnan. Grows in open shrubbery in hilly areas.

Among the many varieties are var. *vittatum* Wils. (zǐ bái wén dùjuān, "purple-white-line rhododendron") which has purple and white striped flowers, and var. *mesembrinum* (Balf. f. et Forrest) Rehd. (zǐ diǎn dùjuān, "purple-dot rhododendron") which has smaller purple-dotted white flowers and is found in Yunnan.

491

4248　亮毛杜鹃

RHODODENDRON MICROPHYTON
Franch.

liàng máo dùjuān   *"shining hair rhododendron"*

Evergreen erect shrub to 2 meters high, densely branched; shoots densely clad with flat red-brown appressed hairs.

Leaves scattered, coriaceous, elliptic, 0.5-3 cm long, apex acute and mucronate, base cuneate, upper surface dark green, sparsely clad with long soft appressed hairs, lower surface light green, with scattered flat red-brown appressed hairs, the hairs more numerous on both sides of the midrib; petiole 2-4 mm long, densely clad with coarse brown appressed hairs.

Terminal inflorescence of 3-6 flowers, often with smaller axillary inflorescences produced immediately below the terminal one; pedicels 3-6 mm long, clad with lustrous chestnut brown hairs; calyx well-developed, 5-lobed, lobes lanceolate, 1-4 mm long; corolla funnelform, 1.2-2 cm in diameter, rose to nearly white tinged pink, the upper three lobes dark red dotted, corolla tube cylindric, 8-10 mm long, lobes spreading; stamens 5, filaments hairy on the lower half; ovary densely hairy, style glabrous.

Capsule 4 mm long, densely clad with coarse red-brown appressed hairs, the long style persistent.

Distributed in Yunnan, southwest Sichuan. Grows in open thickets.

4249　南昆杜鹃

RHODODENDRON NAAMKWANENSE
Merr.

nán kūn dùjuān   *"Nankun rhododendron"*

Semi-evergreen shrub about 50 cm high; branchlets slender and strong, about 1 mm thick, densely clad with flat gray-brown appressed hairs; bud scales not glutinous.

Leaves coriaceous, several clustered together at the branch tips, oblong-obovate to oblong-oblanceolate, 1-2.5 cm long, 5-10 mm broad at the widest place above the middle, acute and mucronate at the apex, tapering downward, cuneate at the base, upper surface subglabrous, midrib and lateral veins impressed, lower surface sparsely clad with coarse appressed hairs, with flat brown appressed hairs on the midrib, lateral veins 3-4 pair; petiole about 2 mm long, with coarse appressed hairs similar to those of the shoots.

Terminal subumbelliform inflorescence of 2-3 flowers; calyx 5-lobed, 2-3 mm long, hairy; corolla narrowly campanulate, 2.5 cm long, rose, glabrous outside, corolla tube slightly enlarged toward the top, about 1 cm long, lobes 5, to 1.8 cm long, 9 mm broad; stamens 5, filaments glabrous; ovary densely clad with flat coarse appressed hairs, style glabrous.

Guangdong (Zengcheng Xian). Grows on shady moist rock cliffs.

495

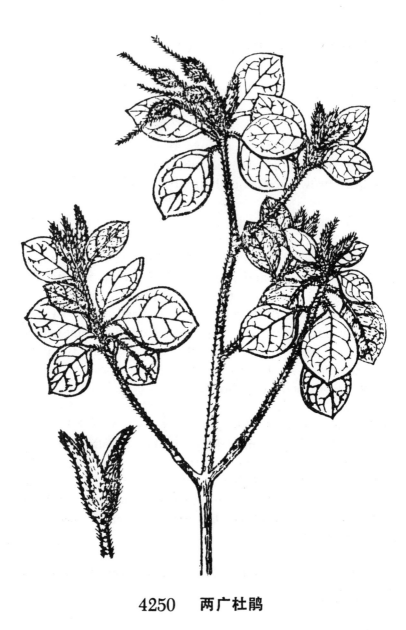

4250 两广杜鹃

RHODODENDRON TSOI
Merr.

liǎng guǎng dùjuān *"two Guang rhododendron"*
(Guangdong and Guangxi)

Semi-evergreen shrub about 1 meter high; twigs fine and strong, cylindric, glabrous, shoots slender, less than 1 mm thick, densely clad with flat chestnut brown appressed hairs.

Leaves numerous, clustered, coriaceous, obovate to broadly elliptic, 5-12 mm long, to 8 mm broad, apex obtuse or rounded, mucronate, base acute, upper surface clad with a few chestnut appressed bristles, lateral veins obscure, lower surface similarly hairy, especially on the midrib.

Terminal umbelliform inflorescence of a few (3-5) small flowers; pedicels to 4 mm long, hairy; corolla about 1 cm long, rose, corolla tube 3-4 mm long, exterior glabrous, interior sparsely and minutely hairy, lobes 5-6 mm long, oblong, rounded, slightly spreading, glabrous; stamens 5, filaments about 9 mm long, minutely hairy; ovary clad with extremely dense appressed chestnut bristles, style glabrous.

Capsule oblong-ovoid, 4 mm long.

Distributed in east Guangxi, north Guangdong. Grows on dry slopes.

4251　岭南杜鹃

498

RHODODENDRON MARIAE
Hance

lǐng nán dùjuān   *"Lingnan rhododendron"*

Evergreen shrub, 1-3 meters high, densely branched; shoots densely clad with appressed red-brown flat coarse hairs which later turn gray and persist for several years.

Leaves coriaceous, dimorphic: Spring leaves elliptic-lanceolate, 3.2-8.2 cm long, 1.8-3.2 cm broad, apex acute and stiffly mucronate, base cuneate, upper surface glossy green, subglabrous, leaf veins impressed, lower surface clad with a few scattered appressed hairs, leaf veins prominent; summer leaves elliptic to obovate, 1.2-3.2 cm long, 5-15 mm broad, apex obtuse and mucronate; petiole 4-8 mm long, densely clad with appressed coarse hairs.

Terminal umbelliform inflorescence of 7-12 flowers; pedicels 6-9 mm long, densely clad with appressed lustrous red-brown coarse hairs; calyx small, similarly hairy; corolla funnelform, 1.8 cm long, lilac-purple, corolla tube slender, about 1 cm long, lobes about 8 mm long, acute, spreading, glabrous; stamens 5, exserted, glabrous; ovary densely hairy.

Capsule 8 mm long, elliptic, densely clad with long appressed red-brown coarse hairs.

Distributed in Guangdong, Jiangxi, Hunan. Grows in thickets in hilly areas.

4252　广西杜鹃

RHODODENDRON KWANGSIENSE
Hu

guǎng xī dùjuān   *"Guangxi rhododendron"*

Subevergreen shrub about 2 meters high, many-branched; twigs slender, brown, densely brown-hairy in the first year, the hairs flat and appressed.

Leaves scattered, coriaceous, elliptic-lanceolate, 2-3.5 cm long, 1-1.5 cm broad at the middle, tapering at both ends, apex acute to short acuminate, base broadly cuneate, margin inconspicuously and sparsely crenate as well as more or less sparsely setose-ciliate, upper surface subglabrous, with sparse flat hairs along the midrib, lower surface slightly setose, the hairs long and appressed, midrib more densely hairy, the hairs similar to those of the branches; petiole 3-4 mm long, densely hairy.

Terminal umbelliform inflorescence of 4-10 flowers; pedicels about 6 mm long, with dense red-brown flat hairs; calyx small, deeply 5-lobed, similarly hairy; corolla narrowly funnelform, about 2 cm long, light purple, corolla tube elongate, 1 cm long, lobes 5, 1 cm long, acute; stamens 4, long-exserted, glabrous; ovary densely hairy, the hairs shining, red-brown, and flat, style glabrous.

Capsule about 6 mm long, densely hairy.

Distributed in Guangxi, Guangdong. Grows in open thickets in hilly areas.

4253　广东杜鹃

RHODODENDRON KWANGTUNGENSE
Merr. et Chun

guǎng dōng dùjuān   *"Guangdong rhododendron"*

Evergreen shrub to 2.5 meters high; old branches glabrous, gray, shoots fine, about 1.5 mm thick, brown, densely clad with bristles and capitate glandular hairs, the bristles to 3 mm long, spreading, the glandular hairs shorter, about 1-2 mm long.

Leaves pseudoverticillate, subcoriaceous, dimorphic, the large form 8 cm long and 2.5 cm broad, the small form 2-3 cm long and 8-14 mm broad, lanceolate to oblong-lanceolate, apex short acuminate, base acute, upper surface glabrous or setose when young, the hairs especially numerous on the midrib and lateral veins; petiole 2.5-4 mm long, setose.

Terminal umbelliform inflorescence of about 12 flowers; pedicels about 6 mm long, clad with bristles and short capitate glandular hairs; calyx small, inconspicuously divided, long-ciliate; corolla about 2 cm long, purple, corolla tube cylindric, about 1 cm long, glabrous, lobes 1-1.2 cm long, slightly spreading; stamens 5, glabrous; ovary densely long-setose, style glabrous, exserted.

Capsule oblong, 9 mm long, setose.

Distributed in Guangdong, Guangxi, Hunan. Grows in thickets.

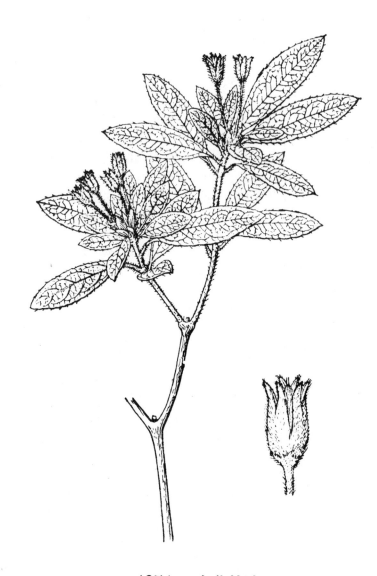

4254　金萼杜鹃

RHODODENDRON CHRYSOCALYX
Lévl. et Vant.

jīn è dùjuān   *"golden calyx rhododendron"*

Deciduous or semi-evergreen shrub about 2 meters high, densely branched; branchlets densely hairy, the hairs coarse, flat, yellowish brown, and appressed.

Leaves chartaceous, lanceolate to oblanceolate, 1.5-4 cm long, 5-10 mm broad, acute at the apex, tapering downward, cuneate at the base, margin sparsely and shallowly crenate, ciliate when young, upper surface dark green, lustrous, glabrous except for a few coarse flat appressed hairs on the midrib, net veins conspicuously impressed, lower surface clad with a few similar hairs; petiole 3-5 mm long, similarly hairy.

Flowers 10-12, terminal; pedicels 1-1.5 cm long, densely hairy; calyx extremely short, hairy; corolla funnelform, corolla tube tubular, 8-10 mm long;* stamens 5, longer than the corolla, filaments pubescent on the lower part; pistil longer than the stamens, ovary densely hairy, the hairs coarse, lustrous, yellowish red, long, and appressed, style glabrous.

Capsule long ovoid, densely hairy.

Distributed in Guizhou, north Guangxi, west Hubei. Grows in thickets. Common.

*No corolla color given; see key.

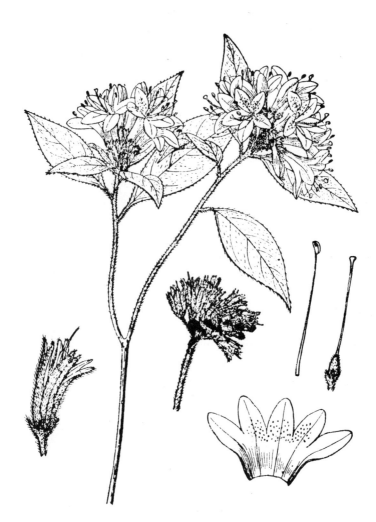

4255　毛果杜鹃

RHODODENDRON SENIAVINII
Maxim.

máo guǒ dùjuān *"hairy fruit rhododendron"*

Semi-evergreen shrub to 2 meters high, densely branched; shoots densely hairy, the hairs gray or reddish gray, flat, coarse, and appressed.

Leaves in terminal clusters, coriaceous, dimorphic: Spring leaves ovate to oblong-lanceolate, 1-6.5 cm long, 8-25 mm broad, apex acuminate and mucronate, base broadly cuneate, upper surface glabrous or subglabrous at maturity, lower surface densely hairy, the hairs red-brown, long, coarse, and appressed; summer leaves much smaller, ovate and acute or broadly long-ovate and ob-tuse; petiole 3-5 mm long, densely clad with coarse appressed hairs.

Terminal inflorescence of 3-10 flowers; pedicels 3-5 mm long, densely clad with coarse appressed hairs; calyx small, densely clad with straight flat red-brown hairs; corolla narrowly funnelform, 1.5 cm in diameter, light purple, corolla tube about 8 mm long, rose-tinged, sparsely hairy outside, lobes longer, spreading, the upper lobes purple-dotted; stamens 5, glabrous; ovary densely clad with coarse appressed hairs, style pubescent at the base.

Capsule elliptic, about 8 mm long, densely clad with coarse appressed hairs.

Distributed in Fujian, Hunan, Guizhou. Grows in hilly areas.

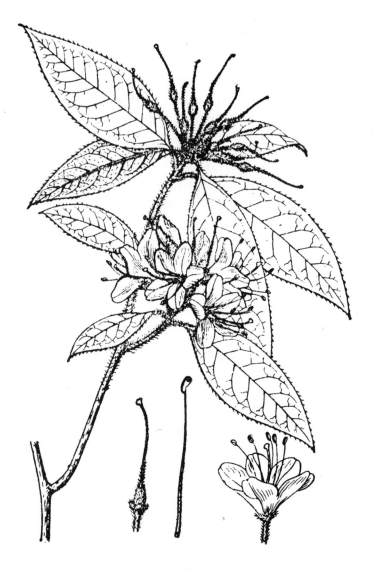

4256 乳源杜鹃

RHODODENDRON LINGII

Chun

rǔ yuán dùjuān   *"Ruyuan rhododendron"*

Semi-evergreen shrub about 2 meters high; branchlets densely clad with spreading bristles.

Leaves in terminal clusters, coriaceous, elliptic-lanceolate, 3-6 cm long, broadest at the middle, 1.3-2 cm, apex short acuminate, base obtuse, upper surface setose only on the midrib, lower surface nearly smooth and glossy, slightly short-setose; petiole about 5 mm long, clad with spreading bristles.

Terminal umbelliform inflorescence of 8-10 flowers; pedicels about 1 cm long, clad with spreading red-brown bristlelike coarse hairs; calyx small, rimlike, similarly hairy; corolla about 1.5 cm long, pink tinged purplish blue, exterior glabrous, corolla tube thick, less than 1 cm long, lobes 5, deep, ovate, and spreading; stamens 5, long-exserted, glabrous; ovary and lower half of the style densely hairy, the hairs similar to those of the pedicels, style shorter than the stamens.

North Guangdong. Grows in forest margins on rocky hills.

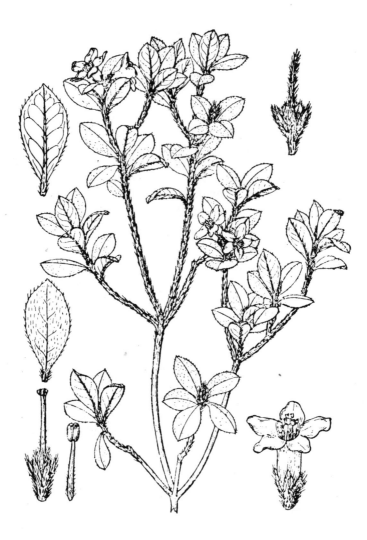

4257 小花杜鹃

RHODODENDRON MINUTIFLORUM
Hu

xiǎo huā dùjuān   *"small-flowered rhododendron"*

Evergreen shrub to 2.4 meters high, densely branched; branchlets clad with flat red-brown stiff appressed hairs.

Leaves in terminal clusters, coriaceous, oblong to obovate, 8-12 mm long, 5-6 mm broad, apex acute, base cuneate, margin recurved and crenulate, upper surface clad with coarse appressed hairs, lower surface similarly hairy only on the midrib and at the margin; petiole about 3 mm long, similarly hairy.

Terminal inflorescence of 1-3(-4) flowers which open at the same time as the leaves; pedicels 6-9 mm long, clad with coarse appressed hairs; calyx about 1.5 mm long, clad with red coarse appressed hairs, lobes conspicuously acute; corolla rotate-narrowly funnelform, about 7 mm in diameter, white, corolla tube about 3 mm long, the exterior clad with minute light red hairs, lobes as long as the corolla tube, glabrous, spreading; stamens 5, filaments minutely hairy on the lower 2/3; ovary densely clad with flat long red coarse hairs, style similarly hairy on the lower part.

Capsule 3 mm long, style elongate, densely clad with flat long coarse hairs.

Distributed in Guangxi, Guangdong, Hunan. Grows in hilly areas.

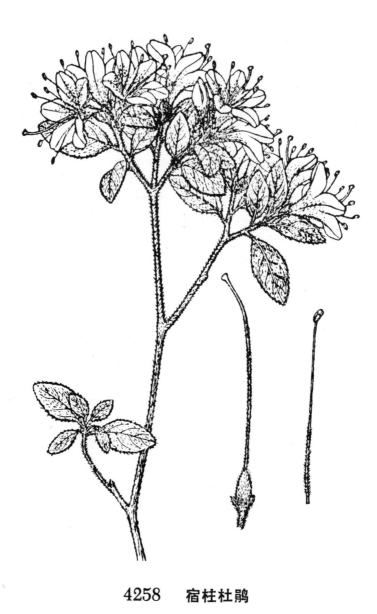

4258　宿柱杜鹃

512

RHODODENDRON CHUNII

Fang

sù zhù dùjuān *"persistent style rhododendron"*

Deciduous shrub to 6 meters high; twigs fine and dense, densely clad with flat red-brown coarse hairs.

Leaves in terminal clusters, subcoriaceous, elliptic to oblong-ovate, 10-18 mm long, 9-10 mm broad, apex bluntly acute, base short cuneate, margin recurved and denticulate, upper surface dark green, both surfaces sparsely clad with long red-brown appressed bristles, the midrib on the lower surface clad with hair similar to that of the shoots; petiole 2-3 mm long, clad with flat brown hairs.

Terminal inflorescence of 3-4 flowers; pedicels 5-7 mm long, brown-hairy and glandular; calyx extremely small, densely clad with flat brown hairs; corolla funnelform, pink tinged purple, the upper three lobes dark purple dotted, exterior brown-hairy and glandular-hairy, interior minutely hairy; stamens 5, of nearly equal length, longer than the corolla, filaments minutely hairy on the lower half; ovary densely clad with fine brown hairs, style glabrous on the upper fifth.

Capsule ovoid, finely hairy, style persistent.

North Guangdong. Grows in thickets.

4259　锦绣杜鹃

RHODODENDRON PULCHRUM
Sweet

jĭn xiù dùjuān   *"splendid rhododendron"*

Evergreen shrub to 2 meters high, sparsely branched; shoots densely clad with flat light brown appressed hairs.

Leaves chartaceous, dimorphic, elliptic to elliptic-lanceolate or oblong-oblanceolate, 2.5-5.6 cm long, 8-18 mm broad, acute and mucronate at the apex, cuneate at the base, clad at first with scattered appressed yellow hairs, the upper surface later subglabrous; petiole 4-6 mm long, clad with hair similar to that of the branches.

Terminal inflorescence of 1-3 flowers; pedicels 6-12 mm long, densely hairy, the hairs flat, red-brown, and slightly spreading; calyx large, deeply 5-lobed, lobes about 8 mm long, margin serrulate and long-ciliate, exterior densely hairy; corolla broadly funnelform, about 6 cm in diameter, rose-purple with dark purple dots, lobes 5, broadly ovate; stamens 10, filaments pubescent on the lower part; ovary densely clad with coarse hairs, style glabrous.

Capsule oblong-ovoid, about 8 mm long, coarsely hairy, calyx persistent.

Widely cultivated; said to have originated in China, but has not been seen in the wild. Cultivars are of many forms and colors, including some with double petals.

4260　溪畔杜鹃

RHODODENDRON RIVULARE
Hand.-Mazz.

xī pàn dùjuān   *"stream bank rhododendron"*

Evergreen shrub more than 1 meter high; twigs slender, shoots hairy, the hairs spreading and ferrugineous, later becoming brown, some of which are long and without glandular tips and others are short and gland-tipped; flower buds narrow, bud scales white-tomentose with a cluster of red hairs at the apex, inner bud scales mucilaginous.

Leaves sparse, chartaceous, ovate-lanceolate, 5-9 cm long, 1.8-4 cm broad, apex acuminate and long-mucronate, base rounded, margin ciliate, mucilaginous when young, upper surface sparsely pubescent at first, the wart-like hair bases remaining after the hairs are dropped, lower surface light yellow, clad with sparse appressed coarse hairs, lateral veins and veinlets prominent, with brown net veins; petiole 4-12 mm long, clad with hairs similar to those of the shoots.

Terminal many-flowered inflorescence; pedicels 1.2 cm long, clad with hairs similar to those of the petioles; calyx about 4-5 mm long, lobes triangular, long-ciliate; corolla funnelform, purplish red, glabrous outside; stamens 10, filaments sparsely and minutely hairy at the base; ovary red-setose.

Distributed in Hunan, Guangxi, Guizhou, Sichuan. Grows in open forests.

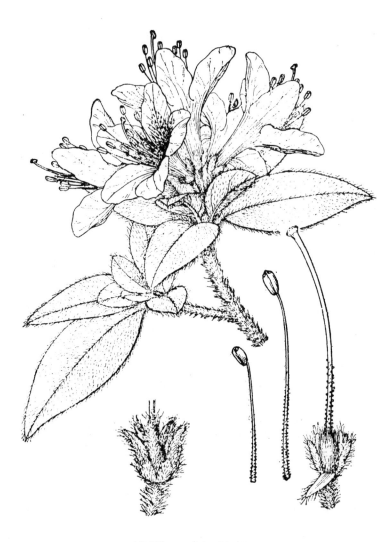

4261　砖红杜鹃

RHODODENDRON OLDHAMII
Maxim.

zhuān hóng dùjuān *"brick red rhododendron"*

Semi-evergreen shrub, 1-3 meters high, densely branched; branchlets densely clad with spreading red partially flattened hairs.

Leaves persistent or partly deciduous, thin-coriaceous, lanceolate-oblong to elliptic-ovate, variable in size, 3-8 cm long, 1.2-4 cm broad, apex bluntly acute, mucronate, base rounded to cuneate, margin spreading-ciliate, upper surface sparsely red-tomentose, some of the hairs gradually dropped, lower surface similarly hairy; petiole to 8 mm long, similarly hairy.

Terminal umbelliform inflorescence of 1-3 flowers; pedicels to 10 mm long, red-tomentose, the hairs partly glandular; calyx large, lobes to 6 mm long, green, clad with long red gland-tipped hairs; corolla broadly funnelform, to 4 cm long, brick red, glabrous; stamens 10, filaments papillate-glandular below the middle; ovary densely tomentose, the hairs gland-tipped, style papillate-glandular below the middle.

Capsule ovoid, 8 mm long, glandular-hairy.

Endemic to Taiwan. Grows in thickets in hilly and mountainous areas from 100 to 2500 meters.

4262　白花杜鹃

RHODODENDRON MUCRONATUM
G. Don

bái huā dùjuān   *"white-flowered rhododendron"*

Semi-evergreen shrub, 1-2 meters high, densely branched; shoots densely pubescent, the hairs spreading and gray, mixed with a few or many flat appressed hairs which are sometimes gland-tipped.

Leaves dimorphic: Spring leaves early-deciduous, membranaceous, lanceolate to ovate-lanceolate, 3.5-5.5 cm long, 1-2.5 cm broad, apex acute or obtuse, base cuneate, upper and lower surfaces hairy, the hairs gray or red, straight, soft, and appressed; summer leaves persistent, chartaceous, oblong-lanceolate, 1-3.7 cm long, 6-12 mm broad, bluntly acute to rounded, clad with hairs similar to those of the spring leaves, often also glandular-hairy; petiole 2-4 mm long, densely clad with soft hairs and flat bristles.

Terminal inflorescence of 1-3 fragrant flowers; pedicels 5-10 mm long, densely pubescent and setose, sometimes also glandular-hairy; calyx large, green, lobes lanceolate, about 1.2 cm long, glandular-hairy; corolla broadly campanulate, 3.5-5 cm long, pure white, sometimes rose or streaked with red; stamens 10, sometimes 8; ovary densely setose, without glands.

Capsule 1 cm long, shorter than the calyx.

A cultivated plant in which the flower color may be rose-purple or the petals semidouble.

4263　马银花

RHODODENDRON OVATUM
Planch.

mǎ yín huā   *"horse silver flower"*

Evergreen shrub to 4 meters high; shoots sparsely stipitate-glandular and pubescent.

Leaves coriaceous, ovate, 3.7-5 cm long, 1.8-2.5 cm broad, apex acute or obtuse, conspicuously mucronate, base rounded, upper surface short-hairy only on the midrib, not scaly; petiole to 8 mm long, pubescent.

Flowers solitary, 1 per flower bud, produced from leaf axils at the branch tip; pedicels 1.6 cm long, clad with short-stalked glands and white powder; calyx large, 5-lobed, about 5 mm long, glabrous except at the base, margin glabrous, only the exterior of the short calyx tube white-powdery and glandular; corolla pale purple, pink-dotted, glabrous outside, corolla tube pubescent within, lobes 5; stamens 5; ovary short-setose, style glabrous.

Capsule 8 mm long, broadly ovoid, short-setose, enclosed within the enlarged persistent calyx.

Broadly distributed throughout the eastern provinces of China. Grows beneath forests or in shady areas at the foot of a hill.

4264　腺萼马银花

RHODODENDRON BACHII
Lévl.

xiàn è mǎ yín huā   *"glandular-calyx horse silver flower"*

Evergreen thin shrub to 6 meters high; shoots and year-old branches pubescent and sparsely glandular-setose.

Leaves scattered, thin-coriaceous, the young leaves red-brown and beset at the margin with conspicuous bristle-like fine teeth, the older leaves entire, ovate-elliptic, 3-4 cm long, 1.5-2 cm broad, apex acute and conspicuously mucronate, base broadly cuneate, upper and lower surfaces glabrous except at the midrib; petiole about 5 mm long, minutely hairy, the edges setose when young.

Inflorescences lateral at the upper leaf axils, flowers solitary; pedicels 1-1.3 cm long, clad with short soft hairs and long gland-tipped bristles; calyx large, deeply 5-lobed, the lobes orbicular-obovate, vein-lined, minutely hairy outside, clad at the margin with gland-tipped hairs; corolla broadly funnelform, about 3 cm in diameter, white tinged with light purplish blue, the upper three lobes finely dark red dotted at the margin; stamens 5, extremely variable in length; ovary densely glandular-setose.

Capsule as long as the persistent calyx, ovoid, clad with coarse glandular hairs.

Broadly distributed throughout Guangdong, Guangxi, Guizhou, Sichuan, Hubei, Hunan, Jiangxi, Anhui, Zhejiang, Fujian. Grows in open forests.

4265　薄叶马银花

RHODODENDRON LEPTOTHRIUM
Balf. f. et W. W. Sm.

bó yè mǎ yín huā   *"thin-leaved horse silver flower"*

Evergreen shrub, 2-6 meters high; shoots light red, clad with spreading soft white hairs.

Leaves thin-coriaceous, elliptic or ovate-elliptic, apex acute and long-mucronate, base broadly cuneate, upper and lower surfaces glossy green, minutely hairy only at the midrib, lateral veins evident on both surfaces; petiole 5-13 cm long, clad with spreading soft white hairs.

Flowers usually 2-4 per branch, solitary from within the leaf axils; pedicels 1-1.2 cm long, densely clad with spreading gland-tipped soft hairs; calyx large, 9 mm long, light green, densely clad with gland-tipped soft hairs and glands, deeply 5-lobed, lobes narrowly ovate, similarly glandular-hairy at the margin; corolla 2.5 cm long, 3.5-4 cm in diameter, rose, deeply 5-lobed, lobes spreading, one upper lobe dark-dotted at the base; stamens 5, unequal in length, filaments glandular-hairy below the middle; ovary globose, glandular-hairy on the upper half.

Capsule ovoid-globose, 7 mm long, clad with gland-tipped bristles, calyx lobes about the same length, fruit-stalk similarly hairy.

Distributed in northwest Yunnan, southwest Sichuan. Grows in thickets.

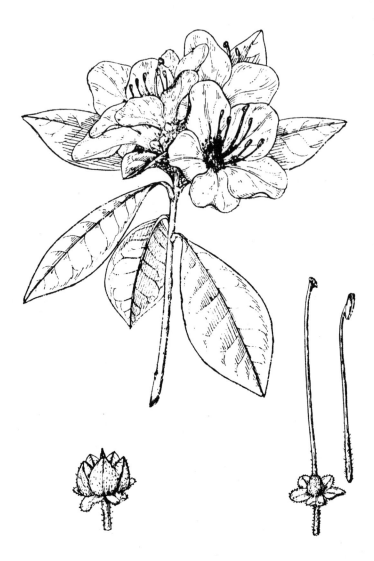

4266　白马银花

RHODODENDRON HONGKONGENSE
Hutch.

bái mǎ yín huā   *"white horse silver flower"*

This species closely resembles the common horse silver flower *(R. ovatum)* of eastern China in habit and several other characteristics, except that the winter-bud scales are glabrous outside and the leaves are more or less oblanceolate or obovate-lanceolate, tapered toward the base, and broadest at or above the middle.

The calyx lobes are smaller, rounded, and densely clad at the margin with short-stalked glandular hairs; the flowers are white, with small purple-lilac spots on the upper part of the corolla-tube interior.

The capsule is verrucose, less than 8 mm long, with persistent calyx lobes which are often reflexed.

Found in Guangdong. Grows in forests.

4267　红马银花

RHODODENDRON VIALII

Delavay et Franch.

hóng mǎ yín huā   *"red horse silver flower"*

Evergreen shrub, 2-3 meters high; shoots short-pubescent.

Leaves coriaceous, ovate-lanceolate or subovate, 3.2-10 cm long, 1.6-3.7 cm broad, apex bluntly acute, mucronate and often emarginate, base cuneate, upper surface finely hairy at the midrib, lower surface finely net-veined; petiole 1.8 cm long, flat and smooth on the upper surface, minutely pubescent.

Flowers solitary, produced from a leaf axil at the branch tip; bud scales minutely hairy, except the glabrous outer layer of scales; pedicels 4-8 mm long, clad with mucilaginous gland-tipped hairs; calyx dark red, large, deeply 5-lobed, lobes oblong, about 5 mm long, densely clad at the margin with sessile glands, setose outside at the base; corolla dark red, corolla tube broadly cylindric, about 1.8 cm long, glabrous, lobes 5, rounded, about 1.2 cm long, somewhat spreading; stamens 5, filaments glabrous or clad with a few minute hairs; ovary 5-loculed, clad with mucilaginous bristles, style glabrous, light red.

West Yunnan. Grows in thickets at 1300-1800 meters.

531

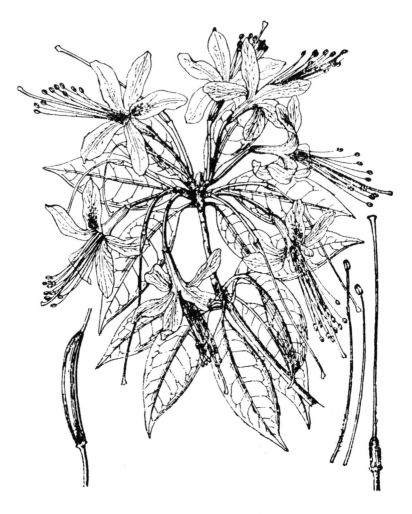

4268　长蕊杜鹃

RHODODENDRON STAMINEUM
Franch.

cháng ruǐ dùjuān   *"long-stamen rhododendron"*
liù gǔ jīn   *"six bone tendon"*

Evergreen shrub or small tree to 5 meters high or more; twigs slender, glabrous.

Leaves usually in whorls of 4-5, coriaceous, elliptic to elliptic-ovate, 6-8 cm long, 2-3 cm broad at the middle, acuminate at the apex, cuneate at the base, glabrous, midrib prominent on the lower surface, lateral veins inconspicuous; petiole 8-12 mm long, glabrous.

Flowers fragrant, usually 3-5 from within a lateral leaf axil at the branch tip; flower-bud scales glabrous except at the margin; pedicels 1.2-1.8 cm long, glabrous; calyx small, minutely 5-lobed, glabrous; corolla white, occasionally rose, yellow-spotted within, glabrous, corolla tube narrowly tubular, 1.5 cm long, lobes 5, long and narrow, 1.5-2 cm long; stamens 10, slender, very long-exserted; ovary sparsely white-hairy, style longer than the stamens, glabrous.

Capsule 2.5-3.5 cm long, cylindric, slightly curved, glabrous.

Distributed in Yunnan, Sichuan, Guizhou, Hubei, Hunan. Grows in thickets or open forests.

Used in the treatment of rabies.

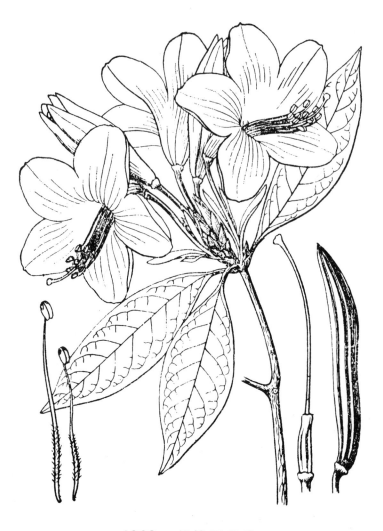

4269　丝线吊芙蓉

RHODODENDRON WESTLANDII
Hemsl.

sī xiàn diào fú róng   *"silk thread hanging hibiscus"*

Evergreen shrub or small tree to 6 meters high; twigs thin, shoots glabrous.

Leaves coriaceous, broadly oblanceolate to elliptic-lanceolate, 6.4-12 cm long, 2.5-4.5 cm broad, acute to short acuminate at the apex, cuneate at the base, glabrous, midrib narrowly grooved on the upper surface, prominent on the lower surface, lateral veins rather inconspicuous on the upper surface; petiole to 1.8 cm long, glabrous.

Lateral inflorescence of as many as 5 delicately fragrant flowers produced from a lateral bud at the branch tip; flower-bud scales large, round-ovate, densely white-hairy only at the margin, caducous; pedicels about 1.5 cm long, glabrous; calyx poorly developed, with 5 shallow undulate lobes, glabrous; corolla narrowly funnelform, lilac-purple, glabrous; stamens 10, shorter than the corolla, filaments pubescent from below the middle to above the base; ovary long, glabrous, style glabrous, slightly longer than the stamens but shorter than the corolla.

Capsule straight, cylindric, to 7 cm long, about 7 mm thick.

Distributed in Hunan, Jiangxi, Guangdong. Grows in open forests at about 700 meters.

535

4270　光脚杜鹃

RHODODENDRON LEIOPODUM

Hayata

guāng jiǎo dùjuān   *"smooth-footed rhododendron"*

Evergreen shrub, 2-3 meters high; branchlets smooth and glossy.

Leaves in terminal whorls, coriaceous, narrowly oblong-lanceolate, 7.5-12 cm long, 1.8-2.6 cm broad, abruptly acuminate or acute at the apex, cuneate at the base, glabrous, midrib impressed on the upper surface, lateral veins and veinlets prominent on both surfaces; petiole about 1.5 cm long.

Lateral inflorescence of 1 flower produced from a leaf axil; flower-bud scales persistent during flowering, short-pubescent at the margin; pedicels about 3 cm long, smooth and glossy; calyx poorly developed, smooth and glossy, with 5 small sharply triangular teeth; corolla narrowly funnelform, about 4.2 cm long, pink to white, smooth and glossy; stamens 10, exserted, filaments pubescent above the middle; ovary cylindric, smooth and glossy, style longer than the stamens, glabrous.

Capsule to 4 cm long, 4 mm thick, cylindric, smooth and glossy.

Endemic to Taiwan. Grows on rocky hillsides.

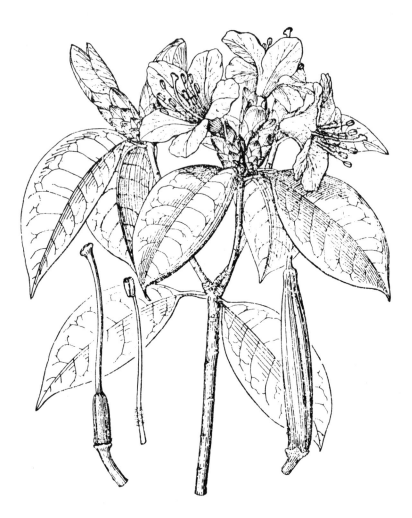

4271　鹿角杜鹃

538

RHODODENDRON LATOUCHEAE
Franch.

lù jiǎo dùjuān   *"deerhorn rhododendron"*

Evergreen shrub to small tree, 1-7 meters high; branchlets long, glabrous, often in whorls of 3.

Leaves verticillate, coriaceous, ovate-elliptic, 6-7.5 cm long, 2.5-4 cm broad, short acuminate at the apex, glabrous, leaf veins obscure; petiole about 1 cm long, glabrous.

Inflorescence axillary, a solitary flower produced from each axillary flower bud; flower-bud scales persistent during flowering, glabrous outside, subglabrous at the margin; pedicels about 1 cm long, glabrous; calyx short, lobes poorly developed; corolla narrowly funnelform, 4.5 cm long, pink, glabrous outside; stamens 10, exserted, filaments pubescent near the base; ovary glabrous, style slightly longer than the stamens, about 3 cm long, glabrous.

Capsule cylindric, about 3 cm long, 4 mm thick, glabrous.

Distributed in Fujian, Zhejiang, Jiangxi, Guangdong. Grows in hilly areas or in low-mountain mixed forests.

4272　多花杜鹃

RHODODENDRON CAVALERIEI
Lévl.

duō huā dùjuān   *"many-flowered rhododendron"*

Evergreen shrub to 5 meters high; twigs quite slender, gray, glabrous.

Leaves thin-coriaceous, oblanceolate, about 7.5 cm long, 2.5 cm broad above the middle, short acuminate at the apex, tapering downward, narrowly cuneate at the base, upper and lower surfaces glabrous, leaf veins inconspicuous; petiole about 8 mm long.

Umbelliform inflorescence from a leaf axil at the branch tip, many-flowered; pedicels slender, 2.5 cm long, with a few fine hairs; calyx inconspicuous, glabrous; corolla narrowly funnelform, 3.2 cm long, white to rose, glabrous outside; stamens 10, exserted, filaments glabrous; ovary tomentose, style glabrous.

Capsule 3-4 cm long, slightly hairy.

Distributed in Guizhou, north Guangxi. Grows in open forests.

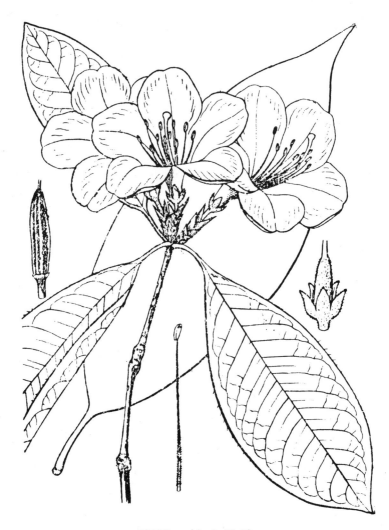

4273　滇南杜鹃

RHODODENDRON HANCOCKII
Hemsl.

diān nán dùjuān   *"south Yunnan rhododendron"*

Evergreen shrub, 1-2 meters high; branchlets glabrous.

Leaves thin-coriaceous, obovate, 10-15 cm long, 3.2-6.2 cm broad, short acuminate at the apex, slightly tapering toward the base, glabrous, lateral veins numerous and conspicuously branched, slightly impressed on the upper surface; petiole 6 mm long.

Inflorescence axillary, one flower produced from each axil; flower-bud scales subpersistent, numerous, very shortly ciliate; calyx deeply 5-lobed, lobes ovate, hairy on the dorsal surface and at the margin; corolla broadly funnelform, 7.5 cm long, white with one yellow-tinged upper lobe, corolla tube glabrous outside, lobes 5, obovate-elliptic, emarginate; stamens 10, long-exserted, filaments pubescent below the middle; ovary 5-6 loculed, densely tomentose, style glabrous, slightly longer than the stamens.

Capsule slightly curved, rostrate, 6.2 cm long, slightly pubescent.

Distributed in southeast Yunnan, Guangxi. Grows in forests.

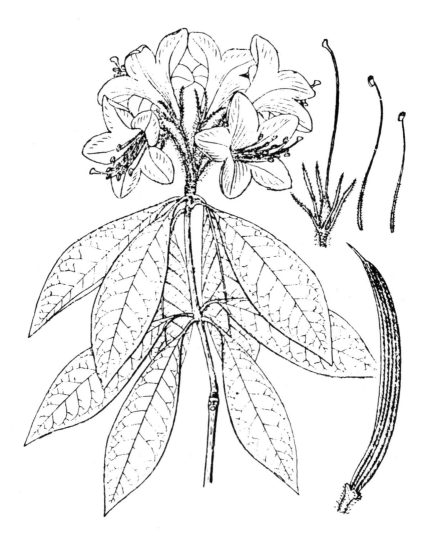

4274 弯蒴杜鹃

544

RHODODENDRON HENRYI

Hance

wān shuò dùjuān   *"curved capsule rhododendron"*

Evergreen shrub about 5 meters high; twigs slender, glabrous, gray.

Leaves in terminal whorls of 5-7, coriaceous, elliptic-obovate, 5-10 cm long, 2.5-3.8 cm broad, acute-acuminate at the apex, cuneate at the base, glabrous, midrib impressed on the upper surface, lateral veins numerous and spreading, lateral veins and net veins impressed on the upper surface, prominent on the lower surface; petiole 1.2 cm long, glabrous.

Inflorescence pseudoterminal, axillary, umbelliform, of 3-5 flowers; pedicels about 2.5 cm long, erect, densely clad with spreading gland-tipped bristles; calyx large, deeply lobed, lobes linear, to 1.5 cm long, glandular-hairy at the margin; corolla narrowly funnelform, 3.7 cm long, pink, glabrous; stamens 10, exserted, filaments pubescent on the lower third; ovary densely hairy, style glabrous.

Capsule cylindric, 5-6 cm long, 4 mm thick, erect, somewhat curved, smooth and glossy.

Distributed in Guangxi, Guangdong, Hunan, Jiangxi, Fujian. Grows in forests.

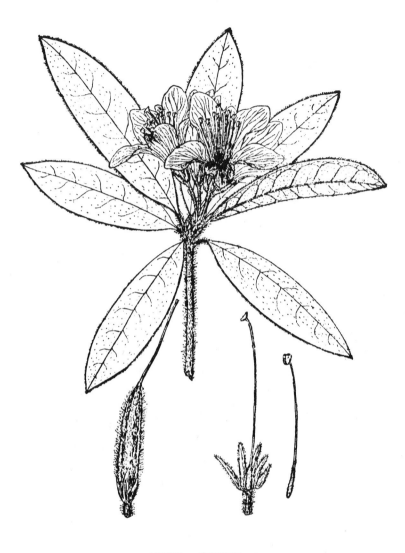

4275　刺毛杜鹃

RHODODENDRON CHAMPIONAE
Hook.

cì máo dùjuān   *"bristly rhododendron"*

Evergreen shrub to 5 meters high; branchlets clad with spreading bristlelike stiff hairs.

Leaves thick-chartaceous, oblong-oblanceolate, 7-15 cm long, 2.5-5 cm broad, apex acute to short acuminate, base short cuneate, upper surface sparsely short-setose, the hairs more numerous and longer toward the margin, lower surface sparsely setose and often sparsely pubescent, the bristles denser on the midrib and lateral veins; petiole 1.2 cm long, densely clad with spreading gland-tipped bristles.

Inflorescence axillary, from a leaf axil at the branch tip, several-flowered; pedicels 1.8 cm long, densely clad with spreading coarse hairs; calyx variable, deeply 5-lobed, lobes linear-oblong, to 1.2 cm long, densely ciliate; corolla narrowly funnelform, to 6 cm long, pink, glabrous; stamens 10, long-exserted, filaments pubescent on the lower part; ovary densely coarse-hairy, style longer than the stamens, glabrous.

Capsule narrowly long-elliptic, 3.8 cm long, coarse-hairy, fruitstalk 3 cm long, clad with gland-tipped bristles.

Distributed in Zhejiang, Fujian, Jiangxi, Guangdong, Guangxi.

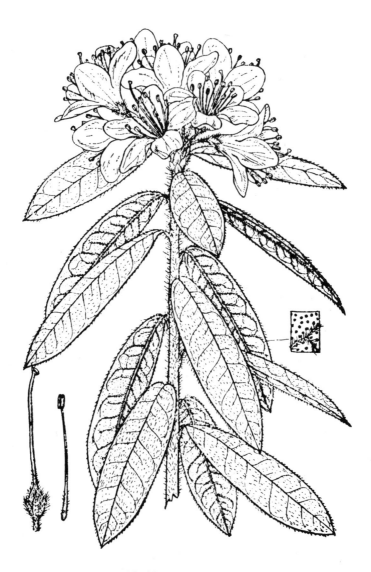

4276　糙叶杜鹃

RHODODENDRON SCABRIFOLIUM
Franch.

cāo yè dùjuān   *"rough-leaved rhododendron"*

Evergreen subshrub, 30-70 cm high; twigs straight and upright, long-setose and pubescent.

Leaves subcoriaceous, broadly oblanceolate to oblong-lanceolate, 3.8-5 cm long, 1.6-1.9 cm broad, apex acute and mucronate, base acute, upper surface scabrous, somewhat bullate, lower surface tomentose and net-veined, also sparsely clad with scalelike glands; petiole 6 mm long, setose.

Inflorescence lateral, produced from within an upper leaf axil, 2-3 flowers per inflorescence; bud scales persistent during flowering; pedicels 1.2 cm long, densely setose; calyx well developed, lobes 4 mm long, densely setose throughout; corolla broadly funnelform, pink or white, corolla tube narrowly tubular, about 1.8 cm long, lobes slightly scaly outside; stamens 10, exserted, filaments pubescent toward the base; ovary densely hairy and scaly, style short-pubescent near the base.

Capsule 6 mm long, pubescent and glandular.

Central and west Yunnan. Grows in open thickets at 1700-2100 meters.

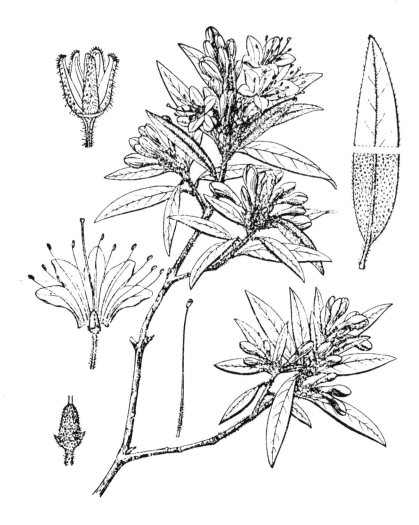

4277　柔毛杜鹃

RHODODENDRON PUBESCENS
Balf. f. et Forrest

róu máo dùjuān   *"pubescent rhododendron"*

Evergreen subshrub about 1 meter high, densely branched; twigs slender, shoots clad with short white hairs mixed with longer stiff fine hairs (about 1 mm long) and short-stalked orange or dark red scales, the hairs more or less persistent on older branches.

Leaves scattered on nonflowering branches, clustered below or among inflorescences on flowering branches, coriaceous, lanceolate to linear-lanceolate, 2-3 cm long, 6-7 mm broad, apex acute, base acute, margin recurved, upper and lower surfaces clad with hairs similar to those of the shoots, also sparsely scaly, the hairs and scales of the upper surface eventually shed, leaving a somewhat scabrous surface, the hairs of the lower surface more dense and persistent; petiole 2-3 mm long, hairy.

Umbelliform inflorescences of 2-3 flowers produced from 2-4 leaf axils near the branch tip; pedicels 6-8 mm long; calyx unequally 5-lobed, hairy, glandular, and long-ciliate; corolla 8-12 mm long, rose, 5-lobed; stamens 10, filaments hairy at the base; ovary densely hairy and scaly.

Capsule 8 mm long, hairy.

Distributed in north and central Yunnan, southwest Sichuan. Grows in thickets.

4278　毛叶杜鹃

RHODODENDRON SPICIFERUM
Franch.

máo yè dùjuān   *"hairy-leaved rhododendron"*

Evergreen subshrub to 1 meter high; twigs thin, clad with long spreading gray-white bristles and short soft hairs; leaf-bud scales caducous.

Leaves scattered, thick-chartaceous, lanceolate, 2.5-3.5 cm long, to 1 cm broad, apex bluntly acute, base short cuneate, upper surface and the margin sparsely setose and pubescent, the hairs similar to those of the twigs, lower surface clad with dense soft gray-white hairs and sparse golden glandlike scales; petiole 2-3 mm long, pubescent.

Flowers axillary on the ends of the twigs, numerous, forming false spikes; flower-bud scales persistent during flowering, clad with small golden glandular scales and soft hairs; pedicels about 6 mm long; calyx well developed, lobes densely ciliate, glandular-scaly outside; corolla narrowly tubular, 1.3 cm long, pink, lobes 5, spreading, clad with golden glandular scales outside; stamens 10, filaments hairy above the base; ovary densely pubescent and glandular-scaly, style hairy toward the base.

Capsule 6 mm long, glandular-scaly and short-hairy.

Distributed in Yunnan, Sichuan. Grows in thickets and beneath open forests in mountain wilderness.

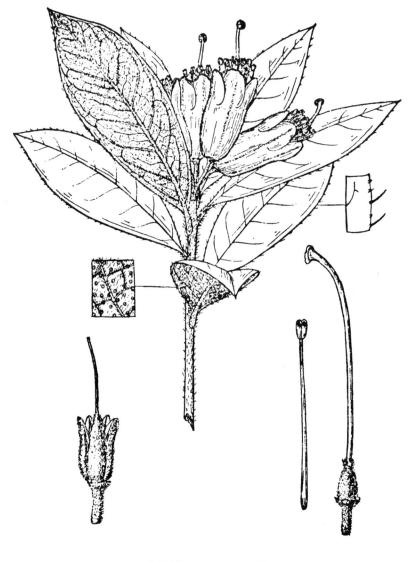

4279　爆杖花

RHODODENDRON SPINULIFERUM
Franch.

bào zhàng huā   *"firecracker flower"*

Evergreen subshrub, 0.5-2.5 meters high; shoots gray-pubescent and setose, soon subglabrous.

Leaves scattered, subcoriaceous, elliptic-oblanceolate to oblanceolate, 3-8 cm long, 1.8-3.2 cm broad, apex acute with a stiff point, base cuneate, upper surface rugose, subglabrous, finely setose toward the margin, lower surface sparsely long-hairy and scaly; petiole about 6 mm long, pubescent.

Inflorescence of about 4 flowers, axillary at the branch tip; pedicels 8-12 mm long, thick, pubescent; calyx small, about 1 mm long, pubescent; corolla tubular, slightly narrowed at both ends, ochre-red, glabrous, corolla tube 1.4 cm long, lobes 5, ovate, erect; stamens 10, exserted, filaments glabrous, anthers black; ovary densely woolly and sparsely glandular, style far longer than the stamens, pubescent at the base.

Capsule oblong, 8-10 mm long, densely woolly, style persistent.

Distributed in Yunnan (central, north, and west), southwest Sichuan. Grows beneath open forests and in thickets at 1900-2500 meters.

4280　腋花杜鹃

RHODODENDRON RACEMOSUM
Franch.

yè huā dùjuān *"axillary flower rhododendron"*

Evergreen shrub about 1 meter high, much-branched; twigs quite fine, shoots clad with small glandlike scales.

Leaves coriaceous, oblong-elliptic, 1.2-5 cm long, 8-25 mm broad, obtuse and mucronate at the apex, obtuse at the base, glabrous, lower surface gray-white, densely scaly, the scales about a diameter apart; petiole about 3 mm long, densely scaly.

Inflorescence axillary at the branch tip, few-flowered, sometimes forming a raceme; pedicels to 1.5 cm long, scaly; calyx small, shallowly 5-lobed, scaly; corolla funnelform, about 1.5 cm long, finely scaly outside, corolla tube glabrous outside, lobes 5;* stamens 10, exserted, filaments pubescent on the lower part; ovary 5-loculed, densely scaly, style slightly longer than the stamens, glabrous.

Capsule elliptic, 6 mm long, sparsely glandular-scaly.

Distributed in central and north Yunnan, southwest Sichuan. Grows in open thickets at 1800-2800 meters.

*No corolla color given, see key.

557

4281　柳条杜鹃

RHODODENDRON VIRGATUM
Hook. f.

liǔ tiáo dùjuān   *"willow branch rhododendron"*

Evergreen shrub about 1 meter high; twigs slender, scaly.

Leaves scattered, firm-coriaceous, broadly lanceolate to oblong-lanceolate, to 6 cm long, to 1.8 cm broad, apex bluntly acute or sharply acute, mucronate, base obtuse, upper surface sparsely scaly, lower surface more densely scaly, the scales slightly separated or nearly contiguous, unequal in size, flaky; petiole about 4 mm long, scaly.

Lateral inflorescence of 1 flower from a leaf axil; flower-bud scales persistent during flowering; pedicels about 3 mm long; calyx well-developed, about 4 mm long, deeply 5-lobed, scaly; corolla funnelform, 3 cm long, light purple, sparsely scaly and sparsely pubescent outside (sometimes rather densely so); stamens 10, long-exserted, filaments pubescent on the lower part; ovary 5-loculed, scaly, style long-exserted, pubescent and scaly on the lower half.

Capsule about 1.2 cm long, elliptic, densely scaly.

South Xizang; also Sikkim, Bhutan. Grows on sandy stream banks at 3000 meters.

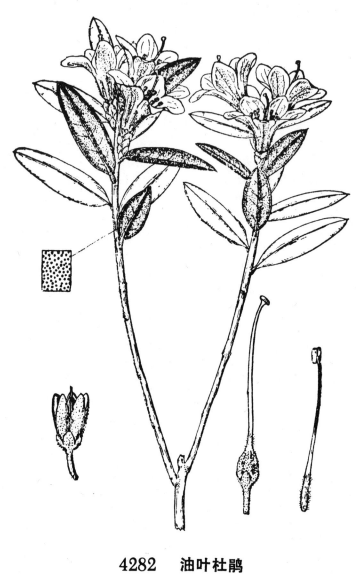

4282　油叶杜鹃

RHODODENDRON OLEIFOLIUM
Franch.

yóu yè dùjuān   *"oily-leaved* rhododendron"*

Evergreen dwarf shrub to 75 cm high, sparsely branched toward the top; twigs slender, branchlets densely scaly.

Leaves sparse, chartaceous, lanceolate to oblong-lanceolate, 2.6-6 cm long, 8-17 mm broad, apex acute, base acute or nearly rounded, upper surface scaly at first, soon smooth and glossy, lower surface nearly gray-white, scaly, the scales fleshy, small, and less than a diameter apart; petiole 3-4 mm long, scaly.

Flowers axillary, 1-2 produced by each lateral flower bud; pedicels extremely short, not longer than the persistent bud scales, densely scaly; calyx light green, 5-lobed, lobes 2 mm long, sparsely scaly outside at the base; corolla campanulate, 2.5-3 cm long, rose, corolla tube 1.5 cm long, scaly on the upper part, pubescent on the lower part, lobes 5, densely scaly on the dorsal surface; stamens 10; ovary densely scaly, style sparsely hairy and scaly at the base.

Capsule 1 cm long.

Central and west Yunnan. Grows in open thickets at 2500-3000 meters.

---

*A confusion of two very similar terms; the translation from Latin to Chinese to English should be "olive-leaved."

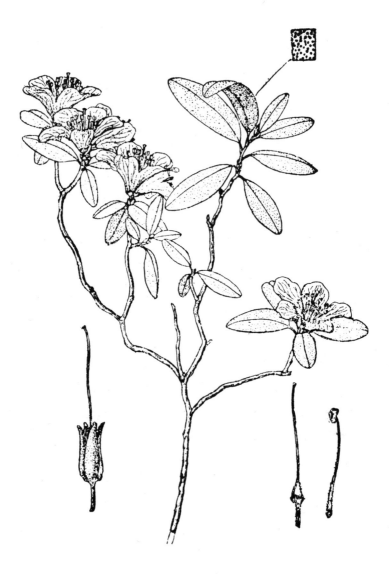

4283　兴安杜鹃

RHODODENDRON DAURICUM
L.

xīng ān dùjuān   *"Xing'an rhododendron"*

Semi-evergreen shrub, 1-2 meters high, much-branched; branchlets scaly and pubescent.

Leaves scattered, subcoriaceous, elliptic, 1.5-3.5 cm long, 1-1.5 cm broad, apex obtuse and mucronate, base obtuse, upper surface dark green, sparsely scaly, lower surface light green, densely scaly, the scales contiguous or imbricate; petiole to 2 mm long, minutely hairy.

Inflorescence lateral (and sometimes terminal) at the branch tip, composed of 1-2 flowers which precede the new leaves; flower-bud scales caducous; pedicels 8 mm long, minutely hairy, not scaly; calyx short, densely scaly outside; corolla broadly funnelform, about 1.8 cm long, pink, pubescent outside; stamens 10, exserted, filaments hairy on the lower part; ovary densely scaly, style glabrous, slightly longer than the stamens.

Capsule 1.2 cm long, oblong, scaly.

Distributed throughout northeast China, Nei Mongol; also Korea, Japan, USSR. Grows on high dry mountain slopes, on mountain ridges, or in forests.

4284　迎红杜鹃

RHODODENDRON MUCRONULATUM
Turcz.

yíng hóng dùjuān   *"welcome red rhododendron"*

Deciduous shrub about 1.5 meters high, much-branched; branchlets slender, sparsely scaly.

Leaves scattered, thin, oblong-lanceolate, 3-8 cm long, 1.2-2.2 cm broad at the middle, margin slightly undulate, upper surface sparsely scaly, lower surface more densely scaly; petiole 3-5 mm long.

Two to five lateral flower buds clustered at the branch tip, one flower per bud, opening before the leaves; flower-bud scales persistent during flowering; pedicels very short, sparsely scaly; calyx very short, scaly, with small triangular teeth; corolla broadly funnelform, 4-5 cm long, pale reddish purple, minutely hairy outside, not scaly, lobes 5, rounded, undulate; stamens 10, inclining, of unequal length, not longer than the corolla, filaments hairy below the middle; ovary 5-loculed, scaly, style glabrous.

Capsule cylindric, 1.3 cm long, brown, densely scaly.

Distributed throughout northeast and northern China, Shandong, north Jiangsu; also Korea, Japan, USSR. Grows in thickets in hilly areas.

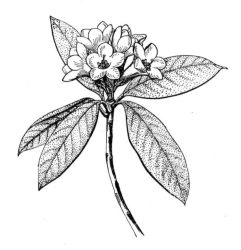

TRANSLATED KEY
TO SPECIES OF RHODODENDRON
IN CHINA

Genus THERORHODION Small: Flowers usually 1-3, terminal on the new growth; pedicels bracteate, the bracts 2 per pedicel and leaf-like; corolla rotate; stamens 10; deciduous repent dwarf shrubs; one species in China, growing in the northeast alpine zone:

Therorhodion redowskianum (Maxim.) Hutch. **4002**

Genus RHODODENDRON L.: Flowers usually several in a racemose-umbelliform inflorescence; pedicels without leaflike bracts; corolla campanulate, funnelform, sometimes rotate or tubular; stamens 5-20(25); mostly evergreen erect shrubs or trees; about 600 species in China, distributed in all provinces and autonomous regions except Xinjiang, especially numerous in Sichuan, Yunnan, and Xizang.

I. SYNOPSIS OF RHODODENDRON SUBGENERA
AND SECTIONS
with illustration numbers

1. Inflorescence terminal, rarely with additional lateral inflorescences produced from subterminal leaf axils.
  2. Plant (including shoots, leaves, ovaries, and other organs) more or less scaly or glandular-scaly.
    3. Foliage evergreen (rarely semi-evergreen to deciduous); flowers opening after the leaves:
Subgenus LEPIDORRHODIUM
    4. Seeds without appendages or slightly appendaged (with only comparatively short, mostly unilateral, appendages of the epidermis margin), or very narrowly winged at the periphery, the wings short and lacerate at both ends; capsule valves woody, hard, not twisted after dehiscence.

567

5. Stamens 10 (occasionally 5), usually exserted beyond the corolla; corolla campanulate to funnelform; scales discoid and entire:
Section LEPIPHERUM
(4003-4098)

5. Stamens 5, rarely 6-8(10), style short and thick, all included deep within the corolla tube, not exserted beyond the corolla; corolla salverform, densely tomentose within at the throat; scales stellately incised at the margin:
Section POGONANTHUM
(4099-4107)

4. Seeds caudate at both ends, the appendages long and threadlike; in the mature capsule the placenta resembles 5 threadlike ribs, separated through the lower common axis and joined only at the top; capsule valves quite thin, more or less twisted after dehiscence and usually reflexed; scales discoid, entire, or irregularly and acutely cleft at the transparent margin to regularly, deeply, and conspicuously stellate:
Section VIREYA
(4108-4110)

3. Foliage more or less regularly deciduous, rarely semi-evergreen, leaves thin; flowers opening before the leaves, yellow:
Subgenus PSEUDAZALEA
(4111-4116)

2. Plant organs devoid of scales or glandular scales.

6. Foliage shoots produced from lateral leaf buds below the terminal inflorescence on year-old branches or at the tips of nonflowering branches.

7. Foliage evergreen; stamens (10-20(24); generally large shrubs or trees:
Subgenus RHODODENDRON
(4117-4240)

7. Foliage deciduous (if the leaves are setose, the hairs are not flat as in Section *Tsutsusi*); stamens 5; small shrubs (in China only one section, one species, *R. molle*):
Subgenus PSEUDANTHODENDRON,
(Section PENTANTHERA)
(4241)

568

6. Foliage shoots produced from within the lowest bract axils of the terminal flower bud on year-old branches (inflorescence and foliage shoots from the same terminal bud); stamens 10-5 (often varying within a species):

Subgenus ANTHODENDRON

8. Foliage more or less (at least partly) deciduous.
   9. Branchlets glabrous or hairy, but mostly gray-tomentose; leaves in terminal verticillate clusters (scattered only on spindly branches), usually large, mostly glabrous or subglabrous by the time the capsules mature (sparsely pubescent only at the midvein and lateral veins), the very young leaves sericeous; flowers opening at the same time as or just before the leaves:

Section BRACHYCALYX
(4242-4244)

   9. Branchlets and leaves clad with flat reddish brown appressed coarse hairs or bristles (often gland-tipped); leaves scattered on the shoots, dimorphic: the spring leaves are broader, thinner, and deciduous; the summer leaves are narrower, thicker, and more or less persistent:

Section TSUTSUSI
(4245-4262)

8. Foliage evergreen, the leaves coriaceous, in terminal whorls of 2-3 (scattered only on spindly branches); (one species, cultivated in China, native to Japan, *R. tashiroi* Maxim.):

Section TSUSIOPSIS

1. Inflorescence lateral, produced only on the upper part of the twigs from within leaf axils (the leaves often degenerate or caducous), or also produced on the lower part of year-old twigs from within leaf axils; the flower buds at the ends of branches are pseudoterminal, actually growing from within the axils of degenerate leaves at the twig tips.
   10. Foliage shoots produced not only from within leaf buds at the branch tips (pseudoterminal buds) but also from leaf axils below the flower buds.
   11. Plant not scaly; foliage evergreen:

Subgenus AZALEASTRUM

   12. Stamens 5; calyx lobes large and broad; seeds without appendages:

Section AZALEASTRUM
(4263-4267)

12. Stamens 10; calyx lobes inconspicuous or rarely well-developed and narrowly lanceolate; seeds short-caudate at both ends; in the mature capsule the valves are joined on the upper part to the style, not dehiscent: **Section CHONIASTRUM** (4268-4275)

11. Plant scaly; foliage evergreen: **Subgenus PSEUDORHODORASTRUM**

13. Leaves clad with dense soft hairs to coarse appressed hairs; stamens 8-10; seeds without appendages: **Section TRACHYRHODION** (4276-4279)

13. Leaves glabrous, the lower surface often grayish white; stamens 10; seeds with or without appendages: **Section RHODOBOTRYS** (4280-4282)

10. Foliage shoots usually produced only from within leaf axils below the flower buds; foliage deciduous to (semi)evergreen; leaves scaly; inflorescence racemose (often reduced to a solitary flower), not only produced from pseudoterminal flower buds, but also produced at the same time from within the subterminal axils of caducous leaves; flowers opening before the leaves: **Subgenus RHODORASTRUM** (4283-4284)

II. KEY TO RHODODENDRON SPECIES

with illustration numbers

A. SUBGENUS LEPIDORRHODIUM

1. **Seeds without appendages or slightly appendaged (with only comparatively short, not all unilateral, appendages of the epidermis margin), or very narrowly winged at the periphery, the wings short and lacerate at both ends; capsule valves woody, hard, not twisted after dehiscence.** p. 588

2. **Stamens 10 (rarely 5), usually exserted beyond the corolla; corolla campanulate to funnelform; scales discoid and entire. (SECTION LEPIPHERUM)** p. 585

   3. Style short and thick, for the most part conspicuously and strongly bent.

      4. Scales of the lower leaf surface of unequal size, some smaller and yellow, the rest larger and dark brown.

         5. Flowers yellow or light greenish yellow; leaves 2-4 cm long.

            6. Scales of the lower leaf surface very few and widely separated; pedicels to 2 cm long (West Yunnan):
            R. brachyanthum Franch. **4003**

            6. Scales of the lower leaf surface very numerous and comparatively close; pedicels 2.5-4 cm long (northwest Yunnan):
            R. hypolepidotum Balf. f. et Forrest **4004**

         5. Flowers pink, sparsely pubescent outside; leaves 4-7 cm long (Yunnan, southeast Xizang): **R. charitopes** Balf. f. et Farrer **4005**

      4. Scales of the lower leaf surface uniform (of equal size).

         7. Pedicels shorter than the corolla; corolla yellow or white.

            8. Inflorescence of 1-2 (rarely 3) flowers; scales of the lower leaf surface very narrowly rimmed, almost bladder-like; terrestrial shrubs (Yunnan, southeast Xizang):
            R. megeratum Balf. f. et Forrest **4006**

            8. Inflorescence of usually 4-10 flowers; scales of the lower leaf surface broadly rimmed, entire; often epiphytic shrubs.

               9. Shoots and petioles setose, the bristles spreading; calyx poorly developed, only rimlike; corolla light yellow, not dotted (northwest Yunnan): **R. chrysodoron** Tagg **4007**

9. Shoots and petioles not setose; calyx large, the lobes leaflike, to 5.5 mm long; corolla light yellow, the interior dotted with orange-yellow on the upper part (west Yunnan):

R. sulfureum Franch. **4008**

7. Pedicels longer than the corolla.
   10. Inflorescence of 1-3 (rarely 4) flowers, corymbose; leaves small, 0.4-2.6 (rarely to 3.8) cm long.
      11. Corolla campanulate, often appearing white-powdery outside, not scaly (Yunnan, southeast Xizang):

R. campylogynum Franch. **4009**

      11. Corolla spreading radially from the tubular base upward, densely scaly outside (south Xizang):

R. lepidotum Wall. **4010**

   10. Inflorescence of 4-18 (rarely 3) flowers, short and distinctly racemose; leaves large, 3-15 cm long.
      12. Scales of the lower leaf surface crenulate and imbricate (south Xizang):   **R. baileyi** Balf. f. **4011**
      12. Scales of the lower leaf surface entire, 6-8 diameters apart (Yunnan, southeast Xizang)

R. genestierianum Forrest **4012**

3. Style long (at least as long as the stamens), slender, more or less straight.
   13. Inflorescence of 1-2 (rarely 3) flowers; corolla exterior densely hairy (except *R. monanthum*); leaves small, 1.2-3.5 (5) cm long; prostrate dwarf shrubs.
      14. Leaf margin undulate, with fine notches that are distinct but not easily seen; calyx large, 5-7 mm long; corolla yellow with light reddish brown dots within the corolla tube (southeast Xizang):

R. ludlowii Cowan **4013**

      14. Leaf margin entire; calyx small, 1-2 mm long, rarely to 3-4 mm.
         15. Flowers bright yellow; corolla exterior glabrous; scales of the lower leaf surface of unequal size, mostly large; erect shrubs of medium size, to 1.2 meters high; leaves large, usually 2.6-5 cm long, 1.3-2.5 cm broad (northwest Yunnan, southeast Xizang):

R. monanthum Balf. f. et W. W. Sm. **4015**

15. Flowers pink, rose, or purple; corolla exterior densely hairy; scales of the lower leaf surface of equal size (of unequal size in *R. pemakoense*), small; dwarf erect or prostrate undershrubs, 15-60 cm high; leaves small, less than 2.6 cm long, less than 1.3 cm broad (rarely broader in *R. pemakoense*).

  16. Leaves elliptic or obovate-elliptic; corolla campanulate, 1.3-1.9 cm long; style about half as long as the corolla (south Xizang, southwest Yunnan):   **R. pumilum** Hook. f. **4014**

  16. Leaves obovate or elliptic-obovate; corolla funnelform, 2.5 cm long; style as long as or longer than the corolla (southeast Xizang):   **R. pemakoense** Ward **4016**

13. Inflorescence of 3-14 flowers; corolla exterior rarely clad with sparse minute hairs, mostly glabrous or scaly.

  17. Lower leaf surface clad with a dense woolly indumentum as well as scales, upper and lower surfaces bullate; ovary and capsule woolly, often also scaly (west Yunnan, southeast Xizang):   **R. bullatum** Franch. **4017**

  17. Lower leaf surface (ovary, capsule) clad only with scales, not with a coexisting thick woolly indumentum.

   18. Style scaly at least at the base, mostly on the lower third, or often throughout the upper part to the tip, sometimes both scaly and villous (or tomentose); stamens often 10.   p. 576

   19. Corolla comparatively small, about 2-3(4) cm long including the lobes, often yellow, whitish pale yellow, or rose.

    20. Flowers bright yellow, corolla exterior quite densely scaly; calyx lobes erect; leaves acute (Yunnan, southeast Xizang):   **R. xanthostephanum** Merr. **4018**

    20. Flowers pink or rose; calyx lobes spreading; leaves obtuse (southeast Xizang):   **R. tephropeplum** Balf. f. et Farrer **4019**

   19. Corolla comparatively large, mostly 5-7-10 (12) cm long, often white, waxy.

    21. Stamens (15)20; calyx quite well developed, of moderate size; ovary 10-loculed.

22. Leaves 10-13 cm long, 2.5-3.5 cm broad, broadly lanceolate to oblong-lanceolate; lateral veins obscure (especially so on the lower surface); petioles grooved on the upper surface, the groove V-shaped; stamens 20, filaments glabrous; style scaly overall (south Xizang): **R. maddenii** Hook. f. **4020**

22. Leaves 15-19 cm long, 4-5.5 cm broad, oblong-elliptic; lateral veins evident; petioles cylindric; stamens 15, filaments hairy on the lower part; style scaly on the lower part (southeast Yunnan): **R. excellens** Rehd. et Wils. **4021**

21. Stamens 10 (rarely to 13); calyx variable, from obscure to very large; ovary 5-7-loculed.

23. Calyx large and more or less leaflike, the lobes quite broad and 8 mm long or longer; petioles convex on the upper surface, not grooved (except *R. megacalyx*).

24. Pedicels and calyx not scaly; calyx divided to the middle, the lobes very broad; style scaly only at the base; capsule very short (6 mm long), not as long as the persistent calyx lobes (southeast Xizang):

   R. megacalyx Balf. f. et Ward **4022**

24. Pedicels scaly at least on the lower part, calyx usually also scaly on the lower part; calyx divided nearly to the base, lobes quite narrow, usually acute or bluntly acute; capsule large, 2-6 cm long.

25. Shoots, upper surface of the new leaves, petioles, pedicels, and calyx exterior quite densely clad at first with long coarse hairs; upper and lower leaf surfaces scaly, the scales almost uniformly dense (Guangdong, Guangxi, Hunan, Fujian): **R. levinei** Merr. **4023**

25. Plant parts not clad with long coarse hairs; upper leaf surface not scaly, or occasionally scaly at the midrib.

26. Corolla exterior more or less scaly overall.

27. Calyx lobes rather broadly ovate, about 12 mm long, vein-lined, scaly but not pubescent outside; corolla about 10 cm long; capsule 4.3 cm long (Guizhou, Guangxi, Yunnan*): **R. liliiflorum** Lévl. **4024**

---

*Hunan, not Yunnan, in the species description.

27. Calyx lobes oblong, 18 mm long, scaly and pubescent outside; corolla to 14 cm long; capsule to 6.5 cm long (southeast Xizang, northwest Yunnan):

R. sinonuttallii Balf. f. et Forrest **4025**

26. Corolla exterior not scaly, or scaly only on the lower part of the corolla tube or at the base.

28. Calyx lobes not ciliate (or with very few hairs scattered at the margin).

29. Corolla 7-7.5 cm long; calyx about 1.5 cm long, scaly.

30. Inflorescence of 1 flower; corolla cream; filaments pubescent on the lower third (southeast Xizang):

R. headfortianum Hutch. **4026**

30. Inflorescence of 3 flowers; corolla pure white; filaments pubescent on the lower half (southeast Xizang): R. taggianum Hutch. **4027**

29. Corolla 10 cm long or longer; calyx 1.5-2.5 cm long, smooth and glossy.

31. Leaves 12-20 cm long, 5.6-10 cm broad, elliptic, mucronate; calyx 2.5 cm long (south Xizang):

R. nuttallii Booth **4028**

31. Leaves 9-12 cm long, 3-3.5 cm broad, elliptic-lanceolate, acute; calyx to 1.4 cm long (north Guangxi): R. chunienii Chun et Fang **4029**

28. Calyx densely ciliate; corolla about 7.5 cm long (south Xizang): R. lindleyi T. Moore **4030**

23. Calyx usually small, often ciliate; petioles grooved on the upper surface, the groove V-shaped.

32. Style quite smooth and glossy overall, glabrous (rarely sparsely hairy at the base) and not scaly.

33. Calyx lobes broad, 8 mm long; corolla not scaly outside; leaves and branchlets setose (south Xizang):

R. ciliatum Hook. f. **4031**

33. Calyx lobes 2 mm long; corolla scaly and pubescent outside; leaves and branchlets not setose (except the young leaves) (Yarlung Zangbo Jiang valley in Xizang):

R. scopulorum Hutch. **4032**

32. Style scaly at the base or above the base.
    34. Corolla tube exterior not scaly, or slightly scaly only at the base of the lobes or at the middle.
        35. Calyx densely long-setose at the margin; scales of the lower leaf surface more than a diameter apart; axillary leaf-bud scales very densely ciliate, the hairs soft and white (west and northwest Yunnan):

                R. ciliicalyx Franch. **4033**
        35. Calyx lobes not ciliate, but usually scaly; scales of the lower leaf surface a diameter or less apart (Guizhou):

                R. lyi Lévl. **4034**
    34. Corolla tube exterior more or less scaly overall or on one side.
        36. Scales of the lower leaf surface contiguous or subcontiguous, less than a diameter apart (west Yunnan):

                R. scottianum Hutch. **4035**
        36. Scales of the lower leaf surface scattered, about a diameter or more apart.
           37. Flowers solitary or rarely in pairs at the branch tip; leaves oblong-lanceolate; calyx small, not ciliate (west Yunnan):   **R. supranubium** Hutch. **4036**
           37. Flowers usually 3 or more at the branch tip; leaves elliptic-obovate; calyx well developed and setose-ciliate, or poorly developed and not ciliate.
              38. Scales of the lower leaf surface not more than a diameter apart; corolla flesh red; calyx well developed, the lobes long-setose at the margin (northwest Yunnan):

                R. carneum Hutch. **4037**
              38. Scales of the lower leaf surface 2-4 diameters apart; corolla white with one large yellow spot at the base; calyx degenerate to rimlike, not ciliate (northwest Yunnan):   **R. taronense** Hutch. **4038**

18. Style devoid of scales throughout; stamens 10 (rarely fewer, as in certain species in Subsection *Lapponica**), sometimes of slightly unequal length.

---

* Several references to "Subsection" occur in this key, but neither definition nor placement is given.

39. Flowers very small, barely 5-6 mm long, scaly outside, in a many-flowered corymb (northeast, northern, and northwest China, southward to Sichuan, Hubei): **R. micranthum** Turcz. **4039**

39. Flowers far larger, mostly in a few-flowered racemose-umbelliform inflorescence.

  40. Calyx relatively large and conspicuous in comparison with the corolla, often reddish, rarely as short as 4 mm even when the corolla is as short as 1-2 cm (as in Subsection *Moupinensia* and Subsection *Saluenensia*), usually to 6 mm long, often persistent and more or less enclosing the capsule.

    41. Prostrate or trailing dwarf terrestrial shrubs, often cushion-shaped, most only a few centimeters high, rarely taller shrubs to 30(60) cm high, not epiphytic; corolla small in most cases, rarely more than 2 cm long, somewhat pentagonal; scales conspicuously crenulate; style nearly always glabrous.

      42. Calyx exterior densely scaly.

        43. Branchlets and usually the pedicels densely setose; corolla exterior densely scaly and pubescent (northwest Yunnan): **R. saluenense** Franch. **4040**

        43. Branchlets and pedicels not setose; corolla exterior short-pubescent, but not scaly (southeast Xizang): **R. calostrotum** Balf. f. et Ward **4041**

      42. Calyx exterior glabrous and not scaly, only ciliate; pedicels densely setose and sparsely scaly (northwest Yunnan): **R. prostratum** W. W. Sm. **4042**

    41. Small and usually epiphytic shrubs; corolla of moderate size, about 3 cm long, fragrant; scales entire.

      44. Flowers white or red; pedicels setose; leaves 10-18 mm long, scales of the lower leaf surface subcontiguous (west Sichuan, Xizang): **R. dendrocharis** Franch. **4043**

      44. Flowers white; pedicels scaly; leaves 2-4.5 cm long, scales of the lower surface about a diameter apart (west Sichuan): **R. moupinense** Franch. **4044**

  40. Calyx relatively short and very small in comparison with the corolla, for the most part barely 3 mm long, not longer than 4 mm, often obscure (except calyx lobes about 6-8 mm long in a very few species in Subsection *Lapponica* and Subsection *Triflora*).

45. Corolla conspicuously fleshy, glabrous outside, narrowly tubular-campanulate, the lobes short and erect or somewhat obliquely ascending; style sparsely pubescent.

  46. Corolla 3-5 cm long, cinnabar red with light yellow or light green lobes; scales of the lower leaf surface very fine, fleshy, and less than a diameter apart (south Xizang):

R. cinnabarinum Hook. f. 4045

  46. Corolla 1.8 cm long, pink with cream lobes (south Xizang):

R. keysii Nutt. 4046

45. Corolla far thinner in texture, in most cases broadly campanulate or funnelform, or the lower half tubular and the upper half spreading.

  47. Prostrate (rarely to 1.5 meters high) shrubs, sometimes dwarf and cushion-shaped; leaves small to very small; flowers often _{p. 580} sessile or with pedicels only to 2-3 mm long (except 4-6 mm long as in *R. parvifolium* and *R. ravum*, or 10-12 mm long as in *R. cuneatum*, all in Subsection *Lapponica*).

    48. Flowers yellow.

      49. Style pubescent; stamens 10.

        50. Corolla 3 cm in diameter; scales of the lower leaf not contiguous, ½ diameter apart (west Sichuan, east Xizang):

R. flavidum Franch. 4047

        50. Corolla about 2 cm in diameter; scales of the lower leaf surface contiguous (southwest Sichuan, north Yunnan):

R. muliense Balf. f. et Forrest 4048

      49. Style glabrous or sparsely hairy at the base; stamens 5 (northwest Yunnan, west Sichuan):

R. chryseum Balf. f. et Ward 4049

    48. Flowers not yellow.

      51. Style pubescent on the lower part.

        52. Inflorescence of 4-10 flowers.

          53. Leaves about 2.5 cm long; calyx lobes 4 mm long, smooth and glossy outside (northwest Yunnan):

R. russatum Balf. f. et Forrest 4050

          53. Leaves 4-5 cm long; calyx lobes to 7 mm long, scaly outside (northwest Yunnan): R. ravum Balf. f. et W. W. Sm. 4051

52. Inflorescence of usually 1 flower, sometimes 2; leaves about 8 mm long, narrowly elliptic (west Sichuan):
R. websterianum Rehd. et Wils. **4052**

51. Style glabrous.
54. Corolla exterior not scaly.
55. Style very short, far shorter than the stamens.
56. Stamens exserted beyond the corolla tube; leaves narrowly oblong-lanceolate (Gansu, Qinghai):
R. thymifolium Maxim. **4053**
56. Stamens included within the corolla tube; leaves oblong-elliptic (west Sichuan, northwest Yunnan):
R. intricatum Franch. **4054**
55. Style as long as or longer than the stamens.
57. Calyx 6-8 mm long; shoots and the lower leaf surface densely setose (south Xizang): **R. setosum** D. Don **4055**
57. Calyx far shorter than the above; shoots and the lower leaf surface not setose.
58. Calyx lobes long-ciliate.
59. Leaves 1.2-2.5(3) cm long.
60. Shoots scaly and finely hairy; leaves to 1.8 cm long; flowers rose (northeastern China, Nei Mongol):
R. parvifolium Adams. **4056**
60. Shoots scaly but glabrous; leaves usually 2-2.5 cm long, sometimes to 3 cm; flowers lilac-purple (northwest Yunnan):
R. hippophaeoides Balf. f. et W. W. Sm. **4057**
59. Leaves 6-8 mm long, rarely slightly longer; flowers mostly purplish blue.
61. Inflorescence of 4-5 flowers; scales of the lower leaf surface usually somewhat separate or slightly contiguous (west and northwest Yunnan, southwest Sichuan):
R. fastigiatum Franch. **4058**
61. Inflorescence of 1-2 flowers; scales of the lower leaf surface densely imbricate (west Sichuan):
R. nigropunctatum Bur. et Franch. **4059**
58. Calyx lobes not ciliate, or sparsely short-hairy toward the apex.

579

62. Leaves 1.8 cm long; inflorescence of 5-8 flowers; corolla narrowly funnelform; calyx lobes 3 mm long, the exterior glabrous, not scaly (Gansu, Qinghai):

R. capitatum Maxim. **4060**

62. Leaves 1 cm long, rarely longer; corolla broadly funnelform; calyx exterior scaly.

 63. Calyx well developed, 3 mm long, the lobes scaly at the margin; flower-bud scales persistent (west Sichuan): **R. nitidulum** Rehd. et Wils. **4061**

 63. Calyx poorly developed, 1-2 mm long, the lobes sparsely short-ciliate toward the apex; flower-bud scales caducous (west Sichuan):

R. violaceum Rehd. et Wils. **4062**

54. Corolla exterior scaly at the lobes.

 64. Inflorescence of 1 flower, sometimes 2; stamens 10; leaves small, barely 6 mm long; calyx lobes not ciliate (south Xizang): **R. nivale** Hook. f. **4063**

 64. Inflorescence of 3-5 flowers; stamens 5(6); leaves 1.6 cm long; calyx lobes densely ciliate (northwest Yunnan):

R. achroanthum Balf. f. et W. W. Sm. **4064**

47. Shrubs of medium height (0.9-1.8-2.4 meters high, to 10 meters); leaves far larger.

65. Umbelliform inflorescence of mostly 4-6 flowers, rarely 8; corolla exterior scaly; stamens often of unequal length; foliage evergreen.

 66. Style glabrous; scales of the lower leaf surface usually contiguous or imbricate.

  67. Leaves elliptic-lanceolate, the lower surface pale red, with scales of more or less equal size (west Yunnan, southwest Sichuan):

R. rubiginosum Franch. **4065**

  67. Leaves oblong-elliptic, the lower surface brown, with scales of very unequal size (west Yunnan):

R. desquamatum Balf. f. et Forrest **4066**

 66. Style hairy on the lower part; scales of the lower leaf surface widely separated or somewhat close.

  68. Scales of the lower leaf surface widely separated; leaves to 10 cm long.

69. Style far shorter than the stamens; leaves tapering toward the base or sometimes rounded (northwest Yunnan):

R. brevistylum Franch. **4067**

69. Style as long as the stamens; leaves rounded at the base (west and northwest Yunnan): R. heliolepis Franch. **4068**

68. Scales of the lower leaf surface subcontiguous; leaves 5-6 cm long (west Yunnan): R. pholidotum Balf. f. et W. W. Sm. **4069**

65. Umbelliform inflorescence of mostly 3 flowers; corolla exterior glabrous or slightly scaly; stamens mostly of equal length; foliage evergreen, except in *R. chartophyllum* and *R. yunnanense*, which are semi-evergreen to deciduous; inflorescence terminal, rarely with lateral inflorescences as well.

70. Flowers yellow, cream, rarely pale greenish white.

71. Scales of the lower leaf surface contiguous, or mostly contiguous near the leaf margin, rarely more than a diameter apart.

72. Leaves oblong or oblong-lanceolate, rounded at the base (south Xizang): R. triflorum Hook. f. **4070**

72. Leaves differing from the above, tapering at the base or cuneate; Sichuan species.

73. Leaves acute at the apex, lower surface light green and scaly, the scales of unequal size and contiguous or no more than a diameter apart (also in Guizhou): R. ambiguum Hemsl. **4071**

73. Leaves acuminate at the apex, lower surface grayish white and scaly, the scales of nearly equal size and a diameter or slightly more apart: R. chengshienianum Fang **4072**

71. Scales of the lower leaf surface 2 or more diameters apart.

74. Calyx very short, not more than 2 mm long; corolla yellow, the exterior hairy and scaly (Sichuan, Yunnan, Guizhou):

R. lutescens Franch. **4073**

74. Calyx well developed, longer than the ovary, calyx lobes about 6 mm long; corolla white, glabrous and only sparsely scaly (Sichuan): R. hanceanum Hemsl. **4074**

70. Flowers pink, purplish blue, light purple, or rarely white, but not pale greenish white, cream, or yellow.

75. Lower leaf surface pubescent at the midrib, the hairs grayish white and usually quite dense.

76. Foliage branchlets scaly and hairy.

77. Branchlets short-pubescent at the most; calyx lobes short-ciliate; leaves hairy only at the midrib (west Hubei, northeast and west Sichuan, south Shaanxi): **R. augustinii** Hemsl. **4075**

77. Branchlets sparsely long-setose; calyx lobes not ciliate; most of the lower leaf surface, including the midrib, clad with bristle-like hairs; corolla densely long-hairy (west Sichuan):

R. villosum Hemsl. **4076**

76. Foliage branchlets scaly but glabrous (northwest Yunnan, southeast Xizang): **R. chasmanthum** Diels **4077**

75. Lower leaf surface glabrous at the midrib, often scaly.

78. Corolla tube exterior scaly overall (or glandular-scaly).

79. Flowers white, pink, or rose, often dotted with red or light greenish yellow.

80. Lower surface of the mature leaves grayish green between the scales, not grayish white; pedicels longer than the corolla; bud scales persistent on the branchlets for a long time (west Sichuan): **R. bracteatum** Rehd. et Wils. **4078**

80. Lower surface of the mature leaves conspicuously grayish white between the scales; pedicels shorter than the corolla; bud scales caducous (west Yunnan):

R. zaleucum Balf. **4079**

79. Flowers light purple, light reddish purple, or dark bluish purple.

81. Leaves narrowly oblong-oblanceolate, the length about 4 times the width, lower surface very densely scaly, the scales imbricate or flaky with a few scattered larger dark scales (west Sichuan, north Yunnan): **R. polylepis** Franch. **4080**

81. Leaves elliptic or ovate-elliptic, the length about twice the width, the scales of the lower surface separate or subimbricate.

82. Petiole margins densely setose; the scales of the lower leaf surface a diameter apart, blackish (west Sichuan):

R. amesiae Rehd. et Wils. **4081**

82. Petiole margins not setose.

83. Leaves quite small, about 3.8 cm long, 1.8 cm broad, the lower surface somewhat grayish white; flowers carmine (Sichuan, Guizhou, Shaanxi, Henan, Yunnan):

R. concinnum Hemsl. **4082**

83. Leaves large, 6.2-7.5 cm long, 2.5-3.2 cm broad; flowers dark purple.

84. Leaves oblong-lanceolate, midrib minutely hairy on the upper surface, upper surface sparsely clad with black scales; pedicels 1.6-1.8 cm long (west Sichuan):

R. pseudoyanthinum Hutch. **4083**

84. Leaves elliptic or long ovate, midrib glabrous on the upper surface, upper surface not scaly; pedicels 5-8 mm long (west Sichuan): **R. hutchinsonianum** Fang. **4084**

78. Corolla tube exterior without scales or sometimes with a few scales only on one side.

85. Leaves broadly ovate or broadly elliptic, the base conspicuously cordate or occasionally rounded.

86. Leaf base rounded, scales of the lower leaf surface 2-3 diameters apart, apex rounded and mucronate (Yunnan, southwest Sichuan): **R. exquisitum** Hutch. **4085**

86. Leaf base cordate, scales of the lower leaf surface scarcely more than ½ diameter apart, apex rounded and mucronulate (southeast Xizang, northwest Yunnan):

R. artosquameum Balf. f. et Forrest **4086**

85. Leaves lanceolate, oblong-lanceolate, or elliptic-oblanceolate, the base cuneate or occasionally almost rounded.

87. Leaves setose on the upper surface or at the margin, the bristles usually persistent for a season or longer; scales of the lower leaf surface usually very scattered, 1½ diameters or more apart; foliage often partly deciduous.

88. Flowers small, about 1.8 cm long; leaves setose only at the margin, especially so at the base (northwest Yunnan):

R. rigidum Franch. **4087**

88. Flowers 2.5 cm long or longer; upper leaf surface setose overall, especially when young (west and northwest Yunnan, southwest Sichuan): **R. yunnanense** Franch. **4088**

87. Leaves not setose on the upper surface or at the margin, except young leaves which may have marginal bristles that soon drop.

89. Scales of the lower leaf surface dense, scarcely 2 diameters apart.

90. Calyx well developed, unequally 5-lobed, the back and front lobes sometimes far longer than the rest (about 4 mm), long-ciliate, exterior scaly overall (Wa Shan in Sichuan):

R. searsiae Rehd. et Wils. **4089**

90. Calyx more or less inconspicuous, at least shallow, and more or less equally divided.

91. Style hairy toward the base; 9-10 flowers per inflorescence; capsule very short, about 6 mm long (Hubei, Sichuan): **R. charianthum** Hutch. **4090**

91. Style glabrous throughout; as many as 6 flowers per inflorescence.

92. A few stamens within the same flower shortly and sparsely hairy, the rest glabrous (central, west, and southwest Yunnan):

R. siderophyllum Franch. **4091**

92. All stamens within the same flower more or less similarly hairy.

93. Scales of the upper and lower leaf surfaces similarly dense.

94. Petiole margins not setose; scales on the leaves brown (northwest Yunnan):

R. stereophyllum Balf. f. et W. W. Sm. **4092**

94. Petiole margins long-setose; scales on the leaves blackish (Sichuan):

R. amesiae Rehd. et Wils. **4081**

93. Scales much denser on the lower leaf surface, the upper surface sometimes without scales or with only a few.

95. Leaves narrowly lanceolate, acute at both ends, the length about 3-4 times the width, the blade often conspicuously V-shaped from the midrib (west Sichuan): **R. davidsonianum** Rehd. et Wils. **4093**

95. Leaves more or less oblong or elliptic, quite rounded at both ends, the length about twice the width or slightly more, the blade flat-surfaced.

96. Flowers small, about 2 cm long; pedicels 1 cm long; scales of the lower leaf surface 2 diameters apart (north Sichuan): **R. heishuiense** Fang **4094**

96. Flowers 3 cm long or longer; pedicels 1.5-2 cm long.
 97. Scales of the lower leaf surface very dense, ½ diameter apart; inflorescence 5-8-flowered; pedicels scaly (Yunnan, southeast Xizang):
    R. oreotrephes W. W. Sm. **4095**
 97. Scales of the lower leaf surface sparse, 2 diameters apart; inflorescence usually 3-flowered; pedicels not scaly (southwest Sichuan):
    R. timeteum Balf. f. et Forrest **4096**
89. Scales of the lower leaf surface very sparse, about 3 diameters apart or more.
 98. Foliage deciduous or subdeciduous; filaments minutely hairy on the lower part; pedicels 1.5-2.5 cm long, not scaly (west and north Yunnan, south Sichuan):
    R. chartophyllum Franch. **4097**
 98. Foliage evergreen; filaments glabrous; pedicels 1-1.4 cm long, sparsely scaly (south Sichuan, north Yunnan):
    R. aechmophyllum Balf. f. et Forrest **4098**

2. Stamens 5, rarely 6-8(10), style short and thick, all included within the corolla tube; corolla salverform, the interior filled at the throat with dense downy hairs; scales stellately incised at the margin. (SECTION POGONANTHUM)

99. Stamens 6-8.
 100. Leaf-bud scales caducous; flowers pink, white, or yellow (south (Xizang):   **R. anthopogon** D. Don **4099**
 100. Leaf-bud scales persistent.
  101. Flowers yellow; lower leaf surface usually medium reddish brown (south and southeast Xizang): **R. hypenanthum** Balf. f. **4100**
  101. Flowers pink or white; lower leaf surface usually light tannish brown to light brown (west Yunnan, southeast Xizang, Sichuan):
    R. cephalanthum Franch. **4101**
99. Stamens 5.
 102. Ovary hairy and scaly.
  103. Corolla tube hairy outside; lower leaf surface chocolate brown; calyx scaly outside; pedicels scaly; flowers palest pink, almost white (southeast Xizang):   **R. laudandum** Cowan **4102**

103. Corolla tube glabrous outside; lower leaf surface light yellow-green or light brown; calyx not scaly outside; pedicels not scaly; flowers greenish yellow or yellow (Gansu, Qinghai, north Sichuan): **R. anthopogonoides** Maxim. **4103**

102. Ovary glabrous and scaly.

    104. Leaves lanceolate to linear-lanceolate, the length 4-5 times the width; calyx small, 1-2 mm long; flowers pink or white (Yunnan, Sichuan): **R. ledoides** Balf. f. **4104**

    104. Leaves broad, elliptic to oblong, obovate, or suborbicular; calyx large, 4-8 mm long (but in *R. rufescens* the calyx is only 2-3 mm long).

      105. Corolla exterior densely scaly.

        106. Corolla tube and lobes scaly outside; leaf-bud scales persistent; flowers lemon yellow (west Sichuan): **R. sargentianum** Rehd. et Wils. **4105**

        106. Corolla tube not scaly, lobes scaly outside; leaf-bud scales caducous; flowers white (northwest Yunnan): **R. primulaeflorum** var. **lepidanthum** Cowan (lín huā dùjuān, ''scaly-flowered rhododendron'')

      105. Corolla exterior not scaly, or sometimes scaly at the lobes.

        107. Corolla tube exterior conspicuously and minutely hairy.

          108. Lower leaf surface chocolate brown; leaf-bud scales persistent (southeast Xizang): **R. laudandum** var. **temoense** Cowan (tiě mù dùjuān, ''Tiemu rhododendron'', presumably a geographic reference.)

          108. Lower leaf surface light tannish brown to light brown; leaf-bud scales caducous (Yunnan): **R. primulaeflorum** var. **cephalanthoides** Cowan (wēi máo dùjuān, ''minutely hairy rhododendron'')

        107. Corolla tube exterior without minute hairs, or sometimes very slightly and minutely hairy.

          109. Leaf-bud scales persistent.

            110. Leaves about 5 cm long, nearly 2.6 cm broad; leaf-bud scales broadly ovate or orbicular; flowers white, occasionally rose-tinged (west Yunnan): **R. platyphyllum** Balf. f. et W. W. Sm. (kuò yè dùjuān, ''broad-leaved rhododendron'')

110. Leaves 1.3-4.2 cm long, 0.8-2 cm broad; leaf-bud scales narrow, linear or lanceolate.
  111. Lower leaf surface usually medium reddish brown; corolla exterior not scaly; flowers yellow (southeast Xizang):
                        R. hypenanthum Balf. f. **4100**
  111. Lower leaf surface usually light brown.
    112. Corolla exterior not scaly; flowers white or rose (Yunnan, Sichuan):   **R. cephalanthum** Franch. **4101**
    112. Corolla exterior sparsely scaly; flowers yellow (Yunnan, Xizang):   **R. cephalanthum** var. **nmaiense** Cowan
                        (huáng huā máo hóu dùjuān, "yellow-flowered hairy-throated rhododendron")
109. Leaf-bud scales caducous.
  113. Lower leaf surface medium reddish brown.
    114. Leaves 1-1.9 cm long; flowers white or pink (Sichuan):
                        R. rufescens Franch. **4106**
    114. Leaves 2.6-3.8 cm long.
      115. Calyx 2-3 mm long; flowers white or pink (Sichuan):
                        R. rufescens Franch. **4106**
      115. Calyx 4-5 mm long; flowers pink, white, or yellow (Xizang):   **R. anthopogon** D. Don **4099**
  113. Lower leaf surface light tannish brown, olive green, or light brown.
    116. Calyx large, 4-5 mm long, sometimes 3 mm.
      117. Pedicels scaly, calyx exterior scaly; leaves narrowly elliptic, 5-8 mm broad, rarely broader, tapered at the base or narrowly rounded; flowers white with yellow corolla tube (sometimes white, light purple, or light rose) (Yunnan, Sichuan, Xizang):
                        R. primulaeflorum Bur. et Franch. **4107**
      117. Pedicels not scaly, calyx exterior not scaly; leaves broadly elliptic, 1.3-1.9 cm broad, broadly rounded at the base; flowers yellow or pale greenish yellow (Gansu, Qinghai, north Sichuan):
                        R. anthopogonoides Maxim. **4103**
    116. Calyx small, 1-2 mm long; flowers pink to white (Yunnan):
                        R. trichostomum Franch.
        (máo zuǐ dùjuān, "hairy-mouthed rhododendron")

1. Seeds mostly caudate at both ends, the appendages long and thread-like; in the mature capsule the placenta resembles 5 threadlike ribs, separated through the lower common axis and joined only at the top; capsule valves quite thin, more or less twisted after dehiscence and usually reflexed; scales discoid, entire, or irregularly and acutely cleft at the transparent margin to regularly, deeply, and conspicuously stellate. (SECTION VIREYA)

118. Calyx large, 3-4 mm long, 5-lobed to the base; leaves spatulate-oblanceolate, 1.3-2 cm long, to 8 mm broad at the upper part (southeast Xizang, northwest Yunnan):   R. vaccinioides Hook. f. 4108

118. Calyx small, finely 5-toothed; leaves long obovate, 2-4 cm long, 8-15 mm broad at the upper part.

119. Leaves obovate, the length about twice the width; flowers 1.3 cm long (southeast Yunnan):   R. emarginatum Hemsl. 4109

119. Leaves cuneate-oblanceolate, the length nearly 4 times the width; flowers about 2 cm long (Guizhou, Guangxi):

R. euonymifolium Lévl. 4110

B. SUBGENUS PSEUDAZALEA

1. Pedicels scaly, or sparsely pubescent, or rarely clad with bristlelike soft hairs.

*2. Pedicels sparsely pubescent and scaly.

3. Hairs of the upper leaf surface persistent; calyx lobes long-ciliate (west Yunnan):   R. trichocladum Franch. 4111

3. Upper leaf surface soon glabrous; calyx lobes not ciliate (Yunnan, southeast Xizang):   R. melinanthum Balf. f. et Ward 4112

2. Pedicels sparsely pubescent but not scaly (west Yunnan):

R. oulotrichum Balf. f. et Forrest 4113

2. Pedicels scaly but not pubescent.

4. Flowers dark yellow; foliage deciduous (northwest Yunnan, southeast Xizang):   R. semilunatum Balf. f. et Forrest 4114

4. Flowers marked with rose; foliage semi-evergreen (northwest Yunnan):   R. rubrolineatum Balf. f. et Forrest 4115

1. Pedicels smooth and glossy, glabrous and not scaly (northwest Yunnan, southeast Xizang):   R. chloranthum Balf. f. et Forrest 4116

*Triple entries numbered in bold type.

588

C. SUBGENUS RHODODENDRON

1. Leaf buds (as well as flower buds) long acuminate, the outer bracts narrow and long acuminate; leaves long lanceolate; shoots and petioles glandular-hairy; corolla funnelform, densely hairy outside, especially on the corolla tube, the hairs glandular or stellate.
   2. Leaves obtuse at both ends, shallowly cordate at the base, indumentum sparse and glandular; corolla 7-lobed (Hubei, Sichuan, Guizhou):

   R. auriculatum Hemsl. **4117**
   2. Leaves tapered at both ends, cuneate at the base, with a dense woolly indumentum; corolla 5-lobed (southwest Yunnan):

   R. griersonianum Balf. f. et Forrest **4118**
1. Leaf buds subglobose or (oblong) ovate, the outer bracts more or less obtuse.
   3. Leaves glandular-hairy (clad with glandular bristles or sparse soft hairs) at least on the lower surface or at the midrib on the upper surface, also often tomentose or woolly (at least when young) on the lower surface; shoots and petioles often similarly setose.
      4. Calyx conspicuous, 5-25 mm long; inflorescence umbelliform, usually compact; shoots clad with bristlelike glandular hairs; young leaves often tomentose or woolly on the lower surface.
         5. Mature leaves glabrous on the lower surface; inflorescence compact; flowers dark red or blood red; stamens and style glabrous; calyx glabrous, the lobes rounded and crenate (south Xizang):

         R. barbatum Wall. **4119**
         5. Mature leaves densely woolly or setose on the lower surface; inflorescence lax; flowers rose or pale lilac purple; stamens and style hairy on the lower part; calyx densely glandular-hairy, the lobes acute, entire, and ciliate.
            6. Leaves 10-15 cm long, 3-4.5 cm broad, slightly cordate at the base, with a dense woolly indumentum on the lower surface; corolla pink (Yunnan, southeast Xizang):   **R. crinigerum** Franch. **4120**
            6. Leaves to 20 cm long, 4-6 cm broad, the lower surface clad with gland-tipped bristles, especially at the midrib and lateral veins; corolla pale lilac purple (Yunnan, Sichuan, southeast Xizang):

            R. glischrum Balf. f. et W. W. Sm. **4121**

4. Calyx small, 1-3 mm long (7-15 mm long and deeply lobed only in *R. longesquamatum*); inflorescence lax umbelliform; shoots neither setose nor glandular-setose; bristles and glandular bristles limited to the lower leaf surface at the midrib (scattered on the shoots and throughout the lower leaf surface only in *R. strigillosum*).

   7. Shoots and petioles usually setose, or rarely glabrous, the bristles long, coarse, and often gland-tipped.

      8. Flowers dark red; corolla tubular-campanulate; lower leaf surface sparsely setose, densely clad at the midrib with interwoven bristles and branching hairs (west Sichuan, north Yunnan):

                        R. strigillosum Franch. **4122**

      8. Flowers white tinged rose; corolla funnelform-campanulate; lower leaf surface glabrous or sparsely glandular only at the midrib.

         9. Corolla 5-lobed; leaves 8-11 cm long, base subcordate, lower surface sparsely glandular only at the midrib (west Sichuan):

                        R. monosematum Hutch. **4123**

         9. Corolla 7-lobed; leaves 19-23 cm long, base obtuse, lower surface powdery-pubescent at first, soon glabrous (north Guangxi):

                        R. chihsinianum Chun et Fang **4124**

      8. Flowers dark red; corolla broadly campanulate; lower leaf surface light yellow with a loose woolly indumentum, floccose and glandular at the midrib; shoots densely clad with glandular hairs of unequal length (west Sichuan):

                        R. ochraceum Rehd. et Wils. **4125**

   7. Shoots and petioles clad with soft fluffy branching eglandular hairs, or at first floccose and glandular-hairy.

      10. Calyx large, 7-15 mm long; bud scales persistent; lower leaf surface densely clad at the midrib with branching hairs, petioles and branchlets similarly hairy (west Sichuan):

                        R. longesquamatum Schneid. **4126**

      10. Calyx small, 1-2 mm long; bud scales caducous.

         11. Pedicels, ovary, and the lower part of the style glandular and floccose; lower surface of mature leaves glabrous throughout (Anhui, Jiangxi):   **R. anwheiense** Wils. **4127**

         11. Pedicels and ovary tomentose; style glabrous; lower surface of mature leaves densely hairy at the midrib, especially on the lower part.

12. Leaves to 3.5 cm broad, apex abruptly acuminate, base rounded (west Sichuan):   **R. pachytrichum** Franch. **4128**

12. Leaves to 4.5 cm broad, apex acute, base more or less cordate (Sichuan, Hubei, Guizhou, south Shaanxi):

R. maculiferum Franch. **4129**

3. Leaves and shoots not setose.

13. Corolla with conspicuous nectary sacs at the base which are dark-colored within, sometimes almost black, and contain nectar glands. p. 594

14. Trees, with a distinct trunk; leaves oblong, apex acuminate, lateral veins numerous, parallel, and usually impressed on the upper surface, lower surface somewhat tomentose, the hairs thinly to thickly layered, white to darkly ferrugineous; inflorescence compact umbelliform; pedicels quite thick, to 1 cm long; corolla tubular-campanulate, usually dark red or silvery red.

15. Leaves oblong-lanceolate or elliptic, apex slightly obtuse, base cuneate or rounded.

16. Indumentum of the lower leaf surface thin (membranaceous) (south and southeast Xizang):   **R. arboreum** Sm. **4130**

16. Indumentum of the lower leaf surface more or less spongy (Yunnan, Guizhou):   **R. delavayi** Franch. **4131**

15. Leaves very narrowly lanceolate, acute at both ends (west Yunnan):   **R. peramoenum** Balf. f. et Forrest **4132**

14. Shrubs, without a distinct trunk.

17. Leaves broad, rounded at the apex, rounded and often cordate at the base, upper surface more or less gray-green, glabrous, but on the lower surface fine hairs or glandular hairs or remnants of them are visible under magnification; inflorescence umbelliform, few-flowered; corolla campanulate to tubular-funnelform, usually 5-lobed, the interior spotted to the mouth; ovary glabrous or clad with glandular hairs, not with simple hairs; pedicels usually clad with stipitate glands.

18. Lower leaf surface clad at the lateral veins with clustered hairs resembling a string of pearls; flowers dark red (south Xizang):

R. hookeri Nutt. **4133**

18. Lower leaf surface not clad as above.

19. Flowers dark red.

20. Leaves orbicular or broadly elliptic (southeast Xizang):
R. **thomsonii** Hook. f.
(bàn tuán yè dùjuān,
"semicircular-leaved rhododendron")
20. Leaves usually obovate or oblong-broadly ovate (west Yunnan): R. **meddianum** Hutch. **4134**
19. Flowers white, yellow, or pink.
21. Leaves orbicular or broadly elliptic, lower surface glabrous; petioles long; corolla white or pinkish (west Yunnan):
R. **cyanocarpum** (Franch.) W. W. Sm. **4135**
21. Leaves obovate or oblong to oblong-obovate, lower surface or the veins of the lower surface hairy or glabrous; petioles to 1 cm long; corolla varying in color from white or light yellow to dark red.
22. Petioles short and thick; lower leaf surface glabrous, but often hairy at the midrib; calyx deeply cleft, the lobes ovate (Yunnan, southeast Xizang):
R. **eclecteum** Balf. f. et Forrest **4136**
22. Petioles 1 cm long; lower leaf surface usually clad with a thin layer of veillike indumentum, or white-powdery; calyx saucer-shaped, the lobes shallow and undulate (Yunnan, southeast Xizang): R. **stewartianum** Diels **4137**
17. Leaves oblong-elliptic to broadly obovate, acuminate or rounded at the apex, not distinctly cordate at the base, glabrous, or the lower surface densely tomentose; inflorescence umbelliform, more or less lax; corolla highly variable in shape, not spotted; ovary pubescent, or hairy and glandular, or glandular only.
23. Procumbent dwarf shrubs with twining crooked stems; leaves small, 2.5 cm long, lower surface purple, glabrous at maturity but clad at the veins with short red glandular hairs (Yunnan, southeast Xizang): R. **forrestii** Balf. f. ex Diels **4138**
23. Erect shrubs, usually of medium height; leaves far larger, lower surface not purple, glabrous, or often clad with thick indumentum.
24. Ovary slender, glabrous, tapering toward the apex to form the style; capsule long and curved.

25. Leaves oblong, apex rounded or obtuse, lower surface glabrous with only traces of hair at the midrib; flowers flame
red tinged purple (west Yunnan):
                              R. neriiflorum Franch. **4139**
25. Leaves lanceolate-oblong, apex acute, lower surface densely
clad with rusty yellow radiate branching hairs; flowers dark
red or rose, or yellow with a broad red margin (northwest
Yunnan):   **R. floccigerum** Franch. **4140**
24. Ovary short and thick, truncate at the apex.
  26. Corolla fleshy; lower leaf surface thickly clad with yellowish
  brown tomentose indumentum.
    27. Shoots woolly-tomentose.
      28. Leaves 4-6 cm long, upper surface smooth; calyx large, to
      1 cm long, dark red (west Yunnan):
                              R. haematodes Franch. **4141**
      28. Leaves 7-13 cm long, upper surface bullate; calyx degen-
      erate, rimlike (Yunnan, southeast Xizang):
                              R. mallotum Balf. f. et Ward. **4142**
    27. Shoots setose (as well as glandular and floccose).
      29. Petioles more or less setose; pedicels long-setose; style
      glabrous (Yunnan, southeast Xizang):
                              R. chaetomallum Hutch. **4143**
      29. Petioles red-tomentose; pedicels densely floccose; style
      stellate-hairy at the base (southeast Xizang):
                              R. beanianum Cowan **4144**
  26. Corolla thin, usually not fleshy; lower leaf surface thinly clad
  with white plastered indumentum (sometimes glabrous).
    30. Corolla orange to orange-red.
      31. Lower leaf surface light grayish brown; pedicels to 2.5 cm
      long; corolla orange-red (northwest Yunnan):
                              R. apodectum Balf. f. et W. W. Sm. **4145**
      31. Lower leaf surface grayish white; pedicels 1.5 cm long;
      corolla orangish purple (northwest Yunnan):
                              R. dichroanthum Diels **4146**
    30. Corolla dark red, red to rose, or blackish red.
      32. Pedicels and ovary glabrous and eglandular; calyx discoid,
      without lobes (southeast Xizang):
                              R. parmulatum Cowan **4147**

32. Pedicels and ovary hairy or glandular; calyx cuplike and lobed.

33. Pedicels and ovary densely glandular; corolla blackish dark red (southeast Xizang, northwest Yunnan):
R. didymum Balf. f. et Forrest **4148**

33. Pedicels and ovary densely tomentose but not glandular.

34. Indumentum of the lower leaf surface thin and plastered; bud scales caducous.

35. Flowers bright dark red (southeast Xizang, Yunnan):
R. sanguineum Franch. **4149**

35. Flowers blackish dark red (southeast Xizang):
R. haemaleum Balf. f. et Forrest **4150**

34. Indumentum of the lower leaf surface dense, thick, and loosely woolly; bud scales persistent on the branches for several years (southeast Xizang, Yunnan):
R. horaeum Balf. f. et Forrest **4151**

13. Corolla without nectary sacs at the base.

36. Corolla lobes as long as the corolla tube; leaves oblong, glabrous, or the lower surface clad at the veins with traces of juvenile hairs; inflorescence corymbose, rachis distinctly elongate; pedicels continuing to lengthen during flowering, elongate and straight when the capsules mature.

37. Dwarf undershrub, 15-30 cm high, stems thick and horizontal, leaf-bud scales persistent on the lateral branches; flowers yellow (northeastern China):
R. chrysanthum Pallas **4152**

37. Erect shrub, 1-3.5 meters high; leaf-bud scales caducous; flowers white (Taiwan):
R. hyperythrum Hayata **4153**

36. Corolla lobes shorter than the corolla tube.

38. Leaves not hairy, even when young, but often clad more or less with stipitate glands, especially at the midrib in young leaves. p. 598

39. Flowers of six to eight parts (rarely 5); leaves broadly elliptic p. 597 (sometimes suborbicular) to elliptic or oblanceolate, apex rounded or rarely acuminate, base cordate or narrowly cuneate; corolla large, mostly funnelform-campanulate, not spotted at the throat (except *R. serotinum*, etc.); stamens 12-25 (rarely 10); inflorescence often glandular, especially the pedicels and ovaries; capsule large, usually oblong, often borne obliquely at the tip of the fruitstalk.

594

40. Style glandular throughout, to the tip.
  41. Stamens pubescent; glands on the style white to yellow.
    42. Corolla not spotted.
      43. Leaves broadly elliptic to suborbicular, 8-11 cm long, 5-7 cm broad, rounded at both ends, the broadly winged base decurrent onto the stout petiole (southeast Sichuan):
                                      R. platypodum Diels **4154**
      43. Leaves oblong to oblong-obovate, the length 2-3 times the width, the base more or less tapered, not decurrent onto the petiole.
        44. Leaves 5-15 cm long; corolla 3-6 cm long (Yunnan, Sichuan):   **R. decorum** Franch. **4155**
        44. Leaves 10-30 cm long; corolla 6-10 cm long (west Yunnan):
                              R. diaprepes Balf. f. et W. W. Sm. **4156**
    42. Corolla conspicuously spotted; leaf apex emarginate and mucronate, base asymmetrically cordate (southwest Yunnan):
                                      R. serotinum Hutch. **4157**
  41. Stamens glabrous; glands on the style white to yellow.
    45. Leaves more or less rounded at the base.
      46. Leaves 7-17 cm long; corolla funnelform-campanulate, 4-5 cm long, pink, or white tinged pink (Zhejiang, Anhui, Jiangxi, Hunan):   **R. fortunei** Lindley **4158**
      46. Leaves 20-25 cm long; corolla broadly funnelform-campanulate, 9-10 cm long, pure white (Guangdong):
                                      R. faithae Chun **4159**
    45. Leaves deeply cordate.
      47. Leaves 10-20 cm long, 6-8 cm broad; petioles and pedicels glandular (west Sichuan):
                                      R. hemsleyanum Wils. **4160**
      47. Shape of the leaves as above but broader; petioles and pedicels smooth, glossy, and eglandular (Emei Shan in Sichuan):
                          R. hemsleyanum var. **chengianum** Fang
                   (wú xiàn dùjuān, "eglandular rhododendron")
    45. Leaves more or less cuneate at the base; leaves oblong-oblanceolate, 13-16 cm long, apex acute (Hubei, Sichuan):
                                      R. discolor Franch. **4161**
  41. Stamens glabrous; glands on the style red to purplish black (Sichuan, Yunnan):   **R. vernicosum** Franch. **4162**

40. Style smooth and glossy, or glandular only at the base.
48. Leaves orbicular or orbicular-ovate.
49. Leaves orbicular or orbicular-ovate, deeply cordate at the base, with bilateral overlapping auricles (west Sichuan):

R. orbiculare Decaisne **4163**

49. Leaves elliptic to orbicular-ovate, slightly cordate at the base, without auricles (east Guangxi):

R. cardiobasis Sleumer **4164**

48. Leaves comparatively long, far longer than broad.
50. Leaves small, 5-10 cm long (rarely longer), more or less symmetrically elliptic, more or less rounded at both ends; rachis usually very short; flowers 3-4 cm long.
51. Ovary smooth, glossy, and glabrous; pedicels glandular (Hubei, Sichuan, Gansu): **R. oreodoxa** Franch. **4165**
51. Ovary glandular.
52. Filaments glabrous.
53. Leaves 9-14 cm long, 3-5 cm broad, subacute at both ends; rachis 3 cm long, eglandular; pedicels sparsely glandular at first, soon smooth and glossy; corolla not spotted (north Guangxi):

R. kwangfuense Chun et Fang **4166**

53. Leaves smaller, 5-8 cm long, 3.5-4.5 cm broad, apex rounded and mucronate; rachis short, glandular; pedicels densely glandular; corolla usually red-spotted (northeast Sichuan, northwest Hubei, south Shaanxi):

R. fargesii Franch. **4167**

52. Filaments hairy; pedicels densely glandular (Sichuan, Hubei): **R. erubescens** Hutch. **4168**
50. Leaves large, 10-30 cm long, more or less oblanceolate, often abruptly short acuminate at the apex, cuneate at the base; rachis usually elongate; flowers 4-6 cm long.
54. Corolla funnelform-campanulate; stamens 10-15; style slender, stigma capitate.
55. Ovary glandular; leaves tapering toward the base to cuneate (west Sichuan): **R. davidii** Franch. **4169**
55. Ovary eglandular, smooth and glossy; leaves tapering slightly toward the base.

56. Midrib more or less hairy.
57. Corolla 5-lobed, minutely and very densely hairy within, dotted or streaked; filaments pubescent on the lower part (Hubei, Sichuan, Shaanxi):
R. sutchuenense Franch. **4170**
57. Corolla 6-7-lobed, glabrous within, not dotted or streaked; filaments minutely glandular-hairy on the lower part (Sichaun, south Shaanxi):
R. planetum Balf. f. **4171**
56. Midrib glabrous; corolla 5-lobed, filaments minutely hairy on the lower part (Hubei, Shaanxi, Sichuan, Yunnan):
R. praevernum Hutch. **4172**
54. Corolla campanulate, swollen at the base; stamens 15-25; style stout, stigma discoid.
58. Leaves 18-20 cm long, 5-8 cm broad, apex obtuse or rounded, lower surface sparsely clad with stellate hairs (Sichuan):
R. asterochnoum Diels
(xīng máo dùjuān, ''star-hair rhododendron'')
58. Leaves 10-15 cm or 20-30 cm long, oblanceolate, apex acuminate or short acuminate, lower surface glabrous.
59. Leaves 20-30 cm long, 4-8 cm broad; petiole about 2 cm long (Sichuan, south Shaanxi):
R. calophytum Franch. **4173**
59. Leaves 10-15 cm long or slightly longer, 2-3.5 cm broad; petiole about 1 cm long (Sichuan):
R. openshawianum Rehd. et Wils. **4174**
39. Flowers of five parts; leaves mostly broad and rounded at both ends, the base sometimes cordate.
60. Corolla funnelform; capsule very slender, falcate; leaves thin-coriaceous, oblong to elliptic (Yunnan, southwest Sichuan):
R. selense Franch. **4175**
60. Corolla cuplike to campanulate.
61. Capsule cylindric, more or less stout, slightly curved.
62. Style stipitate-glandular to the tip; leaves thick-coriaceous, elliptic to orbicular.
63. Corolla bowl-shaped or cuplike, yellow, white, or pink; calyx usually 0.4-1.2 cm long.

64. Flowers bright yellow; leaf base deeply cordate (Yunnan, southeast Xizang): **R. wardii** W. W. Sm. **4176**

64. Flowers white tinged pink; leaf base slightly cordate, truncate, or rounded (west Sichuan):

R. souliei Franch. **4177**

63. Corolla campanulate, pink or rose; calyx small, 1-5 mm long or just a rim.

65. Leaves orbicular; dwarf spreading subshrub; shoots glandular-setose; inflorescence of 2-3 flowers (rarely as many as 5) (west Sichuan):

R. williamsianum Rehd. et Wils. **4178**

65. Leaves oblong or oblong-elliptic; upright shrub; shoots not clad with gland-tipped bristles; inflorescence of 5-7 flowers (southeast Xizang): **R. cerasinum** Tagg **4179**

62. Style glabrous, or stipitate-glandular only at the base; leaves thin-coriaceous, stiff, narrowly elliptic (Xizang):

R. martinianum Balf. f. et Forrest
(shǎo huā dùjuān, "few-flowered rhododendron")

61. Capsule slender, distinctly falcate; leaves coriaceous, orbicular to elliptic.

66. Corolla yellow; lower leaf surface gray-green, minutely papillate, but not stipitate-glandular (south Xizang):

R. campylocarpum Hook. f. **4180**

66. Corolla rose tinged red; lower leaf surface grayish white, glabrous except at the sparsely stipitate-glandular midrib (west (Yunnan): **R. callimorphum** Balf. f. et W. W. Sm. **4181**

38. **Leaves more or less densely pubescent (to woolly or tomentose), often becoming subglabrous, as in Section _Irroratum_.**

67. **Leaves sparsely clad with simple hairs or soft stellate hairs (some becoming subglabrous).**

p. 602

68. Leaves tomentose or pubescent only when young, later subglabrous.

69. Leaves thin and clad with soft simple hairs when young, mostly subglabrous at maturity (but with persistent dot-like hair remnants), more or less oblong or oblong-lanceolate, mostly acuminate at the apex, the margin translucent-cartilaginous, often minutely crenulate, and slightly scabrous; ovary not clad with soft stellate hairs; corolla most often spotted.

70. Lower leaf surface glabrous at maturity or rarely inconspicuously hairy; leaves lanceolate, apex acuminate; ovary glabrous, tomentose, or glandular.

  71. Ovary more or less glandular or glandular-hairy (not smooth and glossy).

    72. Corolla tubular or funnelform-campanulate, 3-5 cm long.

      73. Shoots and rachis clad with short-stalked glands; flowers white or milk white (west Yunnan):

R. irroratum Franch. **4182**

      73. Shoots and rachis glabrous; flowers purple (Guizhou, north Guangxi, Guangdong): **R. brevinerve** Chun et Fang **4183**

    72. Corolla more or less cuplike, 2.5 cm long; shoots and rachis floccose and more or less glandular (Guizhou, east Yunnan):

R. annae Franch. **4184**

  71. Ovary more or less pubescent or tomentose, but eglandular; style glabrous; flowers rose; pedicels and rachis densely tomentose, the hairs reddish brown and branching (west Sichuan):

R. sikangense Fang **4185**

  71. Ovary glabrous and eglandular; style glabrous; flowers dark rose, campanulate, 5-7 cm long (northwest Yunnan):

R. anthosphaerum Diels **4186**

70. Lower leaf surface clad with a thin indumentum which is more or less persistent at maturity; leaves oblong, apex obtuse; ovary more or less glandular-hairy (west Yunnan):

R. agastum Balf. f. et W. W. Sm. **4187**

69. Leaves clad with soft stellate hairs or coarse stellate hairs when young, subglabrous at maturity, mostly large, oblong-broadly elliptic, obtuse to rounded at the apex, thin; ovary clad with soft stellate hairs (Jizu Shan in west Yunnan):

R. eriogynum Balf. f. et W. W. Sm. **4188**

68. Leaves remaining densely pubescent at maturity, the hairs silvery white, silvery gray, or sometimes yellowish brown.

  74. Lower leaf surface clad with a thin layer of usually silvery white or yellowish brown indumentum, the indumentum plastered or parchmentlike, not woolly, thickly felted, nor stiffly hairy; inflorescence lax umbelliform. (It is important to note here that, in comparison, some species in Subsection *Taliensia* are easily differentiated by the shortened rachis.)

75. Indumentum of the lower leaf surface an eye-catching silvery white.

  76. Corolla 3-3.5 cm long, narrow at the base.

    77. Leaves broadly oblong; pedicels and ovary floccose and glandular (Hubei, Sichuan, Shaanxi):

                        R. hypoglaucum Hemsl. **4189**

    77. Leaves narrowly oblong to oblong-lanceolate; pedicels and ovary floccose but not glandular.

      78. Indumentum of the lower leaf surface thin and evenly distributed; inflorescence 7-9-flowered; corolla white, occasionally tinged rose; filaments pubescent on the lower part (Sichuan, Guizhou, northeast Yunnan):

                        R. argyrophyllum Franch. **4190**

      78. Indumentum of the lower leaf surface thicker, thickest along the sides of the midrib, loosely spongy; inflorescence 12-22-flowered; corolla purple to light purplish red; filaments glabrous (west Sichuan):   **R. pingianum** Fang **4191**

  76. Corolla 4-5 cm long, purple, broad at the base (Emei Shan in Sichuan):   **R. rirei** Hemsl. et Wils. **4192**

75. Indumentum of the lower leaf surface bronzy and lustrous (west Sichuan):   **R. insigne** Hemsl. **4193**

75. Indumentum of the lower leaf surface grayish white to light yellowish brown or pale yellow, not lustrous.

  79. Ovary glandular throughout; style glandular overall to the tip, or eglandular.

    80. Leaves broadly recurved at the margin, with dense brown bud scales at the base which persist for several years; flowers white tinged pink; style densely glandular (Sichuan):

                   R. thayerianum Rehd. et Wils. **4194**

    80. Leaves not recurved at the margin; bud scales caducous; flowers purple; style smooth, glossy, and eglandular (Sichuan):

                       R. chienianum Fang **4195**

  79. Ovary glandular and hairy, or elgandular and hairy.

    81. Leaf apex acute.

      82. Leaves 3-4 cm broad, lower surface thickly clad with a light yellow tomentose indumentum; stamens 18-20; ovary densely floccose, style glabrous (north Guangxi):

                     R. haofui Chun et Fang **4196**

82. Leaves 1.5-2.5 cm broad, lower surface thinly clad with a gray-white plastered agglutinate indumentum; stamens 22-24; ovary clad with short branching hairs and scattered small glands (Fujian, Zhejiang, Jiangxi, Guangxi):

R. fokienense Franch. **4197**

82. Leaves 2-4 cm broad, lower surface thinly clad with a light brownish gray plastered indumentum; stamens 10; ovary densely brown-hairy and glandular (southeast Sichuan):

R. youngae Fang **4198**

81. Leaf apex acuminate; style glabrous (west Sichuan):

R. insigne Hemsl. **4193**

81. Leaf apex more or less rounded to obtuse.

83. Leaves 4-9 cm long, veins evident on the upper surface; corolla lobes deeply emarginate; ovary hairy and glandular, style glandular at the base (Guangdong, Guangxi, Fujian):

R. simiarum Hance **4199**

83. Leaves 8-13 cm long, veins obscure on the upper surface; corolla lobes not emarginate; ovary densely pubescent only (north Guangxi): **R. versicolor** Chun et Fang **4200**

74. Lower leaf surface clad with a thicker but still thin and smooth layer of whitish to cinnamon suedelike indumentum composed of stellate woolly hairs; inflorescence umbelliform, rachis very short.

84. Indumentum of the lower leaf surface continuous.

85. Corolla yellow; ovary 9-10-loculed; hairs of the lower leaf surface branching or stellate-radiate.

86. Leaves usually broadly ovate, ovate-elliptic, or broadly elliptic; inflorescence somewhat compact; corolla not dotted; hairs stellate-radiate (west, northwest, and northeast Yunnan):

R. lacteum Franch. **4201**

86. Leaves usually oblong-elliptic, oblong, or oblanceolate; inflorescence usually lax; corolla dotted; hairs branching (south Xizang): **R. wightii** Hook. f. **4202**

85. Corolla white, pink, or rose; ovary 5-11-loculed; hairs of the lower leaf surface long-radiate-branching or stellate-radiate.

87. Ovary densely tomentose.

88. Indumentum of the lower leaf surface suedelike, the radiating hairs oblong or ovate (southeast Xizang, Yunnan, southwest Sichuan): **R. beesianum** Diels **4203**

88. Indumentum of the lower leaf surface usually powdery, the radiating hairs somewhat pear-shaped (northwest Yunnan, southwest Sichuan):

R. traillianum Forrest et W. W. Sm. **4204**

87. Ovary glabrous (or sparsely floccose).

89. Indumentum of the lower leaf surface usually powdery, the radiating hairs somewhat pear-shaped:

R. traillianum Forrest et W. W. Sm. **4204**

89. Indumentum of the lower leaf surface suedelike or agglutinate.

90. Indumentum of the lower leaf surface suedelike or felted; branchlets and petioles eglandular; ovary sparsely floccose or glabrous.

91. Branchlets and petioles usually densely or somewhat tomentose; pedicels usually floccose; ovary sparsely floccose, or glabrous; leaves oblong-lanceolate, apex acute (northwest Yunnan):

R. dryophyllum Balf. f. et Forrest **4205**

91. Branchlets, petioles, and ovary usually glabrous; leaves ovate or elliptic to oblong (Quinghai, Gansu, Shaanxi):

R. przewalskii Maxim. **4206**

90. Indumentum of the lower leaf surface usually felted-agglutinate; branchlets and petioles eglandular; ovary glabrous (southeast Xizang, Yunnan, Sichuan, Gansu):

R. agglutinatum Balf. f. et Forrest **4207**

84. Indumentum of the lower leaf surface not continuous, composed of scattered hairs or a thin veillike layer of sparse hairs, the hairs long-radiate; branchlets, petioles, pedicels, and ovary usually glabrous, also eglandular (Qinghai, Gansu, Shaanxi):

R. przewalskii Maxim. **4206**

67. Leaves conspicuously stellate-tomentose or stellate-woolly on the lower surface.

92. Indumentum of the lower leaf surface woolly and 2-layered, the leaves largest within Genus *Rhododendron*; corolla elongate mortar-shaped, 7-10-lobed; stamens 12-18.

93. Indumentum of the lower leaf surface 2-layered, the upper layer more or less detersile and composed of cupular or funnelform compound hairs, the lower layer suedelike.

94. Petioles long and cylindric, the leaf base not decurrent onto the petiole.
  95. Indumentum of the lower leaf surface rusty red, rarely light yellowish brown.
    96. Leaves broadly obovate, apex broadly rounded and widely emarginate, upper surface distinctly rugose (southeast Xizang, northwest Yunnan):
      R. arizelum Balf. f. et Forrest **4208**
    96. Leaves oblong-oblanceolate, apex rounded and mucronate, upper surface flat and smooth, or rugulose (west and northwest Yunnan, Sichuan): **R. fictolacteum** Balf. f. **4209**
  95. Indumentum of the lower leaf surface gray to light yellowish brown (sometimes rusty yellow, as in *R. hodgsonii*).
    97. Ovary tomentose; leaf-bud scales long acute.
      98. Flowering branches very stout (1.5 cm in diameter); leaves broadly oblanceolate.
        99. Corolla 7-8-lobed.
          100. Flowers rose tinged purple, not dotted (south Xizang):
            R. hodgsonii Hook. f. **4210**
          100. Flowers rose, dotted (northeast Yunnan, southwest Sichuan): **R. rex** Lévl. **4211**
        99. Corolla 5-lobed (southeast Xizang): **R. lanigerum** Tagg
          (mián róng dùjuān, ''woolly-tomentose rhododendron'')
      98. Flowering branches slender (5-8 mm in diameter); leaves narrowly oblanceolate (Yunnan, southeast Xizang):
        R. coriaceum Franch. **4212**
    97. Ovary glabrous; leaf-bud scales rounded at the apex and ciliate (west Sichuan): **R. galactinum** Balf. f. **4213**
94. Petioles short and flat, the leaf base decurrent onto the petiole (northwest Yunnan): **R. basilicum** Balf. f. et W. W. Sm. **4214**
93. Indumentum of the lower leaf surface 2-layered, the upper layer composed of stellate hairs which are somewhat united at the base, the lower layer similar to that of Subsection *Falconera*, thin and suedelike.
  101. Ovary tomentose or glandular; corolla mortar-shaped or funnelform (Xizang and Yunnan species).
    102. Petioles of the leaves beneath the inflorescence 2-5 cm long, more or less cylindric.

103. Indumentum of the lower leaf surface white, thin, and loosely arachnoid, tending to disappear from older leaves; corolla campanulate, rose tinged purple (southeast Xizang):

R. magnificum Ward

(hóng zhuàng dùjuān, "magnificent rhododendron")

103. Indumentum of the lower leaf surface woolly, thin, or absent; corolla funnelform, red.

    104. Indumentum of the lower leaf surface absent, or thin and light gray (northwest Yunnan):

R. protistum Balf. f. et Forrest

(kuí* shǒu dùjuān, "best rhododendron")

    104. Indumentum of the lower leaf surface loosely woolly, light brown (west Yunnan): **R. giganteum** Forrest et Tagg **4215**

    104. Indumentum of the lower leaf surface plastered, silvery white; corolla mortar-shaped, milk white.

        105. Leaves average 7.5-10 cm in width, apex acute; stamens 16; ovary densely glandular and tomentose (south Xizang):

R. grande Wight **4216**

        105. Leaves average 15-20 cm in width, apex rounded and mucronate; stamens 18-20; ovary woolly and eglandular (Yunnan, southeast Xizang):

R. sinogrande Balf. f. et W. W. Sm. **4217**

102. Petioles of the leaves beneath the inflorescence less than 2 cm long, flat and smooth on the upper surface.

    106. Indumentum of the lower leaf surface thin and plastered, gray to light yellowish brown; corolla deep carmine; leaf apex rounded and broadly emarginate (northwest Yunnan):

R. praestans Balf. f. et W. W. Sm. **4218**

    106. Indumentum of the lower leaf surface loosely woolly, not agglutinate, light brown; corolla milk white, dark red spotted at the base; leaf apex rounded, not emarginate (southeast Xizang, northwest Yunnan): **R. semnoides** Hutch. **4219**

---

*In the species description section (with *R. giganteum*), the Chinese name is given as *qiáo* shǒu dùjuān.

101. Ovary glabrous; corolla campanulate; petiole short, flat on the upper surface, with the broadly winged leaf base decurrent along both sides (west Sichuan): **R. watsonii** Hemsl. et Wils. **4220**

92. Indumentum of the lower leaf surface woolly and single-layered, the leaves of medium size; corolla more or less campanulate, 5-lobed; stamens 10.

107. Ovary glabrous, slender, and narrowly oblong; capsule long, slender, and falcate at maturity; leaves long and narrow, oblong to obovate; inflorescence lax umbelliform, 15-20-flowered; pedicels slender

108. Indumentum of the lower leaf surface brown or yellowish brown, more or less granular (composed of finely capitate caespitose hairs) (northwest Yunnan, southeast Xizang):
R. fulvum Balf. f. et W. W. Sm. **4221**

108. Indumentum of the lower leaf surface white or light brown, flat and smooth, not granular, more or less woolly (composed of treelike branching hairs) (northwest Yunnan, southeast Xizang):
R. uvarifolium Diels **4222**

107. Ovary glabrous or sparsely pubescent; capsule oblong-cylindric at maturity, not falcate.

109. Leaves more or less obtuse at both ends; ovary nearly always glabrous.

110. Corolla broadly campanulate, white, rose, or lilac purple.

111. Indumentum of the lower leaf surface not continuous, but in scattered clumps of caespitose hairs (south Xizang):
R. wallichii Hook. f. **4223**

111. Indumentum of the lower leaf surface continuous, flat, smooth, and suedelike, composed of treelike branching hairs (south (Xizang): **R. campanulatum** D. Don **4224**

110. Corolla tubular-campanulate, dark blood red; indumentum of the lower leaf surface thick and floccose, composed of stellate hairs at the tips of long multicellular stalks, the stellate hairs short, thick, and obtuse (southeast Xizang):
R. sherriffii Cowan **4225**

109. Leaves more or less acuminate (rarely acute).

112. Rachis markedly shortened.

113. Shrubs of medium size, neither dwarf nor procumbent; leaves broad in comparison with their length (sometimes narrow, as in Series* *Adenogyna*, but in that series the calyx is conspicuously large); bud scales caducous.

114. Calyx small, eglandular; ovary glabrous or subglabrous, eglandular.

    115. Indumentum of the lower leaf surface loose, without a pellicle and not split, rarely absent.

        116. Lower leaf surface clad with a thick light yellow loose and soft indumentum; petioles densely tomentose; corolla cream tinged rose; ovary glabrous (west and northwest Yunnan):   **R. taliense** Franch. **4226**

        116. Lower leaf surface glabrous; petioles glabrous; corolla white; ovary sparsely clad with white hairs (Shaanxi, Gansu, Henan):   **R. purdomii** Rehd. et Wils. **4227**

    115. Indumentum of the lower leaf surface thick and spongy, with a conspicuous pellicle on the surface (a single-layered membrane) which tends to crack or disappear with age.

        117. Corolla 5-lobed, white tinged rose; stamens 10; leaves lanceolate to oblong-lanceolate, indumentum of the lower surface silvery white (southeast Xizang):
                R. vellereum Hutch. et Tagg **4228**

        117. Corolla 6-7-lobed, deep pink; stamens 12-14; leaves elliptic, indumentum of the lower surface cinnamon (Yunnan, Sichuan):   **R. clementinae** Forrest **4229**

114. Calyx small, eglandular; ovary densely tomentose, eglandular.

    118. Lower leaf surface glabrous, clad only on the lower half of the midrib with fine branching hairs (Gansu, Qinghai):
                R. potaninii Batalin
          (gān sù dùjuān, "Gansu rhododendron")

    118. Lower leaf surface clad with a thick woolly or felted indumentum which is continuous and persistent.

---

*Neither definition nor placement of "Series" is given.

119. Upper leaf surface bullate (the veins deeply impressed, the body of the leaf prominent) (Sichuan).

120. Leaves obovate-oblanceolate, narrowly cuneate at the base, 5-9 cm long, the veins very deeply impressed on the upper surface; flowers white to pale flesh red (west and southwest Sichuan):

R. wiltonii Hemsl. et Wils. **4230**

120. Leaves oblanceolate to oblong-lanceolate, rounded-cuneate at the base, 9-12 cm long, the veins somewhat deeply impressed on the upper surface; flowers pink (southeast Sichuan): **R. coeloneurum** Diels **4231**

119. Upper leaf surface flat and smooth, not bullate.

121. Leaves ovate, rounded or slightly cordate at the base; flowers white, cream, or lemon yellow, the upper part rose-tinged and dark red dotted (west Sichuan):

R. wasonii Hemsl. et Wils. **4232**

121. Leaves oblong to obovate, rounded at the base; flowers white or pinkish purple, dark red dotted (Qinghai, Gansu, north Sichuan): **R. rufum** Batalin **4233**

114. Calyx usually large, clad at the margin with conspicuous stipitate glands; ovary always more or less glandular.

122. Leaves lanceolate, apex acuminate, indumentum of the lower surface thick and spongy, light cinnamon or yellowish brown (Yunnan, southwest Sichuan):

R. adenogynum Diels **4234**

122. Leaves ovate-broadly elliptic to ovate-lanceolate, indumentum of the lower surface thin or thick, loose, of various colors but not red.

123. Indumentum of the lower leaf surface thin and plastered.

124. Leaves oblong-elliptic, indumentum of the lower surface thin and detersile; calyx 3-4 mm long; style glandular on the lower ¾ (northwest Yunnan):

R. detonsum Balf. f. et Forrest **4235**

124. Leaves broadly ovate, indumentum of the lower surface thin and detersile; calyx 6-8 mm long; style glabrous, or glandular at the base (west Sichuan):

R. prattii Franch. **4236**

123. Indumentum of the lower leaf surface thick.
125. Leaves 2.5-4 cm broad, rounded at the base; shoots red-brown-tomentose and eglandular (southwest Sichuan):
R. faberi Hemsl. **4237**
125. Leaves 5.5-6.5 cm broad, distinctly cordate at the base; shoots clad with minute gray hairs and sparse glands (west Sichuan): **R. leei** Fang **4238**
113. Dwarf shrubs; leaves narrowly lanceolate, apex acuminate, margin strongly revolute; bud scales persistent; calyx poorly developed; ovary clad with clavate glands (southeast Xizang, Yunnan, Sichuan): **R. roxieanum** Forrest **4239**
112. Rachis distinctly elongate; upper leaf surface bullate, indumentum of the lower surface thick and coarse, composed of coarse long-stalked stellate hairs (Sichuan, east Yunnan):
R. floribundum Franch. **4240**

D. SUBGENUS ANTHODENDRON*

1. Flowers orange-yellow, usually several flowers produced from a terminal bud, foliage shoots produced from lateral buds below the terminal flower bud, or at the tip of a nonflowering branch; stamens 5.(**SUBGENUS PSEUDANTHODENDRON, SECTION PENTANTHERA**) (eastern, southern, and central China, west to Sichuan, Guizhou, Yunnan):
R. molle G. Don **4241**
1. Flower white, pink, or purple, usually in terminal clusters of 1-3 (sometimes several); foliage shoots and inflorescence produced from the same terminal bud, but foliage shoots are produced on the lower part of the terminal bud from within the bud-scale axils.
   2. Branchlets smooth and glossy, or tomentose; leaves in terminal verticillate clusters of 2-5 (scattered only on spindly branches); corolla usually rotate-funnelform, occasionally campanulate-funnelform.
      3. Foliage deciduous; corolla rotate-funnelform; stamens 5-10. (**SECTION BRACHYCALYX**)

---

*Including Subgenus *Pseudanthodendron*; since there is only one species in China from this subgenus, it has not been separated by the original authors.

4. Leaves ovate to obovate-lanceolate, broader at the lower half; pedicels tomentose.

  5. Leaves small, 3-4 cm long, 2-3 cm broad, subcoriaceous; petioles tomentose; flowers lilac purple; capsule conical-ovate, fruitstalk slightly curved, very tomentose (Fujian, Guangxi, Guangdong, (Jiangxi): **R. farrerae** Tate **4242**

  5. Leaves larger, 4-8 cm long, 2-4 cm broad, subchartaceous; petioles subglabrous; flowers rose; capsule cylindric, fruitstalk erect, subglabrous or more or less hairy (Chang Jiang valley provinces, south to Fujian, Taiwan): **R. mariesii** Hemsl. et Wils. **4243**

4. Leaves obovate or rhomboidal, broader at the upper half; pedicels densely glandular; flowers rose (northeast China):

                             R. schlippenbachii Maxim. **4244**

3. Foliage evergreen; corolla campanulate; stamens 10-12. **(SECTION TSUSIOPSIS)** (indigenous to Japan, cultivated in China):

                             R. tashiroi Maxim.

(yīng sè dùjuān, ''cherry-colored rhododendron'')

2. Branchlets clad with appressed reddish brown coarse flat hairs, or with spreading needlelike bristles (often gland-tipped); leaves scattered on the branches; corolla campanulate-funnelform or narrowly funnelform, not rotate-funnelform. **(SECTION TSUTSUSI)**

  6. Bud scale exterior not glutinous; calyx small, poorly developed; branchlets densely clad with appressed reddish brown coarse flat hairs or with spreading bristles.

    7. Corolla campanulate-funnelform; stamens 10.

      8. Style hairy at the base; leaves narrowly lanceolate to oblanceolate; flowers carmine to dark red (Taiwan):

                             R. kanehirai Wils. **4245**

      8. Style glabrous; leaves mostly oblong or oblong-lanceolate to broadly lanceolate, rarely lanceolate; flowers differing in color from the above-mentioned.

        9. Leaves narrowly oblong-lanceolate to narrowly lanceolate, to 4 cm long, upper surface subglabrous, lower surface light grayish white (Hainan Dao in Guangdong):

                             R. hainanense Merr. **4246**

9. Leaves elliptic-ovate to obovate, upper surface clad with coarse appressed hairs, lower surface light green (Chang Jiang and Zhu Jiang* valleys, west to Sichuan, Yunnan):

R. simsii Planch. **4247**

7. Corolla tube short and cylindric with spreading corolla lobes, the tube rarely long and cylindric; stamens 5, rarely 4.

10. Style glabrous; corolla exterior glabrous.

11. Leaves 0.5-3 cm long; flowers white to rose-purple, corolla tube 3-8 mm long.

12. Lower leaf surface clad throughout with fine reddish brown prickly hairs; flowers 2-3 cm long, corolla tube 8-10 mm long; stamens longer than the corolla, style far longer than the stamens (Yunnan, southwest Sichuan):

R.microphyton Franch. **4248**

12. Lower leaf surface clad only at the midrib with fine prickly hairs; corolla tube 3-5 mm long; stamens and corolla of equal length.

13. Leaves 1.5-2.5 cm long, 3 times longer than broad, oblong-oblanceolate; corolla about 3 cm long (north Guangdong):

R. naamkwanense Merr. **4249**

13. Leaves 5-12 mm long, broadly obovate-elliptic, slightly longer than broad; corolla about 1 cm long (Guangdong, Guangxi): **R. tsoi** Merr. **4250**

11. Leaves 3-9 cm long; flowers purple to lilac purple (purple-violet) or white, corolla tube 1-1.5 cm long.

14. Leaves elliptic or obovate to elliptic-lanceolate, entire; veins inconspicuously impressed on the upper surface.

15. Flowers lilac purple (purple-violet); branchlets, petioles, pedicels, and young leaves clad with appressed reddish brown coarse flat hairs, not with gland-tipped bristles.

16. Corolla lobes obtuse; stamens 5 (Guangdong, Hunan, Jiangxi): **R. mariae** Hance **4251**

---

*"Pearl River" in Guangdong, the estuary of three rivers which form the Guangzhou (Canton) delta; not mentioned in the species description.

16. Corolla lobes acute; stamens 4 (Guangxi, Guangdong):
R. **kwangsiense** Hu **4252**

15. Flowers white; branchlets, petioles, pedicels, and young leaves clad with dense long spreading bristles and shorter glandular hairs (Guangdong, Guangxi, Hunan):
R. **kwangtungense** Merr. et Chun **4253**

14. Leaves lanceolate to oblanceolate, crenulate; veins distinctly impressed on the upper surface (Guizhou, west Hubei, north Guangxi):
R. **chrysocalyx** Lévl. et Vant. **4254**

10. Style hairy at the base; corolla tube exterior clad with appressed bristles, corolla white to rose.

17. Pedicels, corolla, and style eglandular.

18. Flowers white to rose, 1 cm in diameter, corolla tube 1 cm long, exterior clad more or less with appressed hairs; leaves 2.5-6 cm long.

19. Branchlets, petioles, and pedicels clad with appressed long coarse flat hairs; flowers white to rose; style hairy at the base (Fujian, Hunan, Guizhou): R. **seniavinii** Maxim. **4255**

19. Branchlets, petioles, and pedicels clad with spreading bristles; corolla pink tinged purplish blue; style finely setose on the lower half; lower leaf surface subglabrous except at the midrib (north Guangdong): R. **lingii** Chun **4256**

18. Flowers white, smaller, 7 mm in diameter, corolla tube 2.5 mm long, exterior clad with reddish brown hairs; leaves 8-12 mm long (Guangxi, Guangdong, Hunan):
R. **minutiflorum** Hu **4257**

17. Pedicels, corolla exterior, and style glandular and hairy (north Guangdong): R. **chunii** Fang **4258**

6. Bud scales very glutinous; calyx large and deeply divided, the lobes green, 1 cm long or longer; corolla broadly funnelform; style glabrous.

20. Shoots densely clad with appressed coarse flat hairs; leaves dimorphic, highly variable; stamens 10 (seen only in cultivation):
R. **pulchrum** Sweet **4259**

20. Shoots clad with long flat hairs, often with long coarse hairs and glandular hairs; leaves not dimorphic; stamens 5 or 8-10.

21. Foliage evergreen, the leaves ovate-lanceolate, acuminate at the apex; shoots clad with dense spreading long coarse hairs and shorter glandular hairs; stamens 5 (Hunan, Guizhou, Sichuan, Guangxi):   **R. rivulare** Hand.-Mazz. **4260**

21. Foliage evergreen or semi-evergreen, the leaves ovate-lanceolate or lanceolate, acute or somewhat short acuminate at the apex; shoots densely clad with long flat hairs, sometimes somewhat glandular-hairy; stamens 8-10.

    22. Corolla brick red; leaves clad with erect reddish brown long hairs (endemic to Taiwan):   **R. oldhamii** Maxim. **4261**

    22. Flowers white (to light purple); leaves clad with appressed gray or grayish brown soft hairs (sometimes mixed with glandular hairs) (indigenous to eastern China, now seen only in cultivation):   **R. mucronatum** G. Don **4262**

E. SUBGENUS AZALEASTRUM

1. Stamens 5; calyx lobes large and broad; seeds without appendages. **(SECTION AZALEASTRUM)**

    2. Corolla tube quite broad and short, shorter than the lobes; leaves ovate, lanceolate, or obovate-oblanceolate, rarely elliptic; filaments pubescent; calyx lobes glabrous or subglabrous on the back; flowers white or rose tinged pink.

       3. Calyx lobes glabrous at the margin; leaves broadly orbicular-ovate (eastern provinces of China):   **R. ovatum** Planch. **4263**

       3. Calyx clad at the margin with hairs or stipitate glands.

          4. Leaves ovate or elliptic-ovate, broadest below the middle, lower surface distinctly reticulate; calyx lobes orbicular, densely clad at the margin with short-stalked glands (eastern and south-central China, Sichuan, Guizhou):   **R. bachii** Lévl. **4264**

          4. Leaves lanceolate or oblong-lanceolate, base obtuse or nearly rounded, apex mostly more or less triangular-acuminate; calyx lobes clad at the margin with short fine ciliate hairs or short-stalked glands or both (west Yunnan, southwest Sichuan):
    R. leptothrium Balf. f. et W. W. Sm. **4265**

4. Leaves obovate-oblanceolate, with a thick cartilaginous margin, the lower surface only vein-lined; flowers milk white, with fine bluish purple dots on the upper part of the corolla tube interior (Guangdong): **R. hongkongense** Hutch. **4266**

2. Corolla tube broadly cylindric, only slightly broader toward the top, longer than the lobes; leaves obovate-oblanceolate or obovate; filaments glabrous or slightly pubescent; calyx lobes setose outside at the base; flowers dark red (west Yunnan): **R. vialii** Delavay et Franch. **4267**

1. Stamens 10; calyx lobes small and inconspicuous (rarely well developed); seeds short-caudate at both ends; in the mature capsule the valves are joined on the upper part to the style, usually not dehiscent. **(SECTION CHONIASTRUM)**

5. Pedicels glabrous or very rarely hairy.

6. Ovary glabrous.

7. Inflorescence of several flowers (each axillary flower bud producing several flowers).

8. Stamens far longer than the corolla; flowers rose (Yunnan, Sichuan, Guizhou, Hubei): **R. stamineum** Franch. **4268**

8. Stamens of the same length as or shorter than the corolla; flowers purple-lilac (Hunan, Jiangxi, Guangdong):
R. westlandii Hemsl. **4269**

7. Inflorescence of 1-2 flowers (each axillary flower bud producing 1-2 flowers).

9. Bud scales ciliate; leaves narrowly oblong-lanceolate, to 13 cm long (Taiwan): **R. leiopodum** Hayata **4270**

9. Bud scales finely glandular at the margin; leaves elliptic-ovate, mostly 6-8 cm long (Zhejiang, Fujian, Jiangxi, Guangdong):
R. latoucheae Franch. **4271**

6. Ovary tomentose.

10. Leaves oblanceolate, lateral veins obscure; inflorescence of 5-7 flowers (Guizhou, north Guangxi): **R. cavaleriei** Lévl. **4272**

10. Leaves obovate, lateral veins evident; inflorescence of 1 flower (southeast Yunnan, Guangxi): **R. hancockii** Hemsl. **4273**

5. Pedicels densely long-pubescent or setose or both.

11. Leaves glabrous; calyx inconspicuous (Zhejiang, Fujian, Jiangxi, Hunan, Guangdong, Guangxi):   **R. henryi** Hance **4274**
11. Leaves setose on the upper and lower surfaces; calyx large, as long as 1.2 cm (Zhejiang, Fujian, Guangdong, Guangxi):

  R. championae Hook. **4275**

F. SUBGENUS PSEUDORHODORASTRUM

1. Leaves (at least on the upper surface) clad with soft hairs to coarse appressed hairs; stamens 8-10. **(SECTION TRACHYRHODION)**
  2. Corolla broadly funnelform; filaments pubescent toward the base.
    3. Leaves 3.7-5 cm long, veins evident on the lower surface; pedicels densely setose; style pubescent (central Yunnan):

      R. scabrifolium Franch. **4276**
    3. Leaves about 1.8 cm long, upper and lower surfaces densely clad with long soft hairs; pedicels pubescent and scaly.
      4. Style glabrous (southwest Sichuan, north and central Yunnan):

        R. pubescens Balf. f. et Forrest **4277**
      4. Style pubescent (Yunnan, Sichuan):

        R. spiciferum Franch. **4278**
  2. Corolla tubular, slightly narrowed at both ends; filaments glabrous (central, north, and west Yunnan, southwest Sichuan):

    R. spinuliferum Franch. **4279**
1. Leaves glabrous, often grayish white on the lower surface; stamens 10. **(SECTION RHODOBOTRYS)**
  5. Corolla exterior not pubescent, or only very slightly hairy.
    6. Flower-bud scales smooth and glossy outside; leaves short, more or less elliptic, about 2-3 cm long; flowers pink to white, as many as 5 from each flower bud; style smooth and glossy (west Yunnan, southwest Sichuan, southeast Xizang):   **R. racemosum** Franch. **4280**
    6. Flower-bud scales sericeous outside; leaves long, quite long-oblong, 4-6 cm long; flowers light purple, 1 from each flower bud; style pubescent and scaly on the lower part (south Xizang):

      R. virgatum Hook. f. **4281**
  5. Corolla exterior rather densely pubescent and scaly; bud scales smooth and glossy; leaves lanceolate or oblong-lanceolate; flowers pink, 1 from each flower bud; style clad with glandlike scales on the lower half (west Yunnan):   **R. oleifolium** Franch. **4282**

G. SUBGENUS RHODORASTRUM

1. Foliage evergreen to semi-evergreen, the leaves oblong, obtuse at both ends (northeastern China): **R. dauricum** L. **4283**
1. Foliage deciduous, the leaves oblong-lanceolate, acute at both ends, or subacuminate at the apex; flowers opening before the leaves (northeast and northern China, south to Shandong):

R. mucronulatum Turcz. **4284**

TRANSLATORS' CORRECTIONS
OF THE ORIGINAL TEXT

IN THE DESCRIPTIONS

4010 (pedicels) "yǒu *xiān* piàn": with fresh slice, presumed to mean
        "yǒu *lín* piàn": *scaly* (similar characters)
4011 terminal *sessile* inflorescence presumed to mean
    terminal inflorescence (followed by generous rachis
               and pedicel measurements)
    (capsule length) 7 *cm* presumed to mean 7 *mm*
4012 (corolla length) *14* cm presumed to mean *1.4* cm
4018 (pedicel length) 6-14 *cm* presumed to mean 6-14 *mm*
4048 (altitude) *1200-1300* meters presumed to mean *3600-3900* meters
    (*The Species of Rhododendron* gives the altitude
      as 12,000-13,000 feet.)
4144 (leaf shape) "*jù* yuán": distance round, presumed to mean
      "*jǔ* yuán": *oblong*
4149 (flowers) "6-9 *duì*": 6-9 pair, presumed to mean
      "6-9 *duǒ*": *6-9* (flowers)
4180 (leaf shape) "*jǔ* tuǒ yuán xíng": square elliptic, presumed to mean
      "*duǎn* tuǒ yuán xíng": *short elliptic* (similar characters)

IN THE KEY, SUBGENUS LEPIDORRHODIUM

first #22 (lower surface) "*lóng* qí": dragon, presumed to mean
      "*yóu* qí": *especially* (similar characters)
second #30 (corolla color) "*dùn*": blunt, presumed to mean
      "*chún*": *pure* (similar characters)
first #47 flowers often sessile or *petioles . . . petioles . . . petioles,*
    presumed to mean *pedicels*

IN THE KEY, SUBGENUS RHODODENDRON

second #53 (leaf length) 5-8 *mm* presumed to mean 5-8 *cm*
second #52 (filaments) *glabrous* presumed to mean *hairy*, to fit the
    key format and match the description

ENGLISH—CHINESE GLOSSARY

acuminate: Tapered to a sharp point with the sides somewhat concave. 渐尖的 jiàn jiān de

acute: Sharp; ending in a point. 急尖的 jí jiān de
锐尖的 ruì jiān de

agglutinate: Clumped or stuck together. 粘结的 nián jié de

annular: Ringlike. 环状的 huán zhuàng de

anther: The pollen-bearing part of the stamen, usually supported by the filament. 花药 huā yào

apex: The tip or top; the unattached end. 顶端 dǐng duān

appendage: An attached secondary part. 附属物 fù shǔ wù

appressed: Lying flat against another organ. (Variously expressed.)

arachnoid: Cobweblike; clad with fine soft tangled hairs. 蛛丝状的 zhū sī zhuàng de

aromatic: Having a distinctive odor. 有芳香的 yǒu fāng xiāng de

attenuate: Gradually and narrowly tapered. 渐狭的 jiàn xiá de

auriculate: Earlike; with small lobes or appendages, as at the base of a leaf. 耳状的 ěr zhuàng de

awn: A bristlelike appendage.	芒	máng
axillary: Growing from within the angle between the petiole and the stem.	腋生的	yè shēng de
axis: An imagined or real central line of development.	轴	zhóu
bark: The outer layer or covering of the trunk and branches.	树皮	shù pí
base: The lower part; the bottom; the attached end.	基部	jī bù
bilabiate: Two-lipped.	二唇的	èr chún de
bilateral: Of or on the right and left sides.	两侧的	liǎng cè de
bract: A reduced or modified leaf associated with an inflorescence.	苞片	bāo piàn
bracteate: Bearing bracts.	有苞片的	yǒu bāo piàn de
branch: A division of the stem.	枝	zhī
branchlet: A small branch or subdivision of a branch; twig.	小枝	xiǎo zhī
bristle: A strong stiff hair.	刚毛	gāng máo
bud: An undeveloped flower or foliage shoot.	芽	yá
bud scale: One of the thin appressed structures covering a bud.	芽鳞	yá lín

bullate: Blistered or puckered. 泡状隆起的 pào zhuàng lóng qǐ de

caducous: Dropping off early or prematurely, as bud scales. 早落的 zaǒ luò de

caespitose: Tufted; growing in small dense clumps. 簇生的 cù shēng de

calyx: All the free or united sepals of a flower; the exterior perianth. 花萼 huā è

campanulate: Bell-shaped. 钟形的 zhōng xíng de

capitate: Headlike; in a head; having a head. 头状的 tóu zhuàng de

capsule: A dehiscent dry fruit; the mature compound ovary. 蒴果 shuò guǒ

cartilaginous: Hard and tough; gristly. 软骨质的 ruǎn gǔ zhì de

caudate: With a tail-like appendage; tailed. 具尾的 jù wěi de

chartaceous: Papery; of a paperlike texture. 纸质的 zhǐ zhì de

ciliate: Fringed with hairs at the margin. 有睫毛的 yǒu jié máo de

ciliolate: Finely ciliate. 有细睫毛的 yǒu xì jié máo de

clavate: Shaped like a club or bat. 棒状的 棍棒状的 bàng zhuàng de gùn bàng zhuàng de

clustered: Closely gathered together. 簇生的 cù shēng de

619

colors:	black	黑色的	hēi sè de
	blue	蓝色的	lán sè de
	brown	棕色的 褐色的	zōng sè de hé sè de
	carmine	洋红色的	yáng hóng sè de
	chestnut	栗色的	lì sè de
	cinnamon	肉桂色的	ròu guì sè de
	crimson	大红色的	dà hóng sè de
	golden	金色的 金黄色的	jīn sè de jīn huáng sè de
	gray	灰色的	huī sè de
	green	绿色的	lǜ sè de
	orange	橙色的	chéng sè de
	pink	粉红色的	fěn hóng sè de
	purple	紫色的	zǐ sè de
	red	红色的	hóng sè de
	rose	蔷薇色的 玫瑰色的	qiáng wéi sè de méigui sè de
	rusty	锈色的	xiù sè de
	silvery	银色的	yín sè de
	vermilion	朱红色的	zhū hóng sè de
	white	白色的	bái sè de
	yellow	黄色的	huáng sè de

compact: Densely pressed together.　　紧密的　　jǐn mì de

concave: Hollowed like the inside of a bowl; curving inward.　　凹陷的　　āo xiàn de

conspicuous: Obvious; unlikely to be overlooked; plainly visible.　　明显的　　míng xiǎn de
显著的　　xiǎn zhù de

contiguous: Touching but not joined.　　邻接的　　lín jiē de

cordate: Heart-shaped, as in leaves which are notched and roundly lobed at the base.　　心形的　　xīn xíng de

coriaceous: Leathery.　　革质的　　gé zhì de

corolla: All the free or united petals of a flower; the interior perianth.　　花冠　　huā guān

corolla tube: The undivided part of the corolla.　　花冠筒　　huā guān tǒng

corymb: A simple flat-topped or convex inflorescence in which the outer flowers open first.　　伞房花序　　sǎn fáng huā xù

crenate: Scalloped; bluntly or roundly toothed.　　有钝齿的　　yǒu dùn chǐ de
有圆齿的　　yǒu yuán chǐ de

crenulate: Finely or minutely crenate.　　有细钝齿的　　yǒu xì dùn chǐ de
有小钝齿的　　yǒu xiǎo dùn chǐ de
有细圆齿的　　yǒu xì yuán chǐ de
有小圆齿的　　yǒu xiǎo yuán chǐ de

crustaceous: Of brittle texture; crusted.　　脆壳质的　　cuì ké zhì de

621

cultivar: A variety originating and persisting under cultivation.

栽 培 品 种   zāi péi pǐn zhǒng

cuneate: Wedge-shaped.

楔 形 的   xiē xíng de

cupular: Cup-shaped; cuplike.

杯 状 的   bēi zhuàng de

cushion-shaped:

垫 状 的   diàn zhuàng de

cylindric: Elongated and circular in cross section.

圆 柱 形 的   yuán zhù xíng de

deciduous: Falling after a normal season of growth or function, as leaves; nonevergreen, having such leaves.

脱 落 的   tuō luò de

decurrent: Extending down and united with the petiole or stem.

下 延 的   xià yán de

degenerate: Degraded in structure or function.

退 化 的   tuì huà de

dehiscent: Splitting at maturity.

开 裂 的   kāi liè de

dentate: With sharp spreading teeth; toothed.

有 齿 的   yǒu chǐ de

denticulate: Finely or minutely dentate.

有 细 齿 的   yǒu xì chǐ de
有 小 齿 的   yǒu xiǎo chǐ de

detersile: Readily dropped or easily rubbed off. (This term is uncommon in general botanical references but occurs fairly often in rhododendron literature.)

(Expressed in a variety of ways.)

diameter: The width in cross section.

直 径   zhí jìng
口 径   kǒu jìng

dimorphic: Occurring in 2 forms.

二形的   èr xíng de

discoid: Disc-shaped.

盘状的   pán zhuàng de

dorsal: Occurring on or belonging to the back.

背的   bèi de

dwarf: Markedly short or small.

矮生的   ǎi shēng de
矮小的   ǎi xiǎo de

e-: Without; not.

无   wú

eglandular: Without glands; not glandular.

无腺的   wú xiàn de
无腺体的   wú xiàn tǐ de

elepidote: Without scales; not scaly.

无鳞片的   wú lín piàn de

elliptic: Roughly in the shape of an ellipse; regularly oval.

椭圆形的   tuǒ yuán xíng de

elongate: Increased in length.

狭长的   xiá cháng de

emarginate: Notched at the apex.

微缺的   wéi quē de
缺刻的   quē kè de

endemic: Native or confined to a given geographic area.

特产的   tè chǎn de

entire: Not toothed or indented at the margin.

全缘的   quán yuán de

epiphytic: Growing upon another plant, but not as a parasite.

附生的   fù shēng de

erect: Upright; perpendicular to the ground.

直立的   zhí lì de

evergreen: Bearing green leaves throughout the year.

常绿的   cháng lǜ de

evident: Clearly visible; distinct.

可见的   kě jiàn de
明显的   míng xiǎn de
明晰的   míng xī de

exserted: Protruded beyond the surrounding organ; not included.

露出的   lòu chū de

exterior: Outside; the outer surface.

外面   wài miàn

falcate: Sickle-shaped.

镰刀形   lián dāo xíng de

fasciate: Unusually flat and broad.

扁化的   biǎn huà de

fastigiate: Having branches which are erect, parallel, and crowded.

扫帚状的   sào zhǒu zhuàng de

ferrugineous: Rust-colored.

锈色的   xiù sè de

filament: The threadlike stalk of a stamen.

花丝   huā sī

fleshy: Succulent; thick and juicy.

肉质的   ròu zhì de

flexuose: Zigzag; bending in more or less opposite directions.

曲折的   qū zhé de

floccose: Clad with tufts of woolly hairs.

有丛卷毛的   yǒu cóng juǎn máo de

flower: The part of the plant which contains the organs necessary for sexual reproduction, usually surrounded by the perianth; collectively, the pistil, stamens, corolla, and calyx.

花 huā

fragrant: Having a sweet or pleasant odor.

有芳香的 yǒu fāng xiāng de

funnelform: Shaped like a funnel.

漏斗状的 lòu dǒu zhuàng de

furcate: Forked.

分叉的 fēn chā de

glabrous: Without hair; not hairy.

无毛的 wú máo de

gland: A protuberance on the surface of an organ or at the end of a hair which may or may not secrete a sticky substance.

腺 xiàn
腺体 xiàn tǐ

glandlike: Resembling a gland.

腺状的 xiàn zhuàng de

glandular: Possessing or bearing glands.

有腺的 yǒu xiàn de
有腺体的 yǒu xiàn tǐ de

globose: Spherical, or nearly so.

球形的 qiú xíng de

glutinous: Sticky.

胶粘质的 jiāo nián zhì de

granular: Having, composed of, or resembling small grains or particles; finely mealy.

有颗粒的 yǒu kē lì de
颗粒状的 kē lì zhuàng de

grooved: Furrowed lengthwise; sulcate.

有漕的 yǒu cáo de
有沟的 yǒu gōu de
有沟纹的 yǒu gōu wén de

hair: An outgrowth of the cellular covering of the plant, composed of a single elongated cell or multiple cells.

毛　　　máo

hairy: Clad with hairs.

有 毛 的　　　yǒu máo de

horizontal: Level; flat; at right angles to the primary axis.

水 平 的　　　shuǐ píng de
平 展 的　　　píng zhǎn de

imbricate: Overlapping like shingles or roof tiles.

覆 瓦 状 的　　　fù wǎ zhuàng de

impressed: Indented; embossed; lying below the surface.

凹 入 的　　　āo rù de

inclining: Falling or leaning away from the horizontal.

下 倾 的　　　xià qīng de

included: Contained by or not protruded beyond the surrounding organ; not exserted.

内 藏 的　　　nèi cáng de

inconspicuous: Not obvious; not readily noticed; not easily seen.

不 明 显 的　　　bù míng xiǎn de
不 显 著 的　　　bù xiǎn zhù de

indumentum: A hairy covering; in rhododendron descriptions, often used in specific reference to that of the lower leaf surface.

毛 被　　　máo bèi

inflorescence: The arrangement of the flowers on the floral axis; the flower cluster.

花 序　　　huā xù

interior: Inside; the inner surface.

里 面　　　lǐ miàn

internode: The portion of the stem between two nodes.

节 间　　　jié jiān

626

irregular: Incapable of being divided into equal halves along at least two planes; in a flower, having dissimilar petals.

不规则的
不整齐的

bù guī zé de
bù zhěng qí de

juvenile: Young; immature or undeveloped; normal and functional in youth but disappearing later.

幼形的

yòu xíng de

keeled: Ridged lengthwise.

有龙骨的

yǒu lóng gǔ de

lacerate: Torn; irregularly cleft.

撕裂的

sī liè de

lamina: Leafblade; the expanded part of a leaf.

叶片

yè piàn

lateral: Occurring at or belonging to the side.

侧生的

cè shēng de

lateral vein: In a leaf with pinnate venation, one of the veins arising at an angle from the midrib.

侧脉

cè mài

lanceolate: Lance-shaped; relatively long, somewhat broadened at the base, and tapered to the apex.

披针形的

pī zhēn xíng de

lax: Loose; open; not compact.

疏松的

shū sōng de

leaf: One of the lateral appendages of the stem which make up the foliage of the plant; the principal organ of food manufacture by photosynthesis.

叶

yè

lepidote: Clad with scales; scaly.

有鳞片的

yǒu lín piàn de

linguiform: Tongue-shaped.

舌状的

shé zhuàng de

627

lobe: Any division or projecting segment of an organ.　　裂片　　liè piàn

locule: Cavity or compartment of an ovary or capsule.　　室　　shì

lustrous: Having a gloss or sheen.　　光泽的　　guāng zé de
　　光亮的　　guāng liàng de

margin: The edge.　　边缘　　biān yuán

mature: Fully grown or developed; ripe.　　成熟的　　chéng shú de

medial: Occurring in or belonging to the middle; central.　　中央的　　zhōng yāng de
　　中部的　　zhōng bù de

membranaceous: Thin, flexible, and often translucent.　　膜质的　　mó zhì de

metric measurement:　meter　　米　　mǐ
　　　　　　　　　　　　centimeter　　厘米　　lí mǐ
　　　　　　　　　　　　millimeter　　毫米　　háo mǐ

midrib: The principle leaf vein; the main rib, continuing lengthwise from the petiole.　　中脉　　zhōng mài

mucilaginous: Slimy and sticky.　　粘性的　　nián xìng de

mucronate: Tipped with a short sharp point.　　有短尖头的　　yǒu duǎn jiān tóu de

mucronulate: Finely mucronate.　　有小短尖头的　　yǒu xiǎo duǎn jiān tóu de
　　有细短尖头的　　yǒu xì duǎn jiān tóu de

nectary: A nectar-producing gland; a protuberance or other structure containing such a gland.　　蜜腺　　mì xiàn

net veins: Numerous small veins which are interconnected or crossing; reticulate veins.

网脉   wǎng mài

oblanceolate: Inversely lanceolate; broader toward the apex and tapered to the base.

倒披针形的   dào pī zhēn xíng de

oblique: Slanting; lacking symmetry.

斜的   xié de

oblong: Longer than broad with the sides more or less parallel; roundly rectangular.

矩圆状的   jǔ yuán zhuàng de

obovate: Inversely ovate; egg-shaped in outline but with the broader end toward the apex.

倒卵形的   dào luǎn xíng de

obscure: Not clearly visible; indistinct; hidden.

不见的   bù jiàn de
不明显的   bù míng xiǎn de
不显的   bù xiǎn de

obtuse: Blunt; not acute.

钝的   dùn de

opposite: Across from one another at the same node.

对生的   duì shēng de

orbicular: Circular in outline.

碟状的   dié zhuàng de
圆形的   yuán xíng de

ovary: The expanded basal part of the pistil which bears the ovules (young seeds).

子房   zǐ fáng

ovate: Egg-shaped in outline with the broader end toward the base.

卵形的   luǎn xíng de

ovoid: Egg-shaped (a 3-dimensional object).

卵状的   luǎn zhuàng de
卵圆状的   luǎn yuán zhuàng de

papillate: Bearing small rounded protuberances; nipplelike.　　有乳突的　　yǒu rǔ tū de

pedicel: The stalk of one flower in an inflorescence.　　花梗　　huā gěng

peltate: Shield-shaped and stalked at the center.　　盾形的　　dùn xíng de

pendulous: Hanging down; drooping.　　下垂的　　xià chuí de

periphery: The outer wall or margin; the external surface.　　周围　　zhōu wéi

persistent: Not dropping; remaining attached.　　宿存的　　sù cún de

petiole: The stalk of a leaf.　　叶柄　　yè bǐng

pistil: The female organ of a flower, usually composed of the ovary, style, and stigma.　　雌蕊　　cí ruǐ

procumbent: Trailing; prostrate; lying flat.　　平卧的　　píng wò de

prominent: Raised; in relief; standing out or protruding from the surface.　　突起的　　tū qǐ de
隆起的　　lóng qǐ de

pseud-, pseudo-: False; not true or typical; deceptively resembling.　　假　　jiǎ

pubescent: Clad with soft hairs.　　有柔毛的　　yǒu róu máo de

punctate: Marked with minute depressions or with colored or translucent dots; finely pitted.　　有斑点的　　yǒu bān diǎn de

raceme: A simple elongated inflorescence of pedicelled flowers in which the bottom flowers open first.　总状花序　zǒng zhuàng huā xù

rachis: Axis of the inflorescence; the central stalk to which the pedicels are attached.　总轴　zǒng zhóu

radiate: Spreading from a common center.　放射状的　fàng shè zhuàng de

recurved: Curved downward or backward, as a leaf margin.　下弯的　xià wān de　外弯的　wài wān de

reflexed: Bent backward or downward, as a style or corolla lobe.　外弯的　wài wān de　外折的　wài zhé de　反曲的　fǎn qū de　反折的　fǎn zhé de　下弯的　xià wān de

regular: Capable of being divided into equal halves along at least 2 planes; in a flower, having similar petals.　规则的　guī zé de　整齐的　zhěng qí de

repent: Creeping; prostrate and sometimes rooting.　匍匐状的　pú fú zhuàng de

resinous: Containing or producing resin; pitchy.　有树脂的　yǒu shù zhī de

reticulate: Netted; having a netlike pattern or texture.　网状的　wǎng zhuàng de

retuse: Shallowly notched at an obtuse or rounded apex.　弯缺的　wān quē de

revolute: Rolled backward or downward, as a leaf margin.　反卷的　fǎn juǎn de

631

rostrate: Beaked; having a beaklike projection.　　有喙的　　yǒu huì de

rotate: Wheel-shaped; flat and circular.　　辐状的　　fú zhuàng de
　　轮状的　　lún zhuàng de

rugose: Wrinkled.　　有皱纹的　　yǒu zhòu wén de

rugulose: Finely wrinkled.　　有细皱纹的　　yǒu xì zhòu wén de

sac: A pouch; a soft-walled cavity with the opening narrow or absent.　　囊　　náng

saccate: Pouchy; bag-shaped.　　囊状的　　náng zhuàng de

salverform: Shaped like a tall-footed dish; flatly and abruptly spreading from a slender tube.　　高脚碟状的　　gāo jiǎo dié zhuàng de

saxatile: Growing on or among rocks.　　石生的　　shí shēng de

scabrous: Rough to the touch.　　粗糙的　　cū cāo de

scale: A small disclike epidermal hair structure which may occur sparsely to abundantly on nearly any organ in certain groups of rhododendron species and is noticeably absent in others.　　鳞片　　lín piàn

scaly: Clad with scales; lepidote.　　有鳞片的　　yǒu lín piàn de

scobiform: Resembling sawdust.　　锯屑状的　　jù xiè zhuàng de

scurfy: Branlike; chaffy; dry and flaky.　　秕糠状的　　bǐ kāng zhuàng de

seed: The fertilized and mature ovule, containing an embryonic plant usually enclosed by nutritive and protective layers.　种子　zhǒng zǐ

semi-: Half; partly.　半　bàn

sericeous: Silky; clad with silky hairs.　有绢毛的　yǒu juàn máo de

serrate: Saw-toothed.　有锯齿的　yǒu jù chǐ de

serrulate: Finely or minutely saw-toothed.　有细锯齿的　yǒu xì jù chǐ de
有小锯齿的　yǒu xiǎo jù chǐ de

sessile: Without a stalk.　无柄的　wú bǐng de

setose: Bristly.　有刚毛的　yǒu gāng máo de

shoot: A young branch; new growth.　幼枝　yòu zhī

shrub: A relatively low woody plant, branching from the base.　灌木　guàn mù

simple: Not compound or branched; composed of a single unit.　单的　dān de

solitary: Borne singly; not part of a group or cluster.　单生的　dān shēng de

spatulate: Shaped like a spatula; spoon-shaped.　匙形的　chí xíng de

species: The subgeneric taxonomic category to which plant specimens of designated similarity are assigned and upon which the Latin binomial nomenclature is based.　种　zhǒng

spongy: Spongelike in texture; soft and porous.

海绵状的   hǎi mián zhuàng de

spreading: Extended; expanded; standing or opening outward.

广展的   guǎng zhǎn de
开展的   kāi zhǎn de

stamen: The male organ of a flower, composed of an anther and usually a filament.

雄蕊   xióng ruǐ

stellate: Starlike.

星状的   xīng zhuàng de

stem: The main ascending axis of a plant.

茎   jīng

stigma: The part of the pistil which receives the pollen, usually at the tip of the style.

柱头   zhù tóu

stipitate: Stalked.

有梗的   yǒu bǐng de

style: The more or less elongated part of the pistil which connects the stigma and the ovary.

花柱   huā zhù

sub-: Nearly; almost; not quite.

近   jìn

tapering: Narrowing gradually.

渐狭的   jiàn xiá de

terminal: Growing from or belonging to the end; at the tip of a branch.

顶生的   dǐng shēng de

terrestrial: Of the ground; living on land.

陆生的   lù shēng de

throat: The opening into a corolla; the part of the corolla between the corolla tube and the lobes.

喉部   hóu bù

tomentose: Downy; covered with soft matted hairs. 有绒毛的 yǒu róng máo de

tree: A woody plant with a trunk, usually branching into a head well above the base. 树 乔木 shù qiáo mù

triangular: Shaped like a triangle. 三角的 sān jiǎo de

truncate: Squared or straight at the end as though cut off. 截形的 jié xíng de

trunk: The main stem of a tree. 树干 shù gàn

tubular: Resembling a tube; cylindric and hollow. 管状的 筒状的 guǎn zhuàng de tǒng zhuàng de

turbinate: Top-shaped. 陀螺形的 tuó luó xíng de

type: The plant specimen or other material from which the definitive description of a species or other taxonomic group is derived and to which the name of that group is permanently attached. 模式标本 mó shì biāo běn

umbelliform: Resembling an umbel; with a very short rachis, so that the pedicels appear to arise from a common point; umbrella-shaped. 伞形的 sǎn xíng de

undershrub: A small low-growing shrub. 小灌木 xiǎo guàn mù

undulate: Wavy at the margin. 波状的 bō zhuàng de

valvate: Opening by valves. 瓣裂的 bàn liè de

valve: One of the pieces into which a mature capsule naturally separates.

果瓣

guǒ bàn

variable: Not constant in form or size; often not true to type.

多变的

duō biàn de

variety: An infraspecific taxonomic category; a variant of the species; a plant or group of plants within a species differing in form from the type.

变种

biàn zhǒng

vein: A vascular bundle; one of the sap-conveying tubes in a leaf, often externally visible.

脉

mài

veinlet: A small vein; a subdivision of a vein.

小脉

xiǎo mài

ventricose: Swollen or inflated on one side.

一侧肿胀的

yī cè zhǒng zhàng de

verrucose: Warty.

多疣的
有疣状突起的

duō yóu de
yǒu yóu zhùang tū qǐ de

verticillate: Whorled; arranged in a circle around the same point on an axis.

轮生的

lún shēng de

villous: Clad with long soft hairs.

有长柔毛的

yǒu cháng róu máo de

viscid: Sticky.

粘质的

nián zhǐ de

waxy: Waxlike; having the texture of wax; actually or appearing to be coated with wax.

蜡质的

là zhǐ de

wing: A thin flat extension or membranous expansion of an organ.

翅　　　　　chì

woody: With a woodlike texture; fibrous and hard.

木质的　　　mù zhì de

woolly: Resembling wool; clad with soft long curly or matted hairs.

绵毛状的
羊毛状的

mián máo
　　zhuàng de
yáng máo
　　zhuàng de

SOME GEOGRAPHIC TERMS

map	地图	dì tú
north	北	běi
south	南	nán
east	东	dōng
west	西	xī
China	中国	zhōng guó
	中华	zhōng huá
province	省	shěng
autonomous region	自治区	zì zhì qū
county	县	xiàn
city	市	shì
mountain	山	shān
valley	谷	gǔ
	流域	liú yù
island	岛	dǎo
sea	海	hǎi
lake	湖	hú
river	江	jiāng
	河	hé

INDEX TO GEOGRAPHIC NAMES
with illustration numbers

Place names are limited to those within China which occur in the species descriptions listed. The first three groups of names are easily found on any modern map of China. The fourth group includes mountains, smaller rivers, or population centers which are more difficult to locate; approximate latitude and longitude are given for those found in references listed in the bibliography. Most alternative spellings are in Wade-Giles Romanization, the system commonly used on older maps; some non-Chinese names are also included. Sichuan, Xizang, and Yunnan are not indexed, since one or more of these areas is mentioned in over 80% of the descriptions.

It must be stressed that governmental boundaries rarely match those of plant populations; geographic names are used here as a convenient sorting device. China's vast territory contains nearly every sort of terrain and climate and twice the number of *Rhododendron* species described in this book. This material can provide only a rough and incomplete outline of the complex distribution of the genus in that country.

1. MAINLAND PROVINCES OR AUTONOMOUS REGIONS
(see endpaper map)

ANHUI (Anhwei)
    4127 *anwheiense*
    4158 *fortunei*
    4264 *bachii*

ān huī

安 徽

FUJIAN (Fukien)
4023 *levinei*
4197 *fokienense*
4199 *simiarum*
4241 *molle*
4242 *farrerae*
4243 *mariesii*
4255 *seniavinii*
4264 *bachii*
4271 *latoucheae*
4274 *henryi*
4275 *championae*

fú jiàn

福建

GANSU (Kansu)
4039 *micranthum*
4053 *thymifolium*
4060 *capitatum*
(4068) *invictum*
4103 *anthopogonoides*
4165 *oreodoxa*
4206 *przewalskii*
4207 *agglutinatum*
4227 *purdomii*
4233 *rufum*

gān sù

甘肃

GUANGDONG (Kwangtung)
4023 *levinei*
4159 *faithae*
4183 *brevinerve*
4199 *simiarum*
4241 *molle*

guǎng dōng

广东

4242 *farrerae*
4246 *hainanense*
4249 *naamkwanense*
4250 *tsoi*
4251 *mariae*
4252 *kwangsiense*
4253 *kwangtungense*
4256 *lingii*
4257 *minutiflorum*
4258 *chunii*
4264 *bachii*
4266 *hongkongense*
4269 *westlandii*
4271 *latoucheae*
4274 *henryi*
4275 *championae*

GUANGXI (Kwangsi)
4023 *levinei*
4024 *liliiflorum*
4029 *chunienii*
4110 *euonymifolium*
4124 *chihsinianum*
4159 *faithae*
4164 *cardiobasis*
4166 *kwangfuense*
4183 *brevinerve*
4196 *haofui*
4197 *fokienense*
4199 *simiarum*
4200 *versicolor*

guǎng xī

广 西

4242 *farrerae*
4250 *tsoi*
4252 *kwangsiense*
4253 *kwangtungense*
4254 *chrysocalyx*
4257 *minutiflorum*
4260 *rivulare*
4264 *bachii*
4272 *cavaleriei*
4273 *hancockii*
4274 *henryi*
4275 *championae*

GUIZHOU (Kweichow)

guì zhōu

贵 州

4024 *liliiflorum*
4034 *lyi*
4071 *ambiguum*
4073 *lutescens*
4110 *euonymifolium*
4117 *auriculatum*
4129 *maculiferum*
4131 *delavayi*
4183 *brevinerve*
4184 *annae*
4190 *argyrophyllum*
4254 *chrysocalyx*
4255 *seniavinii*
4260 *rivulare*
4264 *bachii*
4268 *stamineum*
4272 *cavaleriei*

HENAN (Honan)
4082 *concinnum*
4227 *purdomii*

hé nán

河 南

HUBEI (Hupei, Hupeh)
4039 *micranthum*
4075 *augustinii*
4090 *charianthum*
4117 *auriculatum*
4129 *maculiferum*
4161 *discolor*
4165 *oreodoxa*
4167 *fargesii*
4168 *erubescens*
4170 *sutchuenense*
4172 *praevernum*
4189 *hypoglaucum*
4254 *chrysocalyx*
4264 *bachii*
4268 *stamineum*

hú běi

湖 北

HUNAN
4023 *levinei*
4024 *liliiflorum*
4158 *fortunei*
4199 *simiarum*
4251 *mariae*
4253 *kwangtungense*
4255 *seniavinii*
4257 *minutiflorum*

hú nán

湖 南

4260 *rivulare*
4264 *bachii*
4268 *stamineum*
4269 *westlandii*
4274 *henryi*

JIANGSU (Kiangsu)
4284 *mucronulatum*

jiāng sū

江 苏

JIANGXI (Kiangsi)
4127 *anwheiense*
4158 *fortunei*
4197 *fokienense*
4242 *farrerae*
4251 *mariae*
4264 *bachii*
4269 *westlandii*
4271 *latoucheae*
4274 *henryi*
4275 *championae*

jiāng xī

江 西

NEI MONGOL (Inner Mongolia)
4056 *parvifolium*
4244 *schlippenbachii*
4283 *dauricum*

nèi měng gǔ

内 蒙 古

QINGHAI (Tsinghai, Chinghai)
4053 *thymifolium*
4060 *capitatum*
4103 *anthopogonoides*

qīng hǎi

青 海

4206 *przewalskii*
4233 *rufum*

SHAANXI (Shensi) *not Shanxi*　　　　　　　shǎn xī
   4075 *augustinii*　　　　　　　　　　　陝 西
   4082 *concinnum*
   4129 *maculiferum*
   4167 *fargesii*
   4170 *sutchuenense*
   4171 *planetum*
   4172 *praevernum*
   4173 *calophytum*
   4189 *hypoglaucum*
   4206 *przewalskii*
   4227 *purdomii*

SHANDONG (Shantung)　　　　　　　　　shān dōng
   4039 *micranthum*　　　　　　　　　　山 东
   4284 *mucronulatum*

SICHUAN (Szechwan, Szechuan)　　　　　sì chuān
   Mentioned in 103 species descriptions;　四 川
   see text.

XIZANG (Tibet, Thibet)　　　　　　　　　xī zàng
   Mentioned in 80 species descriptions;　西 藏
   see text.

YUNNAN (Yünnan)　　　　　　　　　　　yún nán
   Mentioned in 130 species descriptions;　云 南
   see text.

ZHEJIANG (Chekiang)
4158 *fortunei*
4197 *fokienense*
4199 *simiarum*
4264 *bachii*
4271 *latoucheae*
4275 *championae*

zhè jiāng

浙 江

NORTH AND NORTHEAST CHINA
4002 *Therorhodion redowskianum*
4039 *micranthum*
4056 *parvifolium*
4152 *chrysanthum*
4244 *schlippenbachii*
4283 *dauricum*
4284 *mucronulatum*

EASTERN PROVINCES
4263 *ovatum*

2. ISLANDS
(see map)

HAINAN DAO, Guangdong
(Hainan Tao)
4246 *hainanense*

hǎi nán dǎo

海 南 岛

TAIWAN (Formosa)
4153 *hyperythrum*
4243 *mariesii*

tái wān

台 湾

4245 *kanehirai*
4247 *simsii*
4261 *oldhamii*
4270 *leiopodum*

3. MAJOR RIVERS
(see map)

CHANG JIANG (Yangtze River) cháng jiāng
  4241 *molle* 长 江
  4243 *mariesii*
  4247 *simsii*

NU JIANG (Salween River) nù jiāng
  4040 *saluenense* 怒 江

YARLUNG ZANGBO JIANG yǎ lǔ zàng bù jiāng
  (Yalu Tsangpo River, 雅鲁藏布江
  Brahmaputra River)
  4026 *headfortianum*
  4032 *scopulorum*

4. SPECIFIC LOCATIONS

BAOXING (Paohsing, Mupin) 30-102 bǎo xīng
  4044 *moupinense* 宝 兴
  4126 *longesquamatum*

CANG SHAN cāng shān
  mountain 苍 山
  4008 *sulfureum*
  4069 *pholidotum*

647

DALI (Tali) 25-100
    4003 *brachyanthum*
    4226 *taliense*

dà lǐ

大 理

EMEI SHAN (Omei Shan, Mt. Omei)
mountain, 3099 meters (29-103)
    4072 *chengshienianum*
    4160 *hemsleyanum var. chengianum*
    4192 *rirei*

é méi shān

峨 眉 山

ERLANG SHAN (Erhlang Shan) 30-102
mountain, 3212 meters
    4084 *hutchinsonianum*
    4185 *sikangense*

èr láng shān

二 郎 山

GUANGFU (Kuangfu) 26-110
    4166 *kwangfuense*

guǎng fú

广 福

HEISHUI HE (Heishui Ho) 32-103
river
    4094 *heishuiense*
    4238 *leei*

hēi shuǐ hé

黑 水 河

HONG HE (Hung Ho) 23-102
river
    4021 *excellens*

hóng hé

红 河

HUANG SHAN 30-118
mountain
    4127 *anwheiense*

huáng shān

黄 山

JINDING (Chinting) 29-103
  location on Emei Shan, per Fang 1942
    4237 *faberi*

jīn dǐng 金顶

JINFO SHAN (Chinfo Shan) 29-107
  mountain, 2251 meters
    4154 *platypodum*
    4195 *chienianum*
    4198 *youngae*
    4231 *coeloneurum*

jīn fó shān 金佛山

JIULONG (Chiulung) 29-101
    4065 *rubiginosum*

jiǔ lóng 九龙

JIZU SHAN (Chitsu Shan) 26-100
  mountain
    4188 *eriogynum*

jī zú shān 鸡足山

KANGDING (K'angting, Dardo) 30-102
    4061 *nitidulum var. nubigenum*
    4126 *longesquamatum*
    4236 *prattii*

kāng dìng 康定

LIJIANG (Lichiang) 27-100
    4087 *rigidum*

lí jiāng 丽江

LINGNAN   General term for the area
  south of the Nanling mountain range;
  Guangxi and Guangdong.
    4251 *mariae*

lǐng nán 岭南

LONGSHENG (Lungsheng) 26-110   lóng shèng
    4029 *chunienii*
    4124 *chihsinianum*
    4200 *versicolor*

龙 胜

MULI 28-101   mù lǐ
    4048 *muliense*
    4096 *timeteum*
    4175 *selense*

木 里

NANKUN (Nank'un) 23-113   nán kūn
    4249 *naamkwanense*

南 昆

NAN LING (Five Ridges) 25-112   nán lǐng
    mountain range
    4023 *levinei*

南 岭

RUYUAN (Juyüen) 24-113   rǔ yuán
    4256 *lingii*

乳 源

TAIBAI SHAN (T'aipai Shan) 34-108   tài bái shān
    mountain, 3767 meters
    4227 *purdomii*

太 白 山

TAIBEI (Taipei, Taipeh) 25-121   tái běi
    4245 *kanehirai*

台 北

WA SHAN 29-103   wǎ shān
    mountain near Ebian Xian, per Fang 1942
    4089 *searsiae*

瓦 山

XING'AN (Hsing-an) 38-115
4283 *dauricum*

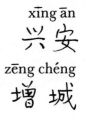

xīng ān

兴安

ZENGCHENG (Tsêngch'êng) 23-113
4249 *naamkwanense*

zēng chéng

增城

GUIDE TO PINYIN PRONUNCIATION
OF CHINESE

In this book, as in the dictionaries, maps, and other printed materials now coming from the People's Republic of China, *Hanyupinyin* is used to represent the pronunciation of the common language of China, the Han dialect or "Mandarin." Like other Romanization systems, it attempts to visually reproduce the sounds of the language by using the Latin alphabet. Many of the letters perform nearly as in English, but a few assume quite different roles. The odd proliferation of Q, X, and Z can discourage even the student who has heard and learned Chinese phonetics, and the tone marks above the syllables add another element of confusion for the person who lacks access to spoken Chinese.

The difficulties of Pinyin fade, however, when compared to the alternative of coping with written Chinese. The study of Chinese characters by Westerners is most certainly possible, as well as infinitely fascinating and rewarding, but the motivation to learn must obviously be strong and sustained.* We will only say here that the written language is essentially the same throughout the country, regardless of the dialect spoken, and that the characters in this book are the "simplified" forms in which the *Iconographia* was printed and which are now in general use in mainland China.

This guide to Pinyin is not complete, does not follow the standard order of presentation for students, and deviates far from the usual IPA pronunciation symbols favored by linguists. It is designed for rhododendron enthusiasts who know nothing about Chinese. Those who are willing to endure several consecutive reviews of this unorthodox material, followed by innumerable references to it, just may find themselves astounding the tour guide on that next trip to Emei Shan.

About Chinese, by Richard Newnham, Penguin Books, 1971, offers much well-organized information for those with either a casual curiosity or a more serious interest in the language.

653

GROUP I
THE FAMILIAR INITIAL CONSONANTS

These initial consonants represent almost the same sounds, as in English:

b ch d f g(*hard*) **h j k l m n p r s sh t w y**

They precede these **final sounds** in the following and many other combinations:

	(*sounds like*)	(*more examples for practice*)
ma	"ma"	fa pa sha wa ya
mai	"my"	bai hai kai tai wai
*fan	"fawn"	chan lan nan shan wan
gang	"gong"	chang fang shang wang yang
nao	"now"	bao mao pao sao yao
*de	"duh"	ge he ke she te
hei	"hay"	bei mei nei pei wei
fen	"fun"	gen hen men pen wen
leng	"lung"	cheng deng feng meng sheng
*bi	"bee"	di ji li ni ti
jia	"je'ah"	lia
jian	"je'en"	bian lian mian nian pian
jiang	"je'ahng"	liang niang
jiao	"jeow"	biao diao liao miao tiao
jie	"je'eh"	bie die lie mie pie
bin	"bin"	lin min nin pin yin
bing	"bing"	jing ling ming ning ping
liu	"Leo"	diu jiu miu niu

654

po	"pu" *as in pull*	bo fo mo wo
tong	"toong", *too as in took*	dong gong hong rong song
gou	"go"	chou kou rou shou you
⋆ chu	"choo"	du fu nu su tu
kua	"kwah"	gua hua
kuai	"kwhy"	guai huai
⋆ kuan	"kwahn"	chuan duan luan nuan tuan
kuang	"kwahng"	guang huang
kui	"kway"	chui gui hui rui shui
⋆ kun	"kwun"	chun dun hun lun tun
kuo	"kwoh"	duo guo huo luo tuo

*Exceptions in Group V.
⋆ Exceptions in Group IV.

GROUP II
THREE STRANGE INITIAL CONSONANTS

Each of these initial consonants has been borrowed to represent a unique Chinese sound, not its own English sound:

c z zh

They precede final sounds from Group I in the following combinations:

		(*sounds like*)
c represents a	ca	"tsah"
sound similar	cai	"tsy" (*rhymes with my*)
to *ts*	can	"tsahn"
	cang	"tsahng"
	cao	"tsow"
	ce	"tsuh"
	cen	"tsuhn" (*rhymes with fun*)
	ceng	"tsuhng" (*rhymes with lung*)

	cong	"tsoong"	(*oo as in took*)
	cou	"tso"	(*rhymes with go*)
	cu	"tsoo"	
	cuan	"tswahn"	
	cui	"tsway"	
	cun	"tswun"	
	cuo	"tswoh"	

z represents a sound similar to *dz*	za	"dzah"	
	zai	"dzy"	(*rhymes with my*)
	zan	"dzahn"	
	zang	"dzahng"	
	zao	"dzow"	
	ze	"dzuh"	
	zei	"dzay"	
	zen	"dzuhn"	(*rhymes with fun*)
	zeng	"dzuhng"	(*rhymes with lung*)
	zong	"dzoong"	(*oo as in took*)
	zou	"dzo"	(*rhymes with go*)
	zu	"dzoo"	
	zuan	"dzwahn"	
	zui	"dzway"	
	zun	"dzwun"	
	zuo	"dzwoh"	

zh represents a sound similar to *j*	zha	"jah"	
	zhai	"jy"	(*rhymes with my*)
	zhan	"jahn"	
	zhang	"jahng"	
	zhao	"jow"	

zhe	"juh"
zhei	"jay"
zhen	"juhn" (*rhymes with fun*)
zheng	"juhng" (*rhymes with lung*)
zhong	"joong" (oo as in took)
zhou	"jo" (*rhymes with go*)
zhu	"joo"
zhua	"jwah"
zhuai	"jwhy"
zhuan	"jwahn"
zhuang	"jwahng"
zhui	"jway"
zhun	"jwun"
zhuo	"jwoh"

GROUP III
TWO MORE STRANGE CONSONANTS

These initial consonants have also been borrowed to represent different sounds:

q   x

They precede the following final sounds, some from Group I plus four **special final sounds**:

		(*sounds like*)
q represents a	**qi**	"chee"
sound similar	**qia**	"che'ah"
to *ch*	**qian**	"che'en"
	qiang	"che'ahng"
	qiao	"cheow"
	qie	"che'eh"
	qin	"chin"

qing	"ching"
qiong	"cheoong"
qiu	"cheo" (*rhymes with Leo*)

qu	"che'ew"
quan	"chwen"
que	"chweh"
qun	"chwn"

x represents a sound similar to *sh*

xi	"shee"
xia	"she'ah"
xian	"she'en"
xiang	"she'ahng"
xiao	"sheow"
xie	"she'eh"
xin	"shin"
xing	"shing"
xiong	"sheoong"
xiu	"sheo" (*rhymes with Leo*)

xu	"she'ew"
xuan	"shwen"
xue	"shweh"
xun	"shwn"

GROUP IV

The **special final sounds** from Group III may also follow these **familiar consonants:**

		(*sounds like*)
y	**yu**	"ye'ew"
	yuan	"ywen"
	yue	"yweh"
	yun	"ywn"

658

j	ju	"je'ew"
	juan	"jwen"
	jue	"jweh"
	jun	"jwn"

And these, marked as shown:

l	lü	"le'ew"
	lüe	"lweh"

n	nü	"ne'ew"
	nüe	"nweh"

GROUP V
IMPORTANT EXCEPTIONS

yan	is pronounced "yen"
ye	"yeh"
yi	"ee"

i	is silent in	zi = "dz"
		ci = "ts"
		si = "s"

i	says "ur" in	zhi = "jur"
		chi = "chur"
		shi = "shur"
		ri = *"jur", but softly, as with the French j.*

However, **er** is not soft at all, pronounced "er" tending toward "ar".

659

VI
THE TONE MARKS

The marks placed above Pinyin syllables help to sort out the many homonyms in spoken Chinese. A difference in the pitch of the pronunciation signals a difference in meaning, with context and grammar providing additional clues. For example, *zhu* marked with each of the four tones can mean the following:

first tone   **zhū**   ''pearl''
second tone   **zhú**   ''bamboo''
third tone   **zhǔ**   ''host''
fourth tone   **zhù**   ''pillar''

The **first** tone is a sustained, slightly elevated pitch.
The **second** tone slides smoothly upward.
The **third** tone dips and rises in pitch.
The **fourth** tone rises very slightly and falls abruptly.

Tone marks are included in this book for increased accuracy, and can be used at least as a visible point of reference for readers who have not had the opportunity to hear and learn the actual tonal differences.

BIBLIOGRAPHY

1. Bailey, L. H. *Manual of Cultivated Plants,* explanation of Latin names pp 8-23 and glossary pp 24-37. New York, 1974.
2. Ding, Guangqi, editor-translator. *Zhiwu Zhongming Shi**, botanical glossary, Latin to Chinese. Kexue Chubanshe, Beijing, 1978.
3. Fang, W. P. *Icones Plantarum Omeiensium*, Vol. I, No. 1, plates 18-36 and descriptions of 20 species of *Rhododendron* in Chinese and English. National Sichuan University, Chengdu, Sichuan, China, 1942.
4. Gould, N. K. and P. M. Synge, editors. *Rhododendron Handbook 1956, Part One, Rhododendron Species.* Rhododendron Group of The Royal Horticultural Society, London, 1956.
5. Gunderson, Karen S., editor, and Stephen L. Gunderson, illustrator. *Rhododendron Glossary and Associated Botanical Terms.* The Pacific Rhododendron Society, Tacoma, 1973.
6. Hansen, C. T. *Glossary*, edited reprint of original glossary from *Rhododendrons 1956.*
7. Hitchcock, C. Leo and Arthur Cronquist. *Flora of the Pacific Northwest,* glossary pp xi-xix. Seattle, 1973.
8. Hou, Kuanzhao, editor. *Zhongguo Zhongzi Zhiwu Keshu Cidian**, botanical dictionary, Latin and English to Chinese. Keshue Chubanshe, Beijing, 1958.

9. Jackson, Benjamin Daydon. *A Glossary of Botanic Terms with Their Derivation and Accent.* London, 1916.

10. Kidd, D. A. *Collins Gem Dictionary, Latin-English, English-Latin.* London, 1977.

11. Lawrence, George H. M. *Taxonomy of Vascular Plants.* New York, 1951.

12. _____. *An Introduction to Plant Taxonomy*, illustrated material selected and reorganized from the preceding text for use by amateur botanists. New York, 1955.

13. Li, Hui-lin, editorial committee chairman and principal author of woody genera, *Flora of Taiwan, Volume Four,* descriptions of *Rhododendron* pp 21-38, in English. Epoch Publishing Co., Ltd., Taipei, 1978.

14. Liang, Shih-chiu, editor in chief. *A New Practical English-Chinese Dictionary.* The Far East Book Co., Hong Kong, 1974.

15. _____, editor in chief; Lu-sheng Chong et al, editors. *A New Practical Chinese-English Dictionary.* The Far East Book Co., Ltd., Taipei, 1973.

16. Rickett, H. W. "Materials for a Dictionary of Botanical Terms—I", *Bulletin of the Torrey Botanical Club,* Vol. 81 (January 1954), pp 1-15.

17. _____. "Materials for a Dictionary of Botanical Terms—II", *Bulletin of the Torrey Botanical Club,* Vol. 81 (May 1954), pp 188-198.

18. _____. "Materials for a Dictionary of Botanical Terms—III, Inflorescences," *Bulletin of the Torrey*

Botanical Club, Vol. 82 (November 1955), pp 419-445.

19. _____. "Materials for a Dictionary of Botanical Terms—IV, Terms to Describe Apices," *Bulletin of the Torrey Botanical Club,* Vol. 83 (September 1956), pp 342-354.

20. Shi, Hu, editor. *Zhongzi Zhiwu Xingtaixue Cidian*,* botanical dictionary, English to Chinese. Kexue Chubanshe, Beijing, 1962.

21. Stevenson, J. B., editor. *The Species of Rhodendron.* The Royal Horticultural Society, 1930 and 1942, reprinted by The Pacific Rhododendron Society, Tacoma, 1973.

22. Swartz, Delbert. *Collegiate Dictionary of Botany.* New York, 1971.

23. U.S. Army Map Service, Corps of Engineers. *Gazetteer to Maps of China, Proper, Southwest.* Washington, D.C., 1947.

24. U.S. Board on Geographic Names. *Mainland China, Official Standard Names, Gazetteer #22,* Volumes I and II. Washington, D.C., 1968.

25. U.S. Defense Mapping Agency. *Gazetteer of the People's Republic of China, Pinyin to Wade-Giles, Wade-Giles to Pinyin.* Washington, D.C., 1979.

26. *Webster's Seventh New Collegiate Dictionary,* pronouncing gazetteer pp 1092-1172. Springfield, 1965.

27. *Webster's Third New International Dictionary of the English Language, Unabridged.* Springfield, 1976.

28. Wong, Sybil. *Dictionary of Chinese Communist Agricultural Terminology,* Chinese to English. Union Research Institute, Hong Kong, 1968.

29. Wu, C. K., et al. *Chinese-English Simplified Characters,* indexed comparative listing of 2296 simplified and conventional characters with Yale Romanization. Chinese Language Research Association, Monterey, 1972.

30. Wu, Jingrong, editor in chief, Beijing Foreign Languages Institute. *The Chinese-English Dictionary,* in simplified characters and Pinyin. The Commercial Press, Ltd., Hong Kong, 1979.

31. Zhongguo Kexueyuan Beijing Zhiwu Yanjiusuo Zhubian (Beijing Botanical Research Institute of Academia Sinica), editors in chief. *Iconographia Cormophytorum Sinicorum Tomus III,* also titled *Zhongguo Gaodeng Zhiwu Tujian Disan Ce**, in simplified Chinese characters, 283 *Rhododendron* species descriptions and key, pp 24-165, 744, 746-780 (the material translated for this book); index to Latin names, pp 1064-1069. Kexue Chubanshe, Beijing, 1974.

32. _____. *Iconographia Cormophytorum Sinicorum Tomus I,* also titled *Zhongguo Gaodeng Zhiwu Tujian Diyi Ce**, in simplified Chinese characters, 23 pages of botanical glossary with 27 pages of black-and-white drawings (Appendix II). Kexue Chubanshe, Beijing, 1972.

ATLASES AND MAPS:

33. *Zhonghua Renmin Gongheguo Fensheng Ditu Ji**, 19x26cm hardbound atlas of China, with discussion and political and topographic maps of each province in color, indexed, all in simplified Chinese characters. Ditu Chubanshe, Beijing, 1974.

34. *Zhongguo Ditu Ce**, 12x17 cm softbound booklet of political maps of each province in color and explanatory notes from the preceding atlas, in simplified Chinese characters. Ditu Chubanshe, Beijing, 1976.

35. *Zhonghua Renmin Gongheguo Ditu**, 70x102 cm map of China in color, place names in Pinyin, with index booklet of place names in Pinyin and simplified characters with latitude-longitude locations. Map is also available in simplified characters. Ditu Chubanshe, Beijing, 1975.

36. Hsieh, Chiao-min and Christopher L. Salter. *Atlas of China,* detailed information on physical, cultural, regional, and historical aspects of China with 273 black-and-white maps and charts, in English with Wade-Giles Romanization of place names. Mc-Graw-Hill, New York, 1973.

37. *People's Republic of China, Atlas,* 26 regional, physical, and cultural maps in color, plus related charts, black-and-white photographs, and text in English with Wade-Giles Romanization. Central Intelligence Agency, 1971. Superintendent of Documents, U.S. Government Printing Office, Washington, D.C., 20402

38. *China,* map in color with Wade-Giles Romanization, National Geographic Society, November 1964.

39. *The People's Republic of China,* 77x95 cm map in color with Pinyin Romanization. National Geographic Magazine, July 1980. Available from the National Geographic Society, Washington D.C., 20036.

*Titles in Chinese:

2. 植物种名释

8. 中国种子植物科属辞典

20. 种子植物形态学辞典

31. 中国高等植物图鉴第三册

32. 中国高等植物图鉴第一册

33. 中华人民共和国分省地图集

34. 中国地图册

35. 中华人民共和国地图

ADDENDA: RECENT RELATED INFORMATION

Luteyn, James L. and Mary E. O'Brien, editors. *Contributions Toward a Classification of Rhododendron*, proceedings of the International Rhododendron Conference, May 1978. The New York Botanical Garden, 1980.

Thorhaug, Anitra, editor. *Botany in China: Report of the Botanical Society of America Delegation to the People's Republic, May 20-June 18, 1978*. United States-China Relations Program, Stanford University, 1979.

Bartholomew, Bruce, Richard A. Howard, and Thomas S. Elias. ''Phytotaxonomy in the People's Republic of China'', *Brittonia*, 31(1), 1979, pp 1-25.

INDEX TO LATIN NAMES

Boldface page number indicates illustrated species description.

669

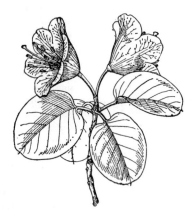

MON

XINJIANG

GANSU

NINC

QINGHAI

XIZANG

NEPAL

Yarlung Zangbo Jiang

Nu Jiang

SICHUAN

KANG-DING • BAOX

ERLAN
∧ SHAN

SIKKIM

BHUTAN

INDIA

MULI •

INDIA

• DALI

YUNNAN

BURMA

VIET

LAOS

THAILAND

CHINA

| 0 | 180 | 360 | 540 | 720 | 900 | 1080 |

KILOMETERS